Where to w

D1647285

Kent, Surrey & Sussex

Don Taylor, Jeffery Wheatley and David Burges

Third edition

Christopher Helm

A & C Black · London

Christopher Helm (Publishers) Ltd, a subsidiary of
A & C Black, 35 Bedford Row, London WC1R 4JH

0-7136-4544-X

A CIP catalogue record for this book
is available from the British Library

Printed and bound in Great Britain by
Biddles Limited, Guildford and King's Lynn

CONTENTS

Contents

INTRODUCTION

The aim of this third edition of *Where to watch birds in Kent, Surrey and Sussex* remains the same — to introduce and guide the reader to the best birdwatching sites in the three counties of Kent, Surrey and Sussex. In addition there is a systematic list of all species recorded in the region since 1900, with a brief statement describing their current status and a few recommended sites where they might be expected.

The first edition was published in 1987. Since then the number of people regularly involved in birdwatching in the widest sense has grown dramatically, perhaps more so in the southeast than anywhere else in Britain. The huge, mainly urban population looks to the countryside for much of its recreational needs and despite the increasing development pressure on the natural environment, these counties boast a wealth of superb birdwatching sites, thus attracting many birdwatchers from outside the region as well.

Birdwatching — even twitching — is now an accepted, if still perhaps poorly understood, part of our national culture. The layman is no longer surprised by the sight of large numbers of people with binoculars and telescopes, sheltering behind sea walls, hurrying down country lanes, or standing around the local gravel pit or reservoir. Birdwatchers now have access to more and better equipment, and information exchange so rapid that it would not even have been considered possible ten years ago.

So what is the role for a book such as this? In addition to providing information about sites, the associated birds, habitats and when to visit, it provides the context within which they sit, within a county and a region. Its aims are two-fold: firstly to provide an efficient tool for those in search of interesting birds, and secondly to fill the gap between the comprehensive county avifaunas, annual Kent, Surrey and Sussex Bird Reports and the vast amount of knowledge held in the heads of local birders. We hope it will encourage birdwatchers both within and from outside these counties to explore sites that they have not previously visited, submit records to their county Bird Recorders, and perhaps support their local Bird Clubs and conservation groups.

The Sites

After careful consideration a few sensitive breeding species have not been specifically mentioned, as even minimal disturbance can cause them to desert. Some of the habitats too can be destroyed by undue disturbance.

We have aimed to be as helpful as possible by distilling this information into an easily accessible format. In choosing the sites, we have been fairly selective and those listed fall into one or more of the following categories:

(1) those which hold a high density of breeding, wintering or migratory birds,
(2) those which comprise habitats supporting a particular assemblage of birds, which may not occur elsewhere,
(3) sites which are representative of a habitat type — for example, a wood with a good range of birds.

The site accounts have been revised since the second edition, and are the result of the authors' own collective knowledge and widespread consultation with local birdwatchers who know these sites well. However, new information is always coming forward, and we hope that any gaps in these site accounts will spur on others to fill them.

Bird identification and optical equipment are outside the scope of this book. There are now many good field guides on the market for both the beginner and expert alike, as well as a number of journals and magazines, which regularly discuss the finer points of identification of particular species or groups. If you are unfamiliar with what is available, it is best to discuss your needs with other birdwatchers, see what they use and decide what is best for you. The same applies to optical equipment, and field trials are essential before purchasing new binoculars or telescopes.

Bird Clubs and Other Birdwatching Groups

The three counties are covered by three Bird Clubs; the Kent Ornithological Society, the Surrey Bird Club and the Sussex Ornithological Society. All produce annual Bird Reports and organise indoor and field meeting programmes for their members. The bird clubs provide a focus for all those interested in birdwatching in the southeast. They also play a crucial role in providing valuable data, which can be used by the conservation bodies for protecting important bird sites and habitats.

In addition to the Bird Clubs, the RSPB has 21 Members Groups and 20 YOC Groups in Kent, Surrey and Sussex. These groups run a very varied programme of events and are particularly helpful to children and beginners of all ages, who want to become involved with birds, wildlife and conservation issues more generally.

The following sections give a brief introduction to the geography and climate of the southeast, and how these influence its habitats and bird communities.

Geography

The area covered by this book is dominated by the eroded Wealden Dome and the North and South Downs. At one time the whole of the southeast was covered by a sea of remarkable purity in which hundreds of feet of white chalk deposits were laid down. The land was later forced up in a broad east to west ridge across the three counties. Over time erosion eventually removed the chalk from the centre of the dome, exposing the sands and clays of what is now the Weald. The clays were once covered by extensive lowland oak forest, and whilst parts of the area are still amongst the most heavily wooded in Britain, much of the early woodland has now been cleared for farmland and building development. The sands, especially in the west and at Ashdown Forest, became heathland after early woodland clearances and low intensity agricultural use, and today represent a significant part of Britain's internationally important heathland resource.

The North and South Downs are all that remains of the overlying chalk. At one time largely used for sheepwalks, the areas not ploughed and converted into arable farmland are, in many places, becoming overgrown with scrub and woodland. The distinctive plant and animal life of the chalk is at risk in the absence of active, traditional management. For example the Downs historically supported Stone Curlews, which depended on a mixture of grazed turf and bare soils provided by spring, rather than winter sown, crops. Today they are exceptionally rare passage migrants. In places the Downs are capped by gravels which are part of an ancient shoreline. These sites support dry, acid heaths, such as at Lullington in East Sussex.

Few substantial rivers cut through the South Downs, but in West Sussex the Adur and particularly the Arun has a substantial flood plain, providing areas of wet riverside pasture subject to shallow winter flooding, which support large numbers of wildfowl. Like so many wetland sites in the southeast, however, these areas have been subjected to drainage and agricultural improvement. Where the chalk reaches the sea there are spectacular cliff exposures, such as at Dover and Beachy Head. These sites formally supported significant seabird colonies, although today Fulmars and now Kittiwakes are expanding again, perhaps supported by man's refuse.

Towards the Thames, the northern slopes of the chalk are overlain by later marine and freshwater deposits. In the west these are mainly the Bagshot series of sands and gravels, making up the commons at Pirbright and Chobham. Where these have been worked they provide extensive areas of gravel pits, especially on the Greater London/Surrey border. Further east they give way to London Clay and the alluvium of the lower Thames. The broad, muddy estuaries of the Thames, Medway and Swale are internationally important for their wintering and breeding bird populations, but are still under very real threat from damaging developments, largely associated with the ports industry. In addition the prospect of a rise in sea level will lead to further direct habitat loss, which will prove very difficult to replace.

The Channel coast has large areas where silt and shingle have built up between the higher ground and the sea, notably on the Romney Marshes, Dungeness to Pett Levels and Pagham Harbour. These are all important for breeding, wintering and passage birds, but some are also much degraded because of extensive drainage over the years. At Pagham the sea breached earlier defences leaving a superb intertidal basin. To the west, Chichester Harbour also supports internationally important numbers of wildfowl and breeding terns.

Climate

The southeast has a warmer and drier climate than most other parts of the British Isles, although there are some surprisingly marked differences due to the alignment of the Downs and Weald, relative to the prevailing southwesterly winds. In Kent the high ground on the North Downs is substantially cooler and wetter. The highest rainfall is at Bedgebury, with 825 mm (32.5 inches), while parts of Sheppey are particularly dry, having less than 533 mm (21 inches). Much of the North Kent coast and the Romney Marshes experience less than 640 mm (25 inches).

Compared with inland areas, most coastal districts are warmer in the winter and cooler in the summer. This relative freedom from frost, in coastal areas, is significant in attracting many birds forced off the Continent by severe winter weather. London, too, has a rather milder climate than the more exposed countryside surrounding it and the really low temperatures in Surrey are usually recorded from places on the Weald.

Whilst the weather is dominated by the prevailing southwesterly winds, proximity to the Continent can have dramatic short-term effects on bird populations and movements. Ridges of high pressure across Europe and Asia produce periods of easterly and northeasterly winds, which are responsible for many of our more eastern visitors, such as the rare warblers in late autumn, or invasions of Smew or Waxwings in hard winters.

FEATURES OF THE REGION'S BIRDLIFE

Kent

For those seeking a genuine wildlife spectacle, the vast numbers of wintering duck, geese and waders on the North Kent Marshes have few equals. Much of the wet grassland has been lost to arable production and 'improved' by drainage. Conservation bodies have acquired or manage significant parts of what is left which provides secure breeding, roosting and feeding sites for many thousands of birds. These sites attract significant numbers of raptors and on a good day in winter the lucky birder could see Peregrine, Merlin, Hen and Marsh Harriers and Rough-legged Buzzard in quick succession.

The region's proximity to the Continent contributes directly to Kent's attraction for the birdwatcher, as some sites have a deserved reputation as migration watchpoints. The unique shingle peninsula at Dungeness provides an excellent opportunity to witness the spring and autumn passage of various seabirds. It is also an arrival and departure point for many passerine species, migrating north in the spring and south in the autumn, when literally thousands of hirundines may be seen flying in or out over the Channel. In a similar fashion, Thanet projects eastwards into the southern North Sea, providing a natural landfall for southbound Scandinavian migrants in the autumn. Needless to say, timing is everything, and the weather conditions have to be just right to produce the birds.

The link with the Continent is further emphasised by the occurrence of more typically European species such as Savi's and Cetti's Warblers, regular spring Serins, and increasingly Penduline Tits. Some or all of these species have already bred, or could breed in the future. Conversely, hard winter weather brings visitors like Red-necked Grebe, Bean and Barnacle Geese, Smew and Goosander from the Netherlands and the Baltic.

Surrey

Unlike the other two counties covered by this book, Surrey — taken here as the administrative county plus Metropolitan London up to the Surrey Docks — has no coastline and no bird observatories. Many seabirds such as the Fulmar, common enough elsewhere, are extremely rare, whilst breeding records for some others, such as Herring Gull, are almost unknown. Two factors go a good way to providing compensating birdwatching opportunities. The first is the very large area of inland water. The Thames forms the northern boundary from the Kent border to Walton-on-Thames. The Thames Valley itself contains large reservoirs and many gravel pits at various stages of exploitation. These are major moulting and winter refuges for wildfowl. When drained for maintenance, the reservoirs provide a rich habitat for waders and dabbling duck. There are more gravel pits in the Blackwater Valley and in a belt across the centre of the county from Send to Godstone.

A number of sewage farms, especially the one at Beddington, have proved of continuing interest at all times of the year and between them, these various wetland sites provide breeding, stopover and wintering sites for many species of waterbirds, migrants and breeding passerines. A second factor arises from the heavily built-up character of the south London suburbs. The northern part of the county is heavily watched because so many observers live there. This has produced excellent grapevine and a pronounced bias in the distribution of reported rarities. London's many parks and gardens, though heavily used for more general recreation, have plenty of interest for the urban birder. Some have stretches of water which hold enough wintering wildfowl to merit inclusion in the national wildfowl counts. Richmond Park is the biggest. Battersea Park, the Surrey Docks and Wimbledon Parks are well worth visiting.

Surrey's most significant feature, and the one which adds most to the value of its birdlife, is the heathland which covers much of the western part of the county. Part of it is used for training by the Ministry of Defence, affording in itself a degree of protection. Much of the rest is managed as public or National Trust open space. There is a major lowland heath reserve, the Thursley National Nature Reserve, and the commons here and elsewhere support important populations of Nightjar, Woodlark and Dartford Warbler, and other typical heathland species such as Hobby, Tree Pipit and Stonechat. There are also one or two pairs of breeding Curlew. Great Grey Shrikes and several raptor species winter regularly.

The countryside is extremely varied. A small area may contain copse, hill, common, pond and field, with a corresponding diversity of birdlife. Surrey is one of the most heavily wooded counties in England. Birds in the woods along the North Downs and the Greensand Hills (which extend into Kent) include owls, raptors, Firecrests and Crossbills.

Sussex

With its long, south-facing coastline, birdwatchers in Sussex, like those in Kent, are well placed to observe the spectacular migration of birds in both spring and autumn. Many birders migrate to the coastal fringe where the headlands at Beachy Head, Seaford and Selsey Bill concentrate the visible migration of seabirds and passerines. These sites, and the coastal wetlands of Chichester, Pagham and Rye Harbours, host tens, if not hundreds of thousands of the more common migrants and winter visitors, whilst many rarities occur each year.

A particular feature of Sussex is its river valley systems, which cut south through the South Downs to the coast. The Arun, Adur, Ouse and Cuckmere each provide some excellent birdwatching areas, even if agricultural improvements have reduced their potential to support breeding birds in particular. The same applies to the the wide lowlands of the Pevensey Levels and Walland Marsh to the east, but their size does make them more attractive to wintering geese. Inland, several reservoirs, mainly in the eastern half of Sussex, and the gravel pits of Chichester provide further opportunities for watching wildfowl.

The rest of the county comprises three main habitats. These are the chalk of the South Downs plunging into the sea at Beachy Head, the Weald with its clay and sandstone outcrops, and the Greensand heaths of the north and west. These are part of the same heathland complex that is found in southwest Surrey and eastern Hampshire.

The chalk downland is an important refuge for many of the widespread farmland birds, such as Grey Partridge and Corn Bunting, that have undergone such dramatic declines in the last thirty years. The Stone Curlew used to breed here and it is hoped that it may yet return.

The Weald is heavily wooded and supports typical woodland bird communities. Where there are outcrops of sandy soils, such as at Ashdown Forest, a more diverse and partly heathland bird community is found. The western heathlands running up to the Surrey and Hampshire borders support important, though smaller, numbers of the typical heathland species found on the Surrey heaths. As in Surrey and Kent, great efforts are being made to restore this important habitat.

ACKNOWLEDGEMENTS

We wish to express our gratitude to the wardens of the Bird Observatories and the RSPB and English Nature Reserves mentioned in this book, for their considerable advice and assistance. Local observers have kindly checked and improved site texts. We apologise to those we may have inadvertently omitted, and especially thank the following: Chris Bond, Chris Bradshaw, Geoff Burton, John Davies, Mick Davies, Andrew Henderson, Ian Hodgson, Murray Orchard, Steve Rowlands, Derek Tutt and Dave Wilson for Kent; Martin Baxter, Frank Cannings, John Clark, Ian Davis, David Dicker, Rupert Hastings, Roger Hawkins, Barry Marsh, Mick Pankhurst, Shaun Peters, John Steer and Roger Suckling, for Surrey; and Peter Burns, John Cooper, Bob Edgar, Robin Edwards, Malcolm Emery, Roger Haggar, Simon Linnington, Leonard Manns, Mike Mason, Owen Mitchell, John Newnham, Sarah Patton, Alan Perry, Ann de Potier, Brian Savage, Alf Simpson, Julian Thomas, Wayne Turner, Barrie Watson and Barry Yates for Sussex.

We are especially grateful to the artists: Dave Beadle, David Boys, David Nurney, John Reaney and Jan Wilczur, whose drawings have so enhanced the presentation. Gill Marriot and Margaret Millner typed most of the original text for Sussex. The maps were drawn by John Holloway and updated by the authors.

The authors will be pleased to receive any information and ideas which might usefully be incorporated in future editions of this guide, and hence benefit future readers. Correspondence (SAE if a reply is required) should be addressed c/o A & C Black (Publishers) Limited, marked for the attention of Don Taylor (Kent), Jeffery Wheatley (Surrey), or Dave Burges (Sussex).

HOW TO USE THIS BOOK

Field guides are essential for critical bird identification but can only give general information on distribution and migration patterns. Although birds are very much conditioned in their behaviour by instinct, and the nature of their perception is remote from our own, their habits and movements will be better understood with more experience and local knowledge. We have attempted to bring out some of the phenomena that affect bird behaviour, especially the influence of the weather, tides and seasons.

THE REGION

The region under discussion in this book consists of the counties of Kent, Surrey and Sussex. Each county is treated separately and each site within the county is numbered, located on a map and described under sub-headings which are explained below.

Also included are a number of additional sites for each county. They may be good sites for specific species, but at only one season; they may be examples of a specialised habitat; they may be included for their general interest; or simply as an alternative to the more popular areas. A lettered map shows the location of each.

Habitat
This section describes the extent of the area covered and the main bird habitat regions. Where relevant, comments on the plant life and other aspects of natural history are included.

Species
The aim is to give a sample of the main species of interest, and what they are likely to be doing — whether resident, breeding, on passage or wintering. Some indication as to the frequency of occurrence and the numbers involved is also attempted, to give the visitor an idea of what to expect — single birds, small parties or large flocks. This section cannot list every species found in an area. For reasons of space, common birds are usually excluded.

At the start of the section, some reference is generally made regarding the ornithological importance of the area. The text, therefore, is written in broadly chronological order, to help the reader to follow the pattern of bird events through the year. In some instances, to end the section, main birdwatching sites have been described where we feel more explanation is needed for a particular area within the main site.

Timing
This is a particularly important section, which should help the reader to avoid wasted visits. It includes such details as the appropriate weather conditions. Visible bird migration is largely dependent on weather and large numbers of birds seen one day may be followed by none the next, if the wind direction or cloud cover has changed. The time of day may also be significant — get there before the birds are disturbed by other

humans and try not to disturb them yourself! At coastal sites the state of
the tide is most important, if you want to see shorebirds well — they
roost at various different localities at high tide, sometimes a long way
from where they feed.

Note: Any information about opening times refers to that which was
in operation in 1996, as does that given for details regarding entry to
reserves, parks and gardens and for tolls.

Access
This section tells you how to get to the site from main towns and A-class
roads; directing you along minor roads, where to park and what paths
to take when you arrive. Maps will often show a maze of roads leading
to a birdwatching site; we have usually described one practicable
route. Also, the distance you need to walk is often included.

Certain areas, such as military firing ranges or wardened reserves,
may have special access restrictions. A number of the more interesting
sites in Surrey, for example, are used for military training, and there are
prohibitions on entry, at least at certain times. Visits to such places
therefore require careful advance planning. Check this section for possible problems in good time. The Thames Valley reservoirs, with some
useful exceptions, require permits from Thames Water and sometimes
prior notification of visits. Public footpaths and roads often permit
access to riversides, marshes and lakes, but do not give the right to trespass on private land through which they may pass. If you wish to stray
from public footpaths, seek permission from the owner first.

Calendar
This is a quick-reference summary section, so the information is of
necessity selective. For convenience, the calendar year has been split
into two–four month periods, which relate in the main to the ornithological seasons, although some species will obviously not fit this pattern. December–February is winter for a large proportion of winter visitors to the region; March–May is spring, covering the migration period,
when the majority of summer visitors arrive; summer, in respect of maximum breeding activity and relatively little migration, includes June–
July, though return migration for some species, that breed within the
Arctic Circle, commences during this period; autumn migration is protracted, with movement throughout August–November.

Within this section we have included peak periods for certain
species. If no further qualifying comment is made, the bird concerned
is likely to be present during that two–four month period, given that
other conditions are right, as often explained in the text. The order in
which species are listed is as in *The Birds of the Western Palearctic*, the
order most often used in field guides. This will facilitate quick reference
to identification points.

Measurements
Throughout this book we have used measurements in those units that
we feel are most readily understood. Distances are normally stated in
miles, like British road signs, followed by the metric equivalent in
metres, as now used on Ordnance Survey maps, while surface areas are
given in acres, followed by hectares (ha).

THE MAPS

The maps have been drawn specifically for this book and each is numbered to cross reference with the sites, and access to the sites described (eg. 1). Sites within the main area may also have a map and this is given a letter reference (eg. Map 1a).

In addition to the above, Ordnance Survey map numbers are also given. These refer, firstly, to the 1:50,000 series sheet number (eg. OS 178) and, secondly, to the 1:25,000 series sheet number (eg. TQ 67/77).

The use of Ordnance Survey maps is recommended as they give a good general appreciation of the nature of many of the sites and access to them via main roads. In the text we have occasionally quoted a map reference (eg. SU 934538) using either of the Ordnance Survey series. (For anybody unsure of how to read these references, a simple guide is often given on the inside back cover of any of the Ordnance Survey 1:50,000 series maps.)

The following are invaluable additional guides: for Kent the A-Z Kent Street Maps, covering 254 towns and villages (produced by Geographers' A-Z Map Company Ltd); for Surrey the 3-inch-to-1-mile Surrey Street Atlas (published by George Philip), which covers virtually the whole of the county, including the London area, shows footpaths, names farms, ponds, woods, hills and other features and indexes over 20,000 roads. A London A-Z street guide may also be helpful.

Key to Maps

▨	Sea/inland water
▥	Area of interest, eg. reserve
★	Viewpoint
▲	Car parking
●	Birdwatching hide
□	Building
⁰⁰	Sewage farm
— - — -	County boundary
— · — ·	Reserve boundary
— — — —	Footpath

KENT

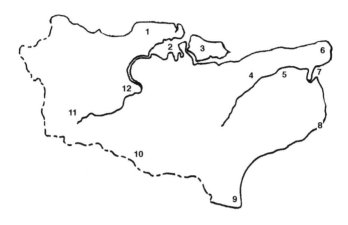

1	Hoo Peninsula	7	Sandwich Bay
2	Medway Estuary	8	St Margaret's Bay
3	Isle of Sheppey	9	Dungeness
4	Canterbury Ring Woods	10	Bedgebury Forest
5	Stour Valley	11	Bough Beech Reservoir
6	Thanet	12	New Hythe

Habitat

The three estuaries and the associated lowlands that make up the North Kent Marshes complex are the Thames, Medway and Swale. Of the three areas, the Hoo Peninsula, bordered by the Thames, provides the greatest variety of habitats. At the eastern end the Isle of Grain and Allhallows look out across the Thames estuary, providing a good site in autumn for observing seabirds and the visible migration of passerine migrants, while the former attracts falls of Scandinavian night migrants in the autumn. Further up the river, there are sand workings; extensive mudflats on one side of the seawall, with grazing marsh and arable on the other; the predominantly oak woodland of Northward Hill RSPB Reserve, containing the largest heronry in the British Isles; wide, reed-lined fleets; the flooded clay pools and North Quarry at Cliffe; and Great Chattenden Wood. The seawall, minor roads and public footpaths give good access to much of the area.

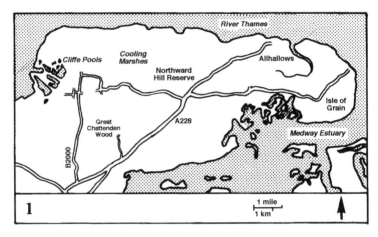

Species

On this stretch of the Thames Marshes, with careful planning, close to 100 species can be seen on a single winter's day, with maybe 120 in May, such is the diversity of habitat. Divers, grebes, wildfowl, raptors and waders, plus most typical woodland species, all occur. The pools at Cliffe are particularly attractive for grebes and a variety of dabbling and diving duck, while good numbers of waders roost there. Small numbers of Bewick's Swans and White-fronted Geese, along with Marsh and Hen Harrier, Buzzard, Peregrine and Merlin, regularly winter on Cooling and St Mary's Marshes, where flocks of Golden Plover also feed. The mudflats attract wintering waders, with particularly large numbers of Dunlin and Knot. A few Long-eared Owls are resident, but immigrant birds join them to form small roosts in winter, when Short-eared Owls also hunt over the marshes. Rock Pipits and Snow Buntings are regular winter visitors, while Lapland Buntings and an occasional Shore Lark may be anticipated.

The tendency we have to associate spring with nesting means that spring comes early on the Thames Marshes, as by February the Grey Herons return to repair their nests in the Northward Hill heronry. The departure of the grey geese often coincides with the arrival of the first Chiffchaff, Wheatear and possibly an early Garganey. By late April, the song of the Nightingale echoes from the Northward Hill reserve, Great Chattenden Wood and the hawthorn scrub at Cliffe. A wide variety of species breed, including duck and waders on the marshes, with migrant warblers on the reserves and woodland birds in Great Chattenden Wood and at Northward Hill.

From midsummer Yellow-legged Herring Gulls *L. a. cachinnans* gather in Higham Bight, often flying across the river to rubbish dumps in Essex to feed, so you need to be there early in the morning to see them. Up to 100 or more of this subspecies (which may well be given specific status by the BOU soon) can be seen at this site during the autumn.

The return of migrant waders is a typical feature of early autumn. When the water levels are appropriate, Cliffe Pools will often attract 20 or so different wader species on any one day. The wetland extension of

Grey Herons

the Northward Hill RSPB Reserve, north of Eastborough Farm, may also attract a good variety of waders. As the autumn progresses and the wind veers northeast, migrant passerines can be expected, while seabird passage may be observed from Grain, Allhallows or Lower Hope Point. The flocking of Little Terns is another regular feature of autumn, but by mid October the majority of summer migrants will have flown south and the winter visitors will be taking their place. Stormy weather in November often brings seabirds into the estuary. Large numbers of Kittiwakes may be involved, often with skuas or auks, and possibly petrels.

Main Birdwatching Zones

Many of the marshland and estuarine species can be expected along the length of the seawall between Cliffe Pools and Yantlet Creek, and on the Isle of Grain, but there are several quite distinct areas, each with its own attractions, that are described in detail. Working down the river they are: Cliffe Pools and North Quarry; Cooling, Halstow and St Mary's Marshes; Northward Hill RSPB Reserve; Allhallows, Yantlet Creek and Stoke Lagoon; and the Isle of Grain. In addition, particularly for woodland birds, Great Chattenden Wood is included, as it too is part of the extensive Hoo Peninsula.

CLIFFE POOLS and NORTH QUARRY (Map 1a)

Habitat

Between the village of Cliffe and the river there is an extensive area of fairly unique habitat, covering some 1700 acres (700 ha) from Higham Marsh to Lower Hope Point. It comprises about 490 acres (200 ha) of water-filled clay pits, one of which is used for sailing and water-skiing; another 245 acres (100 ha) or so are pits filled with river dredgings, some of which are now overgrown with sea aster, while others contain shallow, flooded areas. It is hoped that this area will become another RSPB reserve, with controlled access, habitat improvements and view-

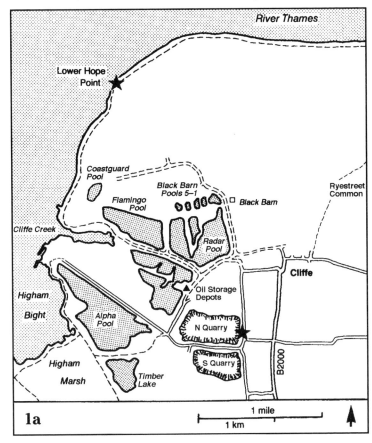

ing arrangements. The level of the water in the flooded areas, that attract many waders in autumn, is at the mercy of the elements. Invariably some have exposed, muddy fringes for part of the autumn at least and with the anticipated RSPB management, there is a possibility of some control over the water levels. There is also a small area of arable and some grazing marsh. Along the river, even at low tide, there is only a narrow foreshore, but there are extensive mudflats in Higham Bight, part of which is owned by the RSPB. Hawthorn scrub and bramble, quite widespread around the pools and along the bank below the radar tower, attract Nightingales, and Long-eared Owls occasionally roost in the denser hawthorn here. To the northeast of Cliffe a footpath forms the northwestern border of Ryestreet Common, an area of grazing marsh owned by the RSPB. Finally, there are two flooded chalk quarries; the North Quarry is virtually a bird reserve, though a limited amount of quarrying still occurs along the northern edge. It is well vegetated, attracts a good variety of species and can be viewed quite well from the road. Trout fishing takes place in the South Quarry.

Species

The flooded pools at Cliffe attract a variety of waterfowl in the winter months. Few winters pass without visits from one of the diver species or the rarer grebes, all three divers and both Red-necked and Slavonian Grebes have made prolonged stays. Up to 100 Cormorants often roost on the Alpha Pool and a few Bewick's Swans can occasionally be seen, though they usually prefer to graze on the marshes. Diving duck, such as Tufted and Pochard, frequently outnumber the dabbling duck species on the pools, where Goldeneye are regular winter visitors, but Scaup somewhat scarcer. Smew and Long-tailed Duck occur from time to time, the former more often when the weather is severe on the Continent. Larger numbers of dabbling duck, particularly Shoveler and Gadwall, favour the North Quarry; Greylag and Canada Geese often feed there too, while 1–2 Little Egrets sometimes roost. From time to time both Greater and Lesser Flamingos have added colour to these pools, but both species are at present presumed to be escapes.

Though the wader roost sites vary, the Alpha Pool frequently attracts several hundred Redshank, while the coastguard pool, close to the river wall, is often favoured by Ringed Plover. A Kentish Plover has been known to winter here and Avocets are now wintering regularly. They feed in Higham Bight when the tide drops, where they can sometimes be difficult to find amongst all the Shelduck, and either roost at the Timber Lake or on one of the Black Barn pools. Common and Green Sandpipers can occasionally be seen in the winter months. Hen Harriers and Short-eared Owls often hunt over the vegetation surrounding the pools, amongst which small flocks of Linnets regularly feed, but the once familiar Twite is now extremely scarce here. During the winter months Ryestreet Common attracts a variety of raptors.

By late March the wintering duck are departing and the local duck are dispersing onto the marshes to breed. The attractive drake Goldeneye can sometimes be observed displaying, before he flies north. Garganey may appear before the end of the month, along with other early migrants, like Little Ringed Plover, Sand Martin, Wheatear and Chiffchaff. The scene changes more dramatically during April, with the arrival of Common Terns and summering passerines, like Yellow Wagtail, Sedge and Reed Warblers, while migrant waders, like

Whimbrel and Greenshank, can also be anticipated. Broad-billed and Marsh Sandpipers, both extreme rarities, have occurred in May. About 20 pairs of Common Terns usually breed at Cliffe, along with a few pairs of Pochard and Gadwall, and occasionally Ruddy Duck, while later in the season creches of up to 50 young Shelduck can be expected.

When the Black Barn pools have muddy fringes, they will attract a good selection of migrant waders in autumn, commencing with species like Little Ringed Plover, and adult Little Stint and Curlew Sandpiper from early July. Greenshank too feature at this time, while small numbers of Ruff, a few Spotted Redshanks and Wood Sandpipers are also regular, with Temminck's Stint now an almost annual visitor. Over the years American vagrants like White-rumped, Pectoral, Stilt and Buff-breasted Sandpipers have all been seen on these pools. With the increase in the Little Egret numbers in the UK, small gatherings of up to nine birds have recently appeared in this area during the summer months.

Although Cliffe is some way from the mouth of the Thames, the autumn passage of seabirds, like auks, skuas, Kittiwakes and terns, can sometimes be quite evident. The bend in the river at Lower Hope Point is a good spot to watch from. Some of the birds continue up the Thames, while others often circle about over the river, before returning east. Storm-driven birds can often be seen here and occasionally on the pools in late autumn, including species like Manx Shearwater and occasionally rarer ones like Leach's Petrel, Grey Phalarope and Little Auk. Another feature of the late autumn at Cliffe Pools is the flocking of Little Grebes, with up to 180 from late October.

COOLING, HALSTOW and ST MARY'S MARSHES (Map 1b)

Habitat

This whole area was once prime grazing marsh, dissected by reed-lined ditches and more open fleets, with small beds of common reed. Access to the marshes is limited to the few public rights of way, but much of the area, which is now arable, can be viewed from the seawall. The fleets and ditches support valuable duck food plants such as common spike-rush, fennel pondweed, soft hornwort and spiked water milfoil. Dragonflies and damselflies are quite common, as is the introduced marsh frog. Along the drier seawall are a mixture of common and unusual plants. Here the meadow barley of the grazing marsh is replaced by the sea barley, which develops a characteristically spiky head as it dries. The small pink flowers of the rare sea clover are difficult to find, but do occur amongst the bright yellow masses of common and narrow-leaved birdfoot trefoil. The slender hare's ear can also be found, if searched for. The ungrazed tall grasses and herbs provide an excellent habitat for moths and butterflies. The common blue and meadow brown are abundant, while the migrant painted lady frequently settles on thistles. Grasshoppers too are numerous and among their relations the Roesel's bush cricket is a Thameside speciality. There is relatively little saltmarsh along this stretch of the river, but the mudflats are extensive, supporting vast numbers of laver spire shells, which are the main food of the Shelduck.

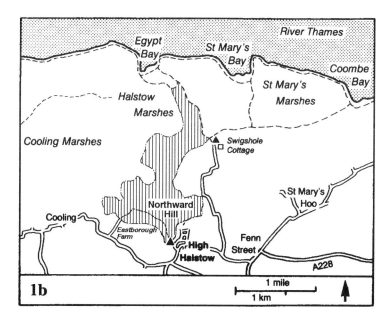

Species

While interesting species can be seen all year round, it is the numbers of wintering wildfowl, raptors and waders that often attract the greatest interest. A few Bewick's Swans are usually present, while up to 100 or so White-fronted Geese regularly graze on the marshes. Larger numbers of Brent Geese now graze on the arable. Well over 1,000 Shelduck may be seen feeding on the mudflats at low tide, or swimming on the river when the mud is covered. At least 1,000 Wigeon and over 600 Teal regularly winter here, usually with at least 200 Pintail, about 150 Shoveler and a similar number of Gadwall. Sometimes they can be seen feeding, or swimming along the river, sometimes over the marshes. Dunlin are by far the commonest wader, with 15,000 regularly wintering on the Thames Marshes, feeding on the exposed mud, from which many fly to roost on the Essex Marshes. Over 7,000 Knot, nearly 1,000 Redshank, similar numbers of Curlew and smaller numbers of Grey Plover also winter. Flocks of Golden Plover regularly feed on the grazing marshes, providing attractive flight patterns against the sky, when disturbed, possibly by Hen Harriers hunting along the ditches. In the reedbeds a few Bearded Tits can usually be seen, or heard, most often in late autumn. Small flocks of Snow Buntings sometimes feed along the seawall, but Lapland Buntings are usually more difficult to locate, often feeding on the grazing marsh, sometimes attracted by the hay that is put out for the cattle, which also attracts flocks of Corn Buntings.

Flocks of over 1,000 Golden Plover may occur during winter and in spring many assume their most attractive breeding plumage. Little Grebes breed along the edges of the ditches, where a variety of duck species also nest, including a few pairs of Pochard and occasionally Garganey, while Redshank favour the damper pastures. Over the meadows, Skylarks, Meadow Pipits and Yellow Wagtails are all quite numerous breeding species, with Reed Warblers favouring the waterside vegetation.

NORTHWARD HILL RSPB RESERVE (Map 1b)

Habitat

The wood is some 135 acres (55 ha) in extent, lying on a ridge of London Clay, rising to about 200 feet (60 m), giving it a commanding view over the marshes towards the river. Oak woodland is the most obvious, with extensive dense hawthorn, some ash coppice, sycamore scrub and clearings surrounded by a dense understorey of bramble and fern. Under the oaks the ground cover is deep leaf litter, but elsewhere dog's mercury, yellow archangel and bluebells proliferate. A pond on the northern fringes adds to the variety. With this mixture of new growth and old and decaying timber it is a bird-rich habitat, and a good site for butterflies, notably the white-letter hairstreak, which flies in early July.

A 460 acre (187 ha) extension to the north, bordered on the east by Decoy Fleet, now includes flooded pasture and reedbeds, which can be observed from Eastborough Farm or the northwest corner of the wood.

Species

Dawn and dusk visits in the winter months will often provide a very different picture of the bird species that use the wood. The shelter of the dense hawthorn thicket not only provides a winter home for Long-eared Owls, but also provides them with a food source in the form of roosting passerines. Several hundred thrushes and finches roost, with on occasion even larger numbers of Stock Doves and Woodpigeons. During the day, these birds will be feeding in the surrounding fields, hedgerows and orchards, and the wood will be comparatively quiet, apart from the thin call-notes from a roving tit flock, probably with attendant Goldcrests, and the gentle tapping of the resident Great Spotted Woodpeckers. A few Woodcock winter and may be seen probing the deep leaf litter with their long bills, if you are very lucky. When the reserve extension is flooded, good numbers of Pintail can be seen. Another interesting recent change is the presence of 1–2 Buzzards, mainly during the winter months. Merlins feed over the marshes during the day and roost in scattered trees on the marsh below the wood.

Activity in the heronry commences early in the year, when returning birds carry branches in to effect repairs to their nests. They can be observed quite well from the road to the northeast, which avoids any disturbance of the heronry. Closer views, on escorted visits, can be arranged in advance with the warden. By mid March, when the first Chiffchaff arrives, many of the 200 or more pairs of Grey Herons will be sitting on eggs, and the resident woodland species will be singing. By late April or early May, the wood will be alive with the songs of Nightingales and the woodland warblers. Very occasionally, rarer species like Golden Oriole may add to the variety of song.

About 50 different species usually breed on the reserve, with 150–200 pairs of Rooks. Avocets breed on the extension scrape, while in the wood several pairs of Shelduck, about 40 pairs of Turtle Doves and up to 20 pairs of Nightingales breed fairly regularly.

In late summer the damp extension, particularly the scrape, will attract a variety of freshwater wader species, but the wood becomes quiet again, as the summer migrants disperse. By October, small influxes of Goldcrests can be anticipated. However, in a woodland habitat such as this, the delights of the subtle seasonal changes can only really be appreciated by those who can visit regularly and frequently. The one guaranteed attraction of Northward Hill is the heronry, and it can be most impressive during the early spring.

ALLHALLOWS, YANTLET CREEK and STOKE LAGOON (Map 1c)

Habitat

This relatively small site contains all of the diverse habitats associated with the general area. To the north and east of the seawall there are small patches of saltmarsh and shingle bays, with an expansive area of mudflats at low tide. To the landward side there are freshwater grazing marshes, dissected by ditches, with small reed-lined lagoons. The seawall below the caravan park faces northeast across the mouth of the estuary, providing a good vantage point for seawatching. Further west, beyond the yachting enclosure, lies Coombe Bay, with more extensive saltmarsh, which occasionally attracts Jack Snipe in early spring, and shingle banks on which waders roost at high tide. South from the mouth of Yantlet Creek lies Stoke Lagoon, an attractive wetland site, essentially formed by a freshwater drainage system and enclosed on all sides by bund walls. The meadows are too heavily grazed for much flora to stabilise, although there is one well-established salsify community along the Yantlet seawall, which flowers in May–June.

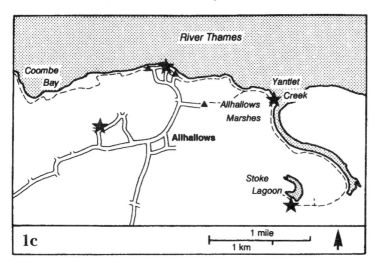

Species

A similar range of species to those upriver can be expected to feed on the mudflats here, with numerous gulls and good numbers of Brent Geese, Shelduck, Grey Plover, Dunlin and Redshank, while Oystercatchers and Turnstone are more plentiful here. At high tide a wader roost forms on the shingle bank at the mouth of Yantlet Creek. The sand and shingle bays, with the adjacent short grass on the seawall, frequently attract a small wintering flock of Snow Buntings. Another speciality that occurs in the same habitat from time to time is the Shore

Lark. Lapland Buntings are fairly regular visitors in the winter months here, preferring the longer grass of the grazing marshes. They can sometimes be seen close to the rough track leading from the British Pilot Inn to the seawall. Throughout the year Stoke Lagoon adds considerably to the attraction of the area. In the winter months good numbers of dabbling duck, like Wigeon, Gadwall, Teal and Pintail feed there, while freshwater waders like Greenshank and Spotted Redshank occasionally overwinter. Hen Harrier, Merlin, Peregrine and Short-eared Owl hunt over the area.

Wheatears can be expected before the end of March and the lagoon is a fairly reliable site for an early Garganey. During April and May a variety of migrant waders can also be expected, though the water level may be too high for the shorter-legged sandpiper species.

Dunlin and Little Stint

By the autumn, the water level in the lagoon is usually lower and the area is consequently more attractive for a wider variety of migrant waders. Freshwater species like Wood Sandpiper, Ruff and Spotted Redshank can be expected, along with Little Stint and Curlew Sandpiper. Rarer species that have occurred include Little Egret, Spoonbill, Blue-winged Teal, Black-winged Stilt, Greater Yellowlegs and Red-necked Phalarope. Another interesting feature of the autumn is the build-up of Little Terns in the mouth of Yantlett Creek, where 50–100 or more may roost by early August.

From August through to November, when the wind blows from the northerly quarter, some seabird passage can be anticipated. Another feature of the autumn here is the visible migration of passerine migrants as they coast westward. Hirundines and pipits are replaced by thrushes and finches as the autumn progresses. The seabird passage is more easily observed when the tide is high, as the birds fly closer to the shore. In August and September species like Arctic and Great Skuas and various terns are regular, while a Mediterranean Gull may be seen amongst the numerous gulls off Allhallows. By October a wider range of seabirds can be expected, including Gannet, Pomarine Skua, possibly Sabine's Gull, Kittiwake and the larger auks, with Puffin possible too. Later in the month flocks of wintering geese, ducks and waders may also be seen arriving. In November northerly storms sometimes produce large numbers of Kittiwakes, while rarer species like Storm and Leach's Petrels, Glaucous Gull and Little Auk are always a possibility.

ISLE OF GRAIN (Map 1d)

Habitat
Much of the northern area, between Yantlet Creek and Grain Village, is grazing marsh, surrounded on three sides by the seawall. To the northeast is the Roas Bank, an extensive area of mudflats, about 1 mile (1.6 km) wide. Rich in invertebrates, it attracts large numbers of feeding waders and gulls, particularly in the winter months. The northeast facing coastline here is a good vantage point for observing autumn seabird movements and the visible migration of passerines. One additional habitat is of particular significance. Between the village and the seawall, adjacent to the school playing fields, is the moat, a natural landfall for autumn passerine migrants. It is an area of scrub covering undulating ground, where sycamore, hawthorn and bramble are dominant. The area south from the moat, on the landward side of the seawall, is essentially pasture, with bramble and hawthorn scrub, reed-lined ditches and pools — another attractive area for passerine migrants.

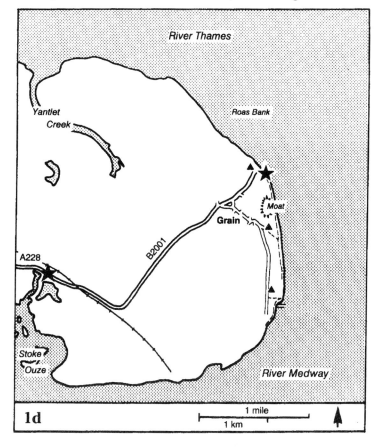

Species
In the winter months, the narrow stretch of mudflats in the mouth of the Medway estuary is a good area for close views of waders, as the tide

ebbs. Species such as Grey Plover, Knot and Bar-tailed Godwit can be expected amongst numerous Dunlin. Flocks of Brent Geese can often be seen 'commuting' between Essex and the Medway. On the grazing marshes, large numbers of Curlew sometimes flock, while Hen Harrier and Merlin regularly hunt.

This site generally is of greater interest in the autumn months. At that time, particularly when the wind veers into the northerly quarter, seabird passage can be anticipated, as described for the previous site. With a northeasterly influence migrant passerines can be expected in the moat and scrub to the south, including pipits, wagtails, chats, common warblers and flycatchers, with the possibility of a rarer species like Red-backed Shrike. By October Goldcrests and a few Firecrests can be expected, and with an influx of these species there is always the anticipation of finding a Yellow-browed Warbler, or even a rarer eastern warbler like Pallas's or Dusky.

In northwest winds, particularly later in the autumn, such species as Grey Phalarope and Sabine's Gull have occurred. Cormorants will be perched on the buoys and old towers in the estuary mouth and as the autumn progresses wintering waders will return to feed on the exposed mud.

GREAT CHATTENDEN WOOD (Map 1e)

Habitat
A deciduous woodland containing sizeable areas of hornbeam and hazel — formerly coppiced — with oak standards. Past coppicing cycles mean that there is no genuinely old timber. Bluebells add an attractive carpet of blue in the spring, when early purple orchids can also be seen. There is limited access, as much of the southern section is MOD land. The main footpath runs along the ridge between Lodge Hill and Cliffe Woods estate. Lodge Hill is an open area with hawthorn and gorse scrub and good views of the surrounding area.

Species
Sparrowhawk, Little and Tawny Owls are resident and the last named may be heard hooting early in the year, when winter visitors like Woodcock and possibly Buzzard may be seen. All three woodpeckers are present, though the Lesser Spotted is scarce. Willow Tit, Hawfinch and Redpoll have all declined and are now rare or absent. Spring is dominated by the song of summer migrants like Nightingale and the six common warblers. In May the 'purring' of Turtle Doves is added to the dawn chorus, but the 'squeaks' of Spotted Flycatchers are less common, while other residents like Treecreeper and possibly Nuthatch can also be heard. Rarer species like Golden Oriole may make brief visits.

In the autumn other passerine migrants like Redstart and Pied Flycatcher may visit briefly, but by early September the woods will be quiet again, apart from the calls of roving tit flocks. By October winter thrushes and finches will be arriving and Lodge Hill should provide a good opportunity to witness visible migration. Of significance during the late autumn and winter months are the enormous roosts of several hundred Carrion Crows and Magpies.

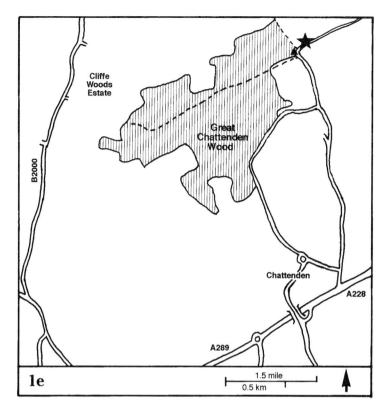

Cliffe
Woods
Estate

B2000

Great
Chattenden
Wood

Chattenden

A228

A289

1e

1.5 mile
0.5 km

Timing

As with all coastal localities, the state of the tide is important in determining where quite a number of the bird species can be seen best. At
low tide all those species that feed on the mudflats will generally be
very distant, but as the tide rises, they feed closer and closer to the seawall. The waders will fly to roost as the mud becomes covered, while
species like Shelduck may simply swim on the river. High tide is also the
best time for seawatching in the Thames, particularly when the wind
veers northwest in the autumn. Visible migration of passerines tends to
be heaviest in the morning, though it can continue throughout the day
in light northwesterly winds (especially when a vigorous depression has
lasted for two to three days; this causes a build-up of migrants in northern Europe). Early morning visits are best to hear woodland birdsong
and migrant passerines are usually best seen at the same time, when
they are feeding most actively. It is also worth being out during the period before dusk for species like Barn Owl. Flocks of corvids gather at this
time before going to roost, and Woodcock may be seen flying from their
daytime woodland roosts to feed in adjacent fields.

Access

For Cliffe Pools (Map 1a) take the B2000 from Rochester. As you reach
the outskirts of the village, turn left towards the North Quarry. Turn left
again and park to view the quarry. Turn right between the quarries and
continue to the end of the tarmac road, turn right towards the oil stor-

age depots, near which you can park. Until the planned RSPB Reserve is opened and new directions are available, you should stick to the public rights of way, as shown on Map 1a and the OS maps. To reach Lower Hope Point, follow the footpath to the seawall, which you follow in a northerly direction until you get to the stone obelisk that marks the point — just over 1 mile (2 km) from Cliffe Creek. The best wader pools in the autumn are numbered 1–5 opposite the Black Barn. To get to the Alpha pool, walk to the end of the tarmac road, turn right and follow the concrete track to Cliffe Fort. From here look south over Higham Bight, then walk back round the southern side of the Alpha Pool along the seawall, past the Timber Lake on the right, where the Avocets sometimes roost in winter. This circuit is about 3 miles (5 km) long.

It is possible to walk the length of the Thames Marshes from Cliffe to Allhallows, along the seawall, a distance of over 12 miles (20 km). From Cliffe village it is also possible to walk alongside Ryestreet Common and beyond to overlook part of Cooling Marshes. The Cooling track, from Cooling Castle, may or may not become a public right of way. There are also public rights of way across Halstow and St Mary's Marshes (Map 1b). To reach Halstow Marshes, continue to drive along the narrow lane through Cooling and High Halstow towards Fenn Street. After about 3 miles (4.8 km) from Cooling, turn left along an unmarked road, via Clinchstreet Farm to Swigshole Cottage, another 2 miles (3 km) or so, where it may be possible to park, but car parking is extremely limited, as it is all along this narrow lane. There are several possible circuits following the tracks and public footpaths. A track to the north takes you to Egypt Bay, alongside a broad, reed-lined fleet. There you can follow the seawall east to St Mary's Bay, then back south across the marsh and west to Swigshole Cottage — a 3.5 mile (6 km) walk. Alternatively, a 4.75 mile (8 km) walk could take you east across St Mary's Marsh to Coombe Bay, then west around the seawall to St Mary's Bay, and south and west across the marsh again. Several other public rights of way, from St Mary's Hoo, across the marshes, are shown on Ordnance Survey maps of this area.

Northward Hill RSPB Reserve (Map 1b) is approached through High Halstow village. Follow the brown RSPB road signs, from the main street to the RSPB car park. Trails start from there. The long one leads to the Saxon Shore Way which you follow to view the scrape on the wetland extension. For details of parking for larger groups (coaches are inadvisable) and arrangements to visit the heronry, contact the Warden at the RSPB Office (see Useful Addresses, p. 289).

To reach Allhallows (Map 1c), follow the minor road off the A228 at Fenn Street for 3.75 miles (6 km), turning right along Avery Way to the British Pilot Inn. There is usually room to park here. For seawatching, in particular, instead of turning right along Avery Way, continue straight ahead into the caravan park (there is usually a charge for entry), then turn right to park at the seafront. From here you can also walk east along the seawall to Yantlet Creek, or west to Coombe Bay. From the British Pilot a track continues east, across the marsh to the seawall, close to the mouth of Yantlet Creek. Follow the seawall south and eventually west, along the creek for about 2 miles (3 km) to find Stoke Lagoon on the right. Keep behind the seawall, as you approach the lagoon, to avoid disturbing the duck and waders.

To get to the Isle of Grain (Map 1d), follow the A228 from Rochester. About 1.5 miles (2.5 km) beyond Lower Stoke, it is possible to park and look over Stoke Ooze to the south, where a variety of waders can be seen in the saltmarsh and muddy creeks. Immediately adjacent, to the east, is a flooded lagoon that attracts duck and occasionally Bewick's Swans in the winter months. Follow the B2001 to Grain Village, continue along Chapel Road, through the village and beyond, until driving south, parallel to the seawall. Park adjacent to the chain-link fence on the left and walk to the seawall. The coastline here provides vantage points for viewing the estuaries of both the Medway and Thames. The moat is between the village and the coast and there is room to park by the playing field, just before you drive south.

Great Chattenden Wood (Map 1e) is best approached from the A228 into Chattenden where you turn north and follow Chattenden Lane along the eastern edge of the residential area for about 1.25 miles (2 km). The road narrows and then makes a sharp turn to the east, at the top of the hill, where there is just room to park a car carefully at TQ 754738. A footpath straight ahead, to the northwest, takes you downhill along the edge of the wood and the open scrubby hillside, or you can take the main footpath through the wood along the ridge towards Cliffe Woods estate.

Calendar

Resident: Little Grebe, Great Crested Grebe, Grey Heron, Greylag Goose, Shelduck, Gadwall, Shoveler, Pochard, Tufted Duck, Red-legged and Grey Partridge, Water Rail, Oystercatcher, Ringed Plover, Snipe, Barn, Little, Tawny and Long-eared Owls, Green, Great and Lesser Spotted Woodpeckers, Bearded Tit, Nuthatch, Reed and Corn Buntings.

December–February: Probably divers and rare grebes, Bewick's Swan, White-fronted and Brent Goose, Wigeon, Scaup, Goldeneye, Hen Harrier, Sparrowhawk, Buzzard, Peregrine, Merlin, Avocet, Golden and Grey Plovers, Knot, Ruff, Jack Snipe, Woodcock, Short-eared Owl, Rock Pipit, Stonechat, Lapland and Snow Buntings.

March–May: Grey Heron (Northward Hill heronry), Garganey, migrant waders including Whimbrel and Greenshank, Wheatear, Whinchat, woodland summer visitors including Nightingale and *Sylvia* warblers.

June–July: Breeding residents, duck and waders including Garganey, Avocet and Common Tern (breeding colony), Yellow Wagtail, Nightingale, Sedge and Reed Warblers, woodland warblers and Bearded Tit. In July Little Egret influx, return wader passage, Yellow-legged Herring Gull.

August–November: Little Grebe (November peak), Manx Shearwater, possible Leach's and Storm Petrel, Brent Goose (from October), Hen Harrier, Buzzard, Sparrowhawk, Peregrine and Merlin (all five from October), migrant waders — Little Ringed Plover, Ringed Plover (August peak), Little and Temminck's Stint, Curlew Sandpiper, Ruff, Black-tailed Godwit, Whimbrel, Spotted Redshank, Greenshank, Wood Sandpiper, returning winter waders (from October), Pomarine, Arctic and Great Skuas, gulls possibly including Mediterranean and Glaucous, Sandwich and Little Terns, auks, Whinchat, Wheatear, winter thrushes, migrant warblers, Goldcrest, finch passage, Lapland Bunting.

2 MEDWAY ESTUARY

Habitat

The huge tidal basin is characterised by large and small saltmarsh islands, a maze of creeks, extensive mud and the brackish freshwater grazing marshes of the Chetney Peninsula. The estuary attracts a wealth of wintering waterfowl and waders, while the islands and grazing marshes support a rich and diverse population of breeding birds. Man's intervention has had a significant impact, but despite threat after threat, a reasonable balance has been maintained to date. The main changes have occurred along the north shore, much of which is privately owned and not accessible to the general public. The construction of the Kingsnorth Power Station is an example of an industrial development which has benefited certain bird species. The jetty joining the tanker terminal off Oakham Ness has been connected to the mainland, forming a sheltered bay, which now attracts huge numbers of duck at high tide. In addition, the ash-settling lagoons are now being used by many waders as high tide roosts. Neither of these sites is open to the public.

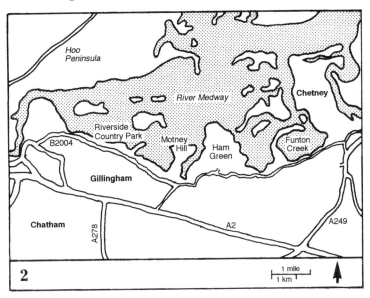

Species

The winter months in the Medway estuary can provide quite spectacular sights, as geese, duck and waders flight across the industrial skyline. It is such a valuable area for thousands of wintering birds that it is not only ranked as internationally important for the total numbers of wildfowl that use it, but also for several individual species, including Brent Goose, Shelduck and Pintail. About 2,500, 5,000 and 1,000 respectively winter there. The attraction of nearby Elmley, as a safe and relatively undisturbed haven for wintering duck, has probably been partly responsible for the reduction in the numbers of dabbling duck now wintering in the Medway, when compared with the early 1970s. But even so, up to 4,500 Wigeon and 3,000 Teal can still be seen flighting over Barksore Marshes. Internationally important numbers of some 500 Ringed Plover, 5,500 Knot, 21,000 Dunlin and 1,700 Redshank also winter here.

Great Crested Grebe and Goldeneye favour some of the deeper channels and can be seen well at high tide from the south shore. Rarer grebes sometimes occur here too and it is one of the more reliable sites for seeing the attractive Red-breasted Merganser. Hen Harrier, Merlin, Peregrine and Short-eared Owl hunt over the saltmarsh and grazing marshes, while Rock Pipits can frequently be seen foraging for food along the edge of the saltmarsh.

As winter progresses, the numbers of duck and waders decline, but many of the species involved are still present in small numbers into early April. By this time, there is usually a peak count of some 1,500 Black-tailed Godwits, while migrant waders like Whimbrel can be expected along with early passerine migrants such as Wheatear and Yellow Wagtail.

The Medway Islands attract an interesting variety of some 35 breeding species, but needless to say they should be left undisturbed while the birds are nesting. Some of the islands attract large colonies of Black-headed Gulls, but comparatively few Common Terns now breed and the small colonies of Little Tern fluctuate considerably. However, up to 200 pairs of Oystercatchers nest.

The return wader passage is a feature of the autumn and for some species the annual peaks occur at this time, with up to 1,000 Ringed Plover, 1,700 Black-tailed Godwits, as many as 6,000 Redshank and up to 600 Avocet. Roost counts of over 100 Spotted Redshank and Green-shank are fairly regular, but these birds often favour the inaccessible pools at Kingsnorth. Of other less common species, the Osprey is a regular autumn visitor. During October, winter visitors like Brent Goose, Hen Harrier and Merlin return while the numbers of wildfowl start to increase again.

Main Birdwatching Zones

Although its size makes the Medway estuary a daunting area to watch, there is ample opportunity to see many of the bird species that occur. Access is limited, but there are stretches where roads provide good vantage points and there are public footpaths, or rights of way, along parts of the extensive seawall system. A boat would certainly make more sites accessible and this is well worth considering (see Useful Addresses, p. 291), though it can be dangerous and knowledge of the estuary and its tides is essential.

The attraction for many visitors to the area will be the wintering wildfowl and waders. Much of the text concentrates on these wintering species. To avoid unnecessary repetition, as many birds will occur at all sites, the information under the named sites will concentrate more on those species that seem particularly to favour them. Four sites are included along the south shore: the Riverside Country Park at Horrid Hill; Motney Hill, Otterham Creek and Berengrave Nature Reserve; Ham Green and Lower Halstow; Funton Creek, Bedlams Bottom and Chetney.

RIVERSIDE COUNTRY PARK (Map 2a)

Habitat

The Horrid Hill Peninsula provides an excellent vantage point for observing the landscape of muddy creeks and saltmarsh islands that is the southern Medway. Nor Marsh, leased by the RSPB, is the nearby large island. If you follow the seawall to the west, around Eastcourt Meadows, you can look out over the saltmarsh of Copperhouse Marsh, with the main channel and Hoo Salt Marsh beyond. The hawthorn and bramble scrub of Eastcourt Meadows provides an attractive habitat, particularly for Whitethroats in the summer, while the small brackish pond is rich in amphibians and insects. A footpath along the edge of the estuary to the southeast, which takes you to Motney Hill, also provides good views over the saltmarsh and estuary mud.

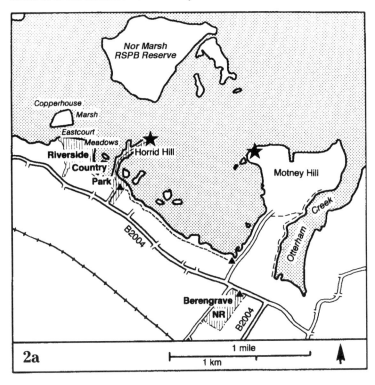

Species

During the winter months, good numbers of waders can be seen as they fly past to roost up to two hours before high tide. When the tide is full, it is a good spot from which to observe Great Crested Grebes and quite often one of the rarer grebes, Red-necked Grebe or Slavonian. Goldeneye and Scaup can also be expected here, with Red-breasted Merganser perhaps more distant. Looking across to Nor Marsh, you may be fortunate enough to see a Hen Harrier hunting. As the mud becomes exposed again, waders will start feeding. Among the numerous Dunlin and Redshank, you may find up to 50 or more Black-tailed Godwits;

100–200 will probably be wintering somewhere in the southern Medway and this is one of their favoured haunts. In March, around 700 may be present, while even larger numbers occur in autumn, but they tend then to feed and roost further east in the estuary. The gulls too are worth studying, the Mediterranean and the rare Glaucous Gull have been seen here. In the summer months, colonies of Black-headed gulls can be observed on the islands.

Red-necked Grebe

Of the smaller birds, the Rock Pipit is common in winter, when a Stonechat might also be seen. In the area of scrub, at Eastcourt Meadows, flocks of tits and finches, and possibly a Great Grey Shrike may occur in winter, while warblers like Lesser Whitethroat and White-throat may be seen or heard in late spring and summer. In autumn this area and the scrub on Horrid Hill attract migrant passerines and falls of Goldcrests have been observed. Another interesting feature of this stretch of the estuary concerns the autumn migration of skuas and waders, some of which fly overland. In northwest winds, Arctic, Great and occasionally Pomarine Skua have been seen heading southwest over Gillingham, often flying over the Riverside Country Park as they leave the estuary.

MOTNEY HILL, OTTERHAM CREEK and BERENGRAVE NATURE RESERVE (Map 2a)

Habitat

The RSPB manages a small Reserve at Motney Hill. Looking west from the Motney Hill Peninsula there are extensive creeks and mudflats at low tide. The sewage works at the northern tip is not open to the public, but there is quite an extensive reedbed alongside Otterham Creek. Here too it is possible to visit a completely different type of habitat. To the south of the B2004 an old chalk pit, rich in wildlife, has been turned into an attractive reserve of some 25 acres (10 ha), managed by the Gillingham Borough Council. There are well established trees such as willow, birch and hawthorn and many different species of wild plants and fungi. The reedbed and pond there attract numerous insects and amphibians, as well as birds.

Species

In the winter months, the estuary mudflats and high water will attract a similar range of species to those seen from Horrid Hill, including Brent Geese and the rarer grebes on occasion. Otterham Creek is also favoured by the rarer grebes and Black-tailed Godwits. The reedbed is a regular Corn Bunting roost and may well hold Water Rail, Snipe, Kingfisher and Reed Bunting, though the first-named species will require some patience before it is seen, except in severe conditions, when it is far more confiding. A better site to observe Water Rail, in the winter months, is in the reedbed in the Berengrave Reserve. Finches, including Brambling, sometimes roost here in winter, while a variety of warblers can be expected in late spring and summer.

HAM GREEN and LOWER HALSTOW (Map 2b)

Habitat

There is a greater variety of habitat on this stretch of the estuary, with some pasture, orchards and hedgerows remaining on the landward side of the seawall. Looking northeast there are extensive areas of saltmarsh islands, surrounded by creeks and mud, including Twinney and Halstow Creeks.

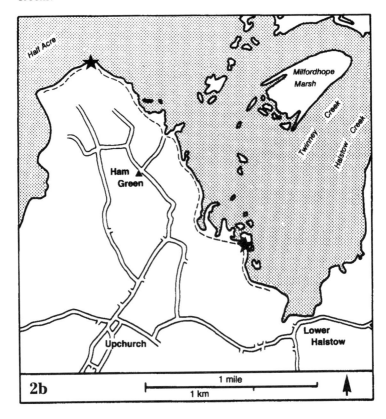

Species

In the winter months, divers can occasionally be seen in the deep channel of Half Acre, which often attracts grebes and diving duck, including Scaup, Goldeneye and Red-breasted Merganser, while the extensive mudflats are much favoured by Brent Geese and Grey Plover.

FUNTON CREEK, BEDLAMS BOTTOM and CHETNEY (Map 2c)

Habitat

The road between Lower Halstow and Kingsferry Bridge runs alongside Funton Creek and Bedlams Bottom, with Barksore Marshes and Chetney to the north. Against the distant industrial backdrop of Grain, the estuary here is a truly impressive sight, particularly when flocks of duck and waders flight across.

The Chetney Peninsula consists of brackish grazing land, divided by fleets and ditches. The vegetation of the surrounding saltmarsh is typical, with common cordgrass, sea purslane and marsh samphire being the dominant species. The pasture behind the seawall has a number of grass species, including common saltmarsh grass, sea barley and marsh foxtail, with patches of sea club-rush, common reed and common spike-rush along the fleets and ditches.

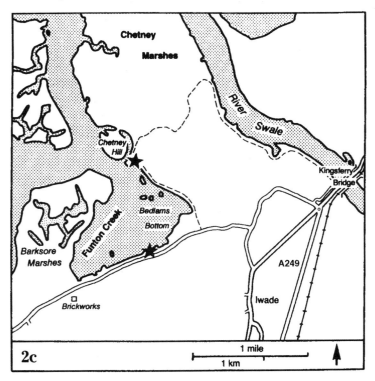

35

Species

The winter months again probably provide the most impressive viewing. Barksore Marsh is not accessible to the general public, but it does hold a large wader roost. Some of the birds flying to and from the roost can be seen from Chetney Hill. Up to 2,000 Grey Plover do occur, as well as about 1,000 Oystercatchers. Funton Creek and Bedlams Bottom is one of the best places to see Brent Geese and Pintail at very close range, using the car as a hide. As the tide rises, the birds are pushed closer to the road. Good views can also be expected of Grey Plover, Dunlin and Redshank, while up to 30 Red-breasted Mergansers have been seen at the mouth of Funton Creek and over 200 Avocets now winter here, with even higher peak numbers in the autumn. Rock Pipits feed in the saltmarsh.

A public footpath across Chetney provides opportunities for good views over the area, where Hen Harrier, Merlin, Peregrine and Short-eared Owl regularly hunt during the winter. Also, there may be a small flock of Bewick's Swans and some grey geese, usually Greylags, but sometimes White-fronts too.

During the summer months, several duck and wader species breed, including Shelduck, Shoveler and Redshank, while large populations of Skylarks, Meadow Pipits and Yellow Wagtails breed successfully on the Chetney Peninsula.

In the autumn, Greenshank and Spotted Redshanks make use of the Barksore roost and they can be seen feeding on the mud along Funton Creek and Bedlams Bottom, when the tide is low, while Avocets and Black-tailed Godwits also frequent this stretch of mud.

Timing

The timing of visits is quite critical, as they should coincide with the period either side of high tide for the best views of most of the wildfowl and waders. Stormy weather may well bring seabirds into the estuary to seek shelter, while winds in the northerly quarter in autumn encourage seabird movements across the mouth of the estuary, and initiate some overland passage. The passerine migrants are most easily seen early in the morning.

Much of the area is shot over by wildfowlers, in season, and they too take advantage of the high tide's influence on the movement of duck.

Access

The western end of the southern Medway is adjacent to the B2004, which can now be reached from the Hoo Peninsula through the Medway tunnel. This avoids the congested Medway towns. Coming from the east, in Rainham, turn north off the A2, along the B2004 for 1 mile (1.6 km). Turn left at the road junction. Motney Hill Road, the turning for Motney Hill, is just over 0.25 mile (0.5 km) on the right, and for the Riverside Country Park just over 1 mile (1.6 km), again on the right (Map 2a). Park in the Country Park car park, then walk out along Horrid Hill Peninsula, or west to Eastcourt Meadows. On OS Map 178, Riverside Country Park is shown as Eastcourt Meadows Country Park. In the new Reception Centre there are toilet and catering facilities. An information board will provide an update on what is being seen in the area.

At Motney Hill, park in the small car park, on the left, about 0.1 mile (0.2 km) along Motney Hill Road. Follow the road and seawall towards the sewage works, looking out over the estuary and Rainham Creek to the left, and at the reedbed on the right. It is possible to walk round the shore line of Motney Hill to the west, for a closer view of Rainham Creek, as far as the sewage works' perimeter fence. To look over Otterham Creek, follow the road almost as far as the no entry signs to the sewage works, where the footpath follows the edge of the field on the right across to the seawall bordering the creek. Back on the B2004, the Berengrave Nature Reserve is just a short way east, with parking on the right just beyond the Berengrave Lane turning. There are also two entrances, with car parking, off Berengrave Lane. On the reserve there are two well-marked nature trails to follow.

To reach Ham Green (Map 2b), follow the road northeast from Upchurch for 1 mile (1.6 km), where there is limited space for parking. A narrow lane to the right leads to the estuary after 0.25 mile (0.4 km). Follow the seawall to the right, towards Lower Halstow, for good views over Twinney and Halstow Creeks, or left out along the peninsula, to find excellent vantage points across the deep channel of Half Acre and beyond. Various passerines may be seen in the scrub and orchards inland of the seawall.

To reach Funton Creek and Bedlams Bottom (Map 2c), return to Upchurch, follow the road east for another 2 miles (3 km) through Lower Halstow. Funton Brick Works are on the right and the estuary opens up before you on the left. The field opposite the brick works often attracts Golden Plover and other waders at high tide in the winter months. Along Funton Creek there are a few narrow places where you can pull off the road. This area can also be reached from the A249, from Kingsferry Bridge or Iwade. Turn into Old Ferry Road, then along the Lower Halstow road to Bedlams Bottom. If there is room, park beside the road. This provides excellent viewing over this important bird area. A public footpath leads along the western edge of the Chetney Peninsula, cutting across the grazing marsh from Chetney Hill to the Swale, and then along the Swale to Kingsferry Bridge — a distance of about 4 miles (6 km). It is another 1.5 miles (2.4 km) back along the road to the start. Alternatively, park close to Kingsferry Bridge by the Ridham Dock road and walk northwest along the Swale, then across Chetney.

Calendar

Resident: Cormorant (non-breeding birds), Greylag Goose (feral population) Shelduck, Eider (some years), Oystercatcher, Ringed Plover, Redshank, Reed and Corn Buntings.

December–February: Great Crested Grebe, possibly Red-necked, Black-necked or Slavonian Grebes, Bewick's Swan, Brent Goose, Wigeon, Pintail, Scaup, Goldeneye, Red-breasted Merganser, Hen Harrier, Merlin, Peregrine, wintering waders including Avocet, Grey Plover, Black-tailed Godwit and Curlew, Short-eared Owl, Kingfisher, Rock Pipit, possibly Great Grey Shrike, Brambling, Snow Bunting.

March–May: Departing winter wildfowl and waders, Whimbrel, Yellow Wagtail, Wheatear, Sedge and Reed Warblers.

June–July: Breeding duck and waders, including Shelduck, Oystercatcher and Ringed Plover, Black-headed Gull colonies, Yellow Wagtail, Sedge and Reed Warblers.

August–November: Brent Goose (from October), possibly Osprey, Hen Harrier and Merlin (from October), Peregrine, returning winter waders, Avocet, Black-tailed Godwit (early autumn peak), Whimbrel, Spotted Redshank, Greenshank, Arctic Skua, migrant passerines including common warblers and flycatchers (August–September), Goldcrest and Firecrest (October).

3 ISLE OF SHEPPEY

OS 178
TQ 97/TR 07

Habitat

The Isle of Sheppey, in the mouth of the Thames, comprises a variety of habitats attractive to birds, including the highly successful RSPB Elmley Marshes Reserve and the English Nature Swale National Nature Reserve. Some traditional grazing marsh is maintained at both sites, while the flooding of other sections is controlled.

The scrub-covered cliffs between Warden Point and Leysdown, and the coastal strip to Shellness facing northeast, form a natural landfall for autumn passerine migrants. The mudflats, along this shore and in the Swale, attract feeding waders, while the saltmarsh and shell spit at Shellness provide a natural high tide wader roost. The path along the seawall provides good views over the Swale NNR, where there are six observation hides. There is saltmarsh to the south and rough pasture to the north, where Marsh and Hen Harriers hunt in winter.

Though much of the pasture has been drained and turned over to arable, increasingly large numbers of White-fronted and Brent Geese

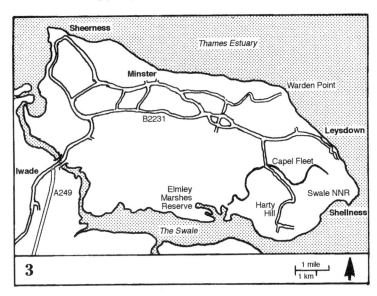

graze in winter. There are pockets of grassland and small reedbeds along the fleets, these attract both Hen and Marsh Harriers, Short-eared Owls and a few pairs of breeding duck. Capel Fleet is quite wide in places and part of it can be seen well from the Harty Road. The level of water and the time of year will determine the species to be seen. The saltings east of the Ferry Inn are now part of the Swale NNR and form another high tide wader roost. There is no public access, but it possible to view it from the pub car park. From Mocketts, on Harty Hill, there is a good view over the marshes towards Bells Creek. The only access here is along the footpath from Harty Ferry to west of Mocketts Farm.

There are few trees and hedgerows in this open landscape and it can be cold and bleak in the winter months, but the rewards are there for those who persevere.

Species

The numbers of wildfowl, waders and raptors present during the winter months are one of the great attractions at that time of year. The variety can also be quite impressive. Offshore, rafts of divers and grebes occur from time to time, seals too can be seen regularly, not only off the point but along the Swale as far as Elmley. Also in the Swale Brent Geese and Red-breasted Merganser are regular, with occasionally, one of the rarer grebes. Over the marshes Marsh and Hen Harriers, Peregrine, Merlin and Short-eared Owls can frequently be seen hunting and though the flocks of White-fronted Geese may often be distant, there are opportunities to study them at closer range. Their evening flights, particularly across the setting sun, provide a memorable picture. In severe conditions, small flocks of other geese can be expected, like Bean, Pink-feet, or more rarely, Barnacle. One or two of both these grey geese species can be expected in late December and early January. Increasingly, the Brent Geese are now feeding on the arable, while flocks of Golden Plover favour the grazing land.

Avocet and young

Wheatears and an early Garganey may be seen before the end of March, at a time when the flock of White-fronted Geese will be departing. One of the highlights of the spring is the flock of Black-tailed Godwits, which may exceed 2,000, while the bubbling call of the Whimbrel is another typical sound, as they stop off to feed *en route* north. The concentration of over 4,000 pairs of Black-headed Gulls in the mouth of Windmill Creek is another impressive, though noisy, experience. A few pairs of Common Terns breed here too.

The summer months are quieter, though Avocets and quite a few duck species now breed successfully on Elmley Marshes Reserve and the Swale NNR, and the downy young are always a joy to watch, particularly the creches of Shelduck.

Autumn commences with the appearance of returning migrant waders, like the freshwater sandpipers and stints. By mid August, the numbers and variety of passerine migrants begin to increase, with species like Whinchat quite widely scattered and the warblers and flycatchers seemingly more concentrated along the coastal strip. When the wind veers northwest in the autumn, it is a good time to seawatch. Movements of both Arctic and Great Skuas are regular. By October, the Pomarine Skua can also be expected. Gannets, auks, terns and flocks of waders returning to winter all add to the interest, along with the visible migration of Skylarks, corvids and finches. Raptors too feature at this time.

Main Birdwatching Zones

The principal areas of interest are largely determined by the available access. There is no public right of way over Eastchurch Marshes, between Capel Fleet and Windmill Creek, an area that frequently attracts the wintering White-fronted Geese, Mute and Bewick's Swans. Several footpaths over Harty and Leysdown Marshes provide better access to the eastern end of the island.

The Elmley Marshes RSPB Reserve (Map 3a) is dealt with specifically, while the eastern block is described in two parts: the coastal strip between Warden Point and Shellness, followed by Capel Fleet and Harty Marshes (Map 3b), inland of the seawall.

ELMLEY MARSHES RSPB RESERVE (Map 3a)

Habitat

The reserve includes grazing land, dissected by reed-lined fleets, and some arable, with no hedgerows and few trees. The area managed by the RSPB, which is bordered by the Swale to the south and Windmill Creek to the north, includes the 'flood', which is essentially flooded grazing land, but the depth of the water is controlled carefully, as is the grazing by the cattle. They are moved and restricted to certain areas at different times of the year, to create either nest-hiding tussocks, particularly for Redshank and wildfowl, or short swards of grass for grazing Wigeon and nesting Lapwing.

As a result of the flooding, the reserve now holds not only a good variety of wintering and breeding bird populations, but also provides a sheltered haven for huge numbers of roosting waders, during the high tide periods.

The hides are strategically sited, not only to overlook the flood, but also for viewing the Swale. The tidal range is significant in the Swale and the vast area of mud attracts feeding waders and dabbling duck at low tide. At high tide, there may well be grebes and diving duck to be seen, depending on the season.

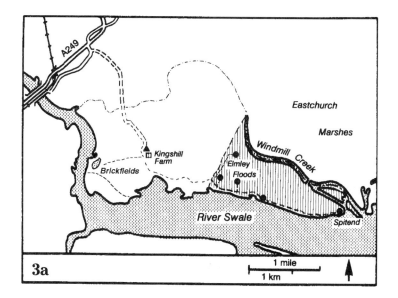

3a

Species

The winter months probably provide some of the most spectacular sights, certainly in terms of sheer numbers. A stooping Peregrine over the flood may disturb thousands of duck and waders. At times there may be up to ten duck species, with peaks in recent years of 22,000 Wigeon, 5,000 Teal, 1,900 Pintail and 650 Shoveler. Such large numbers of Pintail only occur during high spring tides, as they normally feed on the saltmarsh. Waders now use the flood for roosting at high tide and impressive numbers of species like Dunlin, Grey Plover and Bar-tailed Godwit are often present at that time. Migrant freshwater waders like Spotted Redshank sometimes overwinter, while a few Avocets may also be present. Curlew often feed in the grass towards the back of the flood.

It would be surprising if a Hen Harrier or a Short-eared Owl did not appear, as you scan over the Windmill Creek area, while in some winters the rare Rough-legged Buzzard hunts here. From the Swale or Spitend hides, such species as Red-breasted Merganser and occasionally Eider, or a rarer grebe may be seen, when the river is flooded. As the tide drops, the waders leave the safety of the flood to feed again on the mud. Rock Pipits feed along the rocky edges.

Lapland Buntings are fairly regular winter visitors and small groups are sometimes present in the rough pasture, occasionally attracted to the hay that is put out for the cattle. Golden Plover too feed on the pasture; flocks of several hundred are often present in the fields between the A249 and Kingshill Farm.

During March the numbers of wintering duck decrease quite rapidly, though Shoveler numbers may increase for a while, when migrants drop in. Other winter visitors also disperse. By the end of the month, early migrants like Wheatear and Garganey may have arrived, while the build-up of Black-tailed Godwits will have begun; up to 2,000 may be present in March. Other migrant waders will be stopping briefly to feed on their way north. By late April and early May passerine migrants like

Whinchats may be perched on the fenceposts or wire, while Reed Warblers sing from the reed-lined ditches. During May many waders will be in their splendid summer plumages. The Ruff, in particular, are quite spectacular, while the aptly named 'Dusky' (Spotted) Redshank is another most attractive wader worth looking for. It is a good time for rarities, with occasional sightings of species like Marsh Sandpiper, but almost annual visits by Spoonbill and Temminck's Stint, while a trip of Dotterel may stop on the pasture for a few days.

June too produces the occasional unexpected rarity, like Great Reed Warbler, while on a more regular basis it is a time when young duck and newly-fledged waders are evident. Passerine species too, like Yellow Wagtail, will be busy feeding their short-tailed youngsters. The Black-headed Gull colony, which can be viewed from the Spitend hide, is a noisy hive of activity at this time.

As far as waders are concerned, spring moves imperceptibly into autumn, as returning migrants reappear. By mid-June the first Spotted Redshanks and Green Sandpipers appear, followed early in July by Little Stints and Curlew Sandpipers, in varying numbers. The adults appear first, followed by the freshly plumaged youngsters a month or so later. It is not unusual to identify 20 or more wader species during August, and careful scrutiny may occasionally reveal rarer visitors like Pectoral Sandpiper and Red-necked Phalarope.

As the autumn progresses, Marsh and possibly Montagu's Harriers may be seen sailing over the marshes with barely a flap, while delicately attractive Little Gulls and Black Terns also visit the flood. The eclipse plumages of the drakes of various dabbling duck provide identification puzzles, but careful observation may reveal a Garganey resting in the grass or feeding in the shallows. The roost of Spotted Redshanks may number 100 or more birds, while the calls of Whimbrel and Greenshank are frequently heard.

By late September or early October, the wintering waders slowly replace the migrant species, and other winter birds, like Hen Harrier, Merlin and Peregrine start to reappear.

WARDEN POINT and SHELLNESS (Map 3b)

Habitat

The 5 mile (8 km) stretch of coast, either side of Leysdown (Bayview), comprises an interesting variety of habitats. It rises from the shell spit at Shellness to about 100 ft (30 m) at Warden Point, where the London clay forms unstable, crumbling cliffs, which are rich in fossils. The cliff top is grassed, with scrub and bramble, while a few trees and shrubs grow in the mature gardens, all providing shelter and food for migrant passerines, particularly in the autumn. Hens Brook and the sycamores lining Second Avenue, west of Warden Point, are much favoured by warblers and crests.

Between Leysdown and Muswell Manor, there is a small golf course, further grassland, with hawthorn scrub and a few plantations of trees. Towards Shellness, beyond the chalets, is a small sandy beach, backed by marram grass. Beyond the hamlet lies the shell spit. Falls of autumn passerine migrants often concentrate on the vegetation that has been planted in the chalet gardens and the trees surrounding Muswell Manor.

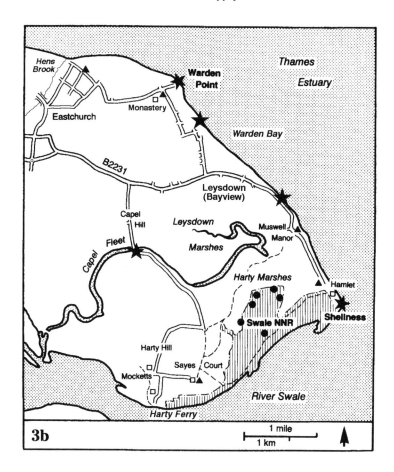

3b

1 mile

1 km

The Swale NNR includes saltmarsh, protected by a 0.5 mile (0.8 km) long spit, composed of cockleshells, which is still extending southwestwards. The shell spit produces a distinctive flora and fauna, including the rare Ray's knottgrass and breeding Ringed Plovers and Little Terns. The broad stretch of tidal sand and mudflats is rich with invertebrate life. In winter, the bivalves, marine worms and snails form the principal food of many hundreds of waders, while the eelgrasses above the low water mark provide an important food source for Brent Geese.

The saltmarsh is particularly rich in plant life. Common cord-grass is dominant, with saltmarsh grasses and glassworts well represented. Other abundant species include sea aster, sea lavender and sea purslane. As well as providing feeding and resting places for thousands of wintering ducks and waders, the saltmarsh also plays host to the scarce ground lackey moth.

Species

Offshore, between Leysdown and the point, flocks of Great Crested Grebes often gather to feed in the winter months, while occasionally 100 or more Red-throated Divers are seen. Small flocks of dabbling duck often rest on the sea, drifting into the Swale as the tide rises.

While the mudflats are exposed, large numbers of waders and Brent Geese feed. As the mud becomes covered with water, many of these birds can be seen well, close to the shore, before they fly towards Shellness and on into the Swale. Good numbers roost on the shell spit at the point, or further up the Swale at Harty Ferry. Others fly further, to Elmley, while some roost on the arable close to the rough road, behind the coastal chalets. A spot to which the Merlin is also attracted. At times, there may be peak counts of 15,000 Dunlin, 5,000 Knot, 4,000 Oyster-catchers, 2,000 Grey Plover, 700 Bar-tailed Godwits and 400 Turnstone. If a Purple Sandpiper is present, it can usually be seen feeding with the Turnstone. Around 2,000 Brent Geese winter, but the feeding flocks may be well scattered. At high tide, however, they often gather in one flock on the arable, where they continue to feed. Careful observation of the Brent Goose flock may produce examples of the pale-breasted race *B. b. hrota*, or the even rarer 'Black Brant' *B. b. nigricans*, while the rare and extremely attractive Red-breasted Goose has occurred.

The sandy beach and small area of marram grass, between the last of the chalets and the hamlet, occasionally attracts a few Twite and Snow Buntings, as does the shingle spit, but the Shore Lark is a rare visitor. A Stonechat or two can be expected along this coastal strip, and often around Muswell Manor, and in the saltmarsh Rock Pipits feed along the ditches. In March, particularly late in the month, it is sometimes possible to witness the departure of wader flocks as they set off for northern Europe. It is then that the first Wheatear of spring can also be expected. Migrant Whimbrel may well be heard calling; they sometimes stop and feed on the musselbeds that are exposed at low tide just off Shellness. Common and Little Terns will arrive from late April and the shingle spit should be left undisturbed during the rest of the spring and summer, if the latter species and Ringed Plover are to breed successfully.

Spring visible migration can be observed well from above Warden Bay during fine weather and light southwest winds, when movements of wagtails, hirundines and finches may occasionally produce a rarity like Serin. Similar winds may produce falls of warblers, including the occasional Wood Warbler, which may be attracted to the sycamores in Second Avenue.

In the autumn months there are frequent opportunities to observe migration. This may involve seabirds, waders arriving from northern Europe, or westerly movements of corvids, finches and other passer-ines, many of which coast — follow the shoreline.

Arctic Skuas can be expected from late July, and by mid August a good passage may involve up to 100 birds or more in a day. The seabird movements are dependent on the wind veering into the northerly quar-ter and even a light wind in August will initiate movement. The best viewing is probably from Shellness, where you can sit below the sea-wall, as the skuas often follow the coast from Herne Bay into the Swale. Some continue up the Swale and probably migrate overland. It is often possible to observe them thermalling high over the mouth of the Swale. Others fly back out of the river, often close to the point, sometimes alighting on the sea, where small flocks will form. Manx Shearwaters can also be seen well, particularly when the tide is up, when they too may fly out of the Swale. Small groups of migrant waders, like Curlew Sandpipers, can sometimes be seen feeding on the mud, while flocks of Knot and Bar-tailed Godwits may occasionally be seen arriving from the northeast, often flying into southwest winds.

In September, peaks of up to 100 Great Skuas may occur and there is always the possibility of identifying the rare Long-tailed Skua. Sandwich, Common and Little Terns are regular, as are a few Arctic, but normally later in the month, while Black Terns occasionally form large flocks, sometimes roosting on the shell spit. In strong, northerly winds and inclement conditions the Sooty Shearwater becomes a possibility.

With a northeasterly influence, falls of migrant passerines can also be anticipated. Common warblers, flycatchers and chats often occur. Any small patch of vegetation, including the trees around Muswell Manor, may also attract rarer species like Red-backed Shrike, or possibly Bluethroat, while October has produced Red-breasted Flycatcher, Pallas's Warbler and Rustic Bunting. On a more regular basis, the low vegetation close to the blockhouse, on the point, may be alive with Goldcrests after a good fall. Another good area to find passerine migrants like Pied Flycatchers, crests and warblers is where the land rises at Warden Point. The Monastery gardens and the trees around the caravan park are all worth checking, as are Hens Brook and the Second Avenue sycamores. The Wood Warbler is regular in August and Yellow-browed Warbler virtually annual here in late September–early October.

Passage in October tends to produce a wider range of seabirds. The Pomarine Skua is regular in small numbers and like the other skuas occasionally rests on the sea in the mouth of the Swale. Strong winds may initiate large movements of Gannets and Kittiwakes, and occasionally produce rarer species, like Sabine's Gull and possibly Storm or Leach's Petrels. In northeast winds, watching from Warden Point can be more profitable, as birds seem to fly more readily into the Thames. Movements of the large auks — Guillemot and Razorbill — are often more obvious from here, partly because of the height. In inclement conditions seawatching from your car may be a practical solution and parking it on the seawall, between Leysdown and Muswell Manor, is often a good alternative. Flocks of Brent Geese can be seen arriving, often with Wigeon and other dabbling duck. Raptors like Hen Harrier, Peregrine, Merlin and occasionally Rough-legged Buzzard, along with Short-eared Owl follow the coast and can best be seen from Shellness. Sea-duck like Common Scoter and Eider often occur, while Velvet Scoter and Long-tailed Duck may occasionally be seen. Movements of the commoner diurnal migrants may involve daily totals of several thousand Starlings and Chaffinches, and hundreds of Lapwings, Skylarks, thrushes and corvids. It is in northwest winds again that the concentration of movement appears to be greatest. Northerly storms in late October and November may produce rarer seabirds, like the petrels and Little Auk, and possibly a Grey Phalarope.

CAPEL FLEET and HARTY MARSHES (Map 3b)

Habitat

This area, once grazing marsh, but now predominantly arable, is dominated by Harty Hill, some 80 ft (25 m) high and the fairly broad, reed-lined Capel Fleet, which stretches from Leysdown Marshes to Bells Creek. Much of the area can be scanned from Capel Hill to the north, or Harty Hill in the south. A few hedgerows and groups of trees remain, to provide shelter for birds and other forms of animal life, but many of the elms that once dominated the landscape have gone.

The Swale NNR includes an extensive strip of some 545 acres (220 ha) of the old grazing marsh, adjacent to the seawall, between Shellness Hamlet and Harty Ferry. Six hides are now open to the public, providing views over an area of flooded marshland, which is particularly attractive to freshwater waders and other waterbirds. Bunds have been built and the water levels in the four main marsh fields can be controlled. Access to the area is signposted from the seawall footpath.

The grazing marsh is intersected by freshwater, or slightly brackish ditches and attracts varied and interesting populations of plants and animals. Grass snakes are fairly common, though rarely seen, whereas slow worms are regularly recorded in the seawall grasses. Shorter grass attracts the common lizard, while the brackish ditches contain smooth newts and a variety of dragonflies. The marsh frog is abundant and extremely vocal during the spring. The seawall is a good area for butterflies during the summer, including gatekeeper, small copper and large skipper.

Species

Though a good variety of species can be seen in this area throughout the year, it is probably the winter months that offer the greatest interest. Between January and late March, over 1,000 White-fronted Geese usually graze in the fields. If they choose the Eastchurch Marshes, they will be distant, but on Leysdown Marshes they are more approachable

Marsh Harriers

along the public footpaths. Scanning from Capel Hill is one way of locating the flocks. In severe conditions, other geese may also be present, plus a few Whooper Swans to supplement the regular small flock of Bewick's. Golden Plover often feed on the pasture that remains below Capel Hill. A few Ruff occasionally winter along Capel Fleet, where Redshank and Snipe are regularly seen from the Harty road. Marsh and Hen Harriers, Merlin, Peregrine and the Short-eared Owl often hunt along the fleet, while one or two Stonechats winter regularly and Corn Buntings gather in flocks to feed. Towards dusk a Barn Owl might appear.

While there are berries in the roadside hedgerows, Redwings and Fieldfares will remain to feed. A Little Owl can often be seen perched in the dead elms close to Sayes Court. From here it is possible to walk to the seawall and along the Swale, or inland across Harty Marshes to Muswell Manor. Within this area, which includes the Swale NNR, one or two Merlins, several Hen Harriers, Marsh Harrier and Short-eared Owl regularly hunt and it is not unusual to see a Merlin associating with a Hen Harrier on a hunting foray. A few Hen Harriers usually roost in the saltmarsh on the reserve and are best seen towards dusk, as they fly in. The car park area close to Shellness Hamlet is relatively close to this site. On occasions, up to 20 roost near the eastern end of Capel Fleet, when they can be seen well from the Harty Road. Twite may be seen feeding in the saltmarsh, while in the grass on the other side of the sea-wall, Lapland Buntings occasionally winter. Hearing their distinctive 'tuc-a-tuc teu' call is often the easiest way to locate this species.

At other times of the year, that part of Capel Fleet visible from the Harty road has attracted a variety of interesting species, including rare waders like Black-winged Stilt and Pectoral Sandpiper, in June and July respectively. In early autumn Marsh and occasionally the rarer Montagu's Harrier may be seen.

Timing

As the state of the tide has a considerable influence on the behaviour of the birds that feed in the estuary, timing is particularly crucial. As the mud becomes covered with water, shortly before high tide, the waders, in particular, will fly to their respective roosts, returning again as the mud becomes exposed. High tide is also the best time to see those species that swim on the sea or in the Swale, as they are then much closer to the shore.

In autumn, passerine migrants are best located in the early morning, while seawatching is generally most productive shortly after the wind veers northwest. Afternoon movements can still be quite impressive, when the wind veers around noon. Some passage will continue the next day, so long as the wind remains in the northerly quarter, but it is likely to be less marked thereafter. Visible migration of passerines tends to be heaviest in the morning, though it can continue throughout the day, when a northwest wind continues to blow. Dusk visits are necessary to see the Hen Harriers coming to roost, and also to observe the Barn Owl hunting, or perched on a fence post.

Access

From the M2 or A2 take the new A249 past Iwade and over Kingsferry Bridge onto the Isle of Sheppey. About 1 mile (1.6 km) beyond the bridge take the rough road to the right, signposted Elmley Marshes RSPB Reserve (Map 3a). Follow the farm track for 2 miles (3 km) to Kingshill Farm, closing behind you any gates you have opened. There is a toilet block and information board at the car park. The reserve is open daily, except Tuesdays, from 9.00 am to 9.00 pm, or sunset when earlier. It is a further 1.25 miles (2 km) to the flood, with its three hides.

The Swale and Spitend hides are a further 0.75 mile (1.2 km) and 1.75 miles (2.8 km) respectively.

To reach the eastern end of the island, continue along the A249, beyond the Elmley turning, for about 0.75 mile (1.2 km). Turn right at the roundabout and follow the B2231 towards Eastchurch and Leysdown (now Bayview).

For Warden Point (Map 3b), take the Eastchurch road rather than the bypass, turn left in the village, then first right after less than 0.5 mile (0.8 km). About 2 miles (3 km) along the road, just 0.25 mile (0.4 km) from the cliff edge, there is ample room to park on the right, where the buses turn. For Second Avenue and Hens Brook drive back towards Eastchurch for about a mile, as you negotiate the second sharp bend turn right into Third Avenue. Second Avenue — lined with sycamore trees — is on the left. Hens Brook is at the northwestern end of First Avenue. A rough track, south from the Warden Point parking area, leads back to the B2231 close to Leysdown.

For Capel Fleet and Shellness (Map 3b) take the Eastchurch bypass for Leysdown. The Harty Ferry road, leading to Capel Fleet and Sayes Court, is a turning to the right off the B2231, about 1.25 miles (2 km) east of Eastchurch. It is about 4 miles (6 km) to the Ferry Inn at Harty. After just under 1 mile (1.6 km), park and look along Capel Fleet to the right. Passing bays, along the next mile or so of narrow road, provide useful scanning points to survey the marshes. There is room to park at the end of this stretch, where Marsh and Hen Harriers sometimes roost. Continue along the winding road, but instead of turning right to the Ferry Inn, carry straight on and park by the old church at Sayes Court. Follow the footpath north, then southeast to the seawall, or further north then northeast across Harty Marshes to Muswell Manor.

To reach Shellness (Map 3b), follow the B2231 through Leysdown to the sea, where you can look over the mudflats. The road runs along the seawall for nearly 0.5 mile (0.8 km), then turns inland to Muswell Manor, then left back to the seawall, where it is possible to park. There is further car parking another 0.75 mile (1.2 km) along the rough road, behind the coastal chalets, before it enters the private Shellness Hamlet. Please respect the privacy of the Hamlet by not trespassing. From here you can walk east to the shore, then south to the point, or directly south to the point alongside the saltmarsh of the Swale NNR. Alternatively, you can walk west, along the seawall public footpath towards Sayes Court. Another right of way leads back across Harty Marsh to Muswell Manor, a circuit of over 6 miles (10 km).

For visible migration in spring, turn left along Warden Bay road just before you reach Leysdown. Continue along Jetty Road where you can park on the low slope, as the land rises towards Warden Point, and overlook Warden Bay.

Calendar

Resident: Little Grebe, Cormorant (non-breeding birds), Greylag Goose, Shelduck, Gadwall, Teal, Shoveler, possibly Eider (non-breeding birds), Oystercatcher, Ringed Plover, Common Snipe, Redshank, Barn Owl, Meadow Pipit, Corn Bunting.

December–February: Red-throated Diver, Great Crested Grebe, Bewick's Swan, White-fronted Goose, Brent Goose, winter duck including peak numbers of Wigeon and Pintail, Red-breasted Merganser, Hen and

Marsh Harriers, Sparrowhawk, Merlin, Peregrine, Golden and Grey Plover, Knot, Sanderling, possible Purple Sandpiper, Bar-tailed Godwit, Turnstone, Short-eared Owl, possible Shore Lark, Rock Pipit, Stonechat, possibly Twite and Lapland Bunting, Snow and Corn Buntings.

March–May: Brent Goose, Garganey, Marsh Harrier, Avocet, Temminck's Stint, Ruff, Black tailed Godwit (peak March–April), Whimbrel, Spotted Redshank, Yellow Wagtail, Wheatear.

June–July: Breeding duck, including Garganey, possibly non-breeding Wigeon and Pintail, Marsh Harrier, breeding waders including Avocet, breeding Common and Little Terns, Yellow Wagtail, Sedge and Reed Warblers.

August–November: Manx and possibly Sooty Shearwaters, possibly Leach's and Storm Petrels, Gannet, possibly Rough-legged Buzzard, Marsh and possibly Montagu's Harriers, Hen Harrier and Merlin (from October), Little and Temminck's Stints, Curlew Sandpiper, Bar-tailed Godwit, Whimbrel, Spotted Redshank, Greenshank, Wood Sandpiper, Turnstone, Pomarine Skua (October), Arctic and Great Skuas, Little Gull, possibly Sabine's Gull, Kittiwake, Sandwich, Common, Arctic, Little and Black Terns, large auks, possibly Little Auk, Short-eared Owl, Whinchat, Wheatear, migrant warblers, Pied Flycatchers, and from October possibly Twite and Lapland Bunting, and Snow Bunting.

4 CANTERBURY RING WOODS

OS 179
TR 05/15 & TR 06/16

Habitat

The Blean woodlands form a broad arc, on the London clay, to the north and northwest of Canterbury. A considerable amount of the once vast Forest of Blean remains, and though there are few stands of really mature oaks, there is quite a lot of 100 to 150-year-old high forest. Oak and sweet chestnut predominate, with smaller areas of other broad leaved trees, like hornbeam — favoured by Hawfinches — alongside a number of well-established, as well as young, conifer plantations.

It is the variety and extent of woodland here that is important. Many woodland birds depend on a range of different aged trees, with mature stands as well as dead wood. Plantations, sometimes dominated by sweet chestnut, usually consist of mixed blocks of coppice, or coppice with standards, separated by wide rides. The blocks are coppiced in rotation, creating open, heath-like clearings; a habitat, that is favoured by Nightjars. To the east of the city there is somewhat similar woodland, on Thanet sands, but now much disturbed by replanting and sand excavation.

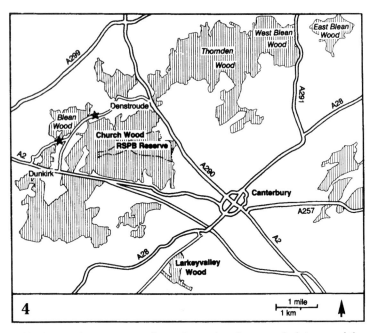

To the south are scattered woods on the slopes and plateaux of the North Downs. Their mainly calcareous nature contrasts greatly with the more acidic Blean. The variety of plant species is typically greater, and it is here you can find the best displays of spring woodland flowers, with at best a profusion of orchids among the more common primroses, bluebells, wood anemones and dog's mercury. Probably the lady orchid is the star attraction for botanists. In Britain this species is only found in Kent, with the best colonies in the woods south of Canterbury.

Species

The downland woods probably hold higher densities of birds throughout the year, but the vastness of Blean is an attraction in itself.

Woodland in the winter months is comparatively quiet. All the resident species are present, but they are less vocal and more difficult to locate. Mixed flocks of tits move quite extensively as they forage for food. Finches and thrushes, including wintering Fieldfares and Redwings, may choose to roost in denser, more sheltered woods, while Crossbills and Siskins are especially attracted to conifers like the Larch. In some winters, the rare Red Kite has occasionally been recorded, but Sparrowhawks are much more likely to be seen, with infrequent visits by a Hen Harrier or Merlin from the marshes to the east, or northwest. Another species, that may be disturbed from the edges of the woodland rides, is the Woodcock; the local population is supplemented by wintering birds from the Continent.

The birdlife is particularly rich in the summer months, with good breeding populations of all three woodpeckers, including the scarcer Lesser Spotted Woodpecker, Tree Pipits, Nightingales and Nuthatches. The whole of Blean has about five per cent of the British breeding population of Nightingales. The Church Wood block alone holds over one per cent, with well over 40 singing males, though the density is patchy, with extensive areas devoid of the species. All the common woodland warblers and tits are well represented, there are a few Redstarts, but the Wood Warbler is a scarce breeding species. Sparrowhawk numbers are increasing and the Kestrel is extremely successful.

Fungi are one of the autumn attractions; the damp woods of the Blean area probably support a richer variety than the drier, chalk woods. Among the more conspicuous species are the colourful russulas and the aptly-named stinkhorn.

Of the butterflies, the purple hairstreak may be seen flying high among oaks, while the pearl-bordered fritillary, which is now scarce elsewhere in Kent, occurs in Blean.

Lesser Spotted Woodpecker

Main Birdwatching Zones

There are several different approaches to woodland birdwatching, depending on the time of the year and the species you wish to see. Raptors often soar over woods and they can best be seen from high vantage points; much of Church Wood can be overlooked from the road between Dunkirk and Denstroude. Feeding flocks of passerines, particularly in the winter months, can often be seen quite easily, by finding a site where the woodland narrows along a valley and a road crosses it. For example, just south of Holly Hill in Blean Wood.

There are many attractive walks along the public footpaths in these woods, but in the summer months, when the foliage is thick, it is often a matter of hearing the birds first. It can be beneficial to sit quietly on the edge of a clearing, where there is a better chance of seeing the birds as they sing, feed, or collect food. When water is in short supply, find where they drink, then sit and wait.

The following two areas between them should produce most of the woodland species that can be expected in the Canterbury 'ring' woods: Church Wood, Blean, which includes both RSPB and English Nature Reserves, and Larkeyvalley Wood.

CHURCH WOOD RSPB RESERVE (Map 4a)

Habitat

About one-fifth of the reserve is sweet chestnut coppice, often with large amounts of silver birch, and occasionally a few beech. There are also extensive areas of oak high forest, with understorey of hazel, hornbeam, chestnut and other species. Management is aimed at establishing greater variety, including the creation of about six hectares of heathland, the cutting of small coppice compartments, conversion of some coppice to oak high forest, creation of glades and ponds, and widening of the rides, many of which are already fairly broad and grassy; while non-management entails allowing many of the oaks to die naturally of old age.

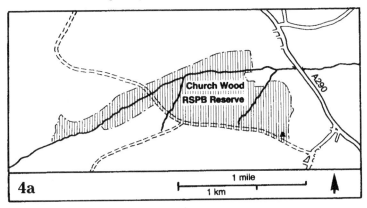

Bracken tends to be abundant and heather is locally quite common. In recently coppiced areas, there is often a good display of common cow-wheat. This attractive plant is the food of caterpillars of the heath fritillary, one of Britain's rarest butterflies, which has scattered colonies throughout the Blean forest, including Church Wood. On the edges of the forest rides, the flora is quite attractive in some places, with a good show of violets in the spring. As the coppice regrows, bramble, honeysuckle and other climbers develop into the tangled undergrowth favoured as nest-sites by such birds as Garden and Willow Warblers, and Nightingales.

Several streams and drains flow through the wood. Most dry up in the summer, but a man-made pond in the northwest part of the reserve remains flooded and attracts a good variety of birds, including an occasional Kingfisher in the summer months.

Species

The quiet winter months are enlivened by parties of tits, as they search busily for food in their quest for survival. Blue and Great Tits are likely to be most numerous, with Long-tailed and Marsh quite frequently seen. These mixed flocks often attract a few Goldcrests and Treecreepers. The drumming of the Great Spotted and the echoing 'yaffle' of the Green Woodpecker, along with the calls and light pecking of Nuthatches are common sounds, more often from the high forest stands. In fact, very few of the typical woodland species occur in the sweet chestnut at any time of the year.

The first Chiffchaff is usually heard in the second half of March and heralds the appearance of the other warblers throughout April and May.

The various species prefer different woodland types: Whitethroats are found in dense young coppice regrowth, with plenty of bramble; Garden and Willow Warblers typically select medium age coppice; while Blackcap and Chiffchaff are found more in high forest. Lesser Whitethroats are very scarce in Church Wood and Grasshopper Warblers, which were formerly almost numerous, have disappeared from there as elsewhere in Kent. Wood Warblers too are scarce, sporadic visitors.

Late April and early May is the best time to see Nightingale and Redstart, shortly after they arrive, but before leaf emergence hides them. Nightingales are easily located in young coppice or other dense undergrowth by their song, which can be heard throughout the day or night. Usually two pairs of Redstarts breed on the reserve; other birds may hold territory for a while, but do not stay to nest. Tree Pipits, another typical woodland summer visitor, are easy to watch as they perform their parachuting songflights in recently coppiced clearings with standards.

In May, the last of the summer visitors arrive. Turtle Doves here are found mainly in coppice and conifer plantations, in the middle years of their growth. Nightjars, however, are present only during the earliest years of the woodland management cycle. A warm June evening is the ideal time to search for this species. The birds are sensitive to disturbance, so it is essential to keep to the rides, from where the churring, wing-clapping and 'goo-ik' calls can easily be heard. Such an evening is also a good time to see and hear roding Woodcock.

From midsummer, as the adult birds become increasingly occupied with feeding their young and full leaf emergence takes place, it becomes much more difficult to observe woodland birds. Song also tails off rapidly. If a Crossbill invasion occurs, this is the period when they will start to appear in the pines. By the end of August, most of the visitors have departed and the long quiet autumn begins.

LARKEYVALLEY WOOD (Map 4b)

Habitat

Located on the slopes of a dry chalk valley, Larkeyvalley Wood has a rich and interesting flora. Mature beech forest is present, as is coppice of hazel, ash, hornbeam and other species, mostly under oak standards.

The thin chalk soils, in particular, support a diverse ground flora with several scarce plants. Where there is heavy shade, this may be sparse, but elsewhere there is a well-developed calcareous flora, including sanicle and sweet woodruff. Among several orchids present are violet helleborine, fly and bird's-nest orchids. The most abundant species of the woodland floor are probably dog's mercury, wood anemone and bluebell, while bramble is very apparent in recent clearings.

The wood is owned and managed, as a public open space, by the enlightened Canterbury City Council. Management is re-establishing a coppice regime, in what had become rather neglected woodland, and developing a system of widened rides about the wood. The vegetation has responded well to the cutting, with luxuriant growth of coppice and ground flora. Particularly noticeable in recently cut areas have been wood spurge and caper spurge, the latter normally regarded as an intro-

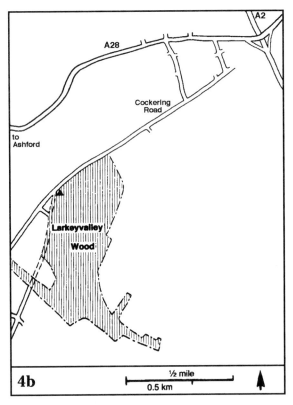

duction to Britain, but quite possibly native here. The great storm of October 1987 affected this wood more than most around Canterbury, especially the areas of beech on thin chalk soils. Along with the coppicing, replanting and natural regeneration, a more varied younger plant structure now exists.

Species

Larkeyvalley Wood in winter can be alive with birds, far more so than many Kent woodlands. One of the most interesting areas are the stands of mature beeches. Especially when there has been a heavy beech mast crop, these areas can hold well over 100 birds of several species. Blue, Great, Marsh and Coal Tits are generally all present, while Nuthatches can be very obvious, as they run up and down the smooth boles of the beeches. Chaffinches and Bramblings add to the lively scene; on occasions 100 of the latter species alone have been seen feeding here.

A circuit of the wood will reveal more species. This is one of the better woods in which to see Hawfinch, although it is almost essential to know the calls, especially the loud 'tic', to locate them. All three woodpeckers are present, but the Great Spotted is the most numerous. Parties of Long-tailed Tits, often with attendant Goldcrests or Treecreepers, are frequently encountered. Jays seem quite common here and winter is probably the easiest time of year to see this colourful species well.

The arrival of spring sees the appearance of the common woodland warblers. Chiffchaff and Willow Warbler, Blackcap and Garden Warbler are the most frequent species here. Their relative abundance is likely to change as the coppicing programme progresses. Tree Pipits rapidly established themselves in clearings, and Nightingales have recolonised the wood.

Timing

In wooded areas, early mornings are generally more productive at all times of year, as birds tend to sing and feed more actively then and it is often less windy. The dawn chorus in May can be dominated by Nightingales, so much so that other species may be difficult to hear. Dusk visits are also recommended: in winter to locate roosts and hear Tawny Owls hooting, while Woodcock circle overhead and call from February onwards; and in late May to early June to hear Nightjars churring and see Woodcock roding — at that time of year it is usually 2100 hours before you can expect to hear either.

Access

To get to Church Wood from Canterbury, take the A290 Whitstable road. After 1.5 miles (2.4 km) turn left into Rough Common and follow the road for about 0.25 mile (0.4 km), where a track that leads off to the right into the wood, is marked by a brown tourist sign 'Church Wood Nature Reserve' (Map 4a). The reserve car park is 0.25 mile (0.4 km) along this track. Three trails are waymarked by red, green and brown arrows on posts beside the paths, which allow a number of walks of varying lengths. Reserve leaflets are on sale at the car park.

For Holly Hill follow the road north from Dunkirk for 0.75 mile (1.2 km), turn sharp left and drive southwest for 0.25 mile (0.4 km) to TR 078601.

For Larkeyvalley Wood (Map 4b) take the A28 Ashford road out of Canterbury. After crossing the bridge over the A2 dual carriageway, take the first left, St Nicholas Road, through a housing estate. At the T-junction 0.25 mile (0.2 km) along this road, turn right and follow Cockering Road for about 1 mile (1.6 km), where the car park will be seen on the left, at the edge of the wood. The many paths allow good access. A leaflet describing the site and the footpaths should be available at the car park.

Calendar

Resident: Sparrowhawk, Kestrel, Tawny Owl, all three woodpeckers, common woodland passerines, including Marsh and possibly Willow Tit, Nuthatch, Treecreeper, and possibly Hawfinch.

December–February: Woodcock, feeding parties of tits, Treecreepers and Goldcrests, possibly Siskin and Crossbill.

March–May: Possibly Hobby, Turtle Dove, Tree Pipit, Nightingale, Redstart, common woodland warblers.

June–July: Breeding residents and summer visitors, including Woodcock, Nightjar (Church Wood), Lesser Spotted Woodpecker, Tree Pipit, Nightingale, possibly Wood Warbler, occasionally Crossbill.

August–November: Most breeding summer visitors depart by late August, winter visitors like Woodcock and Siskin return.

Habitat

The stretch of the Stour Valley that extends eastwards from Sturry to Grove Ferry comprises one of the few remaining true wetland areas in Kent, characterised by extensive reedbeds, shallow lagoons, well established gravel pits, wet woodlands of willow and alders, marsh and grazing meadows.

On the north side of the river there is a footpath from Fordwich to Hersden Lake. The gravel pit at Westbere, used for sailing, is now surrounded by reedbeds and mature willows and alders. Between that pit and the lake at Hersden the reedbeds are extensive, with grazing marsh to the south of the river and the wooded slopes of Trenleypark Wood beyond. In spring, this diverse habitat supports an almost unique dawn chorus of marsh and woodland species in close proximity. There is an equally diverse range of breeding species. Stodmarsh too has extensive reedbeds and shallow lakes, with rough pasture to the east, some of which can now be flooded to attract wildfowl and waders. The three hides on the reserve — Lake, Marsh and Reedbed — all provide good viewpoints, and the last named has wheelchair access. Further east, towards Grove Ferry, the grazing marsh is divided into smaller plots by reed-lined ditches. When heavy rains flood these fields, they too attract dabbling duck and waders.

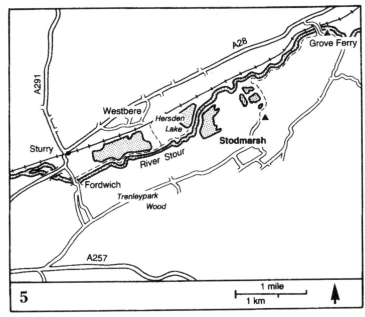

Species

With its proximity to the coast, this variety of wetland habitat attracts many different species. In the winter months it is not too unusual for a diver, and occasionally a rarer grebe, to visit one of the lakes. In severe conditions any wintering Bitterns and Water Rails are often easier to see, while small flocks of Bewick's Swans and White-fronted Geese, and possibly Bean or Pink-footed Geese, may graze on the more open pasture, or flight in to roost on the open waters at dusk. The cold weather sawbills, Smew and Goosander occasionally visit the lakes, which often hold good numbers of wintering Wigeon, Teal, Shoveler and Gadwall. Hen Harriers and the occasional Sparrowhawk, Merlin or Short-eared Owl hunt along the valley, while a Kingfisher might be glimpsed as it flashes along the river. In the reedbeds Bearded Tits will from time to time proclaim their presence.

Bearded Tit

Spring in the valley may be announced by the arrival of an early Garganey or Sand Martin. During April the variety will increase as passage migrants drop in and the summer visitors arrive. Freshwater waders like Ruff, Spotted Redshank, Green and Wood Sandpipers can be expected. Common and perhaps Black Terns may hover over the lakes, while song from the reedbeds should include Sedge, Reed and possibly Savi's Warblers, the first two of which breed in good numbers along the valley. Sadly, the last-named species has declined and is now rare. A Marsh Harrier may flap and glide over the reeds, while in the sky above a migrant Osprey or a Hobby can be anticipated. In late May and early June up to 10 Hobbies may hunt together, while a southern rarity may visit the valley at this time. Over the years extreme rarities like Red-footed Falcon, Caspian Tern, Pallid Swift, Great Reed Warbler and Penduline Tit have all been seen, while Little Egret, Purple Heron and Spoonbill are scarce visitors. Large flocks of non-breeding Mute Swans form.

The volume of song diminishes as the breeding species busily feed their young. All too quickly the marshland waders return on their journey south. Many of the spring migrants can be expected again, some lingering for longer periods, as the autumn journey does not have quite the same urgency about it. Young Hobbies may possibly be seen with the adult birds, as they learn the art of catching prey, while large numbers of hirundines and wagtails may gather to feed and roost in the reedbeds for a few days, before continuing their long journeys south. As the autumn progresses, the winter visitors return again. It remains to be seen whether the Cetti's Warblers, which were wiped out by the severity of successive cold winters, in particular the deep snow of January 1987, will return.

Main Birdwatching Zones

Much of the Stour Valley can be visited along the public rights of way, but human disturbance is one of the principal threats to some of the more sensitive breeding species. Access to the Stodmarsh National Nature Reserve is carefully controlled and more detailed information is given for that site, with a few notes about Westbere under Additional Sites.

STODMARSH NNR (Map 5a)

Habitat

The Stodmarsh National Nature Reserve includes about 650 acres (260 ha) of alluvial marshland south of the Great Stour. There is public access along the flood protection barrier, known as the Lampen Wall and along the river wall east to Grove Ferry. English Nature owns the freehold of the reserve, at the south end of which there is a fine copse of alders. West of the Lampen Wall, where shallow, open water is surrounded by dense reeds and willows, the colliery tip forms a backdrop. Shingle-covered rafts attract Common Terns to breed. Recent bunding work has made it possible to control water levels and English Nature's

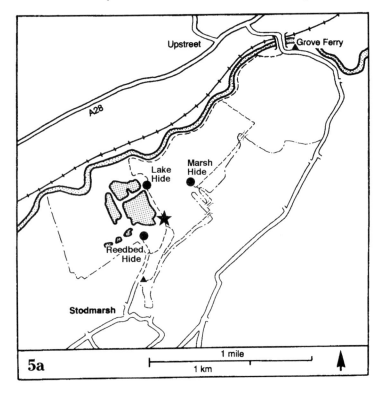

management programme also includes harvesting reed and grazing the meadows with cattle.

The Reedbed hide overlooks lagoons surrounded by reeds, in which you may be fortunate enough to see a Water Rail well and possibly a Bittern. An area of flooded meadow, which can be viewed from the Marsh Hide, attracts dabbling duck and freshwater waders. The drier bramble and hawthorn scrub, either side of the railway to the north of the river, is a suitable habitat for the scarce Grasshopper Warbler.

The wide range of aquatic plants include species like the greater bladderwort, frogbit and flowering rush, which occur in some of the pools; greater spearwort and great water dock grow in the reedswamp, which is dominated by the common reed. Another eye-catching species is the amphibious bistort, whose pink flowers form an attractive spectacle in summer.

Other interesting aspects of wildlife include large numbers of bats, mainly noctules, which feed over the lagoons in summer. The reserve is also rich with invertebrates, notably moths, flies, spiders and dragonflies, including relatively scarce species such as hairy dragonfly and red-eyed damselfly. Of the mammals the water vole is most frequently seen, often noisily crunching reed stems beside the Lampen Wall.

Species

Two of the principal attractions in the winter months are the possibilities of seeing a Bittern, as well as the roosting Hen Harriers. Sometimes up to ten or more of these attractive raptors can be seen flying low over the reeds before they drop in to roost at dusk. The site varies from year to year, often close to the colliery tip, but occasionally near the southern edge of the reedbed, east of the Lampen Wall, where the birds are relatively close, providing excellent opportunities for viewing. Other winter specialities are the Bewick's Swans and White-fronted Geese, the occasional Great Grey Shrike and the more regular Water Pipit, which may be seen from the Marsh Hide, and Siskin, which is usually found feeding in the alders, while the distinctive 'pinging' note from the resident Bearded Tits can often be heard from the reedbeds.

In spring, an early Garganey may be attracted to the flooded meadow in front of the Marsh Hide. Sand Martins can be expected by late March, when Chiffchaffs, which often overwinter, should be singing from the alders, or the dense sallow scrub at the other end of the Lampen Wall. By late April, a wide variety of summer visitors and passage migrants should normally be present. Yellow Wagtails will be feeding in rough pasture, the song of Sedge and Reed Warblers will be echoing round the reedbeds. When they are present, the similar reeling songs of Savi's and Grasshopper Warblers are more difficult to separate. The Savi's sound is lower, slower and more full-toned and the bird is as likely to be singing from a small osier as from a reed stem. The more mechanical sounding Grasshopper Warbler song is more likely to come from bramble in drier habitat, though not exclusively so. One of the most abundant reedbed passerines is the Reed Bunting, which is present throughout the year.

Dawn and dusk visits are important at this time of year to hear rarer species like Spotted Crake and the 'booming' of the Bittern. The latter became purely a winter visitor for a while, but careful management of the reedbeds may well see this wonderful species breeding here regularly again, which will undoubtedly add to the attraction of the site. The intriguing, trilling song of the Water Rail and the fascinating drumming of the Snipe, while displaying, are more commonly heard at these times of the day too.

Several raptors can be anticipated in May, including Marsh Harrier, Hobby and possibly a migrant Osprey, while rarer species like Golden Oriole occasionally occur. As summer progresses, more and more broods of young hatch and the adult birds become increasingly active, as they search for food to carry back to the nest. Sitting on the Lampen Wall can be a delight as Bearded Tits zip by continuously. The Common Terns should also be feeding their young, while Little Terns can be seen teaching their young to feed; they will have come from the nearby coastal colonies. By late August the numbers of Yellow Wagtails and hirundines roosting in the reedbeds increase to hundreds and thousands respectively. In September, following a good breeding season, flocks of up to 100 Bearded Tits may gather, occasionally erupting high into the air. Some move southwest to winter elsewhere. By late October the return of the wintering Great Grey Shrike is eagerly anticipated, but it can be an extremely elusive species, hunting over a wide territory, and it is by no means annual.

Timing

Dusk visits are particularly important during the winter months, while dawn and dusk visits in the spring may well produce a few extra species.

In spring and summer, early mornings are best for songbirds. Visits towards dusk in the early autumn are a must for roosting hirundines, when Hobbies may be seen hunting. Strong winds can be troublesome, fewer birds sing and wildfowl tend to seek shelter in the reeds.

Access

From Canterbury take the A257 Sandwich road (Map 5). After about 1.25 miles (2 km) turn left and follow Stodmarsh Road for just over 3 miles (5 km) to the village of Stodmarsh. Turn left immediately after passing the Red Lion public house. There is a large car park for the reserve (Map 5a) just over 0.25 mile (0.5 km) along this rough track, with a toilet block. Please do not park in the village. There is also a log at the toilet block and a chalkboard, which are worth checking for recent sightings — enter your own observations when you leave. A short nature trail takes you through willows and alders to the Lampan Wall then back to the car park. An alternative is to continue along the track on foot, which provides two options. Either continue straight on to the Reedbed Hide, which is suitable for wheelchair observers, or turn right onto the Lampen Wall, which provides excellent vantage points for looking over the reserve. Walk the length of the Lampen Wall and a similar distance along the river wall to the east, before turning southeast across the grazing marsh, then southwest by the Marsh Hide to complete a circuit of about 3 miles (5 km).

There is also access to the reserve, via the signposted footpath along the river bank, from the Grove Ferry Inn, where there is a large car park and toilet facilities.

Calendar

Resident: Little and Great Crested Grebes, Cormorant, Greylag and Canada Geese, Shelduck, Gadwall, Teal, Shoveler, Pochard, Tufted

Duck, Water Rail, Snipe, Redshank (relatively few in winter), Kingfisher, Bearded Tit, Reed Bunting.

December–February: Bittern, Bewick's Swan and White-fronted Goose, Wigeon, Hen Harrier (regular roost), Water Pipit, possibly Great Grey Shrike, Siskin, Corn Bunting (up to 200 sometimes roost).

March–May: possibly Bittern, Garganey, Marsh Harrier, possibly Osprey, Hobby, migrant freshwater waders (May), Black Tern, Sand Martin, Yellow Wagtail, possibly Grasshopper and Savi's Warblers, Sedge and Reed Warblers, possibly Golden Oriole (May).

June–July: Breeding resident wildfowl, waders and Common Tern, plus resident and summering passerines.

August–November: Hobby, migrant freshwater waders (August–September), Little and possibly Black Terns (August), roosting Sand Martins, Swallows and Yellow Wagtails (August–September), Bearded Tit (eruptive flocks September).

6 THANET

Habitat

Though heavily built-up, the Isle of Thanet (as it is sometimes referred to) has not only considerable interest for local birdwatchers, but much to attract visitors too. A glance at a map of northwest Europe will immediately show the reason for this interest. Situated at the southern end of the North Sea, it is an obvious point for observing the migration of a wide variety of species, from divers over the sea to warblers in the coastal scrub.

The coastline, from Ramsgate in the south round to Margate in the north, is essentially chalk cliffs, with a rocky foreshore and sandy bays. Between Foreness Point and North Foreland, much of the cliff top is grass covered, while lines of trees fringe the North Foreland golf course. These open areas provide an obvious landfall for southbound migrants in the autumn, particularly when inclement weather forces them down. A mile or so inland from Foreness Point is Northdown Park, effectively a sheltered haven for passerine migrants, despite the human disturbance. The large, mature, private gardens of the houses close to the cliff edge will inevitably attract a good variety of migrants too. However, the numerous narrow roads and public footpaths make much of the area accessible for visitors.

Species

The autumn migration can be a most exciting period, producing a wide variety of interesting species in certain weather conditions, but Thanet

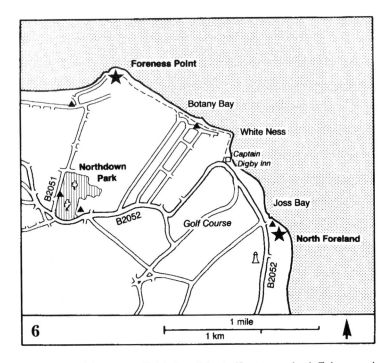

is also one of the most reliable localities in Kent to see both Fulmar and Purple Sandpiper. One might also include Ring-necked Parakeet which has relatively recently been added to the British List, though feral birds have been breeding on Thanet since 1972. The Fulmar only bred for the first time on Thanet as recently as 1973, but since then up to a dozen or so pairs usually breed.

In the winter months, it is often the most inclement weather conditions, particularly northerly gales, that produce the greatest excitement for hardened seawatchers. Large numbers of Red-throated Divers and auks can be expected.

Fulmar, Purple Sandpiper and Ring-necked Parakeet can all be seen during the first quarter, while the spring brings an increase in the variety of birds on sea-passage, as well as a good variety of passerine migrants. The latter half of June and July tends to be relatively quiet, however, the passage of Common Scoters often commences at this time.

Probably the most rewarding period is the late autumn, again when the wind is between northwest and northeast. Such scarce seabirds as Pomarine Skua and Little Auk are virtually annual, particularly in stormy weather, when there is always the possibility of a Leach's or Storm Petrel. Storm-driven birds sometimes find refuge in sheltered spots like Ramsgate harbour, which in recent years has held Shag, Grey Phalarope and Sabine's Gull. Raptors and a variety of passerine migrants also occur at this time and few autumns pass without the occurrence of rarer species like Richard's Pipit and Yellow-browed Warbler.

As with all migration points, regular watching is likely to bring the greatest rewards, though a good understanding of the weather conditions may well enable casual visitors to be there at the right time, when movements of seabirds, or falls of passerine migrants, occur.

Main Birdwatching Zones

The whole area is relatively small, but the time of year, the prevailing weather conditions and the particular interests of the observer will often dictate where effort should be concentrated. Two areas are described in greater detail: the coastal stretch from Foreness Point round to North Foreland, and Northdown Park. However, passerine migrants in particular, are likely to turn up in any patch of vegetation; Ramsgate cemetery, for example, has produced some extremely interesting species over the years. Further west, at Minnis Bay, there is the added attraction of coastal marshes, as well as good seawatching possibilities from Reculver Towers.

FORENESS POINT and NORTH FORELAND (Map 6)

Habitat

The chalk cliffs are approximately 50 ft (15 m) high on this stretch of the Thanet coast, providing excellent vantage points for seawatching. Much of the cliff-top is grassed, with some arable land, particularly close to the cliff edge at North Foreland. At Foreness Point, the open grassland is now backed by a housing development, the gardens of which can already boast of rare vagrants — Booted Warbler for one. The short grass of the pitch-and-putt golf course may attract Mediterranean Gulls, as well as migrant pipits and wagtails, as the North Foreland golf course can, but there is no public access onto it. The rough grass between Foreness Point, along the cliff-top towards White Ness, may conceal tired migrants and autumn visitors like Lapland Bunting. The arable field at North Foreland often attracts roosting gulls, amongst which there may be a Mediterranean Gull. The hedgerows and trees lining the roads that border the North Foreland golf course are most attractive for migrant passerines.

At low tide, the mussel-encrusted rocky platforms provide abundant food for waders like Turnstone and Purple Sandpiper. At high tide these rocks are covered and the narrow sandy strip below the cliff forms a natural roost site for the waders, provided that they are not disturbed. Some of the bays are in fact cut off at high tide, effectively preventing human disturbance, when these birds can be easily seen from the cliff-top.

Species

Foreness Point is undoubtedly one of the most reliable sites in the southeast to see Purple Sandpipers. In the winter months, though they spread out over the mussel covered rocks to feed, they often form into a single flock at each high tide, and a flock of 50 or more birds usually roosts in one of the sheltered bays. If disturbed, they may roost on the harbour walls at Margate.

Small flocks of Eider occasionally feed offshore, while several other waders, like Oystercatcher, Turnstone and Curlew, and the ever hungry Rock Pipit, feed around the rock pools. Black Redstarts occasionally winter, often feeding at the bottom of the cliffs. Winter gales, particularly from the northerly quarter, can produce several hundred Red-throated Divers and larger numbers of Kittiwakes and auks, mainly Guillemots and Razorbills, but occasionally the scarcer Puffin. To seawatch for these species you may find some shelter in the lea of the

Coastguard Station at Foreness Point, or in your own car, which you can park quite close to the cliff edge at Joss Bay. Cold weather movements may occasionally involve geese and duck from the Continent, as well as Lapwings and Skylarks. It is worth checking the gull flocks as they roost in the fields; look for the 'white-winged' species. The Mediterranean Gull is fairly regular, the huge Glaucous Gull virtually annual, but the more elegant Iceland Gull is rare.

The up-Channel seabird passage in spring is really best viewed from Dungeness, as the birds are normally too distant to be seen from Thanet. However, some passage can be expected, with species like Whimbrel and Little Tern flying west into the Thames estuary. The former can be anticipated from mid April, while the latter generally peaks in early May. With the numbers of Purple Sandpipers wintering, there is a tendency for some to remain until early May. Throughout this period the majestic flight of the Fulmar can be studied at close range, as the bird glides along the edge of the cliff.

Purple Sandpipers

Earlier in the spring, passerine migrants like chats and wagtails can be expected, feeding amongst the cliff-top grass, or in the arable fields. It is worth checking the hedgerows and trees that fringe the North Foreland golf course for species like warblers, crests and flycatchers. From mid March Black Redstarts may sit prominently on fences, dropping onto the ground to feed, while White Wagtails (the pale, grey mantled Continental race) are easy to see, as they feed on the short grass. The Firecrest is another early migrant, favouring the denser foliage of evergreen trees — listen for its call-note, which is lower and more powerful than that of the Goldcrest. By the end of the month Wheatears will be feeding in the open, while Chiffchaffs call and sing from the trees. In light westerly winds some raptor passage may be observed from White Ness, where Buzzards and Sparrowhawks that have probably wintered in southern Britain can be seen drifting northeast.

From mid April, Yellow Wagtails can be expected on the short grass of the golf courses, where a migrant Ring Ouzel might also feed, while Whitethroats, Lesser Whitethroats and possibly Pied Flycatchers may forage in the hedgerows and trees. In early May, Whinchats perch on the low bushes, fence wires or fence posts. Overhead a Hobby may occasionally be seen, more often than not on passage, while the visible migration of species like Turtle Dove can occasionally be quite marked, as they coast westwards.

The autumn months invariably provide the greatest opportunity to see a good mixture of seabirds, migrant raptors and passerines. One species that is noticeably absent from the autumn seabird movements is the Fulmar. Once the young have left the breeding cliffs, few will be seen until the adults return in November.

Some seabird passage can be expected during August, with small flocks of Common Scoter flying east off Foreness Point, or south off North Foreland. In periods of northerly winds, the first Arctic and Great Skuas of the autumn can be anticipated. Small numbers of Black Terns can also be anticipated in late August and early September, when the numbers of Pied Flycatchers are generally at their peak, and when the rarer Icterine Warbler has occurred almost annually. Increased numbers of up to 20 Great Skuas and 40 Arctic Skuas can be expected on good days in September, when the Sandwich Tern passage also reaches its peak, with perhaps 300 flying east in a day. Gannet numbers may increase to 100 or more per day, with as many as 1,000 Kittiwakes, while small numbers of Manx and occasionally Sooty Shearwaters can also be anticipated, the latter generally coming closer to shore in inclement conditions. It is a good time too to look for Shags, much slighter looking than the Cormorant, but comparatively scarce.

October sees a further change in the species on passage, with numbers of migrant finches coasting west. At sea, flocks of Brent Geese flying west into the Thames estuary may exceed totals of 1,000 per day late in the month, while small flocks of Velvet Scoter and a few Pomarine Skuas can also be expected. Sparrowhawk, Merlin and also Short-eared Owl can be seen flying in off the sea, or coasting westwards. The Hen Harrier too is fairly regular in October, when rarer species like Rough-legged Buzzard feature as rewards for long periods of observation. Newly arrived Woodcock may be disturbed from patches of cover around the cliff tops in the early morning, while Woodlark and Richard's Pipit are almost annual visitors. Lapland Buntings too may be flushed from the longer grass by the cliff-top path. Other passerines, like Goldcrest and Firecrest, are generally most numerous in the woodland fringes in October, when a Yellow-browed Warbler may also appear.

Northerly storms in late October and early November may well produce movements of auks, including the rare Little Auk, which is almost annual at this time. Petrels too are occasionally driven close to the shore in strong winds.

NORTHDOWN PARK (Map 6)

Habitat

A relatively small town park, much of which consists of short grassed playing fields. However, small parts of it are wooded and there are areas of cultivated gardens. The northeast corner borders on some rough wasteland, which is generally less disturbed and does attract migrant passerines.

Species

This park is one of the most reliable sites for resident Ring-necked Parakeets. They frequently perch in the rows of sycamores that line the footpaths, but are more often located by their raucous calls. Most bird-watchers probably prefer to see and hear them in their native haunts, but if you can accept them, they are attractive and fun to watch. Another species that does occasionally winter here is the Firecrest, most likely to be found in the denser, more sheltered evergreens. By late March, an early Wheatear may be seen feeding on the playing fields, or a Chiffchaff may be singing in the trees, but it is likely to be late April before many spring visitors return and May is the month when the rarer migrants are likely to occur. The arrival of a Collared Flycatcher in May 1984 focused attention on this site, which produced all four fly-catcher species that spring. The Pied Flycatcher and Firecrest are regular spring migrants, as are most of the common warblers, while the open fields may also attract an occasional Ring Ouzel.

The passage of migrants returning south during the autumn months can make visits then most rewarding. In August, species like the Lesser Whitethroat, Wood Warbler and Pied Flycatcher are fairly regular among the commoner migrants, but beware of the confusion that can be caused when migrant Reed Warblers occur away from their natural, reedbed habitat. With a northeasterly influence, Scandinavian migrants like Wryneck or Icterine Warbler may appear. By late September and early October Chiffchaffs have generally replaced Willow Warblers, while an easterly influence may produce the rare Red-breasted Flycatcher. Goldcrest and Firecrest numbers peak during October and, when there has been an influx of these two species, it is worth check-ing the trees and bushes carefully to see if you can find a Yellow-browed Warbler. Listen too for the distinctive call of the Serin, which does occur almost annually on Thanet. By early November numbers of Fieldfares and Redwings can be expected, but they will only remain as long as food is available for them.

Timing

The cliff-top footpath and the park are popular with locals for walking their dogs, so early morning visits are important, particularly during the migration periods when falls of night migrants can be anticipated. Other passerine migrants disperse inland quite quickly, as they feed along the hedgerows and narrow lines of trees close to the coast.

Passerine migration is closely linked with the prevailing weather con-ditions. An easterly wind tends to drift migrants over the Continent west-wards and rain often forces them down. In optimum conditions, after dawn, it is possible to witness migrants actually dropping out of the clouds. If the belt of rain passes through just before dawn, there may be an obvious fall of migrants as dawn breaks. Northeast winds early in the autumn, linked with troughs of low pressure, may well produce condi-tions to bring Scandinavian night migrants to Thanet. Later in the autumn, ridges of high pressure across the Continent and further east are necessary to bring the rarer Siberian warblers closer to Kent's shores.

Visible seabird passage is also dependent on the vagaries of the weather. Thousands of seabirds gather in the North Sea in the autumn and many of them move south through the English Channel. When the wind is northwest, the movement may be more southerly and watching from Joss Bay or North Foreland should be more productive. When the wind is from the north or northeast the birds can be seen well from Foreness Point. Although strong northerly winds often bring birds clos-er to the shore, light winds may have the same effect if the birds become disoriented in fog. A marked passage may also be precipitat-ed when the wind suddenly veers northwest and in these conditions it may commence at any time of the day. While the wind is in the northerly sector, early morning watches tend to be more productive and the movement may cease as the wind drops.

Access

The coastal areas and Northdown Park (Map 6) are boarded on the landward side by the B2052. To visit North Foreland, follow the B2052 north from Broadstairs. Less than 0.75 mile (0.4 km) past the lighthouse there is a car park on the right, opposite Elmwood Avenue, which overlooks Joss Bay. From here you can see gulls either feeding offshore, or roosting in the arable field on the cliff top to the south. Check the hedgerows and bushes for migrants.

Further along the B2052, near the Captain Digby Inn, where the road turns southwest, there is a footpath along the cliff-top to White Ness; from there it leads northwest towards Foreness Point. The wader roost sometimes forms in Botany Bay and the birds can be seen well from the top of the cliff. Access to this stretch of the coast is also possible by car. Follow the B2052 for about 0.5 mile (0.8 km) beyond the Captain Digby Inn, turn right into St George's Road and second right along Kingsgate Avenue.

Northdown Park is bordered by the B2052 to the south and the B2051 Queen Elizabeth Avenue to the west, in which you can park. There is also a small car park in the southeast corner of the park (TR 380702), where the Ring-necked Parakeets can often be heard calling from the Holm Oaks. To drive to Foreness Point, follow Queen Elizabeth Avenue north, turn sharp right and left at the corner of the park into Princess Margaret Avenue, which brings you out by the pitch-and-putt golf course. Park in the spaces provided. Walk along the tarmac road, which leads round the golf course fence, along the cliff top, to the Coastguard Station. This is a good seawatch point, from which you can also see the gulls and other species feeding along the shore. At the appropriate season, check the pitch-and-putt course and the cliff-top grass and arable for migrants.

Calendar

Resident: Fulmar (usually absent September–November), Ring-necked Parakeet.

December–February: Red-throated Diver, Great Crested Grebe, Oystercatcher, Ringed and Grey Plovers, Turnstone, Sanderling, Purple Sandpiper, Curlew, Glaucous Gull, Kittiwake, auks, Rock Pipit, Black Redstart and Firecrest (both almost annual).

March–May: Hobby (April–May), Purple Sandpiper, Whimbrel (passage), Little Tern (peak passage April–May), Black Redstart, Ring Ouzel, Firecrest, Serin (almost annual April–May).

June–July: Breeding Fulmars, Common Scoter (passage), Mediterranean Gull (July peak).

August–November: Manx and possibly Sooty Shearwaters, Gannet, Shag, Brent Goose (October), Common Scoter, Velvet Scoter (October–November), Sparrowhawk and Merlin (October), Woodcock (October–November), Great and Arctic Skuas (September), Pomarine Skua (October), Little Gull (November peak), Mediterranean Gull, Kittiwake (peak passage September–October), Sandwich Tern (September peak), Little Tern, Black Tern (August–September peak), auks possibly including Puffin (November peak) and Little Auk (almost annual late October–November), Short-eared Owl (passage October–November), Woodlark (almost annual October), Richard's Pipit (almost annual late September, early October), Icterine Warbler (almost annual August–September), Yellow browed Warbler (almost annual October), Firecrest and Goldcrest (October peaks), Pied Flycatcher (August–early September peak), finch passage (October peak), Serin (almost annual October–November), Lapland Bunting (October–November).

7 SANDWICH BAY

OS 179
TR26/36 & TR 25/35

Habitat

Much of Pegwell Bay is now a reserve, jointly owned by the National Trust, the KCC, the RSPB and the KWT, comprising Shellness Point, dune pasture, saltmarsh, beach and tidal mudflats to the north and south of the estuary of the River Stour, and Stonelees, a mixture of habitats with a range of unusual and sensitive plants and animals. The areas of saltmarsh and sand dunes are continually being formed from the accretion of silt, sand and shingle. It is the last remaining complex in Kent containing all these habitats.

The lime-rich soils, formed from the sand and shells, attract particularly interesting plants. The dune flora includes sea holly, with its associated broomrape, and sea sandwort, while on the saltings the sharp rush, not found elsewhere in Kent, is abundant.

Adjacent to the coastal strip south of the reserve are the Prince's and Royal St George's golf courses and to the west of them, bordered by the river, an area of arable and grazing land dissected by ditches. At the south end lies the Sandwich Bay Estate and the Bird Observatory, which also includes in its census area part of the Worth marshes.

North of the town of Sandwich, at Great Stonar between the road and the river, is a large sheltered lake, which attracts wintering wildfowl. Just beyond the B2048 turning is the Pegwell Bay Country Park, which is a good spot from which to view the saltings and mudflats of Pegwell Bay, looking eastwards across the estuary to Shellness Point.

Species

The list of winter specialities is considerably increased when the weather is severe on the Continent. The rarer grebes, swans, geese and ducks can then be expected, plus larger numbers of many of the commoner species. In a normal winter, wildfowl feed in the bay, the mudflats attract a variety of wader species, the saltmarsh, dune pasture and shingle beach can be expected to hold a few Twite, both Snow and Lapland Buntings, and possibly Shore Lark, while raptors like Hen Harrier, Merlin and Short-eared Owl can be seen hunting over the grazing

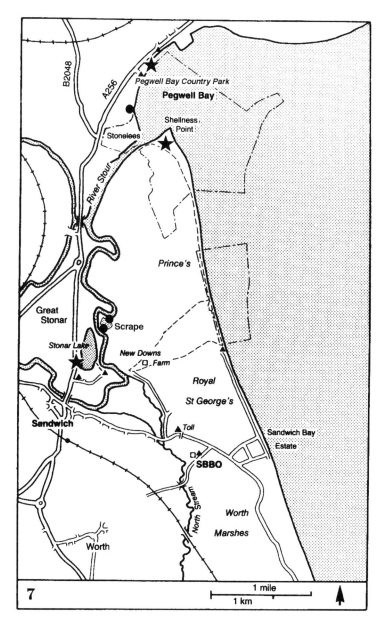

marsh. Much of the up-Channel spring passage is too distant to be observed from the beach, apart from those birds that sometimes follow the coast, like Brent Goose and possibly Avocet, but numbers of several wader species increase during April, when they stop off to feed in the estuary. The Sandwich Tern, which does occasionally winter, is one of the earliest spring migrants, followed by a wide variety of non-passerine and passerine species, while rarer species like Kentish Plover are almost annual in Pegwell Bay.

Kentish and Ringed Plover

Little Terns still breed, thanks largely to the constant attention of wardens, which is minimising the disturbance that has limited their success in recent years.

In autumn, as with other east coast sites, the weather is a major factor in determining the numbers and variety of birds that occur. At some stage, Scandinavian migrants like Wryneck, Icterine Warbler and Red-backed Shrike inevitably appear and at the same time there should be larger numbers of commoner migrants like Pied Flycatcher. On the mudflats there will be a greater variety of waders, including species like Little Stint, Curlew Sandpiper, Whimbrel and Greenshank, that would normally favour freshwater marshes. Offshore, the numbers of terns will increase, when they can be seen feeding in the estuary, roosting at the point, or migrating south. Later in the autumn, flocks of Common Scoter can be seen on the sea, sometimes with Velvet Scoter, Eider and Red-breasted Mergansers, while stormy weather may also bring divers and auks into the bay.

Main Birdwatching Zones

One small site is worth visiting: Stonar Lake, particularly in the winter months, when it often holds rarer grebes and ducks. For convenience, the rest of the region is dealt with in two parts. The area north of the River Stour, known as Pegwell Bay Country Park and the area south of the estuary and east of the river, which is described under the general heading of Sandwich Bay Bird Observatory.

PEGWELL BAY COUNTRY PARK (Map 7)

Habitat

Essentially an area of saltmarsh and mudflats, but there is an open space of grasses and thistles to the south, which attracts finches and buntings in autumn and winter. The hide, which overlooks the estuary, provides excellent viewing across the mudflats, as well as shelter during inclement weather. A little further south is Stonelees, with scrub vegetation ranging from the low growing dewberry and young blackthorn bushes, through to mature hawthorn and trees such as sycamore, ash and a variety of willows. Here a good variety of migrants can be seen during the appropriate seasons.

The saltmarsh reflects a stage in the natural colonisation of the mud-flats by vegetation. Plant species include common cordgrass, sea blite, sea lavender, sea purslane and sea aster, the seeds of which attract various finches.

Species

The mudflats are rich in invertebrate life and support a good number of waders in winter, with over 1,500 Dunlin, about 1,300 Oystercatchers, over 300 Grey Plover and Curlew, between 200–300 each of Ringed Plover, Knot and Redshank, and up to 200 each of Sanderling, Bar-tailed Godwit and Turnstone. They roost either at Shellness Point, on the fields behind the point, or on the old hoverport launching pad. They can usually be seen well feeding close to the saltmarsh both before and after high water. Snipe and the rarer Jack Snipe can sometimes be seen feeding along the ditches in the saltmarsh on the edge of the estuary. Usually about 100 Shelduck winter, with small numbers of Brent Geese and other dabbling duck, but since the closure of the hoverport, numbers have shown an increase. Out in the bay Eider and Common Scoter may be seen, with the occasional Velvet Scoter or Red-throated Diver, but of the more distant species the Cormorant is likely to be the easiest to identify.

Amongst the Linnets and Goldfinches feeding on the seeding plants, not only on the saltmarsh, but also in the open area, there may be a few Redpolls and Twite. Stonechats too favour this stretch of open ground. If the finches, or even the waders, suddenly take flight, look quickly for the cause, it may be a Merlin hunting, or possibly a Hen Harrier gliding over the saltmarsh.

Spring is typified by sudden increases in the numbers of Brent Geese in late March and Bar-tailed Godwits a month later, when they stop off to feed in the estuary, before continuing their long flights north. Other migrant waders can be expected including, appropriately, Kentish Plover; it was first named from a specimen taken here. By May, quite a number of waders are in their more attractive summer plumage, when the brilliant red of the Knot is a pleasure to see. Rarer species like Curlew Sandpiper or Temminck's Stint occur occasionally and in recent years careful scrutiny of the migrant flocks of Ringed Plover, essentially of the northern, tundra race *C. h. tundrae*, has produced one or two Broad-billed Sandpipers.

An easterly wind in May might produce a few Scandinavian passerine migrants in the hawthorn scrub at Stonelees; Icterine Warblers have been heard singing there.

Sandwich and Little Terns are usually present throughout the summer and can be seen feeding in the estuary, while creches of Shelduck ducklings are fascinating to watch as they dive one after the other. A careful study of the gull plumages may reveal the presence of a few non-breeding Mediterranean Gulls, usually in first-summer dress. Several *Sylvia* warbler species breed at Stonelees.

Autumn passage commences with returning waders appearing from mid July. When the tide is low, species like Common and Green Sandpiper can be seen along the ditches in the saltmarsh; Whimbrel and Greenshank also favour this area. The numbers of terns slowly build up at Shellness Point and they are best seen on an incoming tide in the evening, when the light is good. If the flock is suddenly disturbed, it may indicate the presence of an Arctic Skua. From late August it is worth checking the Stonelees scrub for migrants, particularly when a northeast wind blows and it rains, as these conditions might bring rarer Scandinavian migrants like Red-backed Shrike and Wryneck. During August–September there is also a significant passage of Redshank and Curlew, but of the shore waders only the Ringed Plover is seen in numbers markedly higher than those remaining to winter, with up to 500 occasionally. Northerly gales in late autumn may cause rare species like Grey Phalarope or Sabine's Gull to seek shelter in the bay, along with large numbers of Brent Geese and other wildfowl.

SANDWICH BAY BIRD OBSERVATORY (Map 7)

Habitat

The uniqueness of the reserve area around Shellness Point has already been described. South of the point, the golf courses provide extensive tracts of suitable habitat for a variety of ground nesting birds, like Skylark and Meadow Pipit, but access is limited to the public footpaths. Some of the dune slacks are reed-lined and have developed as oases of self-sown willows, which attract many species of migrant birds. Others, close to the Observatory, have been specifically planted with willows and alders and are used very successfully as mist-netting sites. The Sandwich Bay Bird Observatory Trust has recently been responsible for the construction of a wader scrape with islands, close to the river. Visiting is restricted to members, who are finding the hides, including the specially designed photographic hide, quite excellent for viewing waders in particular. The first autumn attracted both Pectoral and White-rumped Sandpipers.

The maturing gardens of the Sandwich Bay Estate attract migrant passerines, as do the small plantations of trees on its southern edge. The SBBO census area includes that part of the Worth Marshes to the east of the North Stream. Covering some 3210 acres (1300 ha) of privately-owned dunes and marshland, it is a complex and fascinating area, greatly attractive to a wide variety of bird species. Its uniqueness also makes it particularly attractive to botanists. Nine native orchids occur, including the rare and fascinating lizard orchid, while the equally rare bedstraw broomrape is another local speciality. The migration of butterflies, like painted lady and clouded yellow, can be witnessed as they cross the coastline, while several uncommon species of migrant moths are caught each summer in the Observatory moth trap.

Species

A walk along the shore towards the point in the winter months may be cold and bleak, but it can be most rewarding. To see the roosting waders well you should plan to be near the point an hour or two before high tide. Offshore there may be a flock of Common Scoter, possibly with Velvet Scoter too, and small groups of Great Crested Grebes. Sanderling will be scurrying along the water's edge. A wintering flock of up to 50 Snow Buntings sometimes leaves the shore to feed on the short grass of the golf course. Shore Larks are generally scarce, but may be found along the sandy beach, while a few Twite are invariably present in the saltmarsh near the point. Looking inland over the arable and pasture you will be unlucky not to see a Short-eared Owl or two and a Hen

Harrier, while a Merlin or a Peregrine might disturb the waders at the point. The wader flocks are worth checking carefully, as species like Little Stint and Avocet have been known to winter.

Back on Worth Marshes, Lapland Buntings can be quite numerous and as many as 1,000 Golden Plover may be feeding. In colder conditions, it is there that you might find some grey geese and a few Bewick's Swans. One or two Green Sandpipers and an occasional Water Pipit may also be present. Cold weather movements will involve Lapwings and Skylarks overland, while offshore a variety of duck and possibly geese may be anticipated.

March generally sees considerable change on a day-to-day basis, with numbers of wintering birds decreasing, influxes of returning winter visitors like Redwing, Fieldfare and Brent Goose on their way north, and the arrival of the first spring visitors. Wheatear and Black Redstart can often be found around the Estate, with Chiffchaff and Firecrest in the scattered clusters of trees. Throughout April and May there are almost daily arrivals of summer migrants passing through, but any 'falls' are

Snow Bunting

usually small compared with those of the autumn. Visits after mid April will almost certainly guarantee an interesting variety of species, even more so when there is an eastern influence in the weather. The visible migration of hirundines, Goldfinches and Linnets coasting north can be quite marked, particularly in light west to northwest winds. Most of the common warblers and chats, like Sedge Warbler, Lesser Whitethroat and Whinchat can be expected, but relatively few Redstarts and Pied Flycatchers occur in spring, unless there are sufficient easterly winds. Raptor passage sometimes involves a good variety of species, including Sparrowhawk and Marsh Harrier, with Hobby and possibly Montagu's Harrier or Honey Buzzard in May. Dotterel can be expected almost annually in early May, usually resting or feeding on arable. The Blue-headed Wagtail, the striking Continental race of the Yellow Wagtail, can be quite numerous and some may stay to breed. Golden Orioles are virtually annual, but their stays are usually brief and they can be difficult to see, despite the brilliant yellow plumage of the male. Another striking species, the Hoopoe, occurs occasionally, as does the attractive Bluethroat.

Although the main migration is complete before the end of May, and one expects June to be a time for studying breeding birds, a number of quite unexpected southern rarities have appeared, like Red-footed

Falcon and Sardinian Warbler. July too has had its highlights. Careful scrutiny of the tern flocks, which can be studied at close range from the point, has produced such extreme rarities as Caspian and Royal Terns. Another interesting aspect of July is the early start of the autumn wader passage. From mid month, on the scrape, along the river and on the marshes, the numbers of Common Sandpipers build up quite rapidly to around 100 by the beginning of August.

Throughout August and September, although the sea and shore will continue to attract an interesting variety of seabirds and waders, including a few Black Terns, Little Gulls and more distant Gannets, the Observatory staff normally concentrate greater activity in the trapping area. There will be a steady flow of passerine migrants, featuring chats, warblers and flycatchers, with the expected, but not always predictable arrival of rarer species like Wryneck, Red-backed Shrike and Icterine Warbler from Scandinavia. Later in the autumn, rarer warblers from farther east, like Yellow-browed and possibly Pallas's Warbler are eagerly anticipated. Visible migration is another impressive feature of October, with hirundines during the first week, followed by finches and thrushes later in the month. Some raptor passage in late autumn may possibly produce a Buzzard or a Rough-legged Buzzard in addition to the regular Hen Harriers, Sparrowhawks and Merlins. Late October and early November can produce excellent seawatching, particularly in east to southeast, and sometimes northeast winds, when good numbers of geese, duck and Little Gulls may occur, with the occasional rare grebe or Little Auk.

Timing

The best time to view waders, gulls and terns in Pegwell Bay is when an incoming tide coincides with late afternoon or early evening. The light then is usually excellent. Early mornings are recommended for passerine migrants, in the Observatory area and elsewhere.

Access

From Thanet take the A256 southwards past the old hoverport in Pegwell Bay (Map 7). Just under 1 mile (1.6 km) from the hoverport turning, the Pegwell Bay Country Park gates can be seen on the left. Drive in, park (for which there is a small charge) and follow the shore path north and south to view the estuary. Using the hide is particularly welcome in inclement weather. At the appropriate time of year, check the open grassland and the scrub to the south of the hide and the mixed habitat at Stonelees.

Drive on south, then keep left at the roundabout. Stonar Lake is 1 mile (1.6 km) or so further south, to the left of the road. Park where there is room on the right. The lake can be viewed from just over the fence, but you will be looking into the sun in the morning. It is possible to drive round to the back of the lake, through the industrial estate. From the east side of the lake you can also view a stretch of the river.

To proceed to Sandwich Bay Bird Observatory, drive a short way south, cross over the bridge and turn left into Upper Strand Street. Turn right at the road junction, then follow the road, turning sharp left, for 1.25 miles (2 km) to the Toll gate. It is possible to park in a small lay-by, on the left just before reaching the gate. (A toll, normally more expensive in the summer months, is payable.) Follow the road for just over 0.25 mile (0.4 km), turn right and the observatory buildings are on the right, where it is possible to park. There are a number of interesting walks along the public rights of way, but it is recommended that you check with the warden regarding access and what can be expected. It is best to book in advance, if you wish to stay at the observatory.

One route to the point, that involves less walking, is to drive on south from the observatory turning and then turn left through the Sandwich Bay Estate. Then left again along the shore, where you can park amongst the dunes on the right, close to the old Prince's Golf Club House. It is about 2 miles (3 km) to Shellness Point, along the shore.

Calendar

Resident: Cormorant (non-breeding birds), Shelduck, Kestrel, Oystercatcher, Ringed Plover, Redshank, Meadow Pipit.

December–February: Red-throated Diver, Teal, Pochard and Goldeneye (Stonar), Eider, Common Scoter, Hen Harrier, Peregrine, Merlin, Water Rail, Golden Plover, Jack Snipe, Green Sandpiper, possible Glaucous Gull, Short-eared Owl, Stonechat, Twite, Lapland and Snow Buntings.

March–May: Brent Goose and Shoveler (March passage), Marsh Harrier, Sparrowhawk, Hobby, Avocet, Kentish and Little Ringed Plovers, Dotterel (almost annual), Woodcock (March passage), Bar-tailed Godwit (peak late April), Whimbrel, Greenshank, Green Sandpiper, Sandwich Tern, Little Tern, common chats on passage including Black Redstart, Ring Ouzel, common warblers on passage, Firecrest, Golden Oriole (almost annual).

June–July: Breeding Shelduck, occasional Quail, Mediterranean Gull and Sandwich Tern (non-breeding birds), Little Tern (small colony), breeding Cuckoo, Turtle Dove, Yellow Wagtail, possibly Stonechat, common warblers.

August–November: Common Scoter, Red-breasted Merganser, Hen Harrier (October–November), Sparrowhawk (peak passage October), Merlin, Little Stint, Curlew Sandpiper, Woodcock (from October), Whimbrel, Spotted Redshank, Greenshank, Green and Wood Sandpiper, Common Sandpiper (peak July–August), Arctic Skua, Little Gull, Sandwich, Common and Black Terns, Wryneck, common chats on passage, Ring Ouzel, wintering thrushes (from October), common warblers on passage, Yellow-browed Warbler (almost annual), possibly Pallas's Warbler (first week November), Firecrest, Pied Flycatcher, Red backed Shrike, returning Lapland and Snow Buntings.

8 ST MARGARET'S BAY

Habitat

The coast here faces southeast, while the valley from St Margaret's Bay runs northeast to southwest, providing a natural funnel for passerine migrants in particular. Below the chalk cliffs, which reach nearly 300 ft (90 m) above Fan Bay, there is a rocky shoreline. On top, the grassy slopes interspersed with scrub, sycamore copses and a small boggy area in a narrow valley, provide a variety of attractive habitats, not only for birds, but also a good variety of butterflies. Twenty-nine species are annual, which is very good for one site, including small, chalkhill and adonis blue as well as dingy skipper. The open, arable fields above Fan Bay provide another habitat, while the coastal path, which is very popular with holidaymakers during the summer months, provides easy access. Similar cliff-top habitat exists to the northeast in the Bockhill Farm area.

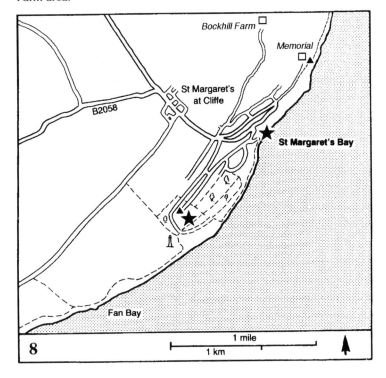

Species

The breeding Fulmars return in December to inspect their nest-sites, but the cliff top area is relatively bleak at this time of year. Common residents will seek shelter in the wooded valley, while the rocky shore line might produce wintering Black Redstarts, which feed along the base of the chalk cliffs. Purple Sandpipers are scarce here, but can be seen a little way along the coast in Dover Harbour, or on the concrete apron at Folkestone Warren. Severe conditions may produce cold weather movements involving wildfowl offshore and flocks of Skylarks, pipits and thrushes coasting along the cliffs, or arriving from off the sea — over 2,000 Skylarks arrived in an hour on 4th January 1985.

Although it is not an ideal spot for seawatching, as the birds are generally very distant, some of the annual up-Channel spring passage can be observed, with flocks of Brent Geese and Common Scoter in March–April and terns, with the occasional skua, in April–May. The northeasterly passage of finches can be quite marked in early spring and Sparrowhawks regularly move out in April. Occasionally there are obvi-

Firecrest

ous increases in the numbers and in the volume of song, from species like Willow Warbler, but unlike more prominent coastal sites, spring falls are rare. However, although their stays are invariably brief, Golden Orioles are almost annual visitors in May. Regular observation has shown that the dips in the coastal cliffs seem to attract raptors on migration. Between 1992–96 there were annual or almost annual arrivals of nearly 50 Hobbys, over 20 Marsh Harriers, nearly 20 Honey Buzzards, over 10 Ospreys, five Montagu's Harriers and four Black Kites. Single Red-footed Falcons were seen twice and a Red Kite once. An extremely good concentration for a single site, where the birds can on occasion be seen arriving low over the sea. The breeding colonies of Kittiwakes are not easily seen, though there are one or two good vantage points, but their onomatopoeic calls announce their presence along the white cliffs. The summer months, however, will produce relatively few species, and they become increasingly disturbed as the human holiday traffic expands. Nevertheless the pleasure gained from watching Fulmars gliding by at eye-level and the occasional glimpse of a Peregrine make visits well worthwhile.

It is the autumn months that frequently attract a greater variety of species, when there are regular marked falls of passerine migrants. 2–3 falls of 500+ warblers are annual and occasionally 1,000 may be present, usually when Chiffchaffs and Blackcaps are at their peak in mid-September.

The visible migration of hirundines, thrushes and finches can also be quite spectacular. As the autumn progresses, the pattern of species occurring changes. The peak numbers of Yellow Wagtails, Tree Pipits, Whinchats, Wheatears, Reed Warblers, Whitethroats, Lesser White-throats, Willow Warblers and Pied Flycatchers occur in August and early September, followed by Swallows, Redstarts and Chiffchaffs in September, with House Martins and Blackcaps in late September and early October. In fact it is October that is often the most exciting in terms of variety and numbers. It is then that the highest counts of finch-es are recorded as they fly southwest, or arrive off the sea. These include Chaffinches, Bramblings, Goldfinches, Redpolls and Siskins. A few Ring Ouzels and the wintering thrushes, Fieldfare and Redwing, often occur in good numbers, while the passage of Goldcrests and Firecrests, the former occasionally in quite large numbers, can be fas-cinating to watch as they search hungrily for insects, slowly moving up the valley as they dart from bush to bush.

One of the pleasures of watching migrant passerines at this site is that they can usually be seen well. Although they are often feeding in the tree-tops, the tops of the trees in the valley can be at eye level for the observer. Another alternative is to spend some time near the lighthouse at the top of the valley in the autumn, as all birds orientate SW.

Other arrivals from the Continent in October may include the greyer mantled Coal Tit *P. a. ater*, with Blue and Great Tits, while different species may dominate from year to year: in 1983 for example over 2,000 Jays flew southwest during October. Of the rarer species, Woodlark and Lapland Bunting are annual, as is Yellow-browed Warbler. Other autumn rarities may include Icterine Warbler and Red-breasted Flycatcher, or possibly Tawny Pipit on the open fields. It is not only passerines that feature during autumn passage, several raptors may also occur, the Sparrowhawk being perhaps the most regular during October.

When autumn migration is late early November can be interesting, with large numbers of winter thrushes, and scarcer finches like Brambling, Siskin and Crossbill. During 1st–3rd November 1993 for example there were over 30,000 Redwings and Fieldfares, with nearly 150 Crossbills between the 1st–8th. In stormy conditions Little Auks sometimes appear close inshore at St Margaret's Bay.

Like everywhere else, it is those that watch one site regularly who can anticipate the excitement of discovering a real rarity. Both Great Snipe and Penduline Tit seem quite extraordinary species for such a locality, but both occurred in October 1983. An almost annual autumn visitor in recent years has been the Dotterel, often attracted to the cropped pea fields before they are ploughed.

Timing

For much of the year, early morning visits are recommended, particu-larly in late summer, to avoid the holidaymakers. It is also the period when newly-arrived night migrants are likely to be more active, while the visible migration of passerines is most marked during the hour after dawn.

An understanding of the weather conditions that influence migration is of great value during spring and autumn passage. The optimum con-ditions for a fall of passerine night migrants of Scandinavian origin involve a northeasterly airflow, with a clear sky at dusk, followed by cloud cover and rain towards dawn.

Access

From Dover take the A258 towards Deal and turn right to St Margaret's at Cliffe along the B2058 (Map 8). Continue through the village towards St Margaret's Bay for about 0.5 mile (0.8 km), then turn right along St Margaret's Road for 0.6 mile (1 km), where there is ample parking space on the left — just before the road turns sharply left. This short stretch of rough road cuts across the top of the valley, with a small sycamore copse on the right, which is worth checking for passerine migrants. Follow the footpath northeast, along the edge of the valley, looking carefully for migrants on the bushy slopes. If there has been an obvious fall, it is worth finding a good vantage point, looking northwest across the valley, and settling down to watch the migrants as they move slowly up the valley. Visible migration is best observed close to the top of the valley. Some migrants tend to coast along the cliff edge, while others will fly up the valley. A footpath leads passed the lighthouse to the cliff edge and southwestwards to Fan Bay, where the arable fields attract wagtails, pipits and chats. Seawatching is best from the beach, near the Coastguard public house, in St Margaret's Bay.

The cliff-top area near Bockhill Farm can be reached by following Granville Road, opposite St Margaret's Road, towards the memorial where there is a car park. The Saxon Shore Way follows the cliff top and there are also footpaths inland, which provide some access to the small copses.

Calendar

Resident: Kestrel, Rock Pipit, Corn Bunting.

December–February: Fulmar (breeding birds return), Black Redstart, Stonechat.

March–May: Brent Goose (up-Channel passage), Sparrowhawk and finch passage (April), arrival of passerine migrants, like warblers and possibly Golden Oriole (May), raptor passage (May).

June–July: Fulmar, Kittiwake, breeding warblers.

August–November: passage of a wide variety of passerine migrants, including Woodlark (October), Whinchat, Ring Ouzel, winter thrushes and warblers, including Wood and Yellow-browed, Firecrest, Pied Flycatcher, finches and Lapland Bunting; Sparrowhawk (October), wildfowl movements offshore (late October–November).

9 DUNGENESS

Habitat

The huge shingle spit at Dungeness forms a unique habitat. With its arid-
ity and relatively sparse vegetation in parts, it is akin to a desert and one
of the few places in Kent where Wheatears regularly breed. Projecting
out into the English Channel and with its close proximity to the
Continent, it makes an important site for studying migration and seabird
passage. In that respect it was a natural choice for the establishment of
the first Kent bird observatory in 1952.

Shingle extraction in the area has produced a number of flooded pits,
which form an important winter refuge for duck. These pits, particularly those under the auspices of the RSPB, attract Smew and Goosander
regularly, while the scattered islands provide nesting sites for a variety
of gulls and terns. In recent years the Sandwich Tern has been encouraged to once again breed in Kent.

The nuclear power stations at Dungeness, strangely enough, have
added to the interest in the area for some bird species. These man-made
cliffs have attracted Black Redstarts to breed and have even been
prospected by Fulmars, while the warm-water outflow — known locally as 'the Patch' — attracts numerous feeding gulls and terns, including
the rarer Mediterranean Gull. Being close to the shore, it offers an excellent opportunity to study the confusing range of plumages, displayed in
particular by the terns.

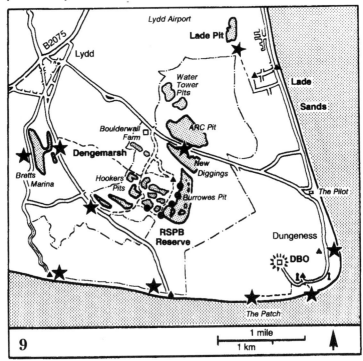

Species

As with all sites that attract birds of passage, the timing of visits is all important to witness major falls of passerines, peak seabird movements, or the all too brief visits of rarities. Even if you can anticipate the optimum weather conditions, how often do they occur when you are free to make a visit? Not often enough, certainly, but at Dungeness, with its interesting variety of habitats, it is usually possible to find something to make a visit worthwhile.

Pomarine Skua

The main seasonal attractions tend to be the rarer grebes and duck on the pits in the winter months; falls of regular passerine migrants and the up-Channel seabird passage in the spring, highlighted by the now eagerly awaited passage of Pomarine Skuas in early May; the possibility of southern rarities in late May and early June, like Red-footed Falcon or Woodchat Shrike; the presence of Mediterranean Gulls and possibly a Roseate Tern on the RSPB Reserve in summer; falls of Scandinavian night migrants in autumn, often accompanied by rarer species like Wryneck, Barred Warbler and Red-backed Shrike; while in late October or early November there is a possibility of rarer warblers from further east, like Yellow-browed or Pallas's.

Main Birdwatching Zones

The Dungeness area can conveniently be sub-divided into a number of different sites, all of which have their own particular attractions. On any one day, depending on the circumstances and your own interests, it is quite possible to visit all of the sites described, but if you are particularly interested in the ringing activities at the Observatory, or seabird passage, then the daylight hours will all too quickly disappear.

The following sites are described in detail: the Observatory area, including the sea; the RSPB Reserve, including Hooker's Pits, the New Diggings and the ARC Pit; the outlying areas of Lade Sands and Lade Pit; and Dengemarsh Road, which cuts through the extensive RSPB Reserve.

DUNGENESS BIRD OBSERVATORY (Map 9)

Habitat

There has been a marked increase in the vegetation during the lifetime of the Observatory. Close to the shore sea kale provides flocks of Greenfinches with ample seeds in the autumn, attracting over 1,000 birds on occasions. The disturbed stretches of shingle in particular now have a rich and varied flora, while in the more sheltered trapping area the sallows have multiplied rapidly.

A private road, running round behind the old lighthouse, leads to the Bird Observatory, which is housed in the end of a row of cottages, surrounded by a dry moat and partly sheltered from the strong winds by a high earth and shingle bank. The thick bramble and other vegetation in the moat attract passerine migrants, which may be trapped in the Heligoland traps by the Observatory staff.

Species

In the winter months the trapping area attracts relatively few birds, though a small flock of Blue and Great Tits may also include a few Goldcrests, with possibly a Firecrest and one or two Chiffchaffs. Woodcock feed and rest amongst the sallows, while Stonechats perch atop the gorse, in which a Dartford Warbler may skulk.

The strip of shore by the fishing boats invariably attracts large numbers of gulls and it is here that the huge Glaucous and possibly the scarce Iceland Gull may be found, sometimes following the fishing boats. On the sea a few Red-throated Divers can usually be seen, the Guillemot is often the commonest auk and Gannets sometimes fish close to the shore, while offshore, movements of these three species may be witnessed in certain weather conditions. Wintering flocks of Common Scoter and Eider are often present further west, off the south-facing shore.

The Observatory enjoys particularly long and varied periods of migration, partly due to the southerly location. The earliest spring migrants are usually Wheatear, Black Redstart and Chiffchaff, with the peak numbers often before the end of March, when Ring Ouzels and Firecrests can also be expected. However, it is often late April before the bulk of the summer migrants arrive and large falls of Willow Warblers — the commonest migrant — can be anticipated. Early May can be particularly exciting, especially when the weather has a southerly influence, though clear nights often mean that the birds fly straight over. A strategically placed belt of rain is an almost essential ingredient for the best falls of migrants.

Witnessing the up-Channel passage of seabirds, duck and waders is also much dependent on certain weather conditions. A change from persistent northerly winds to a southwesterly air flow often precipitates a marked passage, with birds coming quite close to the point. Recording is usually analysed on a numbers per day basis, so figures mentioned will usually refer to peak day totals.

On peak days several hundred divers can be expected, the vast majority of those identified being Red-throated. The spring peak of this species is usually in late March, while Black-throated and Great Northern tend to occur a little later, with peaks in just single figures on average. Brent Goose numbers usually peak in March, when up to 7,000 have been counted, with peaks of 1,000 or more in a day now annual. Common Scoter movements can be most impressive from late March, throughout April and into early May, when several thousand can be seen passing up-Channel in small flocks — a total of 27,000 on 8 April 1979 remains exceptional. Smaller numbers of the larger Velvet Scoter are annual, with peaks of up to 50 occasionally in late April. Other duck species, like Eider and Red-breasted Merganser, and dabbling ducks like Shoveler, Teal and Garganey also migrate up-Channel at this time.

The passage of Bar-tailed Godwits can be highly concentrated and quite spectacular on occasions, with peaks of up to 1,000 in late April or early May. Whimbrel too regularly fly up-Channel, with occasional peaks of several hundred birds in early May. A possibly more attractive sight, if you are lucky, might be a flock of Avocets. The spring passage of Pomarine Skuas has been well documented and many of the flocks that pass Dungeness have been seen some 90 minutes earlier, off the Sussex coast from Beachy Head. Perhaps a portable radio link will soon allow birdwatchers at Dungeness to know when to expect them. Early May is the peak time for these splendid birds, frequently in light southerly winds. The maximum day total is 151, which included a flock of 40, but peaks of 20 or more are seen almost annually. The passage of Arctic and Great Skuas is more prolonged and not as dramatic, with just ones and twos flying past totalling 20 or more in the case of Arctic, but usually fewer than ten Great Skuas per day. An added bonus for a lucky few could be an adult Long-tailed Skua.

The Little Gull is another species that has been recorded with increased regularity in recent years, with totals occasionally reaching 100 or more in late April or early May. Kittiwakes too fly up-Channel in spring, with totals of up to 200, but it is the terns that seem to move almost continuously throughout April and much of May. The usual peak counts of Sandwich Terns are in excess of 200, with over 1,000 exceptionally, while Common Terns frequently exceed 1,000 and exceptionally 3,000. Much smaller numbers of Arctic Terns also occur, usually in late April and early May. The first Little Terns invariably occur in the second week of April and the passage continues into May, with peaks of up to 100, while Black Tern totals occasionally exceed a similar figure.

With all this activity offshore, there are times when the trapping area is deserted, but on occasions falls of migrants coincide with peak passage movements, presenting the visiting birdwatcher with quite a dilemma. As soon as you have left the coast to search for a Golden Oriole, that is the time that the long-awaited Pomarine Skua flock decides to appear!

As May passes and June arrives there is always the possibility of a rarity. Serin and Golden Oriole are almost annual visitors, but other vagrants may include species like Black Kite, Honey Buzzard, Hoopoe, Tawny Pipit, Red-breasted Flycatcher or Ortolan Bunting. On the sea Manx and occasionally Mediterranean Shearwaters occur in June and July, when there are also peak numbers of returning migrant adult Cuckoos.

By late July post-breeding dispersal brings the first autumn passerine migrants to Dungeness and the numbers and variety steadily increase during August. Once again the weather has an important influence on the species present. Early morning rain may well bring down British migrants leaving the country, like Lesser Whitethroats, Wheatears and Willow Warblers, while an easterly wind is likely to drive Continental migrants, like Pied Flycatcher, Redstart and Whinchat, across the southern North Sea. It is in these conditions, particularly during September, that the falls may include rarer species like Wryneck, Icterine Warbler, Tawny Pipit, Bluethroat or Red-backed Shrike.

By early October the pattern changes considerably. The numbers and variety of summer visitors decline, while winter visitors and late autumn migrants like Robin, Goldcrest and Firecrest increase. Diurnal movements of finches are a regular feature at this time; hirundines too migrate through in large numbers. The Dartford Warbler and Woodlark are regular migrants at Dungeness in October, while rarer species that have been recorded include Rustic Bunting and eastern warblers like Dusky, Radde's and Pallas's.

On the sea the Patch is a great attraction from early autumn. A number of the locally-bred terns and gulls can be seen with their parents as they beg for food — an ideal opportunity to study plumages. Among all the Common Terns it might be possible to locate the scarce Roseate Tern, and as the autumn progresses, migrant Arctic Terns can also be expected. Late August is the peak time for Black Terns, on occasions numbering over 100, with the possibility too of the rare White-winged Black Tern, while an Arctic Skua may occasionally cause havoc amongst the birds over the Patch. A check of the gulls is also worthwhile; the Yellow-legged Herring Gull *L. a. cachinnans* is now a regular visitor in autumn, when peaks of 20 or more are recorded.

The down-Channel passage in the autumn is not so marked or reliable as the spring movement, though a few species can be expected in good numbers. Gannets may total 200 or more in a day, with a peak usually in October, Brent Goose peaks vary between 1,000–2,000, but the Common Scoter tends to migrate down the French coast and relatively few are seen. Totals of 100 or more Sandwich Terns are fairly regular, with the peak in September, while similar numbers of Little Gulls pass west, with the highest counts usually in late September, but in some years later. The autumn numbers are sometimes higher than those recorded in the spring. Rarer species include Sabine's Gull and Sooty Shearwater, and in stormy conditions possibly Little Auk or Leach's Petrel.

DUNGENESS RSPB RESERVE (Map 9)

Habitat

By careful management Burrowe's Pit — another flooded gravel pit — has become a site of great importance to wintering wildfowl, breeding gulls and terns, and migrant waders. The vegetation on the islands is controlled to provide suitable conditions not only for the breeding of gulls and terns, but also for grebes and duck. The scrapes prepared for migrant waders are attracting an increasing variety.

Visible from the Lydd–Dungeness road are the ARC Pit to the north and the New Diggings to the south — adjacent to Burrowe's Pit, while on the Reserve there is a carefully marked track which takes you over the shingle through well-vegetated areas of bramble and gorse, much favoured by passerine migrants. The trail takes you by the Hooker's Pits, some of which have dense beds of *Phragmites*. The Reserve area has recently been extended and more wader pools have been created, some overlooked by new hides.

Species

The several hides overlooking Burrowe's Pit provide very welcome shelter in the winter months, while you study the wildfowl without disturbing them. Few winters pass without a visit from a diver or two, while Red-necked Grebes seem to be the most regular of the three rarer grebes. In some winters, Bewick's Swans occasionally come in to roost, but it is the duck that provide the greatest spectacle. Smew now occur annually, increasing in numbers with the severity of the weather. Ruddy Duck too are regular, while Goosander and Goldeneye seem to favour the ARC Pit. Some of the shore waders come in to roost on the low shingle banks, or sandy foreshore close to the hides, while the larger gulls, including Glaucous on occasions, favour the low islands or the shingle for roosting. A large percentage of the wintering Lesser Black-backed Gulls are of the dark, Scandinavian race *L. f. fuscus*. Hen Harrier, Merlin and Sparrowhawk can often be seen hunting over the area. The Merlin in particular likes to hunt the Starlings as they come to roost in the Oppen Pits — to the east of Burrowe's. A Peregrine may also be seen at this time of year.

Mediterranean Gulls

One of the early signs of spring is the raucous cry from a returning Sandwich Tern. In 1978 this species recolonised Kent, here on the RSPB Reserve. The increase has been quite dramatic, reaching 350 pairs in 1985, but they sometimes desert and show preference for the Rye Harbour Reserve. Over 300 pairs of Common Terns also breed here. The number of pairs of Black-headed Gulls is even higher, reaching 1,000 in some years, while amongst them one or two of the larger white-winged Mediterranean Gulls can occasionally be seen. There is quite a cacophony of sound in late summer, when the young are begging for food.

From July onwards a wide variety of wader species visit the Reserve, some, all too often, making only the briefest of stops, though occasionally one or two of the rarer visitors deign to stay for a few days. The list of rare visitors in recent years is quite mouth-watering, not only waders, but rare terns too, including Least and Buff-breasted Sandpipers, Long-billed Dowitcher and both Caspian and Sooty Terns. Sadly, they do not all drop in at the weekend! The Yellow-legged Herring Gull *L. a. cachinnans* is most frequently seen during the autumn.

Many of the regular and rarer autumn passerine migrants can also be expected, and a walk around the shingle track will often produce Whinchats and occasionally a Wryneck or Red-backed Shrike.

LADE SANDS and LADE PIT (Map 9)

Habitat

At low tide a large expanse of sandy mudflats is exposed, providing an attractive food source for thousands of shore waders and gulls. At high tide many of them roost just inland of the coastal cottages, on the fields by Lydd Airport or at Lade Pit. This is another flooded gravel pit, with islands and shallow edges that have attracted natural vegetation such as osiers, sallows and reeds, which provide a sheltered haven not only for a wintering duck, but a wide variety of migrants and breeding species, like the Great Crested Grebe.

Species

In the winter months, when the sandy mud is exposed, up to 1,300 Oystercatchers regularly feed, busily probing the mud. About 350 Sanderling usually feed here, frequently running along the ebbing tide-line. Up to 700 Dunlin, over 100 Grey Plover and a few Bar-tailed Godwits and Curlew help give the impression that much of the sandy surface is alive. Check carefully through the gulls, you might discover a Glaucous or an even rarer Ring-billed Gull amongst them. On the sea, as the tide brings them close to the shore, you can expect a few Red-throated Divers, 200 or more Great Crested Grebes, and possibly Eider and Common Scoter.

Lade Pit at this time frequently attracts one of the rarer grebes, possibly a Bittern, certainly a good variety of duck species, including Gadwall, Goldeneye and Ruddy Duck. In severe conditions numbers of Scaup may also be seen. Over the fields near the airport, a few Curlew and flocks of Golden Plover feed, often to be disturbed by a Hen Harrier as it hunts low over the ground. Chiffchaffs and occasionally Black Redstarts winter here, and they can certainly be seen in early spring, when terns and rarer gulls can also be expected. Little, Mediterranean and the exceptionally rare Laughing Gull have all been recorded.

In the autumn, depending on the water-level, it may also be an attractive site for freshwater waders, like Green and Common Sandpipers.

DENGEMARSH (Map 9)

Habitat

This area includes a mixture of habitats, with arable and grazing land, gravel pits, shingle scrub and gorse. The Dengemarsh Road runs from the Lydd roundabout down to the shore, with farmland to the east and Brett's Marina to the west — several flooded pits now used by wind-surfers and water-skiers. Further south the RSPB lease part of their Reserve to the MOD, while east of the road are a few more flooded gravel workings, with small reedbeds of *Phragmites* and the Hooker's Pits beyond. There are plans over the next few years to create freshwater marsh on this part of the RSPB Reserve, to attract breeding Lapwing and Redshank. It should also be attractive to passage waders. The Dengemarsh gully, which also comes within the RSPB Reserve, is a deepish ditch running parallel to the road, towards the sea, containing more common reed, a few gorse bushes and bramble. It frequently provides shelter from the prevailing winds for tired passerine migrants, including on occasion such extreme rarities as Dark-throated Thrush and Subalpine Warbler.

Species

The arable fields attract a number of geese and swans, particularly in the winter months when, in addition to the resident Greylag and Canada Geese, a few Bean Geese and Bewick's Swans may be seen feeding. In severe conditions flocks of Whitefronts, Pink-feet and Barnacle Geese have occurred. The flooded pits occasionally attract divers and rare grebes, while up to 3,000 Wigeon now graze there in winter, along with other dabbling duck. Common diving duck are also regular visitors and Long-tailed Duck occurs occasionally. Hen Harriers, Merlin and Peregrine hunt over the fields and an occasional Short-eared Owl can be expected, but the flock of Ruff is one of the main attractions. They can usually be seen feeding on the close-cropped pasture by the road. The reedbeds attract Bearded Tits and the Bittern is an almost annual winter visitor to these parts.

During spring, migrant passerines can often be discovered feeding in the fields or scrub. In recent years such rarities as Hoopoe, Black-eared Wheatear and Black-headed Bunting have been found. Shore waders like Grey Plover and Bar-tailed Godwit — in their attractive summer plumage — along with Whimbrel, often rest and feed on the fields between the road and Hooker's Pits. Freshwater waders, like Common and Green Sandpipers, the occasional Greenshank and Spotted Redshank are attracted to the muddy fringes of these shallow pits on both spring and autumn passage.

The protracted return passage in autumn starts as early as mid June and during the next three to four months a good variety of waders can be expected. Of the extreme rarities a Collared Pratincole was present in June 1986, a Terek Sandpiper in August 1982 and a Long-billed Dowitcher in December/January 1990/91, while a Pectoral Sandpiper has been seen twice in more recent years. In early September it may be possible to study Black Terns at close range on Brett's Marina, in more sheltered conditions than the coast often offers, while the rare White-winged Black Tern also favours this area occasionally.

Timing

Several different aspects of timing need to be considered when planning trips to Dungeness. Seawatching can be difficult, due to the southerly aspect, and the angle of light is generally better during the early morning and late afternoon — times that quite a number of seabirds tend to favour too. Onshore winds tend to bring the seabirds closer to the shore, particularly in dull, misty conditions, while the bay to the east and north of the point provides shelter from southwesterly gales for a number of seabirds.

The state of the tide controls the distribution of many of the waders and gulls that feed on Lade Sands. As the tide rises, they will come closer to the shingle bank before flying to roost on the various pits and areas of undisturbed shingle. A rising tide is also a good time to watch for gulls at the fishing boats.

Predicting falls of passerine migrants can be difficult. When there are clear skies they tend to fly straight over. Rain towards dawn may produce falls, if other conditions are suitable — southerly winds in spring and more easterly winds in autumn are best.

Access

Take the Dungeness road from the Lydd roundabout. After 1.25 miles (2 km) you will see Boulderwall Farm on the right and a gravel track leading to the RSPB Reserve (Map 9). It is open daily, except Tuesday, from 9 am to sunset. The Visitor Centre is open from 9 am to 5 pm: the charge for non-members is £2, 50p for children or £4 for family groups. Disabled birdwatchers can drive to four of the hides (ask at the Visitor Centre, or phone beforehand).

Another 0.25 mile (0.4 km) along the Dungeness road you will see the ARC Pit on your left, with the New Diggings on the right. Park beside the road to view these two pits, but take care, the traffic tends to be fast moving.

A further 1.5 miles (2.4 km) and the road bends to the left, leading to The Pilot public house and the coast road to the north, while a right turn leads to Dungeness. After 1 mile (1.6 km) the fishing boats will be visible on the left, with a convenient pull-in for cars on the right. A short walk will take you to the shore by the fishing boats, in the lee of which you can often find shelter from the prevailing southwesterlies.

The Dungeness road continues south, then turns west by the new lighthouse. To get to the Observatory, turn left immediately before the old lighthouse and follow the tarmac surface as it turns northwest by the power station fence and on over the moat to the Observatory building, where there is ample space for parking. Check with the warden to find out what birds can be seen in the trapping area.

'The Patch' may be reached by following the power station fence back to the gate, where there is room to park. Then walk to the shore and about 0.25 mile (0.4 km) west. Seawatching is best undertaken nearer the point in most conditions, and the Coastguard Signal Station building does provide some shelter in inclement weather. This can be reached by walking along the shore, or by parking near the cafe and walking south from the old lighthouse. As a 'Friend of Dungeness' your membership allows you access to the two seawatching hides set into the shingle bank.

Lade Sands extend approximately 4 miles (6 km) northwards from 'The Pilot' to Littlestone. Lade Pit is between the coast road and Lydd airport and can be approached by following the coast road for 1.5 miles (2.4 km) from 'The Pilot'. Turn left into Taylor Road and park near the corner of Williamson and Taylor Road. From here, walk across the shingle to view the pit from its southern shore.

The Dengemarsh Road also leads from the Lydd roundabout and reaches the coast about 3 miles (5 km) south. Footpaths to Hooker's Pits leave this road at approximately 1 mile (1.6 km) and 2 miles (3 km) from the roundabout. The second footpath links the Dengemarsh and Dungeness roads at Boulderwall Farm, via the Hooker's Pits. If using this path, try to avoid disturbing the grazing Wigeon. A turning to the right 1.75 miles (2.8 km) from the roundabout, opposite Manor Farm, leads west then north, following the range fence, and provides good vantage points to look over the largest pool of Brett's Marina.

Calendar

Resident: Great Crested Grebe, Greylag and Canada Geese, Gadwall, Red-legged Partridge, Oystercatcher, Meadow Pipit.

December–February: Red-throated Diver, Great Crested Grebe (wintering flocks on sea from point northwards), Red-necked and possibly Slavonian or Black-necked Grebe, Teal, Shoveler, Pochard, Eider and Common Scoter (on the sea), Goldeneye, Smew, Goosander, Ruddy Duck, Hen Harrier, Peregrine, Merlin, Grey Plover and Sanderling (Lade Sands), Ruff (Dengemarsh), Woodcock, Mediterranean and Glaucous Gulls, Stonechat, possibly Dartford Warbler, Chiffchaff, Firecrest.

March–May: up-Channel passage of divers (Red-throated peak in March, with most Black-throated and Great Northern in late April); Fulmar, Garganey, Shoveler (spring peak in March); up-Channel passage of Eider, Common and Velvet Scoter, and Red-breasted Merganser; Hobby, Avocet (up-Channel passage), possibly Kentish Plover, up-Channel passage of Bar-tailed Godwit and Whimbrel (early May peak), Pomarine, Arctic and Great Skuas; Mediterranean and Little Gulls (up-Channel peak May); up-Channel passage of Sandwich, Common, Arctic, Little and Black Terns; down-Channel passage of Guillemot and Razorbill; Hoopoe (almost annual), Black Redstart, Wheatear, Ring Ouzel, Sedge and Reed Warbler, Whitethroat, Chiffchaff and Willow Warbler, Firecrest, Golden Oriole (annual in recent years).

June–July: Manx Shearwater, Ringed Plover, Mediterranean and Little Gulls (non-breeding birds summer), Black-headed Gull (breeding colonies), Common Gull (a few pairs breed), Kittiwake (post-breeding flock on shore), Sandwich Tern (breeding colony), Roseate Tern, Common Tern (breeding colonies), Cuckoo (peak numbers of returning adults), Yellow Wagtail, Black Redstart, Wheatear, Whitethroat.

August–November: Sooty and Manx Shearwaters (September peak), Leach's Petrel, Gannet (October peak), Garganey, Sparrowhawk (from October), Little Stint, Woodcock (from October), Greenshank, Green and Wood Sandpipers, Arctic and Great Skuas, Mediterranean and Little Gulls, Arctic Tern, Black Tern (peak numbers late August–September), White-winged Black Tern (almost annual on 'the Patch' or the pits), up-Channel passage of Guillemot and Razorbill, Wryneck, Woodlark, large diurnal passage of hirundines, Black Redstart (October peak), Wheatear, Whinchat, Stonechat, Ring Ouzel (October peak), Dartford Warbler (annual in October), Lesser Whitethroat, Yellow-browed Warbler, Goldcrest (October peak), Firecrest (late October–November peak), Pied Flycatcher, Red-backed Shrike, diurnal passage of finches, especially Goldfinch (up to 1,000 daily in October).

Habitat

Just south of Goudhurst, Bedgebury Forest is situated on higher undulating terrain, in sharp contrast to the lowland Weald to the north. Although much of the plantation is coniferous, there is still some Sweet Chestnut coppice. One of the attractions of this area is the Pinetum, with its wonderful and varied selection of conifers set on grassy slopes rising from a small lake. There is also a wide variety of fungi, which increases the interest for visitors. The Forestry Commission plan to extend the Pinetum up to the B2079; they also propose creating another lake and to manage parts of the forest in ways that will benefit a number of bird species. These are extremely welcome proposals and should make visits even more rewarding.

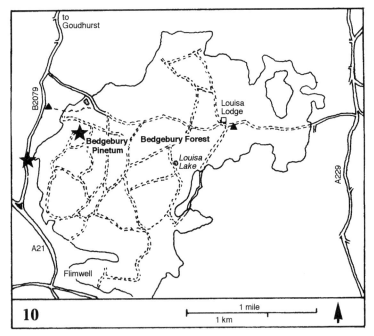

Species

In the winter months, the dense foliage of the cypress trees, within the Pinetum, is much favoured by finches for roosting. This is one of the most reliable localities for seeing the handsome Hawfinch well, but other finches such as Chaffinch and Brambling also fly in to roost. How far these birds disperse during the day is not known, but from high vantage points overlooking the Pinetum small groups may be counted streaming in from outlying areas. Some 50 or more Hawfinches may often be present, though this species is now declining in Kent, probably through loss of cherry and damson orchards. The loud 'ticking' of the

Hawfinch is a characteristic sound of the late afternoon. The numbers of Bramblings fluctuate considerably from year to year, but counts of up to 300 have been recorded. A dawn or dusk visit will probably be necessary to hear the Tawny and possibly Long-eared Owls hooting from the surrounding forest.

There is little obvious birdlife in the forestry conifer plantations, but perseverance will produce its rewards. Woodcock may be disturbed from areas of bracken and there is always a slender chance of seeing the resident Sparrowhawks. Coal Tit and Goldcrest are among the commonest passerines in the conifers, but roving flocks of titmice may contain four or five tit species. The larch plantations are favoured by Siskins and Redpolls, and Louisa lake occasionally attracts species like Little Grebe and Kingfisher, which add to the variety.

Hawfinch

The great storm of October 1987 wreaked havoc with several conifer plantations. Though some are being replanted, the Forestry Commission took the opportunity to allow some natural regeneration. They are also creating wider rides, which will be more attractive for species like the Nightjar, the numbers of which had increased to about 20 pairs by 1996. They are attracted by the open, more heath-like habitat, which other species like Stonechat and Tree Pipit have also found suitable for nesting.

During the spring, the resident species become more vocal and some of the winter visitors, like Redwing and Brambling, may sing before migrating north. All three woodpecker species will be busy pecking new nest-holes, while the Nuthatch lines the entrance of its chosen nest-hole with mud. This is the time to familiarise oneself with the song of the Goldcrest, and to listen carefully for the subtly different, more strident, less variable and shorter song of the most attractive Firecrest. By early May, a good variety of common woodland warblers will be singing and setting up breeding territories. The soft 'purring' of the Turtle Dove is inevitably a late addition to the woodland chorus. From late May through early June is the best period for hearing and seeing both Woodcock 'roding' and Nightjar displaying, though both continue into early July.

Irruptions of Crossbills tend to occur every three or four years, often followed by breeding, which commences early in the succeeding year. Most irruptions consist of two waves, with the first in late June and July, followed by a second which normally peaks in October. The distinctive, hard 'chup-chup' flight call of the Crossbill is often the first evidence of their presence, but look carefully at all larches anyway, the seeds of this conifer are much favoured. Occasionally Siskins may be found in the summer and breeding has recently been confirmed.

Seeing any birds of prey, apart from the resident Kestrels, normally requires a great deal of patience. By selecting a high vantage point that overlooks the forest and scanning diligently over the tree tops, you may be fortunate enough to see the occasional Sparrowhawk, or even a Hobby. The former species may often be accompanied by a flock of Starlings, while the latter may seek prey amongst a flock of feeding House Martins or Swallows, though in spring they are more partial to insects.

The dense plantation areas become very quiet again as the migrants disperse, but mixed flocks of tits and warblers can be seen during August. Though migration will not be obvious at such a wooded inland locality, species like Pied Flycatcher and Whinchat do occur from late August into September. By October the winter thrushes will be replacing the summer migrants and the finches will again be flying in to roost. If there has been an irruption of Crossbills, look at them all carefully, the first Two-barred Crossbill to be seen in Kent was discovered here in October 1990.

Timing

Most woodland species are more active and vocal early in the day, while the roosting birds are best seen from mid-afternoon until dusk. For Woodcock and Nightjar visit some of the young conifer plantations between 2100–2200 hours from late May. Fine weather, with little wind makes it much easier to hear bird calls and song. The Pinetum is popular with the general public, causing considerable disturbance and making listening difficult during the middle of the day, particularly at weekends.

In the winter months, a morning visit to nearby Bewl Water (see p. 188) and an afternoon visit to Bedgebury makes a worthwhile day's outing.

Access

From Goudhurst take the B2079 south towards Flimwell. About 3 miles (5 km) on the left is a public car park (Map 10). From Flimwell follow the A21. Turn right along the B2079 for about 1 mile (1.6 km) to find the car park on the right. To visit the Pinetum a small entrance fee is payable at the shop in the car park, where there are also toilets. Follow the hedge-lined footpath towards the Pinetum, the Cypress trees, usually favoured by roosting finches, are about 0.5 mile (0.8 km) southeast from the gate, just over a sharp rise.

Quite a good vantage point overlooking the forest is to be found further along the B2079, about 0.5 mile (0.8 km) south of the car park. There is just room to park a car on the edge of the road.

There are numerous rides and public footpaths that wind through the forestry plantation, and losing your sense of direction is surprisingly easy. You might find carrying a compass worthwhile! The forest may also be approached from the A229 between Cranbrook and Hawkhurst. Driving south from Cranbrook, just over 0.5 mile (1 km) south of the

B2086 to Benenden junction, turn right into Park Lane and follow the narrow road as far as the 'Road closed to unauthorised vehicles' barrier, and park. The track ahead, passed Louisa Lodge, will take you to the Pinetum, while the track to the south, through Frith Farm and then north through the forest leads you beside Louisa lake. Other reasonable vantage points over the forest can be found along Park Lane, some overlooking clearings within the forest.

Calendar

Resident: Sparrowhawk, Woodcock, Tawny Owl, Green, Great Spotted and Lesser Spotted Woodpeckers, Goldcrest, Coal Tit, Nuthatch, Treecreeper and commoner woodland passerines.

December–February: Fieldfare, Redwing, Brambling, Siskin, Hawfinch, residents and other finches.

March–May: Firecrest (occasionally in winter); Tree Pipit, Stonechat, common woodland warblers, Spotted Flycatcher (early May), perhaps Hobby (May).

June–July: Residents, including Woodcock roding; breeding summer visitors as above, including Nightjar and Turtle Dove. Possibly Firecrest, Siskin and Crossbill (following irruptions).

August–November: Summer migrants leave by mid September. From October Woodcock and winter thrushes, winter finches return to roost.

11 BOUGH BEECH RESERVOIR

OS 188
TQ 44/54

Habitat

This man-made reservoir of some 285 acres (115 ha), first flooded during 1969–70, is the largest stretch of freshwater in Kent. Its irregular, natural shoreline is surrounded by woodland, fields and hedgerows. A road, which runs across the northern end of the reservoir, provides excellent views of the nature reserve, about 65 acres (26 ha) in extent, which is managed by the Kent Wildlife Trust. Water is pumped into the reservoir from the River Eden during the winter months, when conditions allow; but not between May and September, when the water level drops steadily to expose large areas of mud, which is attractive to migrant waders. Footpaths provide access to some of the surrounding mainly deciduous woodland.

With this wide range of habitats it is not surprising that over 230 species have occurred here.

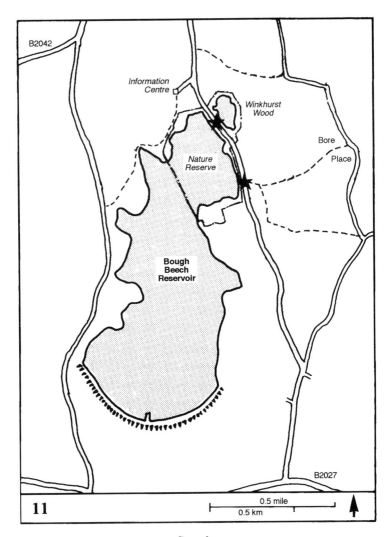

Species

The numbers and variety of wildfowl present on the reservoir in the winter months will depend on the severity of the weather. Great Crested Grebes will be present, with large numbers of noisy Greylag and Canada Geese, which commute between the reservoir and the surrounding fields. Of the dabbling duck, Wigeon, Teal and Mallard are often quite numerous, with smaller numbers of Shoveler and Gadwall, and occasionally Pintail. Pochard and Tufted Duck are often present in good numbers, whilst a few Goldeneye and Goosander are regular visitors. During a prolonged cold spell, the variety of duck may be augmented by a Red-throated Diver, or one of the rarer grebes. Smew and Bewick's Swans most often visit in these conditions. With luck, the resident Sparrowhawks may show over the surrounding woodland. Careful observation should produce views of Snipe, often well camouflaged amongst the vegetated water's edge.

A few spring migrants, including Little Ringed Plover, may be seen before the end of March but, depending on the weather, it may be several weeks before the main arrival of summer migrants. Many of these may be seen from the footpaths that take you through some of the surrounding woodland. This is the time to see the extraordinary courtship display of the Great Crested Grebes and there is also a chance of seeing Goldeneye displaying, before they leave for the north. Ospreys are increasingly regular in spring and one wonders whether the man-made platform will eventually tempt a pair to stay. Other migrant birds of prey, like Marsh Harrier and Buzzard, are being seen with increasing regularity, and Hobbies are usually present in the general area throughout the summer. Common Sandpipers are regular spring migrants, but other waders that pass through, because of the normally high water level as well as the urgency of the season, seldom stay long, if at all. Terns, including the attractive Black Tern, occur regularly, but again they do not linger.

Goosander

In the summer months, it is fascinating to watch the young of the Great Crested Grebe being fed, or riding on the backs of their parents; or to see the young Shelduck diving and following their parents. A duck Mandarin may appear with her brood, as this species occasionally breeds here successfully.

By July, there is often evidence of early autumn migration, as the returning waders drop in to feed at a more leisurely pace than in spring. They will often stay for several days and there is a good opportunity to see Green, as well as Common Sandpipers and the elegant Greenshank at close quarters. Ringed Plover and Dunlin are also regular at this time, whilst other species such as Little Stint, Spotted Redshank and Black-tailed Godwit are virtually annual visitors. Any rarer waders are most likely to occur at this time and over the years these have included five American species, Kentish Plover, Temminck's Stint and Red-necked Phalarope. As numbers of Little Egrets continue to increase in UK southern counties there is a possibility of seeing one here at this time. Ospreys are virtually annual autumn visitors. Garganey should also be looked for, though their identification is more difficult in autumn. In addition many passerine migrants can be expected, such as Wheatear, Whinchat and Yellow Wagtail. The occurrence of a Radde's Warbler here in October 1984 shows that extreme rarities can turn up anywhere.

Timing

Viewing from the road, you look southwest over the reservoir, so morning visits provide the best light. Early morning is also preferable for small passerines, as they are most active then. Evening visits are recommended for roosting birds and possibly Woodcock in the breeding season.

Access

The reservoir and the whole of the nature reserve can be viewed well from the public road just south of Winkhurst Green (Map 11), along which there is ample room to park. From the south, this road can be reached from the B2027, turning north about 1.5 miles (2.4 km) west of Chiddingstone Causeway, following the road signposted to Winkhurst Green and Bough Beech Nature Reserve. From the north, the B2042 runs southwest from Riverhead to Ide Hill. The Winkhurst Green turning is to the east just 1 mile (1.6 km) south of Ide Hill.

The KWT Information Centre, just to the north of the reserve is in an old oasthouse, with car parking and toilet facilities. It is open to the public, free of charge, from 11.00 am–4.30 pm at weekends and on Wednesdays between April and October. For woodland birds, one footpath heads south from here, while another leads from the viewpoint, at the south end of the causeway, to Bore Place, where you can follow the narrow road north, before taking another footpath back towards the Information Centre.

Calendar

Resident: Great Crested Grebe, Cormorant, Grey Heron, Mandarin, Greylag and Canada Geese, Sparrowhawk, Kingfisher, Grey Wagtail, and a good variety of typical woodland species, including the three woodpeckers, Marsh and Willow Tits, Nuthatch and Treecreeper.

December–February: Wildfowl including Wigeon, Teal, Shoveler, Pochard, Tufted Duck, Goldeneye, Goosander and Ruddy Duck, Water Rail, Snipe and a roost of at least 10,000 gulls, mostly Black-headed, but on occasions rarer species.

March–May: Migrant waders and terns, possibly Osprey, passerine migrants and returning summer visitors.

June–July: Breeding Grey Heron, Shelduck, Mandarin, Cuckoo, resident woodland birds, common warblers, including Reed, and Reed Bunting.

August–November: possibly Little Egret, overland migration of Brent Geese (late October–November), possibly Garganey, Osprey, Hobby, Snipe, return passage of migrant waders and terns, with Greenshank, Green and Common Sandpipers quite common, passerine migrants, including Yellow Wagtail and Whinchat.

Habitat

This is an extensive area essentially of old gravel and sand workings. It is surrounded by the tidal River Medway to the east, paper mills to the north, the A228 to the west and to the south more paper mills, a Tesco Superstore (of Golden-winged Warbler fame), a housing estate and the M20. Burham Marsh, a local nature reserve is situated on the other side of the river to the northeast, over which there is a panoramic view of the North Downs. The Abbey Mead pit, between the river and the railway line, is bordered with some mature reedbeds, willows and sallows, which surround many of the other smaller pits. A small area to the north of Abbey Mead also has stretches of marsh, *Phragmites* and mature hawthorn scrub. The Snodland windsurfing lake has some mature willows and small reedbeds. Much of the fishing is concentrated around the Leybourne Lakes in the southwest corner, where the fishermen have long competed with a large roost of Cormorants. Either side of the M20 the Castle and Leybourne lakes are surrounded by mature alders and

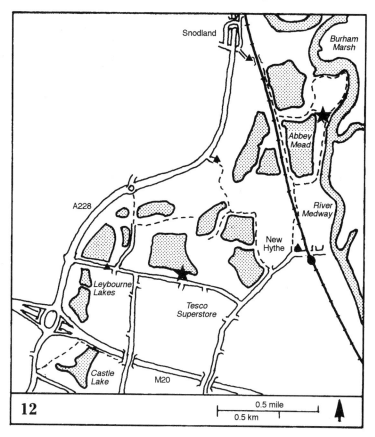

some woodland, which increase the diversity of species that can be seen in the area.

Species

As with many sites it is regular watching that produces the interesting variety of species and this area is no exception. An occasional diver may occur during the winter months and the Red-necked Grebe is fairly regular. The vagaries of the weather have a strong influence, not only on the presence of divers and grebes, but particularly on the wintering duck population. Normally there are good numbers of Gadwall, Teal, Shoveler, Tufted Duck and Pochard, along with a few Shelduck, but in severe conditions rarer species like Goosander, Smew and Goldeneye occur. In most winters a Bittern or two find refuge amongst small beds of *Phragmites*, usually around the Abbey Mead lake, while from the same areas Water Rails squeal and Bearded Tits may 'ping'. Snipe can be seen feeding in the marshy areas adjacent to the river, or on the river mud when the tide is down. The river also attracts good numbers of Teal and in particularly hard weather Water Rails can be seen feeding on the mud at the edge of the reeds. A small roost of Long-eared Owls is occasionally located, but this species is prone to undue disturbance, so avoid getting too close. A Short-eared Owl and wintering raptors like Hen Harrier and Merlin may occasionally be seen. A visit towards dusk should be rewarded with a Barn Owl, towards the Burham area, and is likely to produce numbers of Corn Buntings flying in to roost, either in the Burham Marsh reedbed or the adjacent hawthorn scrub.

Early Sand Martins are usually the first sign of spring, followed by Chiffchaffs in song — small numbers regularly overwinter. Other passerine migrants like Black Redstart and Wheatear are occasionally seen and by mid April Sedge and Reed Warblers will be singing, the latter playing host to several Cuckoos. If you stand between Abbey Mead and the river before dawn, you are likely to be deafened by the volume of Nightingale song — it is magnificent. Several *Sylvia* warblers, like Lesser Whitethroat, Whitethroat and Blackcap will also be in song during the daylight hours. Other woodland species, like Lesser Spotted Woodpecker and Coal Tit regularly occur around the Leybourne and Castle lakes either side of the M20 and Kingfishers are often seen at these lakes too. Displaying Great Crested Grebes are another attraction in early spring. Not many of the lakes or pits have shallow edges, so migrant waders are difficult to see here and early morning visits are essential to see any before they are disturbed.

The summer months are relatively quiet, but one or two pairs of Kingfishers will be breeding, the young Great Crested Grebes are always a delight to observe and the Sedge and Reed Warblers will be actively feeding their broods of young. Flocks of both Greylag and Canada Goose gather to moult, often favouring the Tesco lake.

In autumn large numbers of hirundines can be seen feeding over the lakes, which will again attract a few migrant waders and possibly terns. A wintering Stonechat will usually appear during October. During late October and early November the well established overland passage of Brent Geese can sometimes be witnessed here. The panoramic view of the North Downs to the northeast, from which direction they fly, provides a good opportunity to see a flock. Waders like Redshank and sometimes Dunlin feed on the exposed river mud and both Green and Common Sandpiper are known to winter in the same habitat.

Access

There are several access points and the choice will be determined partly by how long you wish to stay and in part by what you wish to see. The car park at Snodland at TQ 707615 can be reached from the A228 (Map 12). If driving from the M20, turn left, immediately right and drive over the A228, then turn right and filter left, over a narrow bridge into the car park. From the north, turn left by the Royal Mail buildings, left at the roundabout, then sharp right over the narrow bridge. Walk under the railway bridge and follow the footpath by the windsurfing lake. This path takes you around Abbey Mead lake, along the river wall and eventually back to the car park. If you have more time you can cross the railway at the south end of Abbey Mead lake.

For the New Hythe pools and Leybourne lakes there are several spots for parking — by the A228 at TQ 704607, on Leybourne Way at TQ 695598, or by the business park in New Hythe Lane at TQ 710600. A footpath runs north from here to a railway crossing just south of Abbey Mead lake. The Tesco lake can be viewed for wintering duck from opposite Tesco Superstore on Leybourne Way. There are several footpaths around the Leybourne and Castle lakes and in the woodland by the M20.

Timing

For an essentially inland site being aware of the state of the tide may seem strange, but at low tide species like Redshank and Shelduck move upriver to feed on the exposed mud. Windsurfing on the Snodland lake is most popular at weekends, as is fishing on a number of the pools west of the railway. For least disturbance early mornings are best, but late afternoon and dusk visits can also be rewarding.

Calendar

Resident: Great Crested Grebe, Cormorant, Grey Heron, Kingfisher, Lesser Spotted Woodpecker, Reed Bunting.

December–February: possible diver, rare grebes, Bittern, Gadwall, Teal (along the river), Shoveler and good numbers of Tufted Duck and Pochard, possibly Smew and Goosander, Ruddy Duck, Water Rail, Snipe, Redshank, possibly Green and Common Sandpipers, possibly Long-eared Owl and Bearded Tit, Chiffchaff, Corn Bunting (winter roost).

March–May: migrant waders and terns, Cuckoo, Nightingale, Sedge and Reed Warblers, *Sylvia* warblers.

June–July: Greylag and Canada Geese (moult flocks), breeding residents and Sedge, Reed and *Sylvia* Warblers.

August–November: migrant waders and terns, a few migrant passerines like Whinchat and Wheatear, returning winter visitors, including Stonechat.

ADDITIONAL SITES

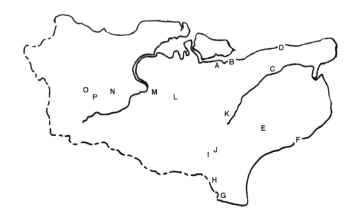

Key & Site	Habitat	Birds of Interest	Peak Season	Nearest Town
A Oare Marshes NR	Grazing marsh, reedbed	Dabbling duck, freshwater and shore waders, Bearded Tit	Spring, autumn	Faversham
OS 178 TR 013647	*This is a KWT Reserve, where there is a hide overlooking the marsh and a small car park. Follow the Saxon Shore Way in both directions.*			
B South Swale NR	Shell beach, mudflats, salt-marsh, grassland	Brent Geese, shore waders, Hen Harrier, Eider, Short-eared Owl, Snow Bunting	Winter	Faversham
OS 179 TR 062647 or OS 178 TR 033631	*A Local Nature Reserve managed by the KWT. Follow the Saxon Shore Way west to the shell spit (Castle Coot) an hour or two before high tide. Alternatively, follow the footpath circuit from Nagden.*			
C Fordwich & Westbere	River, mature gravel pits, reedbeds, wet woodland	Usual reedbed species, Gadwall, Kingfisher, Lesser Spotted Woodpecker	All year	Canterbury
OS 179 TR 179598/ 197610	*Parking is restricted at both ends. Follow the footpaths from either end and northeast-wards along the river towards Hersden Lake.*			
D Reculver & Minnis Bay	Shore, coastal marshes	Eider, Hen Harrier, waders, seabirds, Snow Bunting, possibly Shore Lark	Autumn, winter	Herne Bay
OS 179 TR 226693	*From the car park follow the seawall and other footpaths north of the railway. In autumn, walk towards Bishopstone for passerine migrants, or seawatch from Reculver Towers, when the wind is in the northerly quarter.*			

Additional Sites

Key & Site	Habitat	Birds of Interest	Peak Season	Nearest Town
E Lyminge Forest	Mainly conifer woodland	Sparrowhawk, Tree Pipit, Goldcrest, possibly Firecrest and Crossbill	Spring, summer	Folkestone
OS 179/189 TR 142440	*Early morning preferable to listen for song or calls to locate these specialised woodland species.*			
F Folkestone Warren	Chalk cliff, scrub, rocky coast	Fulmar, possibly Shag, Purple Sandpiper, Mediterranean Gull, Rock Pipit, passerine migrants.	Winter, spring, autumn	Folkestone
OS 179/189 TR 248376 Copt Point TR 240368	*Drive down almost to the concrete apron, below the Warren, where a few Purple Sandpipers winter. Check the gull flock over the sewage outfall, or the rocky foreshore for Mediterranean Gulls — up to 50 in late autumn. Follow paths in Warren for passerine migrants in spring and autumn.*			
G Scotney	Flooded gravel pit	Grebes, geese, Scaup, migrant waders and terns	Winter, spring, autumn	Lydd
OS 189 TR 014191	*View the Sussex end from 008188 and the Kent end from 018197, checking the grassy area, which is full of hollows, as well as all the water edges.*			
H Walland Marsh	Reedbed, grazing marsh and arable	Mute and Bewick's Swans, Marsh and Hen Harriers, Golden Plover, Barn Owl	Winter	Lydd
OS 189 TQ 978244	*Hen Harriers usually roost in the reedbed at TQ 981241, where Water Rail and Bearded Tit also occur. The Bewick's Swans move about a lot, sometimes roosting on the Dungeness RSPB Reserve. Golden Plover often favour the Fairfield area 965263.*			
I Great Heron Wood	Mainly deciduous woodland	Good variety of woodland species, including all three woodpeckers, Nightingale, Marsh and Willow Tits	Spring, summer	Tenterden
OS 189 TQ 954318	*Also known as Parkwood Picnic Site. Eighty acres of attractive woodland. Heronry in southern section.*			
J Fagg's Wood	Mixed woodland	Sparrowhawk, Woodcock, Tawny Owl, Tree Pipit, Nightingale, Willow Tit, possibly Crossbill	Spring, summer	Ashford
OS 189 TQ 987345	*Follow the various rides. Early morning most profitable, with more song and greater bird activity. Dawn or dusk for Woodcock and calls of Tawny Owl.*			
K Challock Forest	Conifer and chestnut coppice	Woodcock, Nightjar, Nightingale, possibly Crossbill	Spring, summer	Ashford
OS 189 TR 030497	*Dusk visits, around 2130 hours to hear and see Nightjar and Woodcock. Coppiced areas with 3–4 years' growth usually preferred.*			
L Leeds Castle	Mixed woodland, lakes	Ornamental waterfowl, possibly Hobby, Kingfisher, Grey Wagtail	All year	Maidstone
OS 188 TQ 837538	*Public footpaths provide reasonable access, through to Broomfield 840527, where cars can be parked. Mandarin can be seen along the River Len. Get to know your duck in beautiful surroundings.*			

Additional Sites

Key & Site	Habitat	Birds of Interest	Peak Season	Nearest Town
M Mote Park	Parkland, lake and reedbed	Great Crested Grebe, Mandarin, migrant terns and passerines, all three woodpeckers, Kingfisher, Grey Wagtail, Siskin in winter	All year	Maidstone
OS 188 TQ 770554	*Early morning to see migrants before they are disturbed by dogs and their owners. Popular with the general public.*			
N Mereworth Woods	Conifer and chestnut coppice	Woodcock, Nightjar, possibly Stonechat	Spring, summer	Tonbridge
OS 188 TQ 630560	*Park by Invicta Cases & Packing 625560, then follow the tracks through the coppice to find a good vantage point around 2130 hours for roding Woodcock and displaying Nightjar.*			
O Sevenoaks Wildfowl Reserve	Managed gravel pits	Wildfowl, passage waders and terns, Kingfisher	Winter, spring, autumn	Sevenoaks
OS 188 TQ 522564	*A private reserve. Open weekends and Wednesdays (1000–1700 hours). Visitors hall with Exhibition Centre. Admission Fee. Membership enables daily visits to be made, apart from Mondays.*			
P Knole Park	Wooded deer park	All three woodpeckers, Tree Pipit, Redstart, Stonechat	Spring, summer	Sevenoaks
OS 188 TQ 541524	*Attractive deer park with fallow, sika and red deer. Old timber much favoured by woodpeckers and Redstarts. Since the October 1987 storm the Stonechat has appeared on the open, more heath-like areas.*			

SURREY

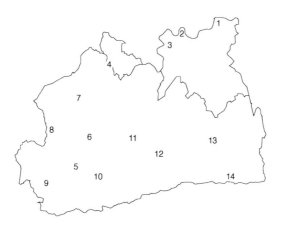

1 The Thames through London
2 Barnes
3 Richmond Park and Environs
4 The Upper Thames Valley
5 The Wey Valley, Eashing to
   Guildford
6 Papercourt Gravel Pits, Send
   and Wisley
7 The Northwest Surrey
   Commons
8 Farnham and the Blackwater
   Valley
9 Southwest Surrey Commons
10 Albury and District
11 Central Surrey Commons
12 Dorking Hills and Lakes
13 Reigate to Godstone
14 Hedgecourt, Wire Mill and
   District

1 THE THAMES THROUGH LONDON

The area described runs along the southern banks of the Thames from its entry into Surrey at the Surrey Docks, west for about 11 miles (18 km) to Putney (Map 1a). Sites are dealt with from east to west.

Habitat

The Thames is tidal for the whole of the area described here and long stretches of mud and stones are exposed at low tide. Old industrial and commercial buildings, including the Bankside and Battersea power stations rise among more modern constructions along the waterfront. The river is crossed by 18 bridges. These, with the numerous buoys, pilings, wharves and moored river craft, provide perches and breeding sites for birds of the district. There are several parks and open spaces with riverside frontages, the largest being at Battersea. River and air pollution levels are much reduced and still improving.

After their closure in the 1970s, the Surrey Docks became a wasteland which was quickly exploited by land and water birds. The docks have been redeveloped with a water sports centre, parkland, industrial buildings and housing (Map 1b). Ringed and Little Ringed Plovers, Skylarks and Yellow Wagtails which bred there during the development phase have been lost. Change has also brought improvements and the area is well worth watching because of the nature of the new habitat, which is unusual so close to central London. Panoramic views of the river can be had from generous lengths of broad footpath. Some of the old docks have been filled in. Most of the dockside buildings have been cleared, though a few have been left to give a flavour of the area as it once was. Greenland Dock is now used for water sports and is effectively a rectangular lake. Canada Dock is full and has an outlet to the Thames. The Ecological Parks Trust has taken over Lavender pond, part of the old Lavender Dock, and created reedbeds, a small wood and some marsh with sluices which lets water wash over a simulated flood meadow. The surrounding area has been landscaped with small mounds, rough grass, copses and patches of scrub. Russia Dock has been converted to woodland. An artificial hill gives views over the entire site.

Southwark Park runs for 0.5 mile (0.8 km) along the west side of the docks. It has mature trees and shrubberies and is heavily used. A pond with an island provides nest sites for waterfowl.

The now derelict William Curtis Ecological Park is 1 mile (1.6 km) upriver, a green area of an acre or two along the waterfront to the west of Tower Bridge. It has produced no records of very unusual species, but provides breeding sites for some of the commoner town and woodland birds and has a Thames frontage. Gorse and bracken grow there, with wild flowers such as lucerne and melilot.

From Southwark Cathedral through Tooley Street to Bankside the streets are noisy and river access is poor but the old commercial buildings provide useful habitat of a kind which is becoming scarcer. The decommissioned Bankside Power Station has a tall brick tower and many ledges. There is small area of grass and bushes open to the public between its entrance and the Thames.

At Southbank tall buildings to the east and west of Waterloo Bridge have attracted various breeding species. Jubilee Gardens provides a green space with spots private enough for Song Thrushes. There are good views of the Thames and the broad ledges on piers of Hungerford

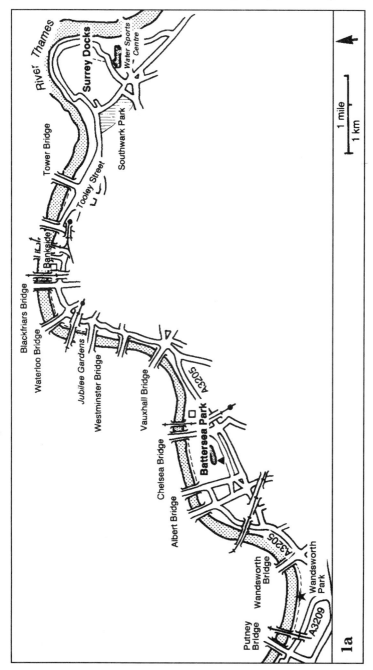

Bridge. Archbishop's Park at Lambeth is a public open space with grass, trees and shrubberies next to the more bird-rich but private grounds of the Archbishop's Palace.

Further up the river, at Battersea, there is a park with a large lake and islands for breeding wildfowl. Its northern boundary is the 0.75 mile (1.2 km) stretch of the Thames embankment between the Chelsea and Albert bridges. The Peace Pagoda, sports track and recreational activities of the many users of the park give it a busy, cosmopolitan atmosphere. A 1.5-acre (0.6 ha) area on an old Battersea Power Station cinder dump at the northeast corner of the Park has been converted to woodland by the London Wildlife Trust and has trees mature enough for woodpeckers and warblers. There is a long river frontage. The power station itself, a well-known London landmark with its four chimneys, one at each corner, is no longer in operation and is likely to be preserved as an exhibition and leisure centre.

The River Wandle passes through King George's Park and joins the Thames at Wandsworth Creek, where there are wooden pilings in the river. Just to the west is Wandsworth Park, mostly playing fields but with a long river frontage looking out to extensive shallows which are exposed at low tide and continue further upriver to Putney Bridge.

Species
The valley is a flyway for seabirds. The bridges are among the more likely places to provide sightings of a few species which are relatively scarce in Surrey, such as the Fulmar, Shag, Kittiwake, Glaucous Gull and Sandwich Tern. Cormorants, Grey Herons, duck and the commoner gulls may be seen at any time of the year. Good places to look for Shags and Cormorants are on the piers of Hungerford Bridge, on buoys in the vicinity of the Festival Hall at Southbank, on the pilings by Battersea Power Station and at the mouth of Wandsworth Creek.

Grey Herons breed in Battersea Park. Tufted Duck breed at the Surrey Docks, Southwark Park, Battersea Park and King George's Park in small numbers. Battersea Park has a breeding colony of feral Greylag Geese which may be the largest in Surrey. Although this species has been widely introduced in the southeast coastal counties of England its colonisation of Surrey has been slow. The park also has a large breeding flock of Canada Geese and creches of up to 50 goslings in the custody of a single adult can be seen in June and July. Black Swans have bred there.

The London parks have had their stock enriched by escaped and introduced wildfowl of many other indigenous and exotic species — a fact which may please the eye but makes recording difficult. Hybrids of the genus *Aythya* are sometimes found. These are usually of Tufted or Pochard origin but can closely resemble scarcer members of the genus such as the Lesser Scaup. Scaup and Ferruginous type hybrids, too, are occasionally found and are at least as common as the real thing. Bill characters are important for distinguishing the species, especially the amount and distribution of black on the nail.

Wintering waterfowl downriver at the Surrey Docks have included one or two Ferruginous Duck which, unlike their cousins in the parks and inner reservoirs, were convincingly genuine immigrants and not escapes or *Aythya* hybrids. Migrant duck such as Common Scoter are sometimes found on the river and other species are forced onto it in hard weather. Winter wildfowl include Pintail (on the foreshore at

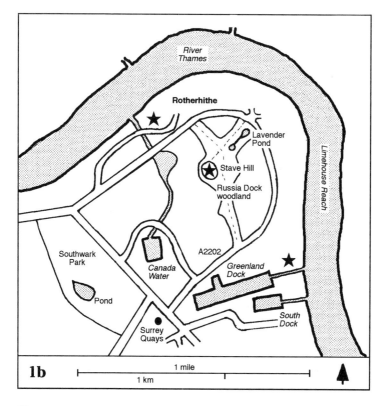

River Thames

Rotherhithe

Lavender Pond

Stave Hill

Russia Dock woodland

A2202

Southwark Park

Canada Water

Greenland Dock

Pond

South Dock

Surrey Quays

Limehouse Reach

1b

1 mile

1 km

Wandsworth), Shoveler and Goosander, and occasionally a Smew or Red-breasted Merganser.

The Kestrel is the commonest raptor but Sparrowhawks are increasing and can be seen carrying prey at the Surrey Docks, Wandsworth and probably elsewhere. Migrant Hobbies appear occasionally. Peregrines are now seen from time to time in winter and have prospected Bankside Power Station. Moorhens and Coots breed on most of the ponds. Migrant crakes and waders are fewer, but a Spotted Crake found in a car park at Waterloo shows that they still pass through. The Purple Sandpiper has appeared as a foreshore bird at Battersea.

Gulls and terns appear along the Thames in due season. A few summering gulls are sometimes found from Chelsea Reach, at Battersea, up to the Surrey Docks and may help the mid May birder along to that elusive Surrey 100 in a day. The Herring Gull, a common enough breeder in coastal counties, has bred once in Surrey, on the roof of the County Hall building at Lambeth. Lesser Black-backed and Herring Gulls breed on buildings on the north side of the Thames and further Surrey colonisation can be expected. Herring Gulls of the yellow-legged races are now being seen along the river fairly regularly. Wintering birds should be sought at Wandsworth.

Auks have appeared at Westminster and other places as part of a wreck after storms and very occasionally odd birds have spent weeks moving up- and downriver with the tides. Stock, Collared and migrant Turtle Doves are sometimes seen in the parks as well as the ubiquitous

Feral Rock Doves and Woodpigeons. Swifts are appearing in central London in increasing numbers as air pollution declines.

The Black Redstart breeds at Bankside and Battersea power stations. Bridgeworks and cleared sites are worth a look. Tooley Street, old buildings between Blackfriars Bridge and Waterloo Bridge and the riverside area up to Vauxhall Bridge can also produce a Black Redstart for the persistent observer. The song, which includes a phrase like the rattling of ball-bearings, may be the first evidence of the bird's presence, and carries well even above the roar of traffic.

Black Redstart

Swallows are rarely seen except as migrants, though their breeding stations are getting closer to the centre of the area. House Martins nest on buildings at the Surrey Docks and have attempted to do so on County Hall at Southbank. Waste ground at the Surrey Docks and on other cleared sites has offered at least a transient site for the Yellow Wagtail, which is extremely scarce as a breeding bird in the more rural parts of Surrey. The species is currently absent but Grey Wagtails have begun to breed in creeks along the waterfront.

Wrens, Dunnocks, Blackbirds, Blue Tits and Magpies can all be found in the breeding season in the parks and at tiny places like the Bankside frontage as long as they have a few bushes and trees. Reed Warblers breed at Lavender Pond. Whitethroats can be found at the Surrey Docks in May. A Firecrest has been found there in November. Sedge and Wood Warblers occur on passage.

Timing

Low tide is best for watching the Thames foreshore. Some of the parks and open spaces are less busy during the week than they are at weekends. Stormy conditions can bring interesting vagrants to the river.

Access

The Surrey Docks and Southwark Park are in the extreme northeast corner of the county, at Rotherhithe. From the north of the Thames the best London Underground station is Surrey Quays, on the East London Line. The bus service from Waterloo is good and preferable to the underground at least until the Jubilee Line extension is completed. The Water Sports Centre is 0.25 mile (0.4 km) along the south side of the A2202

(Redriff Road), which is opposite the station entrance. If you have a car, park in Rotherhithe. Southwark Park has an entrance close to Surrey Docks station, off the A200 (Lower Road).

Steps lead down from the west side of Tower Bridge to the waterside area which includes the William Curtis Ecological Park. Bankside can be approached from Blackfriars Bridge or Southwark Street. Good views of the Thames can be had from there and from the public promenades at the Festival Hall and the National Theatre, both by Waterloo Bridge, at Southbank.

For Battersea Park drive to Prince of Wales Drive outside the entrance and park there or take the train (BR from Waterloo) to Queenstown and walk 0.25 mile (0.4 km) down Queenstown Road. The nearest underground station is Vauxhall (Victoria Line).

A promenade runs along the embankment west of Wandsworth bridge but there is a rather limited space for roadside parking. Adjacent streets offer parking space for King George's Park. There is roadside parking on the east side of Wandsworth Park.

Calendar

Resident: Great Crested Grebe, Greylag and Canada Geese, Mallard, Tufted Duck, Moorhen, Coot, Blackbird, Jay, Magpie.

December–February: Cormorant and sometimes Shag in hard winters, duck on the Thames, chance of Ferruginous. Peak gull numbers. Occasional auks (usually Guillemot or Razorbill).

March–May: Common Gull passage March, terns from about 10 April, most gulls leave by early May. Black Redstarts in territory, most easily found in May and June when the males are singing. Migrant warblers, especially at the Surrey Docks and Battersea Park.

June–July: Breeding wildfowl in the parks, small numbers of feeding Swifts by the river at Vauxhall. House Martins, Yellow Wagtails and Skylarks at the Surrey Docks.

August–November: Return of gulls, with Lesser Black-backed Gull passage. Look for yellow-legged Herring Gulls on the Thames. Migrant terns and passerines.

2 BARNES

Habitat

The 'S' bends of the River Thames, which provide the course for the annual Oxford and Cambridge Boat Race, wind round the Barn Elms and Lonsdale Road Reservoirs just to the south and west of Hammersmith Bridge (Map 2).

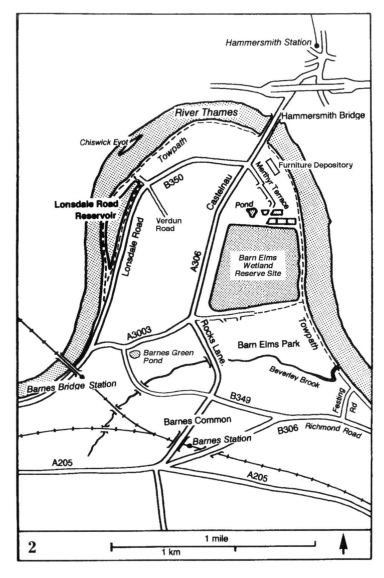

Lonsdale Road Reservoirs used to stretch all along the south side of the river to the west of Hammersmith Bridge. Only the most westerly, shaped like a bulging boomerang, survives, lying north–south against the river. The reservoir is no longer in commercial use and has been converted to a nature reserve. Its banks have become overgrown with thick vegetation. The dam at the north end has a good growth of reeds below it. The elms along the riverbank have now gone but there are some magnificent black poplars with a varied understorey of trees and bushes. Rafts have been moored out in the middle of the reservoir to encourage nesting. There is a footpath around the whole site. Lonsdale Road Reservoir is also known as Leg o' Mutton on account of its shape.

The Barn Elms Reservoirs have been an important site for birds since they were built in the 1890s. Over 190 species have been recorded, which is an excellent total for a small area with a limited variety of habitats. The reservoirs, like others in the Thames valley, were made obsolete by the exploitation of cheaper resources and the completion of the Thames Water Ring Main. Part of the 141 acre (57 ha) site has been redeveloped for housing but most is being converted to a wetland reserve in a partnership between Thames Water, Berkeley Homes and The Wildfowl and Wetlands Trust. The project is due for completion by 2000, when there will be a visitors' centre. In the meantime, access to the southern part of the site is very restricted, though records are still being collected.

On the west side of the Barn Elms there are large Victorian villas and mature gardens. At the north end there are some allotments, a reedy pond and the Harrods Furniture Depository. To the east the riverbank is marked out by willows and acacias. Away to the south are the mature playing fields of Barn Elms Park, with Barnes Common beyond. The common suffers from traffic noise but has rough grass, scrub and trees. There is a pond at Barnes Green. A towpath runs round the whole river frontage from Putney to Barnes Bridge.

The reservoirs freeze over quite easily so that they tend to miss the hard-weather influxes of waterbirds, though scarce species may at such times occur nearby on the Thames.

Essex skipper butterflies occur in some abundance in the rough grass on the riverside at Barn Elms and in the northeast corner at Lonsdale Road. Large and small skippers also occur, as do common and holly blues and meadow browns. Purple hairstreaks occur on Barnes Common and may turn up in the few oaks at the northwest (Barn Elms) end. Great water dock may be found in the Barn Elms pond, wild clary at the Harrods end of the east bank.

Species

Much of the Barn Elms site is inaccessible but the Barn Elms pond and the allotments can be seen from the roadside and the Harrods Furniture Depository from the towpath. The species of most interest at the pond are Sedge and Reed Warblers and other migrants. Chiffchaffs have wintered there. Whinchats, a Melodious Warbler and other migrants have been seen on the allotments. Black Redstarts are sometimes seen on the Furniture Depository.

The charm of Lonsdale Road Reservoir is that the birds may be seen, without hides, at much closer quarters than is usual and residents and long stayers often become quite tame. It is a regular loafing area for duck: Shoveler can often be very close in winter. New or irregular human visitors are not guaranteed scarce or rare birds but the regular observers consider themselves sufficiently well rewarded to keep going back. Spring and autumn migrants tend to stop off for short periods of a day or so and this is where the regular watcher scores. Unless otherwise stated this account refers to Lonsdale Road Reservoir.

Little and Great Crested Grebes are breeding residents. Up to 80 Cormorants roost and feed. Mute Swans breed. Red-crested Pochard are annual and mostly occur in the autumn. These birds are thought to be of feral origin from the London parks. The occasional autumn or winter bird might be a genuine migrant. Pochard, a rare breeding bird in Britain, have raised young at this site. Mallard and Tufted Duck breed annually.

Duck numbers rise in October, reach a peak in the New Year and are usually well down by March. In the winter months there are usually a handful of Wigeon, Teal and Gadwall and up to 50 Mallard. Shoveler numbers peak at up to 200, Tufted Duck rather more. Pintail and Scaup are occasional. Scarcer duck include Ferruginous and Ring-necked. Hard weather brings the highest numbers, provided the water remains unfrozen. Ruddy Duck are now seen regularly.

Common Tern

Sparrowhawks are seen from time to time. Kestrels breed nearby. Hobbies are becoming more frequent. Water Rails occur on passage as do a few waders, mainly Common Sandpipers. Gulls of all the commoner species can be seen on the foreshore east of Hammersmith Bridge. Yellow-legged Herring Gulls often occur there. Common Terns breed on a raft. Barnes Common has produced a Common Nighthawk. Great Spotted Woodpeckers occur in the big trees by the river. Winter thrushes are found in Barn Elms Park. Reed Warblers breed at Lonsdale Road Reservoir. Blackcaps are present in the breeding season. Long-tailed Tits and Bullfinches are more likely in the winter. Reed Buntings sing along the riverbank and at the Barn Elms pond.

The pond at Barnes Green is crowded with wild and feral waterfowl including Mandarin and Shelduck, many of them breeding.

Timing
Lonsdale Road Reservoir can be seen at any time. Since birds on the water can be viewed from all points of the compass, light is generally not a problem. The large parties of Swifts in May and August disperse well before dusk.

Access
Most of Lonsdale Road can be well seen from the towpath and footpath. The accessible parts of the Barn Elms site can be seen from public roads and the towpath. The approach road, Merthyr Terrace, off Castelnau SW13, is not suitable for parking but the site is only a short walk from Verdun Road, which is the best place to park for Lonsdale Road Reservoir. The nearest Underground station is Hammersmith (Piccadilly, District and Hammersmith & City Lines). Buses: 9, 33 and 72. The nearest railway station is Barnes (BR from Waterloo).

Calendar
Resident: Great Crested Grebe, Canada Goose, Mallard, Tufted Duck, Kestrel, Pied Wagtail, Reed Bunting.

December–February: Chance of divers and the scarcer grebes, peak Great Crested Grebe numbers, Grey Heron, peak wildfowl counts including large flocks of Shoveler, good numbers of Teal and a sprinkling of Goldeneye, sawbills, etc. Peak gull counts with chance of rarities, winter thrushes.

March–May: Peak spring passage of waders and terns (Common, Arctic, Black) from the second week of April. Most waders are only infrequently seen and may fly over without stopping. Arctic Terns are scarce, but more likely to be seen in spring than autumn.

June–July: Breeding wildfowl. Sedge and Reed Warbler, Swifts.

August–November: Yellow-legged Gulls on the foreshore. Wader passage (stronger than in spring), mainly Common Sandpipers, with a few Oystercatchers, Godwits, etc. Wintering duck and gulls start returning. Little Gull scarce, but more likely to be seen in autumn. Common and Black Terns also tend to be more frequent in autumn. Pipits, warblers.

3 RICHMOND PARK AND ENVIRONS

OS 176
TQ 07/17 & TQ 27/37

Habitat

Richmond Park and the adjacent gardens and commons extend for about 5 miles (7.5 km) southeast from Kew to Wimbledon (Map 3). The Thames towpath, which has something to offer at most times of the year, marks the western boundary of Kew Gardens. The Gardens cover 300 acres (120 ha) and provides the chance of some relaxing birding. They include a lake with ornamental waterfowl and good stands of mature trees. There is a palm house and an eighteenth-century pagoda.

Three wooded islands (Brentford and Long Aits) in the Thames can be seen from the towpath at the north end of Kew Gardens. The towpath continues past the Gardens to the west end of Old Deer Park, where there is a small nature reserve with willows, water and sedges. It then continues south through Richmond to Petersham meadows, Ham Lands, a secluded marina and Teddington Weir.

Petersham Meadows are not much visited by birdwatchers but Ham Lands, with about 200 acres (80 ha) of rough grass partly invaded by scrub, has been the source of a number of interesting records. A marina with wooded surrounds and a raft for birds can be seen from the towpath. Teddington Weir has ledges for perching and plenty of visitors to feed the birds. Mammals at Ham include fox and badger.

Richmond Park covers about 2350 acres (950 ha) and is 8 miles (12 km) round. The bulk of it is rough grass with plantations of mature mixed woodland. Pollarded oaks are dotted about the open areas.

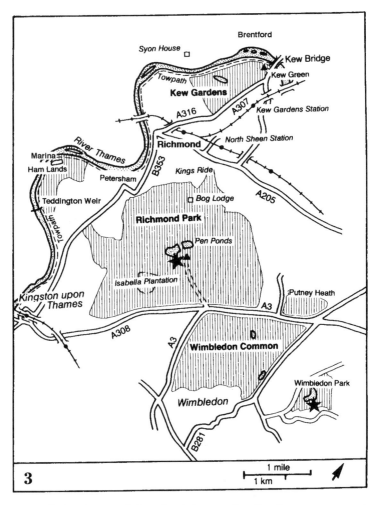

Damp flushes here and there lead down to Pen Ponds, two connected waters in the middle of the park. This area tends to be the most interesting part of the site. The upper pond has a reedbed at one end and is partly surrounded by trees and fenced off. The abundant cover and good grazing supports a famous population of deer, Red and Fallow, which allow close approach though they should, as park notices will remind you, be treated with caution especially in the rutting season (autumn).

Wimbledon Common which, with Putney Heath to the north, covers some 1200 acres (490 ha), is an area of grass, scrub and mixed woodland on a gravelly subsoil. There are some small pools. Wimbledon Park is a rather tatty municipal affair, but it has a good-sized lake with bank cover and is attractive to wintering and breeding wildfowl.

Species

Little and Great Crested Grebes breeding in the parks across the area. Hobbies can be seen in summer. The commoner birds are often very tame. In heavily used places Robins and tits will follow you from bush to bush hoping for crumbs. Nuthatches will feed from the hand.

Ring-necked Parakeets, part of the small feral population in northern and central Surrey, are seen quite often. Parties of up to 20 are not uncommon along the Thames Valley from Kew to Walton and Egham and may most reliably be looked for a few miles upstream at Walton Bridge. The birds appear to be able to survive hard winters. They nest in holes in trees. Sometimes they come into gardens for apples and other fruit. Ring-necked Parakeets have been known to cause confusion with inexperienced birdwatchers, but now appear in most field guides.

There is a heronry on Brentford Ait. Looking across the river to Syon House, one is likely to see many Grey Herons feeding in marshy areas on the other bank, the birds coming from one of the Brentford and other heronries, and possibly a few Snipe. There have been rare winter occurrences of Guillemots on the Thames at Kew, as elsewhere on the Thames and adjacent reservoirs. Common Terns have tried to breed at the marina on the Ham Lands towpath and there are many Ring-necked Parakeets in the area.

Great Spotted Woodpecker

Black Swans and Egyptian Geese have raised young at Kew from time to time. The rather tame Red-crested Pochard often seen at Kew and Richmond are escapes, or possibly feral birds. The Green Woodpecker is most frequent at Kew. Migrants have included Red Kite, Firecrest and Pied Flycatcher.

About 45 bird species breed in Richmond Park. Pen Ponds have the commoner breeding waterfowl including Great Crested Grebes. Grey Herons are regular at the upper pond. Large numbers of Gadwall winter there. Pochard, very scarce breeders in Surrey, have raised young more than once. Mandarin have colonised the Park. Little and Tawny Owls are present. Stock Doves are common round the oaks. This is a good place to see woodpeckers and all three species are to be found fairly easily. The Great Spotted is the commonest. There is a good variety of warblers and woodland passerines. Other breeding birds include Meadow Pipits and Tree Sparrows. Watch the pollarded oaks west of Pen Ponds for the latter. Reed Buntings, which are here all year round, are absurdly tame and will approach to within a few feet in well used areas such as the shore of Pen Ponds, or round the small pond in Isabella Plantation. The area round Pen Ponds is a good one for migrants. Spring overshoots in the Park have included Golden Oriole and Ortolan Bunting. The ponds get wintering flocks of Tufted and other duck. Very occasionally Bearded Tits (a scarce species in Surrey at any time) have been found in the reedbed. Bog Lodge has some attraction for migrants including a Barred Warbler on one recent occasion, Whinchats and Wheatears. Stonechats and the odd Dartford Warbler have wintered. Overall, about 100 species are recorded in the park in an average year.

The bushes on Ham Lands support a good variety of warblers in summer. Winter visitors to the river and meadows at Ham include Goosander, an occasional Short-eared Owl, Fieldfares and Redwings.

Wimbledon Common has breeding Tree Pipits and its warblers include the Wood Warbler. Ornamental rowans with large, persistent berries lining one of the adjacent streets have sustained wintering Waxwings. Wimbledon Park Lake attracts wintering Shoveler and Goosander. Great Crested Grebes and Canada Geese breed. Migrants present in summer include Garden Warblers in lakeside scrub.

Timing

The towpath is most comfortably walked in the downstream direction to keep the sun as far as possible behind you. Kew Gardens and Richmond Park have opening and closing hours which vary according to the time of year. It is best to try Richmond Park early in the day, when there are fewer people about, especially for the occasional migrant wader on the shore of Pen Ponds. The park can get very crowded, particularly on summer weekends. Evenings may be best for Tawny Owls.

Wimbledon Common is best early in the day and is likely to be unrewarding for birdwatching on summer afternoons. Wimbledon Park Lake can only be well seen from the southeast, so mornings are best here too.

Access

Kew Gardens is on the A307 (Kew Road). Park at the main entrance in Kew Green, at the north end or at the riverside car park reached from Kew Green via Ferry Lane. There is an admission charge. The towpath can be reached from a number of points at the Richmond and Kew end, including the riverside car park at Kew Gardens. There is a long stretch from just south of Kew to near Twickenham Bridge where no access is possible. Kew Gardens Underground station is on the District Line.

Richmond Park can be reached from the A307 or the A3. There are several car parks on the perimeter road in the park and one on higher ground in the middle, overlooking Pen Ponds. The nearest train station is North Sheen, a 0.75 mile (1.2 km) walk south along the B353 (Manor Road) and right into Sheen Road to the Kings Ride entrance.

Putney Heath and Wimbledon Common are readily accessed from the A3 by taking the Putney Heath exit just north of the entrance to Richmond Park. Wimbledon Common can also be approached from

Parkside or, from the south, along Cannizaro Road and West Side Common. The entrance to Wimbledon Park is in Wimbledon Park Road, SW19.

Calendar

Resident: Great Crested Grebe, Canada Goose, exotic waterfowl of various origins, Sparrowhawk, Kestrel, Little and Tawny Owls, Stock Dove, Ring-necked Parakeet, woodpeckers, Meadow Pipit, Nuthatch, Tree Sparrow, Reed Bunting, Grey Partridges have been introduced into Richmond Park.

December–February: Wintering Gadwall, Tufted Duck, Pochard, Shoveler, Goldeneye, Goosander, Smew are becoming regular on Pen Ponds. Short-eared Owl has wintered in Richmond Park, so has Dartford Warbler.

March–May: Heronry on Brentford Ait. Southern migrants in Richmond Park. Wintering duck leave but watch for Mandarin and lingering Pochard. Stock Doves active, warblers and Tree Pipits arrive.

June–July: Breeding waterfowl, Hobby, pipits, Blackcap, Garden Warbler, Wood Warbler, Tree Sparrows.

August–November: Wintering duck and Stonechats begin to return. Migrant terns and chats. Fieldfare (small numbers) and Redwing (flocks) from the end of September.

4 THE UPPER THAMES VALLEY

OS 176 SU 86/96, SU 87/97, TQ 06/16 & 07/17

Habitat

The upper part of the Thames Valley from Weybridge west to the Surrey border of Staines broadens out to an extensive plain of low-lying soils and gravels. It has been exploited for various commercial purposes, the most important of which, for the birdwatcher, is the supply of water to the metropolis. The system of reservoirs which now exists has been built in stages since the turn of the century and has had a major impact on the birdlife of the area. The reservoirs are of a distinctive bunded design, being excavated from the gravel floor and built up above ground level with surrounding embankments which have sloping, grass-covered sides up to about 30 ft (9 m) high. The slopes are sometimes grazed by sheep or cattle. From time to time individual reservoir basins are drained, exposing a large expanse of gravelly mud which converts the larger ones, such as Staines, into a kind of tideless estuary.

The gravels have been heavily worked for building materials and there are many pits, some being excavated, others water-filled or at intermediate stages of maturity.

The eastern edge of Windsor Great Park runs down the Surrey border at Egham. It includes Virginia Water, one of the county's larger lakes, set in parkland which is strikingly like that of the native oriental haunts of its colony of Mandarin Duck. Because of the size of the larger waters, a telescope is advisable for reservoir observation, especially in winter when there may be difficult identification problems with divers, grebes or duck. A telescope is best for good views at the reservoirs generally, since binoculars on their own will often not have enough range.

Species

Gulls were scarce in the London area in the nineteenth century but now roost on the western reservoirs in huge numbers. Other seabirds, wildfowl and waders use them on passage or for wintering. The grassy slopes on the reservoir sides provide a suitable habitat for breeding Meadow Pipits.

Little Ringed Plover move in almost at once to drained reservoirs and the basins at Staines have hosted rare waders, some for long periods. The gravel pits provide a more stable habitat for breeding birds and species nesting at least sporadically in suitable places include Shelduck, Pochard, Little Ringed Plover, Ringed Plover and Sand Martin, as well as the commoner duck and grebes.

Main Birdwatching Zones

The reservoirs and gravel pits at Walton are a compact group mostly within sight of one another and these are described first. The Staines area, a little higher up the Thames, is taken next and includes some of the biggest reservoirs in the London area and so many gravel pits as to make it almost more water than land. It straddles the river and includes the Spelthorne district, part of the old county of Middlesex but now in the administrative county of Surrey. Virginia Water, set in old parkland, is quite different from the rest although only 3 miles (5 km) southwest of Staines town centre.

WALTON RESERVOIRS and PITS (Map 4a, TQ 06/16)

Habitat

The main reservoirs at Walton-on-Thames are the Chelsea, Lambeth, Knight and Bessborough group, Queen Elizabeth II and Island Barn, with a smaller group over the river at Kempton. The Walton reservoirs are of various depths. The shallower ones are attractive to diving duck. Chelsea and Lambeth are being decommissioned. They have been drained and their floors have large areas of mud, scrub and shallow water. The future of this part of the site is uncertain. Knight and Bessborough are deeper and among the last to freeze in hard weather.

Field Common gravel and sand pits lie between Queen Elizabeth II and Island Barn reservoirs. Parts are still worked. Elsewhere children and bikers have made many paths. Take care. The southern pit, which can be seen from the railway at Hersham, has been partially filled, leaving an area of badly-drained, made-up ground.

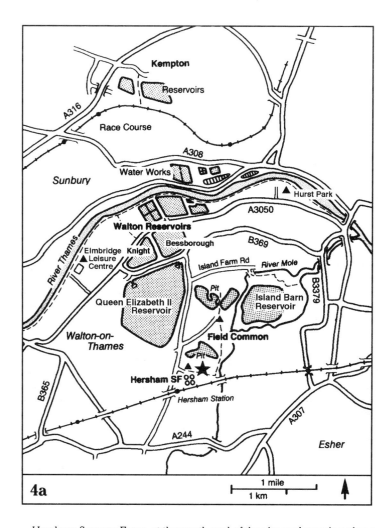

4a

Hersham Sewage Farm, at the south end of the site and running along by the railway to Hersham station, is disused and overgrown. It is worth a scan at any time of the year, but will be most interesting if not dry. Elmbridge Leisure Centre, on the Thames a short distance to the west, has an avenue of poplars by the approach road and a substantial area of scrubland behind the car park. Hurst Park has riverside frontage at the east end of the site and areas of damp meadow and scrub.

Species

Great Northern and other diver species can stay at Walton for long periods, sometimes moving from one reservoir in the district to another. Goldeneye are mainly found on Knight and Bessborough, peaking at over 40 in March or April. A small number of Smew are occasionally present in the winter. The Knight and Bessborough basins are attractive to Goosander, occasional divers and a large flock of wintering Coot. The whole group may be profitably scanned for the scarcer grebes and for Long-tailed Duck, Ruddy Duck and other wildfowl. There is some interchange of duck and waders with a group of shallow, partly drained Greater London reservoirs at Kempton Park, immediately north of the river. Kempton Park also has a heronry, accounting for some of the Grey Herons seen in the district. The shallower water in its reservoirs is better for Garganey and other dabbling duck. Recent migrants have included Avocet, Temminck's Stint and White-rumped Sandpiper. Hobbies are often seen in the area in summer.

Shelduck, Ruddy Duck and Little Ringed Plover breed at Walton in small numbers. Many Reed Warblers can be heard among the flooded scrub in Lambeth Reservoir and a Marsh Warbler has spent a few days there. Queen Elizabeth II Reservoir is important as a winter wildfowl haven, especially for Shoveler, and also attracts unusually large numbers of wintering Cormorant, currently over 500 and still increasing. Common Terns breed on rafts. Island Barn Reservoir, on an island in the River Ember, often has a large flock of wintering Teal as well as other duck, the scarcer grebes and sometimes divers.

Field Common Gravel Pits are interesting for breeding and migrant species, including Great Crested Grebes, waders and Sand Martins. Rough ground round the pits is worth checking for Mandarin. They feed mainly on land rather than water and may be put up from the rough grass, where there may also be a Short-eared Owl in winter. Ring-necked Parakeets breed in the district and may be seen flying over.

Hersham Sewage Farm has breeding Reed Warblers and Reed Buntings and attracts Jack Snipe, Water Pipits and roving flocks of finches in winter. Elmbridge Leisure Centre has become the site of a huge winter Ring-necked Parakeet roost, peaking at over 800 in early 1996. The birds move into a row of poplars by the sports centre and are easily seen from the footpath. Parakeet roosts tend to move every few years but are always close to the river in the Walton area. Scrub behind the centre has many warblers in summer.

There is a large autumn and winter Mute Swan flock on the Thames at Hurst Park, typically peaking at over 100. Various waders and pipits have bred or attempted to breed on rough ground in the area but are subject to considerable disturbance.

Timing

Walton reservoirs are open from 7.30 am to 4.30 pm on Monday, Tuesday, Wednesday and Thursday but close at 1.30 pm on Friday. There is no entry on Bank Holidays. Some of the reservoirs and all the gravel pits can freeze over in long spells of severe weather, driving wildfowl onto the Thames or to more distant unfrozen localities. Deeper reservoirs, which do not normally freeze, include Knight and Bessborough at Walton. Yachting can disturb waterfowl at Island Barn, so go early.

Ring-necked Parakeets fly in to the Elmbridge roost in a 45 minute period starting at about 4.30 pm in December and January, when numbers normally peak.

Access

The entrance to Walton Reservoirs is on the A3050 (Hurst Road), but note that a Thames Water birdwatching pass is needed for access.

Island Barn Reservoir can be approached from Island Farm Road, turning down Ray Road to the entrance. There is room to park a car in adjacent roads. The water can be seen from the top of the steps by the sailing club. A special permit from Thames Water (normally only granted to wildfowl counters) is needed. Field Common Gravel Pits can be reached from Field Common Lane. Park in the housing estate and follow the lane round towards the camping site. Two pits lie on the north side of the path before the entrance to the camping site. An alternative approach is from the North Weylands industrial estate, on the north side of Hersham railway station. Park in the lane on the edge of the estate 0.35 mile (0.5 km) north of the railway bridge over Molesey Road. A footpath from there goes past Hersham Sewage Farm and then turns left along the River Mole, passing the pits.

Access to Queen Elizabeth II Reservoir is by special arrangement with Thames Water. Elmbridge Leisure Centre and Hurst Park have car parks.

STAINES and DISTRICT (Map 4b, TQ 06/16 & TQ 07/17)

Habitat

Heathrow Airport, to the northeast of Staines, provides a noisy backdrop to the district. There are gravel pits on either side of the Thames out to Wraysbury and beyond. Some of the older ones are used for water sports.

Wraysbury, King George VI, Staines and Queen Mary reservoirs are all within a short distance. The first two are not open to public access, though Wraysbury has nature reserve status on account of its wildfowl. The pair of reservoirs at Staines are divided by a causeway with a public footpath along it, from which excellent views can be obtained. The depth of water, about 9 ft (3 m), is very suitable for diving duck. From time to time one or other of the Staines basins is drained for maintenance works, an operation which leaves a rich habitat of shallow pools, shingle bars and mud with deeper channels between. This can be especially fruitful if it is the north basin because of the direction of the light. (The general effect, from the causeway, has been likened to looking across the Channel.) In such circumstances patience can be called for, to wait until the feeding waders move up to the closer expanses of mud and sand.

Staines Moor is a flat valley of the River Colne lying between the Wraysbury and King George VI reservoirs. Parts of the meadow are waterlogged and there is a small gravel pit and a shallow pool at the north end. The moor has an interesting flora and has been made a Site of Special Scientific Interest (SSSI) largely on that account. The M25 now runs along the western edge of the site.

Queen Mary Reservoir, to the east, is over 1 mile (1.6 km) across. A long causeway running north–south almost divides it in two but does not reach the southern side. The causeway separates the west end of the reservoir, which is used for sailing, from the east end, which is a wildfowl reserve. It is a roosting place and is usually off limits to birdwatchers and yachtsmen. Queen Mary tends not to freeze over completely in hard weather because of the turbulent water at the intake. There are gravel pits on the western edge of the site. A water works lies to the east.

Sheepwalk Lake, one of a large and complicated group of pits at Shepperton, 0.6 mile (1 km) south of Queen Mary Reservoir, is to be managed as a reserve. The pits are in various stages of their life cycle and new ones are still being opened up. Some of the older ones are used for water sports, angling and other recreational purposes.

Lying a little to the south of Staines, Thorpe Water Park is a series of old gravel pits which have been landscaped and used for pleasure craft, water sports and passive recreation, with a small reserve area attached. Adjacent pits at Penton Hook are used as a marina. Others at Penton Hook and behind Thorpe are waterfilled and disused, attractive to both wintering and summering species. All are relatively easy of access and can provide productive birdwatching.

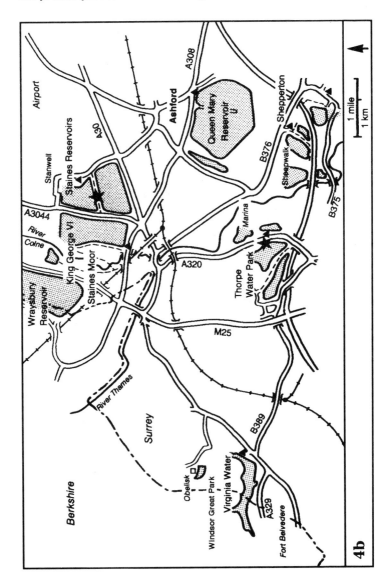

Species

The reservoirs are mainly important as refuges for wintering duck and other waterbirds. Staines and Queen Mary are of national significance for Shoveler, Tufted Duck and Goosander. Queen Mary is a major winter gull roost. The gulls fan out in all directions for 30 miles (48 km) or more each day to feed in the surrounding countryside and their regular morning and late afternoon movements are a common sight across much of Surrey. The reservoirs also provide breeding sites for a few rather local summering species, though in this the gravel pits are more important.

Common Terns breed on rafts in the north and south basins of Staines Reservoirs. Hobbies sometimes appear here in spring and late summer, feeding on hirundines. If the floors of any of the reservoirs are exposed in spring and early summer there will be breeding waders, especially Lapwing and Little Ringed Plover. The Ringed Plover breeds very sparingly in the Thames Valley and might also choose such a site. A flock of Black-necked Grebes can be seen at close range in the autumn. Peak numbers are not so high as they once were, possibly because of the frequent draining and refilling operations, but this is still the best Surrey site for the species. Rare waders which have occurred in drained basins include Americans such as Baird's Sandpiper, Long-billed Dowitcher, Lesser Yellowlegs and Wilson's Phalarope.

Red-necked Phalaropes appear at the reservoir and Staines Moor in autumn from time to time. Little Gulls are regular migrants, sometimes in large numbers. Black Terns beat up and down. Yellow Wagtails appear regularly along the causeway at Staines in spring and autumn.

Wildfowl numbers build up in winter, with good numbers of Smew in some years. Winter duck include over 500 Tufted. Sparrowhawks are regular. A Merlin may occasionally attack any small seed-eating birds feeding on vegetation which has grown up after drainage. There is sometimes a wintering Black Redstart in the vicinity of the towers at the west end of the causeway. Severe winter weather may bring one or two Snow Buntings to exposed parts of the margin of the reservoirs.

Staines Moor is a significant wintering site for Golden Plover and also at times attracts some of the rarer geese, such as the Bean, which has appeared in severe winter weather. Jack Snipe and sometimes Short-eared Owls also occur in winter.

Queen Mary Reservoir has a good record for divers and the scarcer grebes and is a major wildfowl site, especially for Great Crested Grebes and Shoveler. Large numbers of Goosander are often present in cold spells. Other wintering duck include smaller numbers of Gadwall, Teal, Pochard and Goldeneye. Sabine's Gulls and Skuas have been recorded. The causeway has attracted many scarce migrants. Disturbance from sailing has tended to reduce the appeal of the reservoir but it is still a very important site. The adjacent gravel pits can be seen well from the embankment giving views, at suitable times, of spring overshoots such as the Spoonbill, and migrant or breeding waders.

Shepperton Gravel Pits have large numbers of wintering Coot and Tufted Duck and smaller numbers of other wildfowl. Excavations and infilling disturb breeding activities and the water levels are in some places unstable, so that Great Crested Grebes and Coots can be seen nesting high and dry on sand banks. The tree-lined causeways across some of them hold migrant passerines in spring and autumn. Little Ringed Plover and Sand Martins exploit suitable sites. Common Terns can be seen here, as elsewhere in the Staines area, in summer and have bred in this general district when conditions were right. Corn Buntings have breed in fields round the pits but are now hard to find.

Thorpe Water Park and the adjacent pits are worth scanning for migrant terns, which do not seem to mind the boats and water-skiers. Grebes and Canada Geese breed there and are present all year. The site is best in winter when there are occasional divers, Red-necked and Slavonian Grebes, a flock of Smew which may number over 20 and many Goosander as well as other wildfowl and a good mixture of gulls.

Timing

The basins at Staines are very large, but if a day with good light is chosen the north side will be seen excellently from the causeway. The southern basin is more difficult in strong light, and better seen on a duller day or in the morning or evening. Staines is especially good in the autumn, when the Black-necked Grebes peak and there are the chances of seeing a good variety of terns and other migrants. There will not be a large number of waders at Staines unless one of the basins is drained. This seems to happen quite often for maintenance or other reasons, but there is no regular cycle. Many people use the drier parts of Staines Moor for dog walking and exercise and there is some fishing. Early morning is best.

Early morning will also be best at Thorpe on the busier spring and winter days, though for most of the pits disturbance is not a serious problem and any time of day will do. Queen Mary Reservoir is open from 7.30 am to 4.30 pm Wednesday to Sunday.

Access

The Staines reservoirs are best approached from the A30, turning north up Town Lane, which runs along the east side. The two eastern basins have a public footpath between them, from which easy observation can be made. Access from Town Lane or Stanwell Moor Road. Staines Moor lies to the west of King George VI Reservoir and can be accessed from a lay-by on the A30 at the southern end, or from the north at Stanwell Moor.

Wraysbury and King George VI require special permission from Thames Water for access, which is not given by the normal permit.

A Thames Water birdwatching pass is needed for access to Queen Mary Reservoir. It is the one which also gives access to Kempton and Walton. The entrance is at the northeast corner, adjacent to the junction of Ashford Road and Staines Road West.

Shepperton Gravel Pits may be seen quite well from surrounding roads but are most conveniently explored from the public footpath which crosses the main part of the site. This can be started from Fairview Drive, a turning south off the B376 (Laleham Road) 0.5 mile (0.8 km) west of the bridge over the M3. There is room to park a car at the end of Fairview Drive. A path leads out between the Littleton Lane East and Sheepwalk pits. Another approach is from the B375 in Shepperton. Leave the car in the public car park in Church Road, close to the cricket ground. Walk 0.2 mile (0.2 km) back to the Cemetery Lane, on the other side of the road; the cemetery itself is at the end of the lane. Walk through the cemetery and take the public footpath that runs by the Sheepwalk East pits and lake.

Thorpe Water Park is on the A320 between Chertsey and Staines. Alder Valley buses stop outside. There is a car park inside the main entrance, for use by patrons. Alternatively cars can be pulled off the road onto grass. A five-bar gate beside the A320 affords good views over much of the water and more can be seen from a public footpath which runs across the park from St Mary's Church, Coldharbour Lane to the A320. Parking at the Church is possible but congested. Try, obviously, to avoid parking there on Sunday mornings.

A pit on the opposite side of the A320 can be seen well from the footpath and often holds Smew in winter. Other adjacent pits can be seen well from surrounding roads, where there are a number of small lay-bys such as those on the west side of the A320 south of the bridge over the M25 and on the east side opposite the south end of Thorpe Water Park.

VIRGINIA WATER (Map 4b, SU 86/96 & SU 87/97)

Habitat

Windsor Great Park is mature old parkland. The main lake, Virginia Water, is surrounded by gently rising ground, on which are stands of oak, sweet chestnut, beech, ash and pine, dense with rhododendrons in parts. There are patches of heathland grasses and broad lawns of the kind that occasionally attract the overshooting Hoopoe in May or June. It is possible to walk all round the lake and also, on the north side, up to a smaller water, Obelisk Pond.

Species

There is a heronry on private land at Fort Belvedere, to the south. It is the largest in Surrey, with up to 40 nests in good years. Records go back to 1607 and show that the site of the heronry has moved several times. Although it is currently in mixed woodland, virtually all the nests are in Scots pine. There are many species of woodland birds, including the three woodpeckers, Nuthatch and Marsh Tit, but the Mandarin are likely to be the main attraction. Being a tree-nesting species, they may not always be so obvious in the summer, though there are always a few to be seen. They will sometimes rest on the grass by the lake if not disturbed. Numbers build up after the breeding season and up to 100 are possible in December. Wood Duck are occasionally seen. For some reason this close relative of the Mandarin has been much less successful in adapting from its native North America to Britain, but one or two are

Mandarin

sometimes present. The males, which have boldly striped and crested heads and lack the Mandarin's orange 'sails' on the wing, are easily separated in breeding plumage. Females, birds in moult and immatures need more care and are best distinguished by different head markings on the females and traces of a greenish head gloss on the males.

A few Reed Warblers breed in the small stands of reeds established here and there along the water's edge, among the more extensive sweet flag. They should be singing in May or June and easy to hear, though they may be harder to see because their songposts are usually well below the top of the reeds.

Hawfinches have been reported but seem hard to find and the best chances may be in the Berkshire part of the park. Winter will bring Siskins and Redpolls to alders round the lake and other finch flocks may contain Brambling.

Timing

The Fort Belvedere heronry will be very active in May and June. The Mandarin are best seen in December and January. Early morning visits in May will give the best chance of finding migrants and warblers. Avoid afternoons, especially in the summer, when the park can get rather full.

Access

Approach Virginia Water from the A30. There is a very limited amount of parking in lay-bys in Wick Lane and Wick Road, otherwise use official car parks, the most convenient of which is on the west side of the road just north of the junction with the B389.

Access to Fort Belvedere is usually restricted to those carrying out census or research work and is controlled by the Crown Commissioners, Windsor Great Park, to whom application should be made if required. The entrance is in the A329 (Blacknest Road), off the A30 south of Virginia Water. A key from the Commissioners is needed.

Calendar

Resident: Great Crested Grebe, Canada Goose, Mandarin, Tufted Duck, Ruddy Duck, Sparrowhawk, Ring-necked Parakeet, Corn Bunting.

December–February: Black-necked Grebe (Staines), grey geese, Gadwall, Teal, Shoveler, Pochard, Tufted Duck, Goldeneye, Goosander, Red-breasted Merganser, Smew, Golden Plover (Staines Moor). Peak time for gull roosts, including a few Mediterranean and Glaucous gulls. Black Redstart, Fieldfare, Redwing, Brambling, Snow Bunting.

March–May: Spring wader passage. Parties of Avocets are now being seen more often in spring. Common, Arctic, Sandwich, Little and Black Terns, White Wagtail, Yellow Wagtail.

June–July: Overshoots such as Spoonbill and Hoopoe. Hobbies feeding over the reservoirs and pits. Common Terns breeding on rafts at Queen Elizabeth II and Staines.

August–November: Black-necked Grebes and terns at Staines (peak August). Goldeneye return from mid November. Return wader passage, peaking in August.

5 THE WEY VALLEY, EASHING TO GUILDFORD

Habitat

From Eashing, above Godalming, through to the stretch down to Guildford (Map 5a) the River Wey has been spared most of the river improvements commonly applied by water authorities and it winds through a flood plain of water meadows, willow and alder copses. A shallow canal, the River Wey Navigation, runs parallel with part of it and is used by a small number of pleasure craft, mainly in the summer. At Guildford the valley passes through a narrow gap in the North Downs and then broadens out to the best developed section of water-meadow and marsh at Stoke, now being managed as a nature park.

In midsummer the river and canal margins have stands of purple loosestrife, agrimony, balsams and sedges and there are many species of dragonfly. Alders and clumps of thistle provide food for Goldfinches, Redpolls and Siskins later in the year. The Wey Valley Marshes are the largest Surrey remnant of the water-meadow and marshland habitat now threatened in so many parts of England.

The Stoke area has gravel deposits overlaying London clay. Higher levels of the clay support fine fringing woodland in Stoke Park. The A3 runs through the valley but the road is quite well screened by high earth banks. There are examples of four habitats: the river, the marsh and water-meadows, a lake with an island and surrounding hedgerows, and mature woodland with some very old chestnut trees. Guildford Sewage Farm, on the north side of the river, still has a few open lagoons on the older part of the site but most of its bird specialities can be seen in more agreeable circumstances round and near the lake.

Species

At Eashing, approaching from the A3 end, there should be a Grey Wagtail on the river by Eashing Bridge. The riverside path downstream passes a small marsh and an alder copse. The river banks at this point are quite high. Species to look for at appropriate times include Water Rail, Snipe, Kingfisher, Redpoll and Siskin. Some steep hillside woods then lead into Godalming. The Lammas Lands in Godalming may have wintering Lapwings and Snipe. Both species breed here and there along the Wey Valley. Broadwater Lake, at Farncombe, is popular with anglers, notably for its carp, but has an island with breeding waterbirds including grebes. Wintering species include Coot, Mallard, Pintail, Shoveler, Pochard and Tufted Duck.

From Catteshall, on the edge of Godalming, follow the towpath along the River Wey Navigation to Guildford. At Unstead there is a small sewage farm, much of which can be seen from a public footpath across it. The farm has a few Jack Snipe among its wintering birds and produces the occasional Bittern as well as Green, Wood and Common Sandpipers and Water Pipits. Vagrants include Little Egret and Spoonbill. The water-meadows from Unstead down to Guildford flood in most winters and have attracted Bewick's Swans.

At Broadford there is another small marsh tucked up against the railway line. This is not easy to see, but at the right time its open stretches

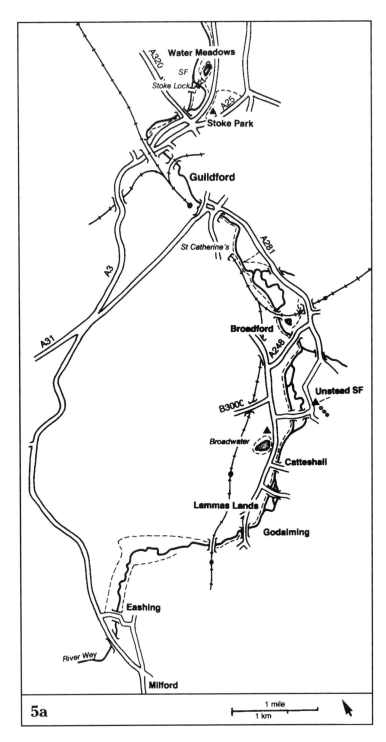

5a

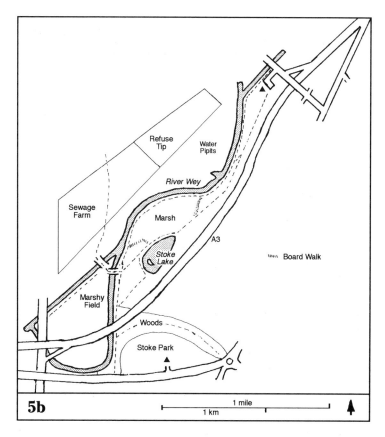

5b

1 mile

1 km

of mud, reeds and rushes will have a few migrant waders and warblers. Reed Buntings will be conspicuous here and along the next stretch of locks into Guildford. Passing under the hill at St Catherine's you are suddenly in a narrow outcrop of Greensand. There is a railway tunnel through the hill, with Sand Martin burrows over the tunnel entrance. Meadows on the opposite side of the river sometimes flood in winter.

The best part of the area is at Stoke (Map 5b), where excavation of gravel for the roadworks has left a landscaped pool with a small island and there is a large variety of waterside and woodland birds. Breeding species on the lake and in the marsh include the Great Crested Grebe, Tufted Duck, Water Rail and, since the provision of a raft, Common Tern. The site has been visited by many of the scarcer Surrey migrants, including Red-throated and Great Northern Divers, Purple Heron, Brent Goose, Eider, Osprey, Peregrine, Avocet, Kentish Plover and Yellow-browed Warbler. There may be an impressive number of birds on winter mornings, with Pochard, Tufted and other duck on the lake, a flock of gulls, up to 200 Canada Geese feeding on the grass and a large party of Stock Doves and Woodpigeons working across the field.

Old hedges provide a varied food supply for members of the thrush family and, in summer, are ideal for Lesser Whitethroats. The marsh by the river supports Reed and Sedge Warblers. Riverside alders provide food for many Goldfinches, Redpolls and Siskins, at appropriate times, and Tree Sparrows like the many woodpecker holes in them. Old pollarded willows provide nest sites for Treecreepers and now and then a Little Owl.

A wet meadow on the north side of the River Wey at TQ 008525 is a major British wintering site for Water Pipits, with the occasional Scandinavian Rock Pipit among them. The woods in Stoke Park usually have all three species of woodpecker and, in summer, a good population of warblers. Migrant Wood Warblers come through in May.

Reed Bunting

Timing

Stoke Water Meadows are best early in the morning because birds on the shore of the lake are then less likely to have been disturbed.

Access

The Eashing stretch can be entered by turning east at the Eashing exit from the A3, 1 mile (1.6 km) north of Milford. Footpaths enable you to follow the river from Eashing to Guildford. A public footpath runs across Unstead Sewage Farm. For permission to explore further, apply to Thames Water, to whom the site is known as Godalming Sewage Farm.

The Stoke area can be approached from a car park in Burpham at TQ 011527. This is the easiest way to get at the Water Pipit area, which can be viewed from the towpath. The woods and the lake can be explored on foot from Stoke Park, starting at the junction of the A25 and the A320 at TQ 010510 and going down through the crescent-shaped wood on the north side of the A25 along a gravel path that leads down to the river. Another approach is along the towpath, from the Woking road. There is also a footpath from Slyfields across Guildford Sewage Farm to Stoke Lock, where there is a bridge.

The unmodernised part of Guildford Sewage Farm can be seen from adjacent footpaths. Permits to enter should be sought from Thames Water, but may not be worth the trouble.

Calendar

Resident: Canada Goose, Mandarin, Tufted Duck, Sparrowhawk, Kestrel, Little and Tawny Owls, Kingfisher, Green, Great and Lesser Spotted Woodpeckers, Grey Wagtail.

December–February: Teal, Shoveler, Goldeneye, Water Rail, Lapwing, Snipe, Jack Snipe, gulls, Water Pipit, Redwing, Fieldfare, Siskin, Redpoll, Brambling, Reed Bunting.

March–May: Green and Common Sandpipers, Redshank, Greenshank, Yellow Wagtail, Water Pipits coming into summer plumage before leaving.

June–July: Common Tern, hirundines, Sedge Warbler, Reed Warbler, Lesser Whitethroat, Whitethroat, Garden Warbler, Blackcap.

August–November: Hobby, Lesser Black-backed Gull passage, Common Tern, waders including Ruff.

6 PAPERCOURT GRAVEL PITS, SEND AND WISLEY

OS 186/7
TQ 05/15

Habitat

Gravel pits and commons are found along the Wey valley from Send to Wisley (Map 6). Some are water-filled, others are still being worked. A few of the exhausted pits have been filled in, and the local geography changes from year to year as fresh pits are opened up.

Land round a newly landscaped pit in Potter's Lane (TQ 025552) has partridges, Turtle Doves and migrants including Quail. Send village has two mature pits with breeding grebes, Sedge and Reed Warblers.

The most interesting pits are a group extending south and west from Papercourt Farm. One has deep water and is used for sailing. Another is shallow, with muddy banks and likely to become a nature reserve. Ripley Sewage Farm is adjacent. The River Wey and the Wey Navigation run to the north and east through a network of channels and water-meadows, controlled by locks and weirs. Newark Priory is an overgrown ruin by the river and adjacent to a meadow which is flooded in winter. There is a second sewage farm at Old Woking, partially modernised. The suburbs of Woking and a golf centre are on higher ground beyond the northern boundary.

1 mile (1.6 km) or so down the river the Royal Horticultural Society (RHS) gardens at Wisley are worth a look on quiet mornings. A bird report for the gardens is currently being produced and is available on site. Wisley Common, to the east of the gardens, has some wet areas extensive conifer woods and a small lake (Boldermere).

Species

Although not large in area, the pits at Papercourt have a good list of breeding birds. Wader passage through the locality is interesting and, among other migrant rarities, Spoonbill and Caspian Tern have both

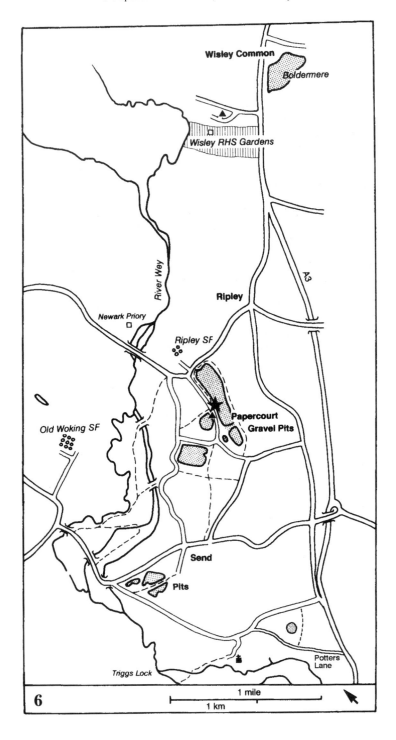

been seen. The largest and deepest pit is the one used by the sailing club. This has attracted a surprising range of sea duck including Eider, Scaup and Velvet Scoter. Goosander winter there, often with one or two Red-breasted Mergansers. The Goosander move around the area and are sometimes seen on Boldermere.

Mediterranean and Glaucous Gulls have been seen in the large gull flocks which feed at Papercourt and on the wet meadow beside Newark Priory in winter. The gulls roost on reservoirs at Staines and the morning and evening flightlines fanning out across Surrey are a conspicuous sight at most times of the year, especially in winter. A flock of several hundred Canada Geese often flights into the pits to roost, having fed elsewhere. In winter and early spring there may be a Firecrest or very rarely a Great Grey Shrike in the scrub round the pits, with flocks of Fieldfares on the rough grass.

Opposite the sailing pit there is a sandy excavation overgrown at one end with willow scrub, which in summer holds a few pairs of Reed Warblers. Fields and nursery land beside this area and outside Ripley Sewage Farm have wintering larks, thrushes and finches, usually including a small flock of Bramblings and sometimes Tree Sparrows. The shallow pit on the west side of the site is attractive to waterfowl, waders and terns. Other pits are still being worked. There are intermittent Sand Martin colonies, including one at the north end on the sailing pit.

Ripley Sewage Farm, at the east end of the complex, is a good place to see Green Sandpipers, which are present in most months of the year, and sometimes has wintering Water Pipits, rather shy birds whose strong flight when you get anywhere near them is one of their better field characteristics.

The more derelict parts of Old Woking Sewage Farm have produced Hen Harrier, Short-eared Owl and Black Redstart, and very rarely a harrier has visited the gravel pits. Black Redstarts are most likely to be seen around towers on the west side of the site. Shelduck and Redshank often move between Old Woking and Papercourt. A muddy scrape outside the fence at the eastern end of the sewage farm is very good for migrant waders in some years. Records include Grey Plover (rare in Surrey), Black-tailed Godwit and Marsh Sandpiper.

Marshland and wet meadows along the river valley are important for wintering thrushes and have breeding Red-legged Partridge, Lapwing, Snipe and Reed Warblers in summer. Grey Wagtails nest at locks and weirs across the area, close to falling water.

The RHS gardens at Wisley can produce interesting woodland birds as well as Kingfishers and Sand Martins on the adjacent river bank. They have, for example, held breeding Firecrests. Wisley Common has Reed Buntings and a few wintering Teal and Snipe in the wetter areas. Redpolls breed among birch scrub and Crossbills may sometimes be found in the pine woods.

Timing

The worked pits are best avoided during weekday working hours, though this is a good time to look at the sailing pit. Watch for sand lorries in the lanes and draw the car off the road onto one of the patches of grass or hard standing when parking. Winter weekends are the time of least disturbance, reflected in the better waterfowl numbers. The sailing pit should then hold Goosander and one or two Goldeneye among the other duck.

RHS members can enter Wisley Gardens free. The gardens are open to the public, with a small entry fee, on most days of the year.

Access

The A3 runs 1 mile (1.6 km) southeast of Send. Approaching from Guildford, leave the A3 at the slip road to Send and turn left at the roundabout. About 0.5 mile (0.8 km) down, on the left, oak trees in Send Hill hold a small rookery. Next, on the left, Sandy Lane leads to the old pits, which are surrounded by mature vegetation. Returning, Send Marsh Road leads to Papercourt. There is a footpath round the sailing pit.

If the area is approached from London, turn off the A3 at the slip road to Ripley and turn right in Ripley High Street, which takes you to the Ripley Sewage Farm end of the site after 0.5 mile (0.8 km). Continuing on this road takes you to Newark Priory and the River Wey after 0.75 mile (1.2 km). A footpath from Send church takes you 0.5 mile (0.8 km) to the water-meadows at Triggs Lock.

A permit from Thames Water is needed for access to Ripley Sewage Farm, or ask at the gate. Carters Lane leads to Old Woking Sewage Farm.

A towpath runs along the River Wey Navigation from Triggs Lock to Newark Lock. The RHS gardens and part of Wisley Common are on the north side of the A3, 2 miles (3 km) south of the junction with the M25. Boldermere is on the east side of the A3. There is a car park in Old Lane at TQ 079586.

Calendar

Resident: Great Crested Grebe, Grey Heron, Mute Swan, Canada Goose, Mandarin, Tufted Duck, Sparrowhawk, Grey Partridge, Lapwing, Snipe, Stock Dove, Little Owl, Kingfisher, woodpeckers, Grey Wagtail, Tree Sparrow.

December–February: Cormorant, chance of Bittern, Bewick's Swan, Wigeon, Shoveler, Pochard, Goldeneye, Goosander, occasional harriers and Merlin, gulls including scarcer species, Short-eared Owl in some winters, Black Redstart (irregular), winter thrushes, occasional Firecrest, Brambling, Siskin, Redpoll.

March–May: Wigeon and sawbills leave by early March, but a few Shoveler and Shelduck stay all through the spring. Grebes and other waterfowl are nesting. Waders and terns pass through, especially from mid April. Avocets have been seen more than once. Sand Martins arrive in March and make burrows in exposed sand cliffs.

June–July: Breeding residents and summer visitors, with occasional late spring overshoots. Return wader passage begins. Turtle Dove. Chance of Hobby hawking over the pits.

August–November: Cormorant, waders including Green, Common and a few Wood Sandpipers, chance of godwits and Curlew Sandpiper. Lesser Black-backed Gull passage, flocks feeding in the pit including dark 'Scandinavian' birds probably of the race *L. f. graellsii.* Yellow-legged Herring Gulls are becoming regular. Sandwich, Common, Little, Black and (very few) Arctic Terns, chats, Yellow Wagtail.

7 THE NORTHWEST SURREY COMMONS

Habitat

Northwest Surrey has some of the more rugged western heaths (Map 7). They lie on the sandy Bagshot Beds, which are related to sands and clays which occur again at Selsey Bill, but are not found elsewhere in the area covered by this book. Cobbett took Bagshot as a benchmark for bad country in *Rural Rides* and used phrases like 'more barren and miserable than Bagshot Heath' to qualify places such as Hindhead and parts of the New Forest that he found even worse.

Exploration still has problems despite better roads, because of military activity on MOD lands in the district, where access can be difficult or impracticable. Trespass can be dangerous and there have been accidents in peripheral areas open to public access, so birdwatching, at least in the Bisley and Pirbright areas, needs care. That said, the northwest commons have long been highly regarded for the birds that breed and winter there, and the restricted access itself provides a degree of protection.

Chobham Common is largely open heath with scattered birch and pine and stands of bracken among the heather. High ground at Staple Hill slopes away to a boggy area at Gracious Pond and there is more wet ground to the north of the M3, which cuts across the common. Chobham has some relatively unusual plants and is nationally important for its varied population of spiders. The army uses part of the land to the north for testing vehicles. It is also a popular site for model aircraft fliers. Being close to London and the M3, the common attracts many visitors for birdwatching and other recreational reasons. The birdlife has tended to suffer under the combined pressure and, as with other fragile habitats, it should be explored with restraint.

Bisley and Westend Commons are on hilly ground 2.5 miles (4 km) to the southwest. They have large areas of long grass as well as heather and bracken and cover an area about 3 miles (5 km) square. The land is used for military training and access to most of it is prevented by an encircling chain-link fence, though good views can be had from high ground on the west side. The Bisley rifle range is at the south end. Live artillery rounds are used on ranges to the west and north. Colony Bog, in the southwest corner, is well known to botanists.

Lightwater Country Park, separated from Westend by the M3, is an extension of Bagshot Heath on higher ground to the north. It is managed by the Surrey Heath Borough Council. The pine woods, rough grassy common and heath are also worth a visit. Nature trails are laid out and there is an information centre. Pipistrelle bats live in hollow trees and buildings. Adders and grass snakes are to be found. There are views to Bisley from Curley Hill.

Pirbright Common is an undulating heath, wet in parts, also used by the military for weapons training at certain times but with public access. Fires break out on the common occasionally, as they do elsewhere in southwest Surrey, leaving dead trees and a variable amount of bare, burnt ground. Mature parts of the common have deep heather and gorse. Pirbright is a valuable site for heathland species, which benefit

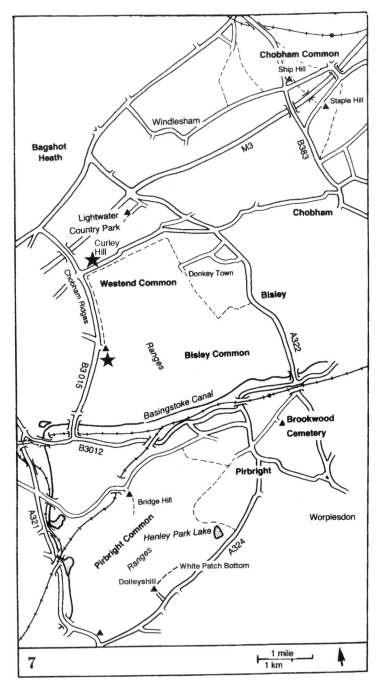

more from the restricted access than they are harmed by disturbance from the army. As on other lands used by the military, observe the notices and warning signs and do not pick up unfamiliar or potentially dangerous objects. Henley Park Lake, at the southeast end, is sheltered by trees. A path continues on past the lake to more open, higher ground which affords good views over the commons.

Brookwood Cemetery is largely mixed woodland with clearings and open heath. It is more overgrown than its name might suggest. Most of the area has been left to develop naturally, apart from some exotic shrubs, mainly rhododendrons. Being mainly quiet and secluded it offers good birdwatching opportunities, though current reconstruction is causing some disturbance.

The Basingstoke Canal runs east–west between Pirbright and Bisley. It fell into disuse with the decline of barge traffic but restoration work is being carried out, to keep it open for pleasure craft.

Species

The district as a whole is a fine area for wintering and migrant birds of prey. Hen Harriers and Merlins occur in the Pirbright/Bisley area and Goshawk sightings have been getting more frequent. There is a good chance of seeing a Hobby on the commons. Long and Short-eared Owls are seen from time to time in winter, as are shrikes.

Nightjars and some other heathland species are present in good numbers in the district as a whole, though thinning out a little at Chobham. Stonechats are found in small numbers throughout. They prefer gorse patches on the heaths and will quickly draw attention to themselves by

Stonechat

their noisy behaviour if present. Dartford Warblers occur in most years and are sometimes very common. Being resident, the species is affected by the severity of the winter and it suffers badly if there in prolonged periods of snow cover or frozen ground. Numbers vary greatly from year to year and can top 40 pairs at Pirbright, which is the main site, after a run of mild winters. Tree Pipits are abundant and, like Redpolls, often associated with the birches. Siskins breed intermittently in the pine woods and Crossbills rather more often. Ring Ouzels come through on passage.

Mandarin are now breeding at Chobham and Woodcock and Cuckoos are a strong feature there. An autumn passage of chats, mainly Wheatears, may be well seen at Chobham and to an extent on the other heaths. Lightwater Country Park has ponds with breeding Canada

Geese and other wildfowl as well as pine wood and heathland species. Feral Egyptian Geese are sometimes seen, as they are in other nearby localities. Grey Wagtails and other waterside species are found along the Basingstoke Canal.

Pirbright has at times had exceptional numbers of Redstarts, which nest in holes in the dead trees. Burnt areas are good for Woodlarks and at Pirbright have attracted migrants rare in Surrey, such as the Stone Curlew and Tawny Pipit. There is a Grasshopper Warbler site at White-patch Bottom. Brookwood Cemetery has Wood Warbler, Goldcrest, Jay and many other woodland species, with a chance of some of the heath-land birds being found.

Timing

For the military lands, normal times for range practice are from 8.00 am to 4.00 pm and there is sometimes firing at night. Occasionally the week-ends are free, especially at Bank Holiday times and there is a two-week free period over Christmas and the New Year. These times are a guide only. Check with site information on the notices displayed and if nec-essary with the military. Watch for red flags and lights indicating danger.

Lightwater Country Park is open all year round. It gets crowded at weekends. Evenings are best for Dartford Warblers.

Access

The southern part of Chobham Common can be approached from Staple Hill, where there is car parking. Take the B383 for 1 mile (1.6 km) north from the centre of Chobham village and fork right up Staple Hill for 0.75 mile (1.2 km). Car parking is on the right. For the northern part of the common, which is on the other side of the M3, continue up the B383 for 1.25 miles (2 km) beyond the Staple Hill turning to the monument on the top of Ship Hill. Public footpaths run from there across the heath.

Access to most of Westend and Bisley Commons is prohibited at all times. However, high ground at Chobham Ridges on the west side affords views over them both, especially good in the vicinity of Colony Gate, on the B3105 2 miles (3 km) north of the junction with the B3012 at Deepcut. There are public footpaths round parts of the perimeter. The best of these, running south from Donkey Town, off the A322 at Westend, provides good views in the vicinity of SU 935595.

Lightwater Country Park can be approached from Junction 3 on the M3. Take the A322 in the Guildford direction and immediately fork right on the minor road into Lightwater. The park is at the end of The Avenue, a turning on the right, signposted, 0.5 mile (0.8 km) from the turn-off.

Pirbright Common may be entered at several points. Bridge Hill, on the unclassified road from Pirbright to Mychett, 1 mile (1.6 km) east of Mychett at SU 905406, is on high ground and has room for off-road park-ing. For the approach via Henley Park Lake, take the track north from the A324 1.25 miles (2 km) south of Pirbright at SU 934538. Another good access point is from Dolleyshill at SU 918519. A path from here leads round to Whitepatch Bottom. The common includes Ash Ranges, which are in regular use and only safely accessible at certain times. The whole area is MOD property with definite, but restricted, rights of pub-lic access. When firing is to take place, red flags are flown in prominent places round the common to indicate danger areas and entry to them is then prohibited.

Brookwood Cemetery is private, but normally open to visitors. If in doubt, check at the office just inside the entrance, which is in Cemetery Pales, a road connecting the A324 and A322 at Pirbright. Limited parking is available outside the entrance.

Calendar

Resident: Canada Goose, Mandarin, Sparrowhawk, Kestrel, Coot, Green, Great Spotted and Lesser Spotted Woodpeckers, Woodlark, Skylark, Meadow Pipit, Grey Wagtail, Dartford Warbler, Redpoll, Reed Bunting.

December–February: Hen Harrier, Merlin, Short-eared Owl, Great Grey Shrike, Stonechats usually absent from the heaths.

March–May: Arrival of Hobby, migrant Goshawk, Buzzard, possible Honey Buzzard. Roding Woodcock, Cuckoo, Nightjar. Return of Stonechats. Nightingales, Redstarts and migrant warblers from mid April (Chiffchaffs earlier).

June–July: Nightjar song in late evenings. Tree Pipit display flights. Stonechats with young. Look for summering Siskins. Possible Crossbill irruption from July.

August–November: Return raptor migration. Whinchat and Wheatear passage. Arrival of winter thrushes.

8 FARNHAM AND THE BLACKWATER VALLEY

OS 186
SU 84/94 & SU 85/95

Habitat

The Blackwater Valley defines the western border of Surrey from just north of Farnham to the Hants/Berkshire border at Camberley (Map 8). There are disused sand pits with shallow pools at Wrecclesham, on the outskirts of Farnham. Cliffs suitable for Sand Martins have been left in older parts of the workings. Some of the land is being back-filled with refuse. The River Wey runs through Wrecclesham and floods low-lying meadows in winter. Sand deposits on the east side of Farnham at Runfold and Seale are being worked and selectively filled. Some are flooded. A recently landscaped pit at Tongham has gravelly shore areas. Farnham Sewage Farm is on the Aldershot side of the town. Surrounding meadows may be interesting in winter.

The Blackwater Valley forms the western boundary of the county from Camberley to Aldershot. The river itself is hardly more than a stream but it runs through gravel deposits which have been extensively worked, leaving pits of different ages and a consequent variety of habitat. The best are in the area from Aldershot up to Frimley, which is fair-

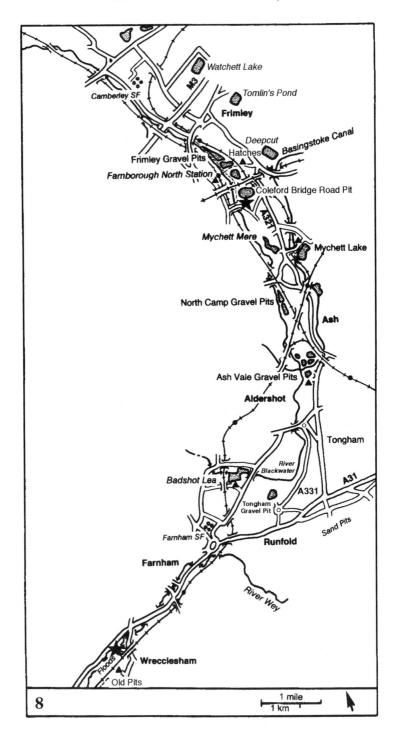

Watchett Lake

Tomlin's Pond

Camberley SF

M3

Frimley

Deepcut

Basingstoke Canal

Hatches

Frimley Gravel Pits

Farnborough North Station

Coleford Bridge Road Pit

A321

Mychett Mere

Mychett Lake

North Camp Gravel Pits

Ash

Ash Vale Gravel Pits

Aldershot

Tongham

River Blackwater

Badshot Lea

A331

A31

Tongham Gravel Pit

Sand Pits

Farnham SF

Runfold

Farnham

River Wey

Floods

Wrecclesham

Old Pits

8

1 mile
1 km

ly heavily built-up and crossed by several railway lines. Badshot Lea Gravel Pit is a large, mature water between Aldershot and Farnham. It is surrounded by trees, mainly willow and alder, and patches of reeds. There are small islands at the northern end.

The Basingstoke Canal enters the county at Ash and runs north up the valley to Frimley, where it bends east towards Woking and Weybridge. The canal is used by pleasure craft and has lush waterside vegetation. The section through Ash is elevated and provides a good vantage point from which to see adjacent areas, especially Ash Vale Gravel Pits, which lie either side of it and straddle the county border. These are mature pits used by anglers and, in the case of the one south of the canal, by windsurfers. North Camp Gravel Pits, 1 mile (1.6 km) to the north, also lie on the border and are similar.

The gravel pits at Frimley are a superb series of landscaped and overgrown workings running down the Blackwater Valley between Frimley and Ash Vale. The pits are of various sizes, most have islands for breeding waterbirds and other species. The three best are the Coleford Bridge Road, Hatches and North pits. There are smaller and more mature waters along the Basingstoke Canal at Mychett and Deepcut. Mychett Lake is an extension of the canal and is rather lush, with yellow flag and water lilies. There is a pounding lake with reedbeds, Greatbottom Flash, a little to the south. Mychett Mere, an old gravel pit 0.5 mile (0.8 km) to the west, is reedy and surrounded by long grass and scrub. Deepcut (Wharfendon) Lake, to the north, is a smaller water adjacent to the canal.

Tomlin's Pond and Watchett Lake, both in Camberley, are small and lined with trees. The Royal Military Academy at Camberley has two sizeable lakes. Camberley Sewage Farm is on the edge of the York Town industrial estate. There is rough grass and scrub and a tip at the back of the site, which drains into the Blackwater River. Adjacent meadows alongside the A331 from the M3 interchange to Blackwater, by the side of the River Blackwater, have proved interesting, especially in winter. Waders and a Shag have appeared there in cold spells.

Species

The most rewarding parts of the area are currently Wrecclesham and Frimley. Gulls on the flooded fields by the River Wey at Wrecclesham include some that have begun to roost at Frensham in recent years and are reinforced by the daily outward movements of those roosting in the Thames Valley. Close observation has revealed the fairly regular presence of one or two Mediterranean and Glaucous Gulls as well as the five common species. Iceland Gulls have also been recorded there. Waders can be found there in winter and early spring. Records include Avocet, Knot, Ruff and Black-tailed Godwit. Tongham Gravel Pits are also good for gulls, including Mediterranean and Yellow-legged Herring, from a tip at Seale.

The sand and gravel pits between Farnham and Camberley attract many kinds of duck and have a significant wader passage, now best observed at the Frimley North and Hatches gravel pits. The pits are perhaps most interesting for the wintering wildfowl, with good numbers of the commoner duck and the chance of seeing a few scarcer species, along with winter-visiting grebes. The Hatches has a wintering Wigeon/Gadwall flock with a few Goosander and brief visits from Surrey rarities such as the Brent Goose. Coleford Bridge Road is one of the last pits to freeze because of disturbance from water skiers and is one of the better places to look for scarce grebes and scoter. Badshot Lea is used by wintering wildfowl and has produced some good records over the years.

Overgrown areas round the pits hold warblers and resident woodland species. Breeding birds which are frequent on waters throughout the district include Little and Great Crested Grebes, Canada Geese, Tufted Duck and Coot, all of which, as in other parts of Surrey, have greatly benefited from the habitat provided. Water Rails winter at Frimley and may stay through the summer to breed. Where conditions are right there may be Little Ringed Plover, though given their preference for the more open conditions present in pits which are being actively worked, numbers and locations vary from year to year. They are most likely to be seen at Frimley.

Grey Wagtails are frequent, especially at suitable spots along the canal. Reed Warblers breed at Ash Vale and Frimley. Sedge Warblers now seen to be mainly on passage though they have bred at Frimley in earlier years. A few Willow Tits are found here and there, for example at Frimley.

Timing

Wrecclesham floods are best on mornings from November to March, avoiding very dry spells. Sand Martins will be at the pit from about mid April onwards, with a few earlier arrivals in some years. Winter and passage times are the most interesting at Frimley. For Ash Vale, the south pit will be best early in the day if watched from the canal because of the direction of the light, except on dull days. Windsurfing disturbance is also greater later in the day, especially in the summer.

All the pits can freeze up in severe weather though Ash Vale, which may be deeper than the others, has maintained a small open area even in the most severe of recent winters. Small holes in the ice can be crowded with the commoner wildfowl or, as has happened at Ash Vale, might hold something less common such as a Ring-necked Duck.

Access

Wrecclesham floods can be seen from the A31, on the southbound side 0.5 mile (0.8 km) beyond the roundabout on the west side of Farnham. Draw off the road onto the grass and watch from inside the car so as not to disturb the gulls. Alternatively turn down River Lane and park there. Continue down River Lane for 0.5 mile (0.8 km) to a road junction and turn right, for the disused sand pit. After 0.25 mile (0.4 km) turn right again to the recreation ground (signposted) where there is car parking. A footpath that goes past some rugby pitches leads to the site.

Tongham gravel pits can be viewed from the northbound carriageway of the A331. Take the Tongham turning from the A31 and turn left down Manor Road to park at the end and walk a short distance west to the pits. There is room to pull off the A331 to cut out the walk but the road can be busy, so if you do this, take care.

Farnham Sewage Farm is in Monkton Lane, off the A324. View from outside or ask at the gate for permission to look round. The Runfold and Seale sand pits can be accessed from minor roads south off the A31 at Runfold. For Badshot Lea approach via Tongham and park in Lower Weybourne Road, preferably off the road itself, or in the car park at the entrance to the pit (SU 862489). A footpath runs between the pit and the

Farnham/Aldershot railway line and leads to Boxall's Lane. The pit is easily observed from the footpath or the car park. (Permission of Farnham Angling Society is needed to walk round — see the notice at the entrance.)

Approaching Ash Vale Gravel Pits from the A31, turn off north at Tongham and fork right after 0.75 mile (1.2 km). On reaching the round-about by the Greyhound public house go straight over. The pits are 0.5 mile (0.6 km) down, on the left. They can be seen from the Basingstoke Canal, at SU 887514. The canal has towpaths on both sides, readily accessed where the rail and road bridges cross it by the pits. A permit from the angling society is needed for access to the pits north of the Basingstoke Canal. The pit south of the canal can be seen from Culverlands Crescent. If admittance to this one is wanted, it should be sought from the Windsurfing Club. The entrance is on the south side, in Willow Park. North Camp Gravel Pits lie behind North Camp railway station and are most easily accessed from the Hampshire side.

Access to the main part of Frimley Gravel Pits is by well maintained footpaths from Farnborough North Station, where there is a car park, on the west side, or The Hatches, where parking is tight, on the east side. A footpath joins the two access points and branches to run up the west side of the pits. This to a third access point near Frimley Station and on the way gives very good views over North Pit, where there is a seat.

The Coleford Bridge Road pit, located south of the railway, can be accessed from Coleford Bridge Road or by a footpath running south from the footpath between The Hatches and Farnborough North Station.

The Basingstoke Canal towpaths have many points of access. There is car parking at Mychett Lake (SU 892545) and the whole lake is readily seen. Greatbottom Flash is just to the south, easily seen from the towpath. Mychett Mere is a private gravel pit but Amey Anglers may give permission for a look round. The entrance is on the west side of the A321 at SU 889543 and limited views are available without entering.

Tomlin's Pond (SU 385587) can be approached from Chobham Road and Watchetts Lake (SU 887589) from Watchetts Drive, both in Camberley. The Royal Military Academy, Sandhurst, is on the north side of the A30 in Camberley. The lakes cannot be seen from outside the grounds and permission from the Commandant will be needed for entry. (At the present time access is very restricted.)

The entrance to Camberley Sewage Farm (Thames Water, Camberley) is in Doman Road, on the industrial estate. Ask at the office for permission to visit, or view the rough ground at the back from Blackwater Road.

Calendar

Resident: Little and Great Crested Grebes, Canada Geese, Mallard, Tufted Duck, Kingfisher, woodpeckers, Grey Wagtail.

December–February: Duck numbers build up at the gravel pits. Occasional wintering Green Sandpipers at Frimley, gulls (but no roost), Winter vagrants including Shag and Bearded Tit.

March–May: Great Crested Grebe numbers peak at the larger pits in March or April. Wader passage from about mid March. Little Ringed Plover are often early. Whimbrel in May. Warblers taking up territory.

June–July: Reed and Sedge Warblers at the pits. Lapwings beginning to flock up. Mid July sees the beginning of the return wader passage, Greenshank, Green and Common Sandpipers.

August–November: Wader passage peaks in August, mainly Green and Common Sandpipers but with Wood Sandpipers, Ruff etc., also. A few Goldeneye from late October or early November.

9 SOUTHWEST SURREY COMMONS

OS 186
SU 83/93 & SU 84/94

Habitat

The western commons (Map 9) are mainly on dry, sandy soils with heathers, birch and pine the dominant plant cover. Left to themselves they would mostly revert to pine or birch woodland and steps are taken to check tree intrusion in a few places. Bogs make an important variation to the habitat. The one at Thursley NNR is carefully managed to maintain a suitable water level on the reserve throughout the year. It should be obvious from the dryness of the light sandy soils and the expanses of heather and gorse that there is a serious fire risk for much of the year and visitors should act with appropriate caution. As it is, outbreaks are far too frequent.

Species

The damage done by fires to the habitat of species such as the Nightjar, Stonechat and Dartford Warbler can be very great. One species, the Woodlark, sometimes benefits, and seems to like breeding on the burnt-out ground. In more normal times Woodlarks are best looked for along the edges of the many broad sandy paths and in spring are most easily found by listening for birds in songflight, the song being briefer and more musical than that of the Skylark, with a characteristic 'tu-lu-lu'

Dartford Warbler

144

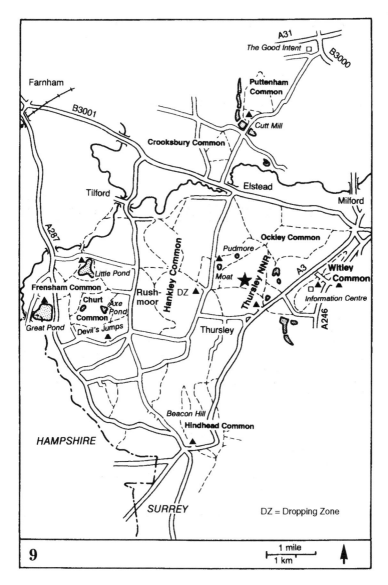

9

DZ = Dropping Zone

1 mile
1 km

phrase. Woodlark numbers vary considerably from year to year, dependent on ground conditions and the severity of the previous winter.

Winter conditions affect other heathland residents such as the Wren. The Dartford Warbler, which is on the edge of its range in Surrey, can suffer especially badly and has in certain years been wiped out. The damage may be done by snow alone if the heather is covered for a long period, as in 1961. Prolonged spells of very low temperatures, as in 1985/6, can be fatal to the species even if the heather and gorse remain exposed and may be the bigger threat, by the effect on its food supply. Fortunately recolonisation takes place within a few years. Under favourable conditions the total Surrey population of Dartford Warblers has exceeded 250 pairs. There is no conclusive evidence as to the origin of the new colonists, but they probably come from more protected populations to the southwest. Stonechats are not much seen on the heaths in winter and most move to sites where there is a more reliable food supply, in coastal areas or on sewage farms and marshes. Crossbills are irregular breeders on the western heaths, but may more often be seen flying over in small parties in irruption years.

Main Birdwatching Zones

The commons have been treated in separate sections to bring out their distinctive features. The core area is the nature reserve at Thursley. Hankley is adjacent, bleaker and drier. Witley is a dry heath. Frensham and Hindhead are detached, with fine ponds at Frensham. The Puttenham area has tree-lined pools.

THURSLEY and OCKLEY (Map 9a, SU 84/94)

Habitat

Thursley and Ockley Commons (Map 9a) make up one of the finest pieces of lowland heath in southern Britain. Much of the area is in the Thursley NNR. The central part of the reserve is a peat bog. Once, as old maps show, there was a cart track across it, passing north–south by Pudmore Pond, but this has long since been impassable, the more so since the water level in the bog is now managed by an effective system of dykes and sluices. Stick to the board walks in the this area, however firm the ground may look.

A line of low pylons runs across the bog and there are quite a few isolated dead trees, some of them the victims of fires. Local names for features include 'Pine Island' (an isolated group of pines by the board walk), 'Pine Avenue' (an avenue of pines which is part of a circular walk round the bog) and 'Shrike Hill' (a low, heather-covered hill east of the avenue of pines).

The commons are rich in dragonflies and 26 species have been recorded, believed to be a record for southern England. The Nature Conservancy Council says there are up to 10,000 insect species present, rather dwarfing an otherwise impressive bird list. There are also many unusual plants, the most distinctive of which, perhaps, are the insectivorous sundews on damp tracks and other places where there has been standing water on the peaty soil. The round and long-leaved species are both to be found, the former being the commoner. Cotton grass, scarce in the southeast, is a good marker of wet ground when it is in flower. Heathland fungi, mosses and lichens are well represented.

The bog is surrounded by heather moor, which rises steeply at the southern end and there are scattered copses of pine and birch. The higher ground gives good views across west Surrey. On the east side of the reserve a stream was dammed in earlier times to form a series of pools — the Hammer Ponds, Forked Pond and Warrenmere. Drier ground in the southwest corner, at Truxford, was used as a site for army huts during the Second World War. These have long since been cleared and have given way to a little hawthorn scrub. In the northeast corner a similar area exists at Rodborough Common, with access off the west side of the A3.

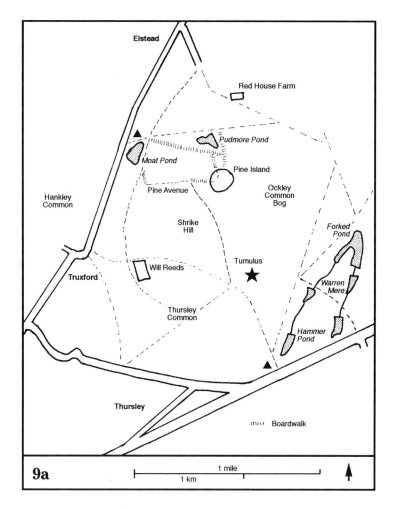

9a

Species

A tumulus on the south side of the bog at SU 912408 provides a good vantage point. Thursley Common is a nationally important site for wintering Great Grey Shrikes. Dead trees and pylons should be scanned for these and other birds of prey. Hen Harriers and Merlins are regular in autumn and winter, Buzzards, Kestrels and other falcons in spring and summer. Hobbies feed over the bog area on dragonflies and hirundines. Many other birds of prey have been seen here, including the Honey Buzzard, Marsh Harrier, Goshawk, Red-footed Falcon and Osprey.

Little Grebes breed on Moat Pond. There are often a few Teal at the Pudmore pools, though not normally in the breeding season. Waders are sometimes found there. Green Sandpipers and Little Ringed Plover are the most frequent but others include Pectoral Sandpiper. Waders may also be seen flying over on passage. More surprisingly several maritime species including a Fulmar and a Leach's Petrel, both extremely rare in Surrey, have been recorded. Common and Velvet Scoter have appeared on the ponds here and at Frensham.

This is a very fine area for breeding heathland species. Redstarts, Siskins and occasionally Crossbills nest in the pine woods around the Moat Pond car park and elsewhere. Pine Island and Pine Avenue are also good for Redstarts. Stonechats are conspicuous on the gorse. Dartford Warblers can be seen from the board walk and are commonest to the south of the reserve where the older age-classes of heather and gorse are established. Care should be taken to keep to paths so as

Hobby

not to disturb them. Woodlark can be heard and seen over Shrike Hill and other places, especially where the heather is short In good years there can be at least 15 pairs. The best time is from March to July. Again, care should be taken to avoid disturbing them. The Nightjar is quite common, with several birds sharing a feeding ground near Moat Pond. Tree Pipits and Redpolls will be found among the birches and there are a few Meadow Pipits. Reed Buntings are numerous along the margins of the bog.

Hammer Pond should produce Grey Wagtails at the outfall, and the occasional Kingfisher as well as resident grebes, Mute Swans, Canada Geese and duck. Wigeon sometimes linger into May. Flocks of up to 100 full-winged Mandarin are now being reported from a private lake in the district and reports from Thursley are becoming more frequent. Thorn bushes at Truxford and Rodborough hold a few Nightingales.

Timing

Birds of prey are best looked for early soon after dawn or from late morning. Hobbies may well be seen at midday, when they are chasing dragonflies. May is outstandingly good for breeding species and there will be noisy family parties of birds later in the summer. Redstarts begin singing before first light. Dawn and dusk are best for Snipe, Cuckoo, Nightjar and Woodcock. Nightjars often do not begin churring until after 9.15 pm. Warm calm days in spring and early summer are best for Dartford Warblers.

Neither spring nor autumn passage is very noticeable apart from a passage of chats.

Access

The best approach is from Elstead, taking the unclassified road to Thursley that runs between Hankley and Ockley commons. Park at Moat Pond, on the east side of the road, after 1.5 miles (2.4 km). This is a small water with some interesting plants. From here, well-marked paths and a board walk lead round the reserve and give vantage points over the best areas. There is a map on a notice board.

Another approach is from Thursley village, where there is a very limited space for parking. Walk north to the commons on a footpath by the cricket pitch.

There is an entrance gate on the A3 at the southern end of the reserve (look for the brown NNR sign and map). This is closer to Hammer Pond but parking space is very restricted.

While in the area, observe the common-sense rules, which are there to protect the fragile ecology of the site against fire, the trampling of the heather, disturbance of scarce breeding species and havoc caused by uncontrolled dogs. Since the area is disused army land, care should be taken not to handle any suspicious objects. It is best to keep to well-worn paths.

HANKLEY (Map 9a, SU 83/93 & SU 84/94)

Habitat

Hankley Common is predominantly open heath with scattered pines. It has some low, but striking sandy ridges at its southern end, where the steep slopes are covered by deeper heather and gorse. Updraughts along the ridges are sometimes used by model glider enthusiasts, and also by various raptors. The undulating terrain, with its bleak exposures, has been popular among film-makers. The common has no warning flags or access restrictions but is frequently used for army training exercises including parachuting. Visitors and especially children should be careful about spent flares, cartridge cases and other bits of military litter which may be on the ground. These should be left where they are. Also keep out of the Dropping Zone (DZ) when it is in use. There are wide paths round DZ and the rest of the common, and they provide good views of the parachuting if you want to watch it.

Species

Hankley is well known for Nightjars, which at the right time can be heard and seen even without leaving the car park. The birds nest on the ground among the heather and it is important not to cause disturbance by walking thoughtlessly through it. Nightjars perch in trees, or sometimes on power lines, to churr, moving their heads slowly from side to side so that the direction can be hard to locate. The males also fly low over the heath, giving a sharp 'goo-ick' call which makes them easier to find.

Woodlarks and Dartford Warblers are usually present, though they may not be too easy to see outside the breeding season, when they are not in song. The common supports a large population of Tree Pipits and Yellowhammers, as well as a few Meadow Pipits. The display flights of the Tree Pipits, climbing and then parachuting back to a perch on a low pine or birch, are a frequent sight from April to July. As on the other western heaths, the Hen Harrier, Merlin are among the more likely winter visiting birds of prey. Great Grey Shrikes rarely go there.

Timing

Nightjars are rarely active before it is almost dark. The evening chorus closes as the sun does down. There will be Woodcock then, perhaps at 9.15 pm in mid June, the first churring will be heard. Military training exercises may start at dusk and can be noisy, involving flares, blank ammunition the blockage of access lanes by vehicles. This is not normally a problem, but at such times try somewhere else.

Access

Approach from Elstead along the Thursley road between Ockley and Hankley Commons (Map 9). About 0.75 mile (1.2 km) south of Moat Pond there is a zigzag bend from which a lane goes off on the right signposted to the DZ. Follow this for 0.5 mile (0.8 km) to a car park on the left. There are also footpaths onto the common from Tilford, at the northeast end. From the south take a footpath on the north side of the unclassified road between Thursley and Churt, immediately west of Pitch Place (SU 883391).

MILFORD and WITLEY (Map 9, SU 84/94)

Habitat

Milford and Witley Commons lie to the south of Milford, between the A246 and the A3, opposite the Thursley group of commons. At the Milford end the light, rather gravelly soils carry extensive hawthorn scrub, heather and areas of short grass. Further down, pine and deciduous woodland predominates, with scattered clearings. Small areas where chalk has been dumped enrich the flora, which includes aliens such as the Turkey oak, and the curious little New Zealander, pirri-pirri bur, the seeds of which reached Britain by clinging to imported wool. About 30 species of butterfly can be found, including green hairstreak, purple emperor and white admiral. Rabbits are usually conspicuous and there are a few deer. Reptiles include adder, grass snake and slow worm.

The commons are managed by the National Trust (NT), who run a well-appointed information centre. Nature trails have been laid out and pamphlets are available.

Species

Milford Common is best known for its Nightingales. They breed mainly among the hawthorn scrub and are not always easy to see. Woodlarks can be found in good years. Warblers, especially Whitethroats, Garden Warblers, Blackcaps and Willow Warblers, are numerous among the scrub and birch. The pine woods at the southern end of the commons are good for Sparrowhawks and woodpeckers.

Timing

Nightingales will be in good voice from about mid April to the end of June. They can be heard at most hours of the day and night, but are least active in the afternoon. If you really want to hear them perform at midnight, this can be done comfortably from Webb road, which connects with the A246, 0.75 mile (1.2 km) down the A246 from Milford. A May or June morning visit will find numerous Willow Warblers, as well as Cuckoo, Tree Pipit, Garden Warbler, Blackcap, Whitethroat and many other birds in song.

Access

Approach by A246, where there is a car park near the entrance to Webb Road. Walk towards the information centre (follow signposts along Webb Road). The Nightingales are in scrub on the right. Be careful not to park on the main roads or to block access points to the common.

FRENSHAM (Map 9, SU 83/93)

Habitat

Frensham Common lies on undulating ground. Frensham Ponds mark the western edge of the Surrey heaths, and the Great Pond itself is, at one end, partly in Hampshire. Like most of the waters in Surrey, the ponds are artificial, made by damming a stream. This gives them a characteristic shape, shallow and reedy at one end and deeper, with an embankment, at the outfall. The contiguous area of Churt Common has marshy pools including Axe Pond, a heronry, pine woods and heather moor.

Species

If starting from the Little Pond car park, take the path up the east side of the pond, taking note of the Great Crested Grebes, Tufted Duck and other wildfowl on your right, while keeping an eye on the heath and sandy fields of Tilhill Nurseries to your left, where there is excellent habitat for Woodlarks and wintering finches. The path round the head of the pond crosses boggy ground on a boardwalk and gives a view of the secluded nature reserve in the southeast corner of the pond, where Garganey and migrant waders might be found. Early in the year there is a chance of Crossbills. They breed intermittently and are also seen in irruption years, then appearing most often in July and August, when their hard 'chip-chip-chip' flight call draws immediate attention.

At the south end of the Little Pond some dead birches provide attractive perches for a Great Grey Shrike if one is wintering on the common. Shrikes have been less regular in recent years but, if not seen at the Little Pond, may be found further over on the western slope of Kings Ridge, a shoulder of high ground to the west which is the watershed for the catchment areas of the two ponds. Great Grey Shrikes may best be found by searching likely looking posts and dead branches, though they may also be noticed when they make a quick downward sally for an insect or small bird.

There are substantial reedbeds around both ponds, and especially the south end of the Little Pond. These accommodate one of the county's largest Reed Warbler colonies. Sedge Warblers are annual on passage but scarce breeders. There are good numbers of Reed Buntings. Water Rail are often seen, mostly in winter, and they may be heard squealing in the reeds at the end of the Little Pond in summer. They are known to have bred. The best place and time to look is at the base of the reedbed in the southeast corner of the Little Pond when water levels are low. The fortunate observer might then see a dusky, narrow-bodied rail with a long red bill make a quick dash for cover between the reeds.

Following one of the paths up Kings Ridge will get you to the ridge path which affords excellent views over the commons on either side, and out over both ponds. The depth of the heather and development of the gorse varies somewhat from year to year. In spite of all efforts and no doubt partly because of sheer thoughtlessness on the part of some of the many users of the common there are occasionally serious fires in the later days of hot summers. These cut the heather back, kill the pine and birch saplings and leave clear burnt areas which are highly attractive to Woodlarks but very damaging to the breeding needs of other heathland species. In winter there may be little to be seen on the open heath, apart from a few Wrens and Dunnocks mousing round the gorse clumps, but as the year advances every one seems to provide a songpost. Stonechats are mostly absent in winter, but good numbers are present at Frensham, as on other Surrey heaths, from March to October. The noisy family parties of young birds are conspicuous during the summer. The spectacular songflight of the Tree Pipit, with its 'parachute' stalled descent onto a birch or pine branch is also not likely to be missed. The Meadow Pipit, incidentally, is not a common breeding bird in Surrey. A few pairs may be found in the Thursley/Frensham area, but much less frequently than Tree Pipits. The rough grass that the species prefers is found only sparingly in the county. Linnets are plentiful. Another conspicuous species among the birches is the Yellowhammer.

Continuing over the ridge and down to the Great Pond, the paths cross the A287 and reach a rather eroded area, the subject of some determined reclamation work in parts, at the shore of the Great Pond. Migrant waders may be found on the sandy shore here at suitable times. Frensham is one of the two places in Surrey which have provided most of the Oystercatcher records, the other being Barn Elms. Not that the numbers are more than tiny compared with coastal areas, but they are fine birds to find on a Surrey heath. Whimbrel, Curlew and godwits might also be seen here, feeding or flying over. Both ponds are worth scanning for migrant terns. These are mostly Common, but a few individuals of scarcer species each year and flocks of Black Terns may be present for several days. Little Gulls may also be seen, and the occasional Kittiwake.

On the south side of the Great Pond, where a small stream marks the border between Hampshire and Surrey (and along which a Spotted Crake once walked, thoughtfully putting a foot into both counties), is an alder copse which is a good place to search for Lesser Spotted Woodpeckers, Marsh Tits, Willow Tits and Siskins. In some years, when a Siskin flock collects in March or early April, birds may be heard in full song before they finally leave. And perhaps not all go, for a few now breed in west Surrey. At the west end of the Great Pond a footpath leads past the small Outlet Pond to the banks of the River Wey, where Grasshopper Warblers sometimes sing from rough grass on the far bank. Other possible species here are Lesser Spotted Woodpeckers, Garden Warblers, Marsh Tits and Willow Tits.

Frensham Common has its share of migrant and resident birds of prey. Most spectacular, perhaps, is the Osprey which calls at the ponds annually on its way north or south. Buzzards of various species have been seen moving through and some of the summer occurrences may be of birds wandering from more distant breeding areas. Merlins sometimes appear in winter, though they may be more reliably picked up on some of the damper commons, such as Chobham or Pirbright. Hen Harriers come across from the other commons from time to time.

Wildfowl wintering at Frensham now include a few Goldeneye and sometimes Ruddy Duck among the Mallard, Tufted Duck and Pochard. A good many other species have occurred and should certainly be looked for, as should divers and Red-necked, Black-necked and Slavonian Grebes. The divers are sometimes in perplexing plumages and separation of Red and Black throated can require care. Bitterns and Bearded Tits are scarce winter visitors. Autumn brings more gulls, and a winter roost of several thousand has built up in recent years, mostly Black-headed. This is the only Surrey gull roost away from the Thames Valley reservoirs and is probably connected with the large numbers now found a few miles away at Seale rubbish tip and Wrecclesham.

Churt Common is not much watched but Axe Pond has produced a Little Egret.

Timing

Local birders find it best to get to the Great Pond very early in the day if possible, because of the popularity of the spot for dog walkers. The sandy shoreline attracts migrant waders, especially in May, July and August — usually Sanderlings, Ringed or Little Ringed Plovers or sandpipers, but sometimes Oystercatchers. Note that the Frensham car parks may be locked overnight until 9.00 am. This complicates arrangements for early morning visits because of roadside parking restrictions.

Access

One way of approaching the Common is to take the A287 south from Farnham (Map 9). Note that this does not directly link with the A31 but can be accessed from the traffic lights at Farnham by forking left into Tilford Road and taking the first on the right (Alfred Road). After 2 miles (3 km) down the A287, take Priory Lane, the entrance to which is 100 yards south of the Mariner's Hotel, on the left. The lane leads through woodland to a car park at the outfall end of the Little Pond. From here there are good paths out onto the heath. Alternatively, continue down the A287 from Farnham and take the signposted turning on the right to a car park on the north side of the Great Pond.

For the Devil's Jumps and Churt Common follow the A287 south past the Great Pond and after 0.5 mile (0.8 km) turn left up Jumps Road. There is a car park among the pines on the left, after 1.5 miles (2.4 km). Axe Pond (SU 867402) is most easily reached from a bridle path off Sandy Lane, in Rushmoor.

HINDHEAD (Map 9, SU 83/93 & SU 84/94)

Habitat

Hindhead Common is a National Trust property with wet and dry heath and woodland. It includes the Devil's Punchbowl, a steep-sided and partly wooded valley running north towards Farnham and some high ground at Gibbet Hill. Nature trails have been laid out on Gibbet Hill and in the Punchbowl. South of the hill there is some damper ground. There are mature pine woods on Beacon Hill.

Species

The woods and heather hold the usual resident and summer visiting heathland species and are more reliable than most for Wood Warblers. Firecrests and Crossbills have had good breeding success in the district, though not every year. Siskins breed.

Timing

Best in spring and early summer, when Stonechats and warblers are established in territory. Avoid summer afternoons. The area is not so interesting in the winter months, attracting fewer birds of prey than Thursley or Frensham.

Access

Approaching from Hindhead or Frensham, park at the head of the Punchbowl, on the north of the A3. Nature trail leaflets are available from a cafe in the car park. Good paths lead over most parts of the common.

PUTTENHAM, CUTT MILL and CROOKSBURY (Map 9, SU 84/94)

Habitat

Puttenham Common is a mixed habitat of rough grass, bracken and birch with some oak woodland, on sloping ground. A series of tree-lined ponds runs down from the slopes of the Hog's Back to Cutt Mill House, between Puttenham and Crooksbury commons. The lower pool is private, with a public footpath on two sides. Take care not to walk through the gates of Cutt Mill House. Crooksbury Common lies to the west of the ponds. It is waterlogged in places but its heather and boggy areas are becoming overgrown with birch.

Species

Cutt Mill is an outstanding site for Mandarin with 70 or more there in winter, mainly on the lower pool. Wood Duck are sometimes seen. Great Crested Grebes and Tufted Duck breed. Listen for Willow Tits in alders and oaks at the north end. The second pool is used for fishing but also has breeding waterfowl, including grebes. The upper pool, visible only from the dam between it and the second, often has Grey Herons perched in trees on the west side. Wintering species include Goosander and more occasionally scarcer wildfowl such as Bewick's Swans and Pintail. There are good numbers of Tree Pipits, Marsh Tits and Yellowhammers and a few Redpolls out on the commons in summer. In good years at Puttenham there are Stonechats at the northern end and Nightingales near the car park at the south. Crooksbury Common is good for Woodcock, Cuckoos, Tree Pipits and Yellowhammers with, as elsewhere in west Surrey, a chance of finding a Hobby or Nightjar.

Timing

Puttenham Common is a good place for roding Woodcock, which may be seen at dusk from March to July. It gets crowded in the vicinity of the pools at weekends, especially in the summer. Crooksbury is less disturbed.

Access

From the A31, take the signposted turning south to Puttenham, along the B3000. Turn right after 0.5 mile (0.8 km) and then left after another 0.25 mile (0.4 km) opposite The Good Intent public house. This will take you to the lakes after 1.5 miles (2.4 km). There are good car parks on high ground to the east of the lakes and under trees on the west side of the second pool. Crooksbury Common is immediately to the west.

Calendar

Resident: Little and Great Crested Grebes, Grey Heron, Mandarin, Teal, Tufted Duck, Sparrowhawk, Kestrel, Water Rail, Snipe, Woodcock, owls, woodpeckers, Kingfisher, Woodlark, Meadow Pipit, Grey Wagtail, Stonechat, Dartford Warbler, Siskin, Redpoll, Crossbill in some years.

December–February: Divers, Red-necked, Slavonian and Black-necked Grebes, peak Mandarin counts at Cutt Mill, Goldeneye, sawbills, Ruddy Duck. Gull roost at Frensham Great Pond, Hen Harrier, Merlin, Short-eared Owl, Great Grey Shrike on the commons.

March–May: Crossbills breed very early. Tree Pipits begin arriving from end March, main warbler arrivals in early April, Nightjars and Nightingales a little later. Migrant waders passing through Frensham, terns from mid April. Heathland species are well established by May.

June–July: Hobby, Nightjars very active, Nightingale song tailing off as the birds get down to raising young. Stonechats have second broods. Reed Warblers and Water Rails at Frensham.

August–November: Young Hobbies on the wing in August. Autumn passage of duck, terns, raptors, Whinchat, Wheatear. Redwing, Fieldfares arrive early October. Hen Harrier, Merlin, Great Grey Shrike possible from October onwards.

10 ALBURY AND DISTRICT

OS 186/7
TQ 04/14

Habitat

The country round Albury (Map 10) has three ridges of hills. Furthest north are the North Downs, running from Pewley Down east through Newlands Corner to Netley Heath. The chalk is in most places capped by shallow plateau gravels where heathy patches, usually dominated by gorse, bracken and scrub, have developed. The south-facing scarp has turf and a good range of chalkland flora. The Greensand elevations of St Martha's Hill and The Chantries are immediately to the south of the downland. Beyond them are some lower sandy heaths at Blackheath and Albury, rising gradually to the third area of elevated ground, with peaks at Pitch Hill and Winterfold.

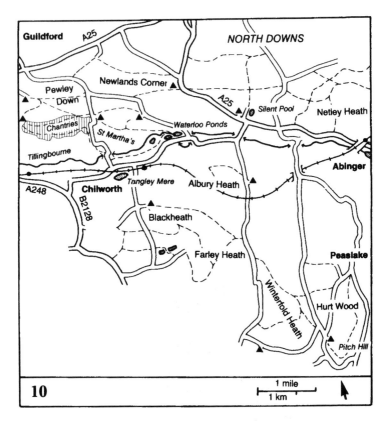

Blackheath has open areas of deep heather, mature conifer plantations and scattered copses, mainly of pine, running east into the brack-
en and pine of Farley and Albury Heaths. It is a district of substantial
country properties along the lanes. There are cricket pitches on the
edge of the heath at Blackheath and Albury. Deer abound and are easily seen on summer evenings, especially towards dusk. A birder listening intently for the first Nightjar might hear a lion roar in a distant
menagerie.

There are several private lakes. Tangley Mere is reedy and can be
glimpsed from the railway at Chilworth. Waterloo and Postford Ponds,
at the foot of St Martha's Hill, are readily seen from public footpaths.
The Tillingbourne is a stream with exceptionally pure water which has
been the basis of the watercress industry in the district. Cress beds at
Abinger are still in use though others elsewhere have been converted to
fish farms. The cress is grown in shallow, gravel-bottomed pans of water
enclosed by low concrete walls, continuously irrigated from the adjacent stream. A spring in the chalk at Albury rises to form the Silent Pool,
a shallow pool of clear blue water overhung by trees, well known as a
Surrey beauty spot.

Species

The stretch of North Downs from Pewley Hill to Netley Heath is now
largely interesting for its breeding birds. Lesser Whitethroats are found

in the dense old hedges on Pewley Down and elsewhere. Marsh Tits are frequent. Migrant chats and Ring Ouzels can be found, especially if sought early on spring or autumn mornings. In a way this is a sad place, illustrative of the decline of some traditional southern species. The last Surrey stronghold of the Cirl Bunting was at Pewley. Newlands Corner, further along, was once famous for its Nightingales, all of which now seem to have gone, and in earlier days this would have been typical habitat for Red-backed Shrikes. The Collared Dove, graceful though it is on garden bird tables, can seem poor compensation for the losses. Other new colonists are noticeable in the district though, including birds of prey and the more regular summer occurrences of Firecrests and Siskins with, perhaps, the Serin to follow. Sparrowhawks are now much more common and are very likely to be seen along the Downs or the Greensand hills. A few Woodlarks are reappearing on downland and set-aside sites.

Blackcap

The Chantries is a ridge of mixed woodland, readily approachable from either end, though with a car it is better to start in the west. Along with all the expected woodlands species there are good views over the surrounding farmland, with Grey and Red-legged Partridges and Little Owls and the evening appearances of the roe deer on the fields. The south slope of The Chantries has open turf and hawthorn scrub and is a place for Nightingales and warblers. Migrant or wandering Hobbies may be seen as well as Kestrels. There is a pleasant walk eastwards along The Chantries, either continuing along the ridge to St Martha's or dropping down on the south side to Waterloo Ponds via the old gun-powder works, an enterprise which blew up before the First World War to leave a group of interesting but overgrown ruins by a stream. There are ponds, old culverts and other relics which have something to offer industrial historians, anglers and birds alike. A circular route can be made by going via the gunpowder works to Waterloo and Postford Ponds, up the hill to St Martha's and then back via paths on the north side of The Chantries to the car park at the west end.

St Martha's Hill has Tree Pipits in summer. Stands of Scots Pine and other conifers should be examined for Crossbills in good years. Firecrests are sometimes found in the district, usually at places where there is mixed pine and oak, and in spring may give themselves away by their song, which is a distinctive and flattened version of that of the Goldcrest, an abundant bird in most parts of Surrey. The steep hillside down from St Martha's through the beech woods of Colyers Hanger to Waterloo Pond is excellent for warblers including the Wood Warbler, which should be sought among the mixed woodland on the higher slopes.

Waterloo and Postford Ponds have Sedge and Reed Warblers, and Reed Buntings as well as Grey Herons, Kingfishers and other waterbirds. Like a number of well-stocked, tree-lined ponds in Surrey, Waterloo has attracted a migrant Osprey which lingered, as some others have when conditions are right, for several weeks.

Little and Great Crested Grebes breed on ponds and lakes in the district, as do Canada Geese and a few Tufted Duck. Mandarin are spreading up the streams. Reedy stretches along the Tillingbourne have sometimes, as at Abinger, held a wintering Bittern. Heronries have been established and lost, as at St Martha's, and are unpopular with fish farming interests, whose managers have to protect their stock against the hungry Herons. The Abinger cress beds attract a few waders, most regularly Green Sandpipers which have sometimes wintered there. Grey Herons and Kingfishers may also be seen there. Both may perch on the concrete causeways between the beds to fish.

Blackheath is a reliable place for Nightjars. An evening visit to hear them will also produce roding Woodcock and appearances of Cuckoos, and roe deer. During the day Tree Pipits and Redpolls will be active where there is birch and the pines may in some years hold Crossbills. Winter birds are not so interesting. The area does not seem particularly attractive to raptors and is not much visited by birdwatchers out of season. Albury Heath, nearby, is a good place for roding Woodcock on summer evenings. They can be seen at or below eye-level if watched from the high ground on the west of the road 1 mile (1.6 km) south of Albury Church.

Winterfold is heathy but overgrown and has extensive conifer woods with occasional Firecrests and Crossbills. This is an attractive but under-watched area which may have more in it than present records suggest. The land rises from Winterfold to the top of Pitch Hill, which is tree-covered and has Redstarts. The farming country south of Pitch Hill, around Ewhurst, is typical of the relict Barn Owl habitat still in the country.

Timing

Most of the places discussed will be more rewarding in spring and summer than at other times of the year. The more heavily walked routes along the Downs and hills will be best early in the day. Blackheath and Albury are interesting if visited in the late afternoon and evening, when species such as the Woodcock, Cuckoo and Nightjar are active.

Access

For Pewley Downs there is roadside parking at the top of Pewley Hill (TQ 006491). From here footpaths lead 0.5 mile (0.8 km) south to The Chantries, 2 miles (3 km) east to Newlands Corner and 1 mile (1.6 km) southeast to St Martha's. There is a car park under trees in Echo Pit Road, at the west end of The Chantries. Take the Pilgrims Way along the north side of the woods, or others leading to the eastern end. Newlands Corner and Netley Heath can be approached from the car park at

Newlands corner (TQ 041493). Other ways onto Netley Heath are from a car park at Hackhurst Downs, an area well known in its own right for its chalk flora and butterflies, or by a footpath up from the Silent Pool. Car parking for the Silent Pool is on the north side of the A25 opposite the turning to Albury (TQ 059485).

St Martha's has a car park on the west side of Halfpenny Lane (TQ 021484) and another, more convenient for getting at Waterloo Ponds, on the east side of White Lane at TQ 034484.

Blackheath has various bits of roadside parking and a proper car park off Sampleoak Lane at TQ 040463. Look for the sign to The Villagers public house at the crossroads 1 mile (1.6 km) south of Chilworth railway station, turn right and drive past it and on to the car park. Walk east along the broad track from here to reach Farley Heath. Albury Heath has parking space on the east side of the road at TQ 060469, 1 mile (1.6 km) south of Albury Church, down the Farley Heath road. Walk across to the other side for the Woodcock.

The Hurt Wood lies 2 miles (3 km) south of Albury Heath, taking the Winterfold road in Farley Green. The western part of it, Winterfold Heath, has plenty of parking spots including one looking down over the Weald from the crest of Winterfold Hill at TQ 062428. The Hurt Wood continues over the heights of Pitch Hill and Holmbury Hill and is crossed by other roads running south from Shere and Peaslake. There is a car park below Pitch Hill at TQ 080429, 3 miles (5 km) south of Shere, for those who want to make a start from there.

Calendar

Resident: Grebes, Grey Heron, Mandarin, Tufted Duck, Sparrowhawk, Woodcock, Stock Dove, Barn Owl, Little Owl, all three woodpeckers, Grey Wagtail. Firecrest and Crossbill in some years. Redpoll.

December–February: Wildfowl at Waterloo and Postford Ponds, chance of wintering Bittern and Green Sandpiper at Abinger.

March–May: Migrants chats and occasional Ring Ouzels on the downs. Arrival of warblers, best heard in song in May.

June–July: Woodcock and Nightjars at Blackheath and Albury. Tree Pipits on most of the downs and heaths. Sedge and Reed Warblers at Waterloo Ponds. Crossbill irruptions from July.

August–November: Green Sandpipers and perhaps other waders at Abinger. Winter thrushes on the North Downs from early October.

11 CENTRAL SURREY COMMONS

Habitat

A group of commons along the north slopes of the Downs (Map 11) are distinguished by mainly clay or calcareous soils, with some shallow gravels. Those in the Bookham and Epsom districts support mixed but primarily oak woodland, scrub and rough grass with a few boggy areas and pools. Stands of hawthorn are frequent and some of the land has been used for forestry. Higher ground around Epsom Downs is drier, with short turf growing on the chalk. The River Mole meanders north-west across the district.

Springs rise at Fetcham to fill old mill ponds.

Species

Woodland and scrub species predominate, with breeding and wintering waterbirds and occasional rarities at the ponds. The commons are traditional Surrey Nightingale localities; the species though is rather dependent on the state of development of the scrub and plantations and numbers are currently low. Pochard and Garganey have bred. Mandarin are increasing.

Main Birdwatching Zones

There are three main areas of interest. Effingham Fish Ponds and the surrounding woods and commons provide a habitat for waterbirds, woodland birds and passage migrants. Commons, riversides and ponds from Bookham through to Fetcham support a good variety of breeding species. Commons and Downland in the Ashtead and Epsom areas offer opportunities for observing inland migration and gull movements.

EFFINGHAM PONDS and COMMON (Map 11)

Habitat

A chain of fish ponds on marshy land at Effingham has good cover for wildfowl, with well-covered banks round the pools, and small islands. The surrounding ground is bushy, with mature hedgerows. Effingham Common has mixed woodland and scrub with stands of hawthorn. Woodland nearby at East Horsley includes hornbeam.

Species

Canada Geese and Tufted Duck are resident and other wildfowl winter. Little Grebe and Pochard have bred. Gadwall and Garganey should be looked for among the duck in spring and autumn. Lapwings are often seen on an adjacent meadow. This is a good place for passerine migrants, especially hirundines and warblers. Yellow Wagtails of various races have been reported in spring. Scrub on Effingham Common has a few Nightingales. The woods at East Horsley are one of the best Hawfinch localities in Surrey.

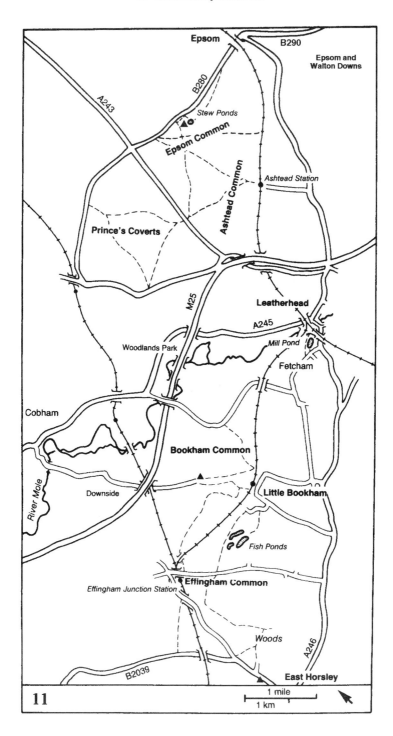

Epsom

B290

Epsom and
Walton Downs

B280

A243

Stew Ponds

Epsom Common

Ashtead Common

Ashtead Station

Prince's Coverts

M25

Leatherhead

A245

Mill Pond

Woodlands Park

Fetcham

Cobham

Bookham Common

River Mole

Downside

Little Bookham

Fish Ponds

Effingham Junction Station

Effingham Common

Woods

A246

B2039

East Horsley

11

1 mile

1 km

Access

The ponds may be approached on foot from Effingham Common Road, taking a turning 0.5 mile (0.8 km) southeast from Effingham Junction Station which leads to the public footpath crossing the site. Alternatively pick up the other end of the footpath in Little Bookham. Private parking at the ponds themselves is for anglers with permits. The public footpaths provide good views. Effingham Common runs out to Effingham Common Road, on the south side of Effingham Junction railway station.

The woods at East Horsley may be entered by walking 0.5 mile (0.8 km) south down a public footpath starting from Effingham Common. Alternatively start at East Horsley, parking at the tennis courts or shops in Ockham Road South (B2039) 0.5 mile (0.8 km) north of the junction with the A25 at Horsley Towers and take the signposted bridle path.

BOOKHAM and FETCHAM (Map 11)

Habitat

Great and Little Bookham Commons have a long record of scientific recording under the auspices of the London Natural History Society and there is a large survey literature. The clay soils on the higher parts of the commons are covered by deciduous woodland, mainly oak, and the damper low-lying parts have rough grass and hawthorn scrub and small ponds. Survey work has revealed many interesting plant and insect species. Mammals present include fox and roe deer. The River Mole runs across the back of the commons, with old parkland at Cobham and Woodlands Park. There are mill ponds by the Mole at Fetcham.

Species

Little Grebes, Kingfishers and Grey Wagtails breed and frequent small pools along the River Mole, which forms the northern boundary of the site. Mandarin breed in adjacent woodland.

There is a heronry at Bookham. Raptors which have been seen there from time to time include Goshawk, Buzzard and Hobby. Sparrowhawks have bred and are often seen. Green, Greater Spotted and Lesser Spotted Woodpeckers are resident on the Bookham commons as are the Tawny Owl, Marsh Tit, Nuthatch and Treecreeper. Stock Doves are present in small numbers. Summer visitors include Turtle Doves, a few pairs of Nightingales in the hawthorns, a good population of the commoner British scrub and leaf warblers and a few Wood Warblers. Grasshopper Warblers may sometimes be found in the open areas. A Cetti's Warbler once took up territory in thorn scrub along a stream and a Night Heron has lingered at one of the ponds. Dense blackthorn stands have at times held winter roosts of Short-eared and Long-eared Owls. Winter flocks of Redwings and Fieldfares are regular in the scrub areas.

Woodlands Park, on the other side of the River Mole, can be approached from Leatherhead and offers a chance to see more of the Mandarin habitat. Fetcham Mill Pond has small numbers breeding and wintering waterfowl and attracts migrants.

Access

Bookham Common is managed by the National Trust. There are many footpaths and access is unrestricted. One approach is over the footbridge at Bookham railway station. If approaching from the A245 at Cobham, take the minor road to Downside. This leads to a car park on the north side of the commons at TQ 120566.

Footpaths from Leatherhead run along the bank of the Mole and past Fetcham Mill Pond.

ASHTEAD and EPSOM COMMONS, EPSOM and WALTON DOWNS (Map 11)

Habitat

Ashtead Common is an area of rough grass, conifer plantation and ancient oak wood to the north of Ashtead station. Butterflies include green hairstreak and silver-washed fritillary. Epsom Common is adjacent. Woodland and scrub continues up to the Stew Ponds, which have been the subject of conservation work. Epsom and Park Downs are on higher ground, partly taken up by Epsom Race Course. The Downs are dry, with turf, rough grass and gorse. Prince's Coverts, immediately to the northwest of Ashtead Common, on the other side of the A243 is mainly plantation woodland.

Species

Mandarin are now breeding on Epsom Common. Hobbies are seen occasionally. Migrant Little Bittern, Garganey and Osprey have been found at Epsom Stew Ponds. Gull flocks on the Downs reflect migratory patterns, with large numbers of Lesser Black-backs in late summer.

Lesser Whitethroat

Nightingales breed sparingly throughout, but have also become scarcer. Redstarts should be looked for in Ashtead Woods. Garden Warbler, Blackcap, Lesser Whitethroat and Whitethroat are found in suitable places throughout. Longer grass on Ashtead Common has held Grasshopper Warblers, though they have recently become scarce. The Downs have proved to be good for visible passerine migration, mostly Lapwings, gulls, chats and leaf warblers.

Timing

Visits early in the day are advisable, especially in the Epsom localities, because of heavy public use of the Downland sites but timing is not in general critical. Grasshopper Warblers may be most easily found by listening for them in the early morning or evening.

Access

Convenient points from which to explore Ashtead Common are Ashtead railway station, from which public footpaths fan out over the common, and a turning east off the A243, 1 mile (1.6 km) north of Leatherhead.

There is a car park at the Epsom Common Stew Ponds on the B280 0.75 mile (1.2 km) west of the junction with the A243. For Epsom and Walton Downs take the B290 for 2 miles (3 km) south from the centre of Epsom to the racecourse.

Calendar

Resident: Little Grebe, Grey Heron, Mandarin, Tufted Duck, Sparrowhawk, Kestrel, Woodcock, Kingfisher, Green, Great and Lesser Spotted Woodpeckers, Grey Wagtail, Marsh Tit, Redpoll, Hawfinch, Reed Bunting.

December–February: Shoveler, Fieldfare, Redwing, Siskin, Lesser Spotted Woodpecker calling from February.

March–May: Redshank, Common Sandpiper, Yellow Wagtail, Nightingale, Grasshopper Warbler, Spotted Flycatchers may not arrive until the second week of May. Best time for Hawfinches.

June–July: Lapwing and Lesser Black-backed Gull flocks reappear on the Downs from July. Nightingale song to about mid June. Tree Pipit.

August–November: Chance of migrant raptors, Goshawk, Buzzard, Osprey and Hobby. Good numbers of Whinchats and Wheatears in open situations such as Epsom Downs. Pied Flycatcher.

12 DORKING HILLS AND LAKES

OS 187
TQ 04/14 & TQ 05/15

Habitat

Dorking lies among the highest of the Surrey hills, at the point where the River Mole cuts through the North Downs and the Lower Greensand Ridge (Map 12). Some of the water runs underground through swallow holes in the stony river bed so that in dry weather the water level can

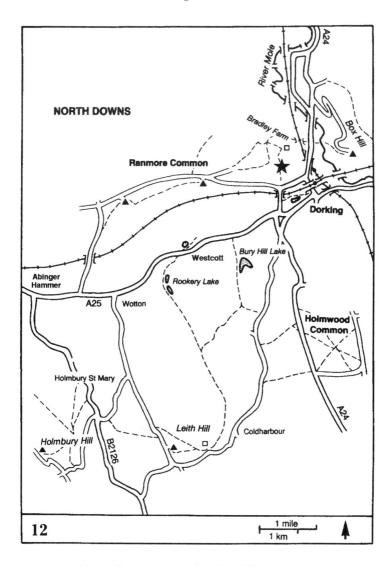

12

1 mile
1 km

appear very low or disappear altogether. Box Hill and Ranmore Common command the heights of the Downs to the north of the town. Leith Hill and Holmbury Hill, formed of sands and the harder, flint-like chert, are to the west. Streams running off the sandy slopes have been dammed in several places to form lakes, of which the largest are at Westcott and Bury Hill. Holmwood Common is an extension of the Greensand on lower ground east of Leith Hill. There is a small mill pond at Dorking.

Box Hill (National Trust) is a pleasant but heavily-used vantage point with some 800 acres (325 ha) of woodland and chalk Downland and it is designated a Country Park. Nature walks have been laid out. A cliff on the west side is famous for its cover of box trees. Other plant specialities include orchids and stinking hellebore. There are old chalk quarries in the southern slopes.

Ranmore Common (National Trust) is on high ground west of Box Hill, on the opposite side of the Mole valley. It is one of the better places in Surrey for orchids and other chalk flora, including green hellebore. Mixed woodland and bracken-dominated heath on the plateau gravels give way to chalky soils and beech glades on the northern slopes. Rough grass and scrub cover much of the south-facing scarp.

Leith Hill (National Trust) is the highest elevation in Surrey and the high point in the Weald for the Lower Greensand. A folly tower at the summit takes it to a height of over 1000 ft (305 m) and is conspicuous for many miles around. Most of the hill is wooded. There is some oak coppice. The dip slopes have been extensively planted, mainly with conifers and there are a few monkey puzzle trees. The scarp woodland includes naturally regenerating holly, yew, rowan and beech. Part of the area is an SSSI, designated for its geology, botany (including mosses) and birds. There is a hill fort, Anstiebury Camp, at Coldharbour. Holmwood Common (National Trust) is a rather overgrown area of sandy heath dominated by bracken, birch and oak.

Holmbury Hill, to the west of Leith Hill is mostly wooded and there are broad rides through the conifer plantations. A large area of *Amelanchier* scrub, an alien from North America, gives it a place in the botany books. Birds are said to take the fruit, which appears in mid-summer, helping the tree to spread to other parts of the county. There is a hill fort on the summit.

Species

Birds on the tree-covered parts of Box Hill include Sparrowhawk, Kestrel, Woodcock, woodpeckers, Wood Warbler and Nuthatch and the more open areas have a good variety of scrub and leaf warblers and finches. Kestrels and Jackdaws nest in the chalk quarries. Mandarin are to be found along the Mole and migrant Common Sandpipers occur on the stonier stretches.

Open fields at Bradley Farm are a good place at which to observe visible migration, especially in autumn, the species involved being mainly Skylarks, chats, thrushes and finches. One of the winter gull flightlines from the Thames Valley roosts passes through the Mole gap at this point, fanning out south, east and west at Dorking.

Ranmore Common is similar to Box Hill for birds, though being less crowded it is more rewarding to visit. The heath areas have good numbers of Tree Pipits and used to have Nightjars before being overrun by bracken. Wood Warblers are to be found in the beech glades northwest of the old Post Office. Redstarts seen from time to time suggest that they summer up there too. Hawfinches are present but hard to find. They are thirsty birds and an early morning watch at a waterhole might provide good views. Or else listen for them. Woodcock also come for water, and may be found roding on summer evenings.

The woods on Leith Hill are full of tits, Goldcrests, finches and the commoner warblers in the breeding season. More interestingly, there are also good numbers of breeding Redstarts and Wood Warblers, Sparrowhawks should be seen and there may be a fleeting glimpse of a Hobby. Woodcock and Tawny Owls are present in the thicker parts of the woodland. Stonechats have bred at a clearing near the cricket pitch at Duke's Warren (TQ 140440).

Holmbury Hill is similar but has at times supported extraordinary numbers of Nightjars, feeding over the woodland rides. The fairly

Great Tit

secluded scattered woodland is worth looking at. Holmwood Common has Tree Pipits and a variety of warblers but few real heathland species.

The lakes at Westcott have breeding and wintering Tufted Duck. Bury Hill Lake has reedbeds and an island. It is heavily fished from the shore and from boats, but is worth a look, nevertheless, early in the day or as part of a longer excursion towards Leith Hill. Dorking Mill Pond has the usual collection of urban wildfowl and attracts a few passerine and non-passerine migrants.

Timing

Box Hill gets crowded at weekends. Early in the day is best, unless you can go during the week. Leith Hill and Holmbury Hill are best in spring and summer. Like Box Hill, Ranmore and other places on the higher ground in Surrey tend in the winter to be deserted by birds, except for a few tits, thrushes and finches.

Access

Box Hill can be climbed by the footpath starting from the A24 on the north edge of Dorking at TQ 173513 or by the zigzag minor road behind the Burford Bridge Hotel, 1 mile (1.6 km) north of Dorking at TQ 174523. A good path starting on the north side of Dorking at TQ 162500 goes across the fields for 0.6 mile (1 km) to Bradley Farm where it turns left up to Ranmore Common. An unclassified road running northwest from the town leads to car parks on Ranmore south of the road at TQ 127501 and TQ 140503.

Possible approaches to Leith Hill are by footpath from Dorking, commencing at Milton Street (TQ 149488) and going north past Bury Hill Lake, or by car or bus to Coldharbour. A network of paths leads down the back slopes to Wotton, Westcott and Holmwood Common. Paths over the common start at various places along the A24 immediately south of Dorking.

For Holmbury Hill take the B2126 from the A25 at Abinger Hammer and follow it for 2 miles (3 km) to Holmbury St Mary, then walk south along a track from TQ 108451. Small lakes at Westcott are reached by public footpaths northeast and southwest from the A25 at TQ 133483.

Calendar

Resident: Little and Great Crested Grebes, Mute Swan, Mandarin, Tufted Duck, Sparrowhawk, Kestrel, Woodcock, Stock Dove, Little Owl, Tawny

Owl, woodpeckers, Grey Wagtail, Nuthatch, Jackdaw, Redpoll, Hawfinch, Reed Bunting

December–February: Thrush and finch flocks on the lower ground. Ranmore, Leith Hill and other more elevated locations tend to hold fewer birds.

March–May: Woodcock roding. Redstart, warbler arrivals. Wood Warblers on Box Hill, Leith Hill and Ranmore. Chance of Firecrest. Best time for Hawfinches.

June–July: Great Crested Grebes and Tufted Duck with young. Bird song eases off in July.

August–November: Summer visitors leave, starting with Swifts in August. Daily movements of gulls out from the Thames Valley to Dorking and beyond begin. Visible migration across lower ground at Dorking, especially Skylarks, Fieldfares, Redwings and finches flying east from early October.

13 REIGATE TO GODSTONE

OS 187
TQ 24/34 & TQ 25/35

Habitat

Like the Dorking district, the country round Reigate and Redhill straddles the North Downs and the sandy soils further south (Map 13). A narrow belt of Gault Clay lies between the two. Deposits of Fuller's Earth occur among the sands and these, together with the sand and chalk, have been worked for many years. There are a number of lakes and water-filled pits. Further east the ridge of sandy hills runs on to Godstone, a pleasant village of small shops and country eating places where there are more pits, active and exhausted, and several ponds.

Gatton Park, on Gault Clay on the north side of Reigate, holds the largest water in the district, Gatton Lake, and one of Surrey's largest heronries. There are smaller waters at Reigate Priory and Earlswood Common. Sand and Fuller's Earth pits to the east of the town at Holmethorpe provide an unstable habitat of waste ground, sand cliffs, pools and stretches of drying silt while being worked. In their later stages they may be landscaped or used as tips and filled.

Mercer's Lake is a landscaped pit used for sailing. It belongs to British Industrial Sand Limited (BIS). A picnic area has been provided and there are toilets. A car park which is open to the public commands a fine view over the whole water. It is possible to walk round on a footpath. A small part of the lake has been zoned as a nature reserve and is protected by a line of buoys. Holmethorpe Sewage Farm is on the north side of Mercer's Lake.

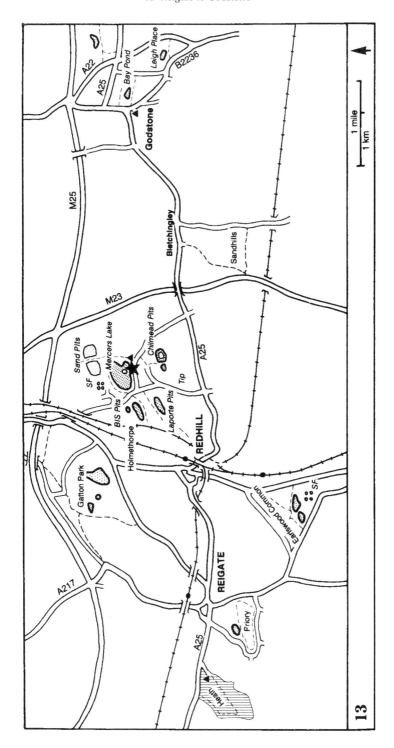

A large new pit has been opened to the north of Mercer's Lake. This has sand cliffs and pools and is proving to be a useful addition to the area.

The BIS Holmethorpe Quarry is opposite Mercer's Lake, in Nutfield Road. It contains a number of pits, one of which is flooded, with significant areas of sandy shoreline. Part of the site is still being worked. Mercer's Lake, the new pit to the north and the BIS pits are the ones to concentrate on, though the evolution of other good areas may be expected. There are abandoned pits on the west side of Cormongers Lane, where Laporte Industries have a number of Fuller's Earth and sand workings. These are currently difficult of access and unrewarding. Cormongers Lane has bends and is on a hill. Watch for sand lorries. Two small pits accessible from a footpath running south at the end of Chilmead Lane, off Cormongers Lane, have been landscaped, and Laporte have set up a nature trail.

Reigate Heath is a small, hilly piece of sandy common on the south side of the A25 west of Reigate. Most of it is laid down as a golf course but there are large stands of pine, birch, oak and alder which attract good numbers of the commoner golf course species. The elevations, one of which is topped by a windmill, make it a pleasant place to walk, in summer or winter. Reigate Heath is an SSSI. Reigate Priory has a small ornamental lake and woods. There used to be hornbeams but some or all of these have been felled.

Earlswood Common has two lakes. Earlswood Sewage Farm is on the south side of the common. Agricultural land between Redhill and Godstone, to the east, can offer good birdwatching. An example is around the Sandhills Estate in Bletchingley.

At Godstone, two old sand pits at one time used as reservoirs by the East Surrey Water Company have now been filled. Other sand pits there are still being worked. Godstone has another Surrey Wildlife Trust reserve, Bay Pond, an artificial lake with reedy margins and an alder swamp. Some adjacent sandy lagoons were formed by silt pumped out of Bay Pond. They are suitable for migrant waders but might be a short-lived feature of the site. Ponds at Rooks Nest Farm and Leigh Place should be worth a quick inspection in winter.

Species

The pits at Holmethorpe have from time to time produced divers and more frequently the scarcer grebes, usually Red-necked or Black-necked. These sometimes appear on other waters in the district. A Great Northern Diver stayed on Earlswood lakes for several weeks. There are large numbers of Canada Geese. A few feral Barnacle and Snow Geese are now regular. Greylags are appearing more frequently following their recent colonisation of the county from introduced stocks elsewhere and flocks of 50 or more are sometimes on Mercer's Lake. Red-legged Partridges are occasionally seen round the pits. Fair numbers of wild-fowl winter in the district, mostly Teal, Mallard, Pochard and Tufted, but with the occasional Wigeon, Long-tailed Duck or other wanderer. Bean Geese of the race *A. f. rossicus* have been seen. One or two Shelduck may be seen at odd dates during the year and at times have bred, though the habitat is rather marginal. The Osprey is sometimes seen on passage, most often in autumn. Hobbies appear over the pits at Holmethorpe and Godstone from time to time in summer. Bay Pond, being easy to observe, is worth scanning for wintering Water Rails, which occur sparingly throughout. The pits produce a good spring and autumn wader passage, mostly sandpipers and Greenshank, with a few Whimbrel and godwits. The Green Sandpiper is a characteristic bird of the district and might be seen at Mercer's Lake in any month of the year, with up to five in winter. Common Sandpiper are also frequent, but more confined to passage seasons. The Little Ringed Plover is a summer visitor in suitable localities.

Many gulls are attracted to the Holmethorpe pits, including Mediterranean, Glaucous and the occasional Iceland. Lesser Black-backs now linger through May and returning immatures are present in good numbers as early as mid June. Tern migrants are mostly Common but with a few others. Terns should be looked for perched on the buoys at Mercer's Lake. Large flocks of Carrion Crows may be found in winter.

There are small Sand Martin colonies at the Redhill Quarry, Holmethorpe and the Godstone. Black Redstarts have bred in Redhill, though they more commonly occur at Holmethorpe on passage. Reed Warblers breed at a number of the lakes and pits where conditions are right. Hawfinches used to breed at Reigate Priory when the hornbeams were there but appear to have left the area. As at other sites, patience may be needed to find them.

Breeding birds at Sandhills include Red-legged Partridge, Pheasant, Cuckoo, Little Owl, Tree Sparrow and the usual field and woodland edge species, with the chance of seeing Sparrowhawk and Hobby.

Timing

The scarcer birds tend to be seen at the pits in winter or on passage, though the area has something to offer at most times of the year. Breeding birds on the farmland around Sandhills will be best seen in May and June. This is also the time when the Gatton heronry is most active.

Migrant Black Redstarts arrive earlier and leave later than the common species, often a helpful point when females or immatures are found in unusual places in March, October or November.

Access

Holmethorpe Sand Pits can be reached from Cormongers Lane, left off the A25 0.5 mile (0.8 km) east of Redhill. Small roadside parking places give views over various parts of the area but do park OFF the road because of the lorry traffic. There is a car park above the sailing pit at Mercer's Lake, entrance in Nutfield Marsh Road, off Cormongers Lane. This is open to the public and is the best place from which to explore the more important parts of the Holmethorpe area. A circular walk can be made from here, beginning along the path round Mercer's Lake to the BIS Redhill Quarry pits. Good views of these and adjacent meadows can be had from the entrance in South Nutfield Road but the best way of seeing them is to follow the footpath which runs south of the BIS pits to the railway line. Returning to the road, follow it south to Chilmead Farm and then go east along Chilmead Lane to the landscaped pits. From here the Mercer's Lake car park can be reached via the cricket ground at the end of the lane. For details of the nature trail, which starts in the church car park at TQ 307508, phone Laporte on 01737 765050.

The new pit to the north of Mercer's Lake can be seen from a bridle path which passes the west end of the lake, behind the windsurfing centre. A public footpath marked as running across the area west of Cormongers Lane is overgrown and not recommended.

Reigate Priory and Earlswood Common are on the west and south margins of the town respectively. There is no public access to Gatton Lake though public footpaths through the grounds of the Royal Alexandra and Albert School, from Tower Lane and Gatton Park Road to Rocky Lane, run quite close to it. Limited access, for example for wildfowl counts or the heron census, is by arrangement only. Try asking for access at the water bailiff's cottage, entrance in Temple Wood, Gatton Park Road. In the interests of birdwatchers generally, do not trespass.

Car parking for Reigate Heath is available down Flanchford Road, on the south side of the A25 immediately west of Reigate. For Sandhills, park in Castle Square, just off the A25 in Bletchingley (TQ 324507). Follow the footpath east along the woodland edge (signposted to Nutfield), then south to meet a bridle way. Explore along this southwards to the motorway, then retrace steps to the car. A map is advisable. The return distance is 2.5 miles (4 km).

Godstone is 0.5 mile (0.8 km) south of the M25, leaving it at Junction 6. Park by the village green. Bay Pond is behind the White Hart public house at Godstone and can be well seen from footpaths to the north and south of the site, running between the High Street and Church Lane. Leigh Place is 1 mile (1.6 km) southeast, down the B2236. Rooks Nest farm is off the A22 at TQ362522. View from the road.

Calendar

Resident: Little Grebe Great Crested Grebe, Grey Heron, Greylag Goose, Canada Goose, Tufted Duck, Red-legged Partridge, Grey Partridge, Sparrowhawk, Kingfisher, woodpeckers, Grey Wagtail, Tree Sparrow, possible Hawfinch.

December–February: Occasional divers, Red-necked and Black-necked Grebes, Cormorant, Shelduck, Teal, Pochard, Goldeneye, possible Wigeon, Gadwall, Long-tailed Duck and Smew, Water Rail. Look for Golden Plover among the Lapwings at Holmethorpe. Possible wintering Green Sandpipers. Gulls of various species. Redwing, Fieldfare, Tree Sparrow (flocks of up to 100 at Nutfield Marsh at one time but now rare), Brambling, occasional Corn Bunting.

March–May: Sand Martin and Wheatear arrivals from mid March. Look for Garganey on the pits in April. Godwits, Whimbrel and sandpipers mainly in May. Terns, mostly Common but with a chance of Arctic, from mid April. Lesser Whitethroat, Whitethroat, Garden Warbler, Blackcap, Chiffchaff and Willow Warbler in hedges and copses round the pits.

June–July: Lapwings flocking up. Lesser Black-backed Gulls return to Holmethorpe.

August–November: Autumn wader passage, chance of Spotted Redshank at the pits. Redwing and Fieldfare from early October, Goldeneye from mid November.

14 HEDGECOURT, WIRE MILL AND DISTRICT

OS 187
TQ 24/34

Habitat

The low-lying country north of East Grinstead is drained by closely spaced tributaries of the River Eden (Map 14). Old mill ponds along the waterways reflect a bygone industrial structure. The largest of these are at Hedgecourt and Wire Mill, on the Eden Brook. The district has a number of small woods and copses accessible by footpaths. There is some unimproved grassland, best seen at Blindley Heath.

Hedgecourt Pond, a 43 acre (17 ha) stretch of water lying on a bed of Tunbridge Wells Sands, is the most important wildfowl refuge in south east Surrey. It is relatively secluded and has reeds along the south side and round the west end. The outfall at the east end runs off through damp woodland and meadow. The Pond is not very deep and freezes over in hard weather. It is used intermittently for sailing. The site is an SSSI. Ten acres (4 ha) at the west end of the pond are managed as a nature reserve. Botanical specialities include touch-me-not balsam and various pond weeds.

Wire Mill, 1 mile (1.6 km) to the northeast, is smaller. It has extensive beds of reed and sedge along the edges and woodland round two sides. Blindley Heath is a flat, 64 acre (26 ha) area of tall grasses 1.75 miles (2.8 km) north of Wire Mill. Drainage is poor and there are several small ponds. Oak and hawthorn scrub has begun to invade. The ponds have interesting sedges and other plants.

Species

Winter Cormorant numbers at Hedgecourt have been peaking at over 20 and in January and February there is just a chance of a Bittern in the reeds. Wintering duck include Mandarin, Shoveler and Pochard. Water Rails are sometimes seen there and may stay to breed. Greylag and Canada Geese have bred fairly regularly in recent years. Grey Wagtails may be seen at the outfall of the pond, which passes under a narrow roadway along the dam. Kingfishers, which are to be found here and along the many streams in the district, will also appear at Hedgecourt. The reedbeds attract Sedge and Reed Warblers, the former scarce in south Surrey, and also a few Reed Buntings. Birches and alders round the lake provide food for Goldfinches, Siskins and Redpolls in winter.

Wire Mill has rather fewer waterfowl, but, like Hedgecourt, may have Water Rails in winter and the surrounding reedbeds and scrub hold Sedge and Reed warblers and Reed Buntings in the breeding season. Woodcock are to be found in copses such as those near Hedgecourt Pond. Tawny Owls and Nightingales occur here and there among other woodland species. As in some other parts of Surrey, Nightingales have become rather scarce in recent years.

Blindley Heath provides a relict habitat for some fairly local species. Snipe winter there. Summer visitors include possible Grasshopper Warbler.

Timing

Hedgecourt is used for sailing, mainly at weekends but on most days during the summer. This drives duck and Coot into shallow bays at the

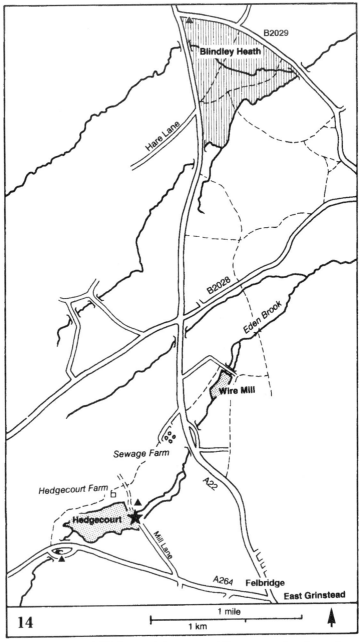

west end. Wire Mill is used for water-skiing at weekends and on Wednesdays. Early morning is best at both sites, especially when disturbance is expected. Nightingales will be easiest to find from late April to early June, their period of most consistent song.

For Blindley Heath an approach at dusk might provide the best chance of hearing Grasshopper Warblers.

174

Kingfisher

Access

Hedgecourt Pond is at Felbridge, on the western outskirts of East Grinstead. Approach via the A264 (Copthorne Road) and turn off on the north side up Mill Lane. The road passes the east end of the lake, where there is room to park a car. Alternatively, continue past Mill Lane and park in the slip road south of the A264, at the west end of the lake. Cross the road and follow the footpath through Domewood, which will take you round the west and north sides.

Approach Wire Mill via Wire Mill Lane, on the east side of the A22 1.5 miles (2.4 km) north of Felbridge. The lane is deeply potholed so take care. If walking from Hedgecourt, stay on the Domewood footpath, which continues past a sewage farm to the A22, crosses it and goes on to Wire Mill. The path returns to the A22 through woods on the other side of the lake. Blindley Heath lies east of the A22 between Godstone and East Grinstead. There is a small car park north of the heath, at the A22 end of Danemore Lane. Footpaths start from here and from the northeast and southwest corners.

Calendar

Resident: Great Crested Grebe, Mute Swan, Greylag and Canada Geese, Mandarin, Mallard, Sparrowhawk, Water Rail, Woodcock, Tawny Owl, Kingfisher, woodpeckers, Grey Wagtail, Marsh Tit, Willow Tit, Reed Bunting.

December–February: Cormorant flock. Chance of Bittern, Shoveler, Pochard, Tufted Duck, Goosander (wildfowl mainly Hedgecourt), Redwing, Fieldfare, Siskin, Redpoll.

March–May: Mandarin disperse from ponds to streamside breeding sites. Woodcock roding at Hedgecourt, warbler arrivals, including Grasshopper, Sedge and Reed.

June–July: Wildfowl, Warblers and Grey Wagtails with young.

August–November: Terns and Common Sandpipers possible at Hedgecourt. Departure of summer visitors. Gulls return.

ADDITIONAL SITES

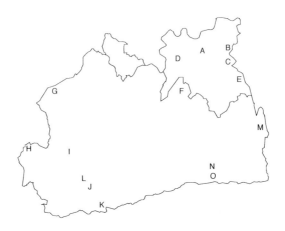

Key & Site	Habitat	Birds of Interest	Peak Season	Nearest Town
A Beddington	Sewage farm and power station	Wader passage, breeding Black Redstart, Yellow Wagtail, winter Corn Bunting flock and migrants	May, Aug–Sep	Croydon
OS 176 TQ 286661		*A site with a long history of scarce migrants, Killdeer, Lesser Yellowlegs, etc. Stints in September/October. Yellow Wagtails, including blue-headed types, have bred. Some have wintered. Black Redstarts at adjacent Croydon Power Station and other Croydon localities. Strong passage of chats. Tree Sparrow colony. Being redeveloped. Nearby Waddon Ponds have unusual numbers of breeding Coot.*		
		Current access very restricted but views of lake and other areas possible from the bridge north of Hackbridge railway station and car park (small charge). Roadside parking possible. Special access arrangements made for national rarities — listen for announcements on Birdline Southeast.		
B Dulwich Woods	Deciduous woodland	Warblers, wintering Firecrests	Jan–May	Dulwich
OS 176 TQ 345725		*Park in Sydenham Hill Road. Access through Sydenham Hill Nature Reserve.*		
C Crystal Palace	Park with lake	Breeding Shelduck, Spotted Flycatcher, migrants	All year	Penge
OS 176 TQ 345705		*Park at the National Sports Centre. Weird atmosphere with lifesize model dinosaurs in the bushes. Interesting winter visitors including Firecrest. Shelduck are feral.*		
D Berrylands	Sewage works	Passage migrants	Spring	Surbiton
OS 176 TQ 198681		*Adjacent to Berrylands railway station. View filter beds from Up platform or apply for permit to explore.*		

Key & Site	Habitat	Birds of Interest	Peak Season	Nearest Town
E S Norwood Country Park	Rough grass and wetland	Migrants and winter visitors	All year	Croydon
OS 177 TQ 352680	*Park near the sports stadium. On the Kent/Surrey border, best part in Kent. Used to be Elmers End sewage Farm. Migrant Marsh Warbler, Red-backed Shrike, Twite in winter have been recorded. Corn Bunting, Tree Sparrow possible. Nearby Norwood Lake has breeding waterfowl, recorded migrants include Sandwich Tern.*			
F Headley Heath	Acid heath on downland	Woodcock, Tree Pipit, heathland migrants	May–Sep	Leatherhead
OS 187 TQ 205535	*Approach on the B2033. There are car parks on the west side of the road, 2 miles (3 km) from Leatherhead.*			
G Olddean Common	Heath and pine woods	Woodlark, Redstart, Stonechat, Wood Warbler, Crossbill, Great Grey Shrike.	Dec–July	Camberley
OS 186 SU 893625	*Approach from roads north of the A30 on the London side of Camberley. Area near radio tower fenced off for bikers, best avoided. Great Grey Shrike site at Wishmoor Bottom, on the Surrey/Berks border.*			
H Bricksbury Hill	Heath and pine woods	Heathland species including Nightjar	May–July	Camberley
OS 186 SU 827492	*Park off the A287 near the radio tower and walk northeast. Fine views, and good birds, at Caesar's Camp.*			
I Wanborough	Open corn fields, wire fences	Stock Dove, Skylark, Corn Bunting	Jan–June	Guildford
OS 186 SU 934485	*A good example of Corn Bunting habitat on chalk downland. Flocks of up to 100 Stock Doves in winter. Corn Buntings now hard to find but Grey Partridge, chats and Quail possible.*			
J Hascombe	Mixed woods on sandy hills	Woodcock, Wood Warbler, Crossbill	Apr–Oct	Godalming
OS 186 TQ 002394	*Hascombe Camp is an Iron Age hill fort approached by footpath from Hascombe, on the B2130 3 miles (5 km) south of Godalming. Hydons Ball is a small hill to the west.*			
K Dunsfold	Plantations and farmland	Nightingales and other summer visitors	Apr–Oct	Haslemere
OS 186 TQ 016353	*Tracts of Forestry Commission woodland with clearings south of Chiddingfold and Dunsfold. Well known for butterflies. Frillinghurst Wood, between Grayswood and Chiddingfold, is similar.*			
L Winkworth Arboretum	Lake and ornamental woodland	Breeding Water Rail and Red-crested Pochard	All year	Godalming
OS 186 SU996413	*National Trust. Admission charge. 2 miles (3.2 km) southeast of Godalming, on the east side of the B2130. Good for summer and winter migrants.*			

Key & Site	Habitat	Birds of Interest	Peak Season	Nearest Town
M Limpsfield Chart	Acid heath on hill	Woodcock, Nightjar, Redstart	Apr–July	Oxted
OS 187 TQ 407519	*Approach on the B269 from Limpsfield. It is 2 miles (3 km) to the Chart.*			
N Hookwood	Farm fields, sewage works	Tree Sparrow, migrant waders	All year	Horley
OS 187 TQ 262430	*Park on roadside grass. Footpath at Hookwood leads over farm fields with winter/spring Tree Sparrows and finches. Nearby Horley sewage works has several lagoons attracting migrant waders.*			
O Povey Cross	Airport, wetland, lake	Summer visitors and migrants	All year	Gatwick
OS 187 TQ 265328	*Access from Povey Cross Road for riverside and views of Gatwick Airport. Little Ringed Plover and Black Redstart occur on rough ground near Cargo terminal. Summer migrants by river and in woods. Breeding Reed Warbler at the Hilton Hotel Lake, approachable by road.*			

SUSSEX

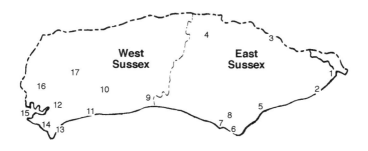

1 Rye Harbour and Pett Level
2 Hastings Country Park
3 Bewl Water
4 Ashdown Forest
5 Pevensey Levels and
   Pevensey Bay
6 Beachy Head
7 Cuckmere and Seaford Head
8 Lullington Heath and
   Friston Forest

9 Cissbury and the Adur Valley
10 The Arun Valley
11 Climping
12 Chichester Gravel Pits
13 Pagham Harbour
14 Selsey Bill and Bracklesham Bay
15 Chichester Harbour
16 Kingley Vale
17 Iping and Stedham Commons

1 RYE HARBOUR AND PETT LEVEL

Habitat

Lying at the southwestern end of the vast complex of Romney/Walland Marsh and Dungeness Peninsula, these areas provide a wide range of habitats. Most of Rye Harbour SSSI, within which lies the Rye Harbour LNR, comprises a large marine deposited shingle bank. Near to the sea, the shingle is on the surface, but further inland it is overlain by a thin layer of soil. The bare shingle supports some rare plants such as sea pea and least lettuce, as well as more typical species like yellow horned poppy and sea kale. Inland an interesting semi-natural grassland has developed. Insects, too, are notable, with nationally rare beetles being recorded. A substantial volume of shingle has been extracted over the years and wet gravel pits left; these add substantially to the wildlife interest of Rye Harbour.

Running to the sea along the eastern boundary of the Rye Harbour SSSI is the mouth of the River Rother, just to the east of which are other areas of ornithological interest such as Northpoint Pit and Camber Dunes. The Rother discharges into Rye Bay which is a shallow sandy

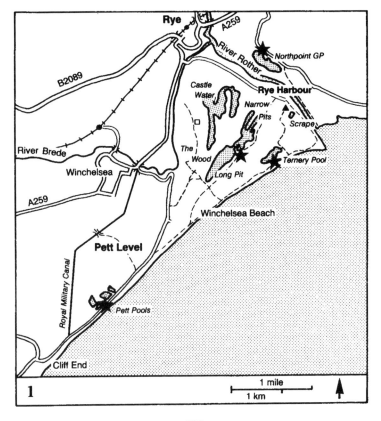

bay with, at low tide, an expansive foreshore. Rye Harbour Local Nature Reserve is managed by a warden on behalf of a Management Committee, comprised of Local Authorities and conservation bodies, but large areas within the SSSI are still managed by private landowners.

Pett Level, which is backed by an old sea-cliff, is mainly a sheep-grazed grassland criss-crossed with narrow dykes. Patches of reed have developed in some ditches and they prove to be an important habitat. Just behind the seawall near the western end is a series of four pools. Three are reed-fringed and are used for fishing, but the water level in the fourth is normally reduced in July by pumping carried out by the Sussex Ornithological Society. This pool has wide muddy margins throughout the autumn and attracts many waders which can be watched at very close range.

Species

Over 265 species of birds have been recorded in the Local Nature Reserve and others have been seen on Pett Level. An annual report is published for the LNR and also by Sussex Ornithological Society members for the Pett Pools project.

This area, being flat, can feel very exposed. In some severe winters all of the pits can be frozen over; at such times few birds remain, except for those which feed on the sandflats. These conditions are rare and usually there is a wide range of waders, wildfowl, raptors and passerines present. Out in the bay a calm day will reveal the telltale sight of groups of dark ducks, Common Scoter with perhaps a few Velvet among them. In winter up to 2,000 may be present and with them may be the low-slung shapes of Red-throated Divers, their heads distinctively upslanted; in some severe winters several hundred enter Rye Bay — they are often seen best off Pett Level where they find food in the productive shallow waters. Unfortunately the English Channel has a chronic oil pollution problem and when strong winds occur, a few disconsolate oiled individuals make for the sheltered waters inland, particularly the Ternery Pool, Castle Water and Long Pit. Here they join in with flocks of ducks. Hundreds of Shoveler, Teal, Mallard, Tufted Duck and Pochard dot these waters, concentrating in the lee of islands or the shoreline when the wind is chilling. Small numbers of the upright Gadwall, so often associating with Coot, the beautifully elegant Pintail, Long-tailed Duck and Goldeneye are regularly seen.

In most winters a few Scaup appear, but they are nearly always females or immatures and so have a large white patch around the base of the bill. Do beware of similar patterns on some female Tufted Duck and, therefore, check for the rounded crown, the barrel-shaped body and the paler, richer brown coloration of the former. Recent severe winters have drawn in that gem of winter ducks, the Smew. A patient search through all of the waterbirds may reveal many other species of divers, grebes or duck. In severe weather several species of geese have appeared, including apparently wild Barnacle Geese.

Out on the sand flats or in the channel of the Rother, Shelduck can be seen sifting the sand for the tiny snails on which they feed, while waders forage in their diverse ways. Over 200 Sanderling feed here along with up to 700 Oystercatchers and up to 2,000 Dunlin. Small numbers of most of the other commoner species may be picked out although Bar-tailed Godwits and Knot are scarce. As the tide floods in, they get pushed close to the shore and roost on the beach or come onto the sheltered islands of Ternery Pool. At Pett, there is usually a concentration of Turnstone, although whether they come from the Rye or Fairlight areas is not certain. On Pett Level many Curlew feed, but at night up to 900 roost at Rye Harbour with birds coming from Pett and Romney Marsh. Wherever the grassland is short there are small flocks of wintering Lapwing and Golden Plover; severe weather often temporarily increases numbers, but if it lasts, these are some of the first species to leave for warmer latitudes.

Among the passerines, the seed-eating finches and buntings remain in good numbers. Flocks of 10 to 30 Corn and Reed Buntings, Tree Sparrows and Chaffinches are regular, and 100 or more Linnets can usually be found. On the saltings, especially where small patches of sea aster grow, a few Twite can sometimes be located; they mix well with Linnets, so careful scrutiny is needed to identify this darker, yet buffier, relative. Among the few insectivorous birds are the Rock Pipits, which scavenge along waterlines on the shore and the pits. Grain stores attract an unwelcome yet spectacular flock of 300 Collared Doves as well as finches and buntings.

With this range of birds present, it is to be expected that many raptors include this area in their hunting range. Merlins, Peregrine, Hen Harriers and Sparrowhawks are regularly seen, in addition to Barn and Short-eared Owls.

At the same time as some of the winter waterbirds start to slip away, come the first signs of spring passage. Small flocks of Brent Geese pass east and then by mid March a few migrants appear which are the vanguard of the summer rush to the coast: a Wheatear standing boldly upright, a Sand Martin feeding low over the pits, or a Black Redstart shivering in the cool wind. Before long the harsh calls offshore draw attention to the chalky white Sandwich Terns moving past. Seawatching at Rye, which lies right at the head of Rye Bay, is not particularly good, but nevertheless strong southeasterlies will bring in a fraction of those passing offshore. So, as April progresses, a few Arctic and Great Skuas, Gannets, terns and other seabirds are seen. The gulls are worth checking, as Glaucous, Iceland and Mediterranean occur most years. At most sites, birds are just observed going by, but at Rye there are some unusual features not seen elsewhere in Sussex. The pits attract small groups of Little Gulls and Black Terns, where they twist and turn feeding on flying insects. Of particular interest is the build-up of Bar-tailed Godwits, Whimbrel and Turnstone. These stop off here in late April and early May with roosts reaching 500, 600 and 350 respectively. Obviously feeding conditions are very good.

While the seabirds are moving up-Channel, so the passerines are steadily arriving. Bright canary-yellow male Yellow Wagtails feed, actively chasing flies, and in most years a few of the Blue-headed continental race are seen among them. In the same vein it is worth checking through Pied Wagtails for their White cousins. Spring passage of warblers and chats is often poor, although by May many Reed and Sedge Warblers will be singing from the reeds, and Swallows hawking around the pits. In most years a rarity or two stops off, often in June or early July. Recent examples include Sooty, Bridled, Whiskered and Caspian Terns, Wilson's Phalarope, Alpine Swift and Black Kite.

By far the most spectacular feature of the breeding season is the terns on and around the Ternery Pool. Enormous efforts to protect the vulnerable colonies have been made here, several miles of electric fences have been erected and long hours of wardening put in by volunteers and wardens alike. Little Terns have steadily increased, so up to 70 pairs breed each year on the shingle, with up to 150 pairs of Commons on the islands. Similar numbers of Sandwich Terns also breed (having first bred here in 1986), but numbers fluctuate as birds move between this site and Dungeness. These pale grey and white birds are so graceful and their behaviour so fascinating that an hour or two can pass very quickly when watching them. Roseate Terns, with their very long tail streamers and long, all-black bills, are regular in spring and summer, often dropping in to the Ternery Pool for a bathe and a rest.

Out on the shingle other specialist breeders have taken advantage of protection, up to 55 pairs of Ringed Plovers, 20 pairs of Oystercatchers and six to eight pairs of Wheatears nest. The increase in their numbers since electric fencing was introduced in 1979 can be no coincidence. Up to 15 pairs each of Tufted Duck and Shelduck, six pairs of Great Crested Grebe and ten pairs of Little Grebe breed on the pits. Their success is variable; some years most pairs produce young, but in others there is almost total failure.

A large number of duck species may be seen in July or August, usually a few Wigeon, Teal, Shoveler or a Garganey can be present, although once they are in moult (eclipse plumage) they can be quite difficult to identify. Even a Long-tailed Duck or Scaup may remain over the summer. Autumn migration is much more pronounced and involves many more species than it does in spring. At Pett Pools and at the wader pool at Rye Harbour, the muddy margins attract many waders. Late July brings in juvenile Little Ringed Plovers, a few adult Wood Sandpipers and Little Stints, but it is late August to late September which is most productive. Then up to ten Little Stints, Common and Curlew Sandpipers and smaller numbers of Black-tailed Godwits, Wood Sandpipers, Greenshank and Spotted Redshank can be seen. Rarities occur with surprising regularity, including up to three Pectoral Sandpipers together, Least, Buff-breasted and Semipalmated Sandpipers and Wilson's Phalarope. The nocturnal roosts of Curlew and Whimbrel, which were a feature in the spring, reappear in the autumn at Rye Harbour.

Many migrant passerines move through Rye Harbour. In August Willow Warblers, with the occasional Wood Warbler, Whitethroats and other warblers are prominent and at the end of the month and into September come a scattering of Redstarts, Whinchats, Spotted and Pied Flycatchers and many other species. Flocks of hirundines reach several thousand and often roost in the reedbeds. They attract passing Hobbys and the resident Sparrowhawks. In addition, other raptors move through. Marsh Harriers are regularly seen. Ospreys and Peregrines are less frequent.

By October another change is on the way. Most of the warblers have gone and, when easterly winds set in, rarer species appear. Firecrests, Black Redstarts and Ring Ouzels are not unusual, and a careful examination of warblers may reveal a Yellow-browed. Then a Short-eared Owl may be seen hunting, or a Long-eared Owl hiding in a bush. Many of the seed-eating passerines build up to a peak at this time of the year. The Greenfinch flock may exceed 500, and a very substantial coastal passage of Linnets, Goldfinches, Chaffinches and other finches is to be seen. Just occasionally the grasslands attract down a few Lapland Buntings, or the shingle some Snow Buntings. After southwesterly storms Grey Phalaropes are occasionally driven onto the pits at Rye Harbour or Pett Pools.

Timing

Rye Harbour is well worth visiting at any time of the year. The migration periods, especially in May and again in autumn bring the greatest range of species, especially if the wind is easterly, but winter can provide excellent birdwatching. However, a visit in June, when the activity in the ternery is at its peak, will provide a memorable occasion. As always morning visits are best, before too many people are out walking and when the birds are most active. In winter, activity extends throughout the day. To see the waders and any ducks, divers or grebes on the sea, it is best to seek a high tide which coincides with mid-morning. Because Rye is very exposed, a strong wind or heavy rain is going to make bird-watching uncomfortable and usually unproductive. Pett Level can be overlooked from the road, but it is most productive when the pool nearest to the road is partly drained, between mid July and mid October. In midwinter a climb up onto the seawall here can reveal large numbers of scoter, divers and Great Crested Grebes on the sea.

Access

The Rye Harbour LNR can best be reached by taking the A259 to Hastings and before leaving Rye, take an unclassified road to the left, signposted Rye Harbour. Follow this for 1.5 miles (2.4 km); it ends in a free car park in which stands a small information centre which provides further details on the nature reserve. (There are public toilets just before reaching the car park.) From here it is possible to take two circular walks. A 2-mile (3 km) walk following the concrete road alongside the river at first and then right parallel to the coast, leads past the hide (with wheelchair access) overlooking the new wader pool and to the two hides at Ternery Pool. A footpath winds back through agricultural land past the eastern hide. To see more of the area it is possible to start on this route but keep on past Ternery Pool to a footpath running north towards The Wood, a small copse, and the grassland near Camber Castle before retracing steps and picking up the track which runs past and overlooks the Long and Narrow Pits, back to Rye Harbour. This route totals 5.5 miles (9 km).

Pett Level and Pools can be easily overlooked from an unclassified road running from Winchelsea Beach to Cliff End immediately behind the seawall. To reach this, follow the A259 towards Winchelsea and turn left just after crossing the River Brede, 2 miles (3 km) from Rye on the road to Winchelsea Beach. The Pools are near to the western end. Park here and climb up on the seawall to get a good view of the Levels, beach and sea.

Calendar

Resident: Little and Great Crested Grebes, Grey Heron, Gadwall, Ruddy Duck, Tufted Duck, Sparrowhawk, Oystercatcher, Ringed Plover, Redshank, Stock Dove, Barn and Little Owl, Green Woodpecker, Tree Sparrow, Goldfinch, Linnet, Reed and Corn Buntings.

December–February: Divers, Shelduck, Wigeon, Eider, Scaup, Goldeneye, Smew, Hen Harrier, Merlin, Water Rail, Golden and Grey Plovers, Sanderling, Dunlin, Snipe, Long-eared and Short-eared Owls, Rock Pipit, Fieldfare, Brambling, Snow Bunting.

March–May: Gannet, Brent Goose, Garganey, scoters, Avocet, Bar-tailed Godwit, Whimbrel, Common Sandpiper, Arctic and Great Skuas, Mediterranean, Little and Glaucous Gulls, Sandwich and Black Terns, Cuckoo, Yellow Wagtail, Black Redstart, Wheatear, Sedge and Reed Warblers, Whitethroat, Willow Warbler, Firecrest, rarities.

June–July: Sandwich, Roseate, Common and Little Terns, Turtle Dove, Wheatear, rarities.

August–November: Garganey, Marsh Harrier, Hobby, Peregrine, Little Ringed Plover, Knot, Little and Temminck's Stints, Pectoral and Curlew Sandpipers, Ruff, Black-tailed Godwit, Spotted Redshank, Greenshank, Green and Wood Sandpipers, Grey Phalarope, rarer waders, Arctic Skua, Little Gull, Black Tern, Turtle Dove, Grey Wagtail, Black Redstart, Redstart, Whinchat, Stonechat, Ring Ouzel, warblers, Firecrest, Spotted and Pied Flycatchers, Bearded Tit, finches, Lapland Bunting.

2 HASTINGS COUNTRY PARK   OS 199
TQ 81/911

Habitat
This unusual area lies between Fairlight and Hastings. It comprises out-crops of sandstone plus sandstone seams which are mixed with bands of clay. The cliffs are therefore very unstable and large cliff-falls occur every year. Where they are more stable, large ledges are to be found. There are three narrow glens each covered by woodland or scrub alongside a ghyll stream. Joining them along the cliff-top are areas of bracken, bramble, gorse and open fields. The foreshore is a mixture of sand and mud with some rocky outcrops. The park is managed by Hastings Borough Council.

Species
Sheltered from most winds, the glens can be relatively mild and it is not surprising that a few insectivorous migrants winter here, in most years one or two Chiffchaffs and a Firecrest can be found. The latter often searches through the ivy, which covers many of the trees, along with parties of tits which can include Marsh and Long-tailed Tits, Treecreepers and Nuthatches. In the woodland, Tawny Owls are setting up territories and it is possible to find any of the three woodpeckers although Green is the most frequently seen. With such a range of crevices on the cliffs, Black Redstarts can be found on migration, and used to winter here. While most are dull females or immatures, some-times a well-marked male with a sharply black face and a large white wing panel can be seen. In recent years Dartford warblers have win-tered. The cliffs also provide resting and roosting places for the

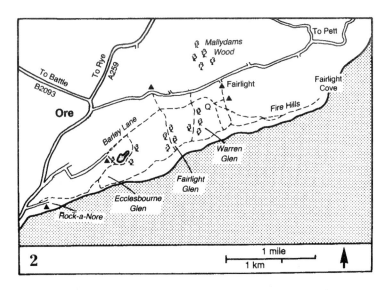

Cormorants which feed offshore, and Fulmars begin to prospect for breeding ledges in December. Small flocks of Eider and scoter can usually be found offshore, but generally few other birds are regular on the sea. When a strong south or southeast wind blows divers, auks, Kittiwakes and a few Gannets may pass by. These are usually best seen from Fairlight Cove. With virtually no access to the foreshore the small number of waders there are difficult to see, but up to 35 Purple Sandpipers and Oystercatchers, and over 100 Turnstone, may be feeding there.

The first signs of spring migration are at sea in late February and early March when divers and Brent Geese fly northeast along the coast. Black Redstarts are one of the first migrants to arrive at the Park, and the Firecrests become more obvious. Chiffchaffs emerge from the woodland glens and begin to sing in early March, although it is not clear if these are new arrivals. Because Fairlight is on a bulge midway between the first-rate seawatching headlands of Beachy Head and Dungeness, a strong southeasterly pushes a wide variety of seabirds, duck and waders quite close inshore. April and May in particular produce movements of Arctic Skuas and Terns, together with the odd Roseate Tern and summer plumaged Black-throated Diver. The main problem is to get a low enough vantage point — the most accessible cliff-top area is between Fire Hills and Fairlight, whilst Rock-a-Nore to the west is also good. As spring proceeds, a steady trickle of Wheatears, Whinchats, warblers, Cuckoos and other migrants pass through this area. Unusual species can appear, although the amount of cover may make them difficult to find. A Hoopoe, Ring Ouzel or Pied Flycatcher might be encountered, while Hobby and Marsh Harrier have been seen overhead.

Many summer migrants breed here, including Whitethroats and Willow Warblers in the open, scrubby areas, while Turtle Doves, Garden Warblers, Blackcaps, Chiffchaffs and Spotted Flycatchers can be found in the woodlands. Nightingales also occur from time to time. Other typical scrub- and gorse-loving species such as Yellowhammers and Linnets can be seen singing from their open perches and Stonechats breed on the cliff-tops. In the old trees in the glens, Tawny Owls breed; their endearing and vociferous young, still covered in a cloak of down, can often be spotted in late June staring down from high branches. Sparrowhawks and Kestrels also hunt the area in summer, the latter using the updraughts created by the cliffs. Often out of sight on the cliff-crevices are 30 or more pairs of Fulmars and up to 100 pairs of breeding Herring Gulls. Usually one or two pairs of Lesser Black-backed Gulls are there too. Cormorants breed between Rock-a-Nore and Fairlight Glen: the former is the best place to watch Fulmars. In some years the parachuting songflight of Rock Pipits can be seen and heard from the cliff-tops.

Autumn is a fascinating time with many common migrants passing through in good numbers. If there is a touch of easterly in the wind, especially between late August and early October, a wide range of scarcer species drop in. Redstarts, Pied and Spotted Flycatchers, Tree Pipits and Reed Warblers are among the earlier species. Later on, the harsh chuckle of Ring Ouzels, the sharp call of Firecrests mixed with the thin notes of Goldcrests and quivering Black Redstarts on the cliff-top fence may provide a most rewarding walk. Strong southeasterly to southwesterly winds can bring passing seabirds well inshore; Arctic Skuas, hordes of Kittiwakes, Gannets, auks and divers can pass by especially late in the autumn. Among the raptors which have been seen recently are Black Kite, Honey Buzzard, Buzzard, Osprey, Peregrine and Hobby. October and early November mornings can bring substantial movements of Chaffinches, Bramblings, Goldfinches, Linnets and Siskins, even a few Crossbills. Their calls can be confusing, however, especially when mixed flocks pass rapidly overhead. As the leaves fall so the woodpeckers again become obvious, and then it is worth looking for both Lesser and Greater Spotted.

Timing

The best birdwatching is undoubtedly to be had during the migration periods of April to early June and again from August to October. Light winds in the eastern sector from south through to northeast bring the best range of migrants, but it is essential to be out early in the morning. The Country Park attracts hordes of visitors, especially on fine weekends, so disturbance of all open areas can be severe by mid-morning. Later in the day many of the warblers, chats and flycatchers will be inside the woodlands, and then they demand patience if they are to be found. Another good site for migrants is the overgrown quarry (Q on the map) southwest of the Fairlight car parks. Seawatching is not ideal, for one looks out southeast, ie. directly into the light for the morning, and it can be difficult to find a good, sheltered position, but it is sometimes productive.

Access

About 1.5 miles (2.4 km) from Hastings seafront, in the centre of Ore, an unclassified road leaves the A259 to the right; it is signposted to Hastings Country Park. Two good car parks are found on this road, one about 0.6 mile (1 km) from the A259, near to the Wireless Tower, and the other 0.75 mile (1.2 km) further on near Fairlight Church. For Ecclesbourne Glen, there is a new car park along Barley Lane, 1 mile (1.6 km) northeast of the seafront; follow the signs for Shear Barn Caravan Park. From here, footpaths to the south take the walker down to the maze of coastal paths, some of which pass through the wooded glens. A full round walk, including all the glens and the cliff-top path, totals approximately 5 miles (8 km) and is strenuous walking. As some of the paths are very steep, they can be slippery after rain. Under these conditions good boots are essential.

Calendar

Resident: Cormorant, Sparrowhawk, Kestrel, Stock Dove, Tawny Owl, Green and Great Spotted Woodpeckers, Nuthatch, Treecreeper, Yellowhammer, Long-tailed and Marsh Tits.

December–February: Fulmar, Eider, Oystercatcher, Purple Sandpiper, Turnstone, auks, Fieldfare, Redwing, Chiffchaff.

March–May: Red- and Black-throated Divers, Gannet, Brent Goose, Hobby, Peregrine, Whimbrel, skuas, Kittiwake, terns, Cuckoo, Hoopoe, Rock Pipit, Yellow wagtail, Redstart, Stonechat, Whinchat, Wheatear, *Sylvia* and *Phylloscopus* warblers, Firecrest, Linnet, Yellowhammer.

June–July: Fulmar, Lesser Black-backed Gull, Turtle Dove, Spotted Flycatcher.

August–November: Hobby, skuas, terns, Lesser Spotted Woodpecker, Tree and Meadow Pipits, Grey and Yellow Wagtails, Black Redstart, Redstart, Whinchat, Stonechat, Ring Ouzel, Redwing, migrant warblers, Goldcrest, Firecrest, Spotted and Pied Flycatchers, Tree Sparrow, Brambling, Goldfinch, Siskin, Linnet, Redpoll.

3 BEWL WATER

OS 188
TQ 68/33

Habitat

Bewl Water is the largest reservoir in any south coast county of England. In area it covers 770 acres (312 ha) and it was completed in 1975; thus many of the trees and shrubs planted around its perimeter are still young. However, existing woodlands along the northern shore of Hook Straight and south of the dam provide an additional habitat. On the grass margins some patches of scrub have started to develop and adjacent to the reservoir is a wide range of farmland. With such a wide range of habitats, it is perhaps not surprising that 212 species have been recorded to date, and new species are continually added. Recent additions to the site list have included Marsh Harrier, Ring-necked Duck, Tawny Pipit and Blackpoll Warbler.

Water levels drop a little in summer and autumn, so exposing gravelly or muddy margins. This fluctuation results in relatively poor condi-

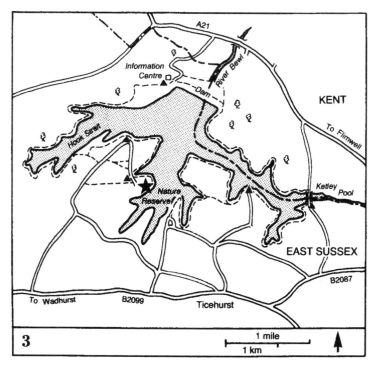

KENT

To Flimwell

Information
Centre

River Bewl

Dam

Hook Street

Nature
Reserve

Ketley Pool

EAST SUSSEX

B2087

To Wadhurst   B2099   Ticehurst

3

1 mile
1 km

tions for marginal vegetation, although this has been encouraged in the
nature reserve, managed by the Sussex Wildlife Trust. Apart from the
reserve, the reservoir is a major water sport area and it is managed by
Southern Water.

Species

Wildfowl are the main attraction in winter. Up to 1,000 Mallard, 1,500
Coot and 1,500 Canada Geese are present, and these draw in a good
range of other species. Among the dabbling duck, Wigeon are prominent, sometimes feeding on water plants, but often grazing on short,
bankside grass. In a normal winter, some 300 to 400 birds are usual, but
numbers can easily double in cold spells. Gadwall have been increasing in numbers throughout southern England during the last decade
and over 200 have been seen here. Their upright, rather delicate shape,
floating high on the water, is reminiscent of a Wigeon, but it is slightly
larger and has a longer neck. Small groups of Teal feed along the tide-
line, but only a few Shoveler and Pintail are present. Over the years,
many diving duck have visited the reservoir, but because it is relatively
deep, the species such as Tufted Duck and Pochard which are bottom
feeders, are relatively few in number and total fewer than 200 of each.
Up to ten Goldeneye, mainly females, join with them. Midwinter usually brings interesting waterfowl: a few Smew and Goosander provide a
very wintry sight, especially the predominantly white males. Many of
the Great Crested Grebes which breed here appear to remain for the
winter and, unusually, few others join them. In severe weather rarer
grebes may join them, particularly Red-necked. This often also brings in
a Black-throated or Red-throated Diver or possibly a Bittern. However,

if very cold weather persists, the reservoir can virtually freeze over and most waterfowl have to leave. A small flock of Cormorants is sometimes present and their smaller, more slender relative, the Shag, sometimes occurs; exceptionally up to ten may appear.

In general, other species are relatively unobtrusive. Flocks of Fieldfare and Redwing occur each year, but they are usually in the fields or hedgerows which are adjacent to the reservoir. A few hundred Lapwing may come down to the water's edge to bathe. Sometimes, too, a Sparrowhawk can be glimpsed flying low and fast.

Spring's approach is first noted by the wintering ducks slipping away, while the Mallard and grebes start to display. By the end of March, the first Chiffchaff is singing from the woodland or calling loudly from the shoreline willows. Soon Willow Warblers are in, singing their liquid cascade of notes from the top of bushes. They find the mixture of grass, scrub and taller bushes particularly attractive and over 100 pairs breed. Also from this area many Yellowhammers and Reed Buntings utter their

Osprey

high-pitched songs, and by late April Whitethroats, often dancing in their songflight, start to join in. The woodland provides a very different bird community. Both Blackcaps and, in May and June, Garden Warblers confusingly sing from similar areas, although the latter prefers thick scrub edges. From within the woods, thin songs of Treecreepers and Goldcrests emerge, sometimes also confusingly similar, especially when Goldcrests are not in full voice. Mid May sees the first Spotted Flycatchers and Turtle Doves to seal the arrival of the summer visitors. On the water, migrants are also obvious. First, in April, hirundines pass through and if cold, windy weather persists, thousands may be down, feeding. Late in the month and through May there is usually a passage of Common and Arctic Terns, and a few Little Gulls and Black Terns. Sometimes, particularly in a northeasterly wind, Whimbrel, Curlew or other passage waders which are normally passing off the coast may fly over or drop down for a few hours. Breeding waterfowl are not particularly numerous, although Great Crested and Little Grebes, Canada Geese and a few Tufted Duck and Pochard try. Success tends to be poor due to a combination of fluctuating water levels and natural factors. Sometimes a pair or two of Teal remain for the summer.

By late July and August, many of the duck are going into eclipse plumage and sitting out on the exposed mud margins. The occasional Garganey is difficult to spot. This area attracts passing waders, so a few Little Ringed Plovers and Green and Common Sandpipers soon appear. During August and September a wider range may be seen, with Greenshank being very vocal. During this time, migrant passerines are moving through, but numbers of warblers and Whinchats are small. Yellow, Pied and later Grey Wagtails are very obvious, feeding on insects in the reservoir margins; this provides an excellent opportunity to look at the similarities and differences between them. Insects attract Swifts and hirundines and also a few Black and Common Terns most autumns. Bewl Water is one of the best places to see Ospreys in the region. Three or four pass through each autumn, mainly mid August to mid September; sometimes they remain for a week or more. A Hobby, too, is quite likely to be seen. A flock of 11 Little Egrets in August 1996 is perhaps not surprising, given their dramatic increase in the southeast. By late October, other waders start to appear, such as Dunlin, Snipe and Grey Plover. At this time, finch flocks are noticeable, particularly Goldfinches and Chaffinches, but early morning movements bring Siskins, Redpolls or Linnets.

An occasional Swallow or House Martin remains into November. That month can bring some remarkable movements of sea or coastal birds. This takes place in northeast winds, especially when combined with fog or rain. Every year, several hundred Brent Geese fly over going southwest, sometimes a few stop for an hour or two. Ducks, too, may appear. Red-breasted Mergansers and both Velvet and Common Scoter have been seen in recent years. It is well worth looking out for other storm bound birds such as Leach's Petrel or unusual grebes. Around the edge of the reservoir, finch, tit and thrush flocks can still be very obvious, but they are starting to seek sheltered feeding areas by then.

Timing

With such a large area and with its diversity of habitats, Bewl Water is worth a visit at any time of year. However, birds can be difficult to find at times, especially in strong winds. Using the long-distance footpaths around the reservoir, it is usually possible to leave behind the many visitors and just encounter the odd fisherman. Early morning is best at migration times. Severe winter weather can bring unusual waterbirds in, but the reservoir can freeze over.

Access

The main access point lies on the A21, 3 miles (5 km) north of Flimwell and 1.25 miles (2 km) south of Lamberhurst. This leads into a pay-barrier car park near the visitor centre. Here can be found information leaflets, toilets and other facilities. It is possible for the active to walk almost all of the 15 miles (24 km) of shoreline and this provides excellent views of all the habitats. There are very few other access points available by car. It is possible to stop at the causeway over Ketley Pool, but the best alternative is to take Wards Lane off the B2099, 2 miles (3 km) west of Ticehurst and follow this narrow lane a similar distance to a small car park in a quarry. From here, it is a short distance down to the public hide which overlooks the mouth of the Sussex Trust's nature reserve. A short walk north from this along the shoreline path will reach toilets and a longer walk of 2.5 miles (4 km) will provide a view over Hook Straight, another good area for waterbirds in winter.

Calendar

Resident: Little and Great Crested Grebes, Canada Geese, Teal, Pochard, Tufted Duck, Sparrowhawk, Tawny Owl, Great Spotted Woodpecker, Mistle Thrush, Yellowhammer, Reed Bunting.

December–February: Scarce divers and grebes, Cormorant, Shag, Wigeon, Gadwall, Shoveler, Goldeneye, Smew, Goosander, Lapwing, Siskin.

March–May: Osprey, Little Ringed Plover, Whimbrel, Little Gull, Common, Arctic and Black Terns, hirundines, Wheatear, *Sylvia* warblers, Chiffchaff, Willow Warbler.

June–July: Turtle Dove, Swift, Spotted Flycatcher.

August–November: Brent Geese, Garganey, scarce sea ducks, Osprey, Hobby, Little Ringed Plover, Dunlin, Greenshank, Green and Common Sandpipers, other coastal waders, Common and Black Terns, Green Woodpecker, Yellow and Grey Wagtails, Whinchat, Fieldfare, Redwing, passage warblers, finches including Goldfinch, Siskin, Linnet and Redpoll.

4 ASHDOWN FOREST

OS 187 & 188
TQ 42/52 & TQ 43/53

Habitat

The unique and fascinating assemblage of habitats on this 8000 acre (3238 ha) area provides very many walks which are rich in wildlife and extremely attractive. It is the largest heathland in southeastern England with some large patches of heather-dominated heath remaining. However, extensive areas have been invaded by bracken, gorse, birch and pine, while the wetter sections are dominated by moor and cotton grass. Some substantial oak and beech woodlands are found, but elsewhere conifer plantations blanket the ground. One extremely valuable habitat is the ghyll woodland. Many streams run off this high sandstone block, which rises to 715 feet (218 m), and they cut deep valleys through the soft substrata. In places bare sandstone is exposed and the steep slopes have become clothed in woodland; here high humidity provides ideal conditions for many plants which are more typical of western Britain, particularly ferns and mosses. The conflicting uses of the Ashdown Forest commonland are reconciled by the Conservators of Ashdown Forest, who appoint a Clerk and rangers to carry out its day-to-day management.

Species

Open heathland is inhospitable in winter and in severe weather it is often almost birdless. A scurrying Wren under the shelter of gorse or

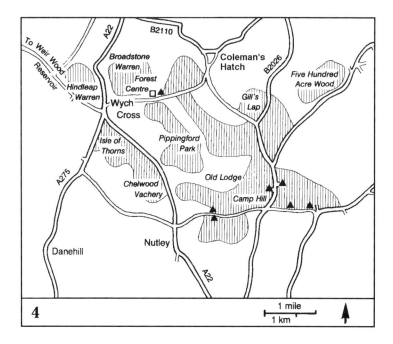

dead bracken, or a small party of tits or Chaffinches venturing out may be all that is seen, apart from a Hen Harrier gently and, apparently, effortlessly quartering the ground. Most of the birds withdraw to the woodlands or the sheltered valleys. In some areas such as the Isle of Thorns or the Sussex Wildlife Trust's Old Lodge Nature Reserve, large flocks of Reed Buntings gather, sometimes 100 or more can be seen in damper zones. The woodland holds large parties of tits including many Marsh and Coal, and a few Long-tailed. After years with good crops of beech-mast, hordes of the larger tits can be found along with Chaffinches and the occasional Brambling, searching through the leaf litter in the beech woodlands. All three woodpeckers are present, although the Great Spotted tends to be the most obvious. Other typical woodland species such as Treecreeper and Nuthatch are common, as are Coal Tit and Goldcrest in the conifers. The warning rattle of Mistle Thrushes or the loud scolding of many species may reveal the presence of a Tawny Owl roosting in an ivy-covered tree or a Sparrowhawk dashing through looking for small birds. In the 1970s Great Grey Shrikes were regular, but numbers have slumped since then and there are now only occasional sightings. Streamside alders often hold flocks of Siskins and Redpolls, and it is here that Lesser Spotted Woodpeckers are most often seen.

Many of the resident passerines start to sing by mid March, but it is not until the end of that month that the first real sign of spring migration can be detected. The weak, onomatopoeic song of the Chiffchaff may then emerge from the woodland. By late April the whole area is transformed into activity. Out on the gorse-dominated heathland the Yellowhammers, which spent the winter on nearby farmland, join with Linnets from Iberia and Whitethroats from south of the Sahara. Stonechats here vary in numbers with perhaps as many as 100 pairs after a series of mild winters, but following severe weather fewer than ten pairs may survive; presently there are about 50 pairs. That real heathland specialist the Dartford Warbler also occurs on the Forest, at the eastern extremity of its current UK range. Up to 30 territories have been recorded in recent years, but like the Stonechat, this species is particularly vulnerable to hard winters, and numbers can crash dramatically. The open heather supports just Meadow Pipits and Skylarks, though migrant Wheatears are most obvious here. At the heathland edge where pine, birch and bracken have encroached can be found many pairs of Willow Warblers and Tree Pipits; the latter usually sing from a high perch rather than undertake their distinctive tail-up parachute songflight. Where over-mature birch, pine, beech or oak with holes are present it is worth listening for the short song of the Redstart. The spectacular males, with shivering flame tails, sing from high up in the trees. Ashdown Forest supports up to 70 pairs of them. At times the sky seems criss-crossed by the trilling songflights of Redpolls, but it is often impossible to decide just how many males are involved. In June a dusk visit may reveal the presence of Nightjars, either hawking around the tree-tops or low over the ground.

Nightjar

For such a large area with many wet flushes, waders are unusually scarce. A few Snipe still hang on, and drumming is heard on calm spring evenings. Up to two pairs of Curlew occasionally breed, their evocative bubbling song, given while almost hanging in the air, provides a real summery experience. Down in the stream valleys it is worth looking for Grey Wagtails, especially where water bubbles over rock, but also keep an eye open for the electric-blue flash of a Kingfisher or the dark, long-tailed whirring Mandarins moving between ponds. Several pairs of Sparrowhawks and Kestrels breed and a glimpse may be had of a passing Buzzard.

Deciduous woodland is always good for birds. Here, in addition to the many commoner species, a few pairs of Hawfinch and about 5 pairs of Wood Warblers are to be found. The former are most obvious in late April and May before the trees are out in leaf and when their sharp 'tschit' can be heard overhead. The latter appear to move around from year to year but the strength of their trilling song can penetrate several hundred yards through woodland. Sometimes a Woodcock can be flushed, jinking away low through the trees but looking like a rufous owl; normally they can only be seen at dusk and dawn during their distinctive roding flight. In some years the coniferous plantations are of interest, for after irruption years a few Crossbills stay to breed or a Firecrest may stop to sing for a few days. While the plantations are young they can support many Blackcaps and Garden Warblers, although once they are older than ten years much of the bird interest disappears.

Initially in autumn the masses of young warblers and tits, and family parties of finches and buntings, provide life everywhere, but soon the summer visitors slip away. A few passage Wheatears and Whinchats are seen, perhaps together with a Hobby stopping off either to chase the local House Martins, or leisurely take dragonflies or large moths. It is fascinating to watch as they clip off the wings of the insects while flying along, leaving them to drift back to earth. By mid October finches are beginning to fly through, especially noticeable are Chaffinches and Siskins, and a short while later early Fieldfares and Redwings start to appear. Then, as the frosts of November set in, so we are left with the winter remnants.

Timing

There is always something to look for in Ashdown Forest, but the spring and early summer is undoubtedly the time for several visits. A beautiful warm and calm spring day is ideal, for then not only are the birds active but the fresh green plant growth is very attractive. On summer weekends it attracts hordes of day visitors, but given the will to walk it should be possible to spend many hours without too much disturbance. An evening visit in summer is most likely to reveal Nightjars and Woodcock. Severe winter weather will probably push many birds out to lower altitudes and is unlikely to force much else in in recompense. Should it be a very dry summer, the forest becomes tinder dry and is at great risk from fires: almost every year serious burns occur. Great care should be taken under these conditions.

Access

Ashdown Forest is crossed by many roads including the A22, A275 and B2026. Perhaps the best place to start a visit, unless arriving early in the morning, is at the Ashdown Forest Centre run by the Conservators. This provides a wealth of background information on the Forest and lies 0.5 mile (0.8 km) along the unclassified road running east from Wych Cross to Coleman's Hatch. There are small parking areas on many of the roads but large car parks, which are good starting points for walks, can be found a few hundred yards east of the Forest Centre and along the roads running east and north of Camp Hill. There are many tracks which enable one to explore the Forest, but there are several large private estates which are not commonland, and also a military training area near Pippingford Park where access is not permitted.

Calendar

Resident: Sparrowhawk, Buzzard, Woodcock, Stock Dove, Tawny Owls, woodpeckers, Grey Wagtail, Nuthatch, Hawfinch, Redpoll, Reed Bunting.

December–February: Hen Harrier, possibly Great Grey Shrike, Siskin.

March–May: Mandarin, Snipe, Curlew, Cuckoo, Kingfisher, Tree Pipit, Redstart, Whinchat, Stonechat, Wheatear, Dartford and other *Sylvia* warblers, Chiffchaff, Willow Warbler, Spotted Flycatcher, Linnet Yellowhammer.

June–July: Turtle Dove, Nightjar, Crossbill.

August–November: Hobby, Lapwing, Stonechat, Wheatear, Fieldfare and Redwing (November), passage warblers, Brambling, Goldfinch, Siskin.

5 PEVENSEY LEVELS AND PEVENSEY BAY

OS 199
TQ 60/70 & 61/71

Habitat

Not long ago the 9884 acres (4000 ha) of the Pevensey Levels were unimproved wet grassland with a maze of floristically rich ditches. Such areas still exist within this area but substantial sections have been converted to cereal production, by pumped drainage systems, or otherwise 'improved'. The dyke system still contains many nationally rare water-plants, particularly pondweeds, and is very good for several groups of insects and molluscs. Many of the dykes contain narrow fringing reedbeds and, to add to the overall interest, many also have scattered large hawthorn bushes next to them; in some areas quite dense hedgerows have developed. Pevensey Bay has a narrow strip of sand exposed at low water and is backed by the broad shingle area of the Crumbles and a narrow shingle beach from the village to Pevensey Bay to Bexhill. The southern part of the Levels include a NNR wardened by English Nature and a Sussex Wildlife Trust reserve.

Species

The Levels used to support many thousands of Lapwing, Snipe and Golden Plover in the winter months, but recent survey work has shown that numbers average about 1,800, 440 and 150 respectively. Numbers may increase if the weather becomes more severe further north or east, but the key determinant of numbers is the extent of shallow winter flooding, which today is less frequent and extensive than it probably used to be. They are spread widely over plough, winter cereal and grass-land fields, but the Snipe tend to be concentrated in 'hot spots' where there is a mixture of shallow water and marshy vegetation or leftover stubbles. The lucky observer may flush a Jack Snipe from such locations. Occasionally other waders such as Dunlin, Curlew, Redshank and Ruff may take advantage of the wetter areas. Look for Little Grebes in the open channels on Pevensey Bridge Levels. The fields within 0.5 mile (0.8 km) of the sea sometimes attract a few waders more regularly seen

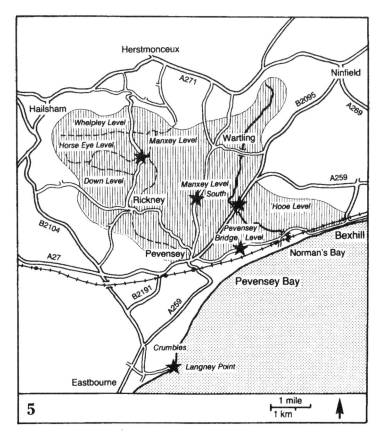

on the shore, such as Ringed or Grey Plover, Bar-tailed Godwits or Turnstone. Ducks tend to be relatively scarce with only a few hundred Teal, Wigeon and Mallard being regular, a few Shelduck, Shoveler, Gadwall and Pintail may join them. The major drainage channel for the eastern part is Wallers Haven, which discharges to the sea at Norman's Bay; the water level on this is high enough to attract small numbers of Tufted Duck and Pochard, sometimes a Goldeneye, too. It also acts as a refuge for many of the dabbling duck if they are disturbed.

Hard winter weather can produce exciting birdwatching; Bewick's and Whooper Swans have been recorded but it is much more likely that the visitor will come across some of the 160 or so Mute Swans that winter here. Geese are more fickle, but White-fronts, Bean and Pink-footed Geese have been recorded. Severe weather may also drive a flock of real Barnacle Geese to Pevensey from their Dutch wintering grounds; such a pleasant sight after so many escaped birds which now dot our landscape. Geese and wild swans are mostly seen on Horse Eye and Pevensey Bridge Levels. A few Brent Geese graze the Levels in most winters.

A sudden mass or panic flight of birds on the Levels provides a clue that a raptor is about. In winter several Hen Harriers, Sparrowhawks and Merlins and Short-eared Owls hunt the area, with an occasional Buzzard, Goshawk or Peregrine being seen as well. The Short-eared

Owls do not cause such a panic, for several can be seen quartering the fields which have rough grass or rushes in them. Little Owls may be flushed from the hedgerows and a dusk visit could reveal a floating Barn Owl. Until their sharp national decline in the 1980s, wintering Great Grey Shrikes were regularly seen sitting on the top of bushes, the sharp whiteness of their underparts standing out brightly against a dull winter's day. To feed this range of birds of prey there must be plenty of mammals and passerine birds. On some days every field with short vegetation seems to be alive with Redwings and Fieldfares, plus the resident thrushes. As the weather gets colder and Redwings weaker, it is not unusual to see a Kestrel or Sparrowhawk drop onto one of these unfortunate birds. Small flocks of Greenfinches, Linnets, Yellowhammers and Corn Buntings are found, especially in the northern parts of the Levels. Near to the beach a few Stonechats find food and shelter. The shingle, sand and breakwaters add another dimension, for here 1,000 to 3,000 Dunlin, Ringed Plovers and Turnstone winter with a few Sanderling and Purple Sandpipers, on the sandstone rocks near Bexhill. On the sea Red-throated and the scarcer Black-throated Divers are regular, along with Razorbills, Guillemots, Eider and Red-breasted Merganser. Many other species occur as irregular visitors, such as Great Northern Diver, Slavonian Grebe and scoters. Gulls find Langney Point particularly attractive, a sewage outfall offshore and fishing boats helping to provide food. As a result, Glaucous and Mediterranean are regular and Iceland and Ring-billed have been seen in recent years.

As spring approaches, the wildfowl and waders start to leave, but the Grey Herons in the three heronries on the Levels start to display and repair their nests. Then, by mid March, Redshank hang on quivering wings and Lapwings twist and turn in display, just as the first Wheatears and Chiffchaff make landfall. Small numbers of most common migrants are seen passing through. Yellow Wagtails are frequent, and in many years one or two Blue-headed Wagtails appear. Garganey are regular but very elusive, and in several recent years a White Stork has been seen. Other scarcer birds noted include Hobbies, Marsh Harrier, Montagu's Harrier, Black Kite, Crane, Purple Heron, Great White Egret and Black-winged Stilt. Exceptional national rarities have been found, such as an Oriental Pratincole a few years ago.

Langney Point is not a good seawatching site in spring, for birds pass far offshore, but a patient observer should see a small percentage of many divers, Brent Geese, scoters, waders, skuas and terns which are flying east. In a northeast wind some of the waders, particularly Whimbrel, will fly inland over the Levels and a small feeding flock might be encountered anywhere on the wetter grasslands. English Nature have raised water levels on part of Pevensey Bridge Levels and flooded a small area. When water levels are just right, this area can attract many migrants: in recent years several Temminck's Stints, and both Pectoral and Broad-billed Sandpipers, have been noted. Regular passage waders include Wood Sandpiper and Spotted Redshank, and up to three Water Pipits have been recorded together in recent years. Breeding communities of particular interest are associated with the wet grassland, the reedy dykes and the thick hawthorn hedgerows. As the area of grassland has decreased so the numbers of breeding Snipe, Redshank and Lapwing have decreased dramatically, and now occur in very small numbers. Yellow Wagtails still occur in moderate numbers, and sometimes Blue-headed Wagtails are also recorded in the spring. In

June, the reedbeds resound with the songs of Sedge and Reed Warblers and to the thin jumble of notes from Reed Buntings, while from the hedges comes the rattle of Lesser Whitethroats and the purr of Turtle Doves. Above the fields Skylarks and Meadow Pipits stake out their territories. It is also worth checking the larger willows near to habitation, for there the now scarce Tree Sparrows find their nesting holes.

By mid June gathering flocks of Lapwings herald the autumn, but it is not until late July that the yellow juvenile Willow Warblers start moving through, and Green Sandpipers can be found on open, muddy cattle drinking places. Thereafter Wheatears, Whitethroats, Whinchats and other common migrants can be seen; Yellow Wagtails gather in flocks of 10 to 20 feeding among the feet of grazing cattle, every now and again circling round uttering their distinctive 'seeip' calls. By late September thousands of Swallows gather to feed over the Levels and seek out a reedbed in which to roost, but not before marauding attacks from a late Hobby or a Sparrowhawk. Seawatching at Langney Point is better in autumn than in spring, strong southwesterlies bring in Great and Arctic Skuas and sometimes a Pomarine, too, or a Manx or Sooty Shearwater.

As mid October is reached so the summer visitors have nearly all left and the westward movement of Meadow Pipits, Chaffinches, Goldfinches, Linnets and sometimes Siskins, provide notice of winter's approach. This is soon confirmed by the thin calls of Redwings as they seek out the ripening haws.

Timing

This large area can provide fascinating birdwatching at any time of the year, but it needs plenty of time to get the best out of it. In winter it is at its best during or just after a severe spell when the chance increases of more duck, geese, swans and raptors being present. Throughout migration periods and the breeding season it is best to arrive as early as possible so that the passerines are at their most active, but passage raptors tend to wait until the day has warmed up a little. A visit to Langney Point may reveal birds on the beach or the sea at any time of day, but it is usually best when the tide is full. To see birds well on the water or feeding around the off-shore outfall, a bright but cloudy day is best. Seawatching is best in strong winds, southeast in spring or south to southwest in autumn.

Access

The A259 connects Eastbourne and Bexhill/Hastings and runs through the centre of Pevensey Levels. However, this is a fast and dangerous road, so the area is best explored from the minor roads which radiate from the roundabout just east of the traffic lights in Pevensey village. The southern section is reached by the narrow road to Norman's Bay: this runs for 2.5 miles (4 km) past good, often wet, grass fields and reedy dykes. There are two access points over the railway line to the beach and it is worth a check, especially in winter. It is not worth proceeding to Bexhill, but coming back to the A259. Then cross the roundabout onto the other minor road, signposted Herstmonceux and Wartling. The Wartling road provides good views over Manxey Level South. However, the narrow winding road which leads via Rickney to Herstmonceux gives the best range of habitats, and ends up at Horse Eye Level before climbing off the Levels. Here there is a good bridleway 3 miles (4.5 km) long which is often well worth walking.

Langney Point is isolated from the rest of the Levels and is on the outskirts of Eastbourne. There is a large roundabout at the southern end of Willingdon Drive, by the swimming pool, from which a road is signposted to Langney Point. But note that vehicular access is not allowed beyond this point. The seawall however does give an excellent and comfortable vantage point. The large shingle area and its wet gravel pits inland are private.

Calendar

Resident: Grey Heron, Mute Swan, Sparrowhawk, Ringed Plover, Lapwing, Snipe, Redshank, Little Owl, Meadow Pipit, Skylark, Mistle Thrush, Yellowhammer, Reed and Corn Buntings.

December–February: Divers (on the sea), Cormorant, Bewick's and Whooper Swans, White-fronted (and other) Geese, Brent Goose, Shelduck, Wigeon, Teal, Shoveler, Pintail, Pochard, Tufted Duck, Eider and Red-breasted Merganser (on sea), Hen Harrier, Merlin, Peregrine, Golden and Grey Plovers, Sanderling, Dunlin, Ruff, Snipe, Jack Snipe, Curlew, Turnstone, Glaucous Gull, auks, Stock Dove, Barn and Short-eared Owls, Kingfisher, Stonechat, Fieldfare, Redwing.

March–May: Gannet, Brent Goose and scoters (at sea), Garganey, Marsh Harrier, Avocet, Temminck's Stint, Spotted Redshank, Wood Sandpiper, Black-tailed and Bar-tailed Godwit, Whimbrel, skuas, Mediterranean Gull, Kittiwake and terns (at sea), Cuckoo, Yellow Wagtail, Whinchat, Wheatear, warblers, Goldfinch, Linnet, possible rarities such as White Stork.

June–July: Turtle Dove, Sedge and Reed Warblers, Lesser Whitethroat.

August–November: Passing seabirds, Buzzard, Hobby, Greenshank, Green and Common Sandpipers, Tawny Pipit, Yellow and Grey Wagtails, Whinchat, Wheatear, Redstart, migrant warblers.

6 BEACHY HEAD

OS 199
TQ 49/59 & 69

Habitat

The impressive chalk cliffs of Beachy Head rise to 535 ft (163 m) and protrude several miles out into the English Channel, these features undoubtedly contributing greatly to the impressive range of birds seen on, or from them. The cliffs are still eroding actively, which limits the number of safe breeding ledges for seabirds, but from the sea they are sparkling white. At their base is a ridged platform of chalk 200–300 yds (250 m) in width, which is exposed at low water. Originally the whole of the land surface was chalk downland and chalk heath of outstanding quality, but this has mostly disappeared under the plough. Some, how-

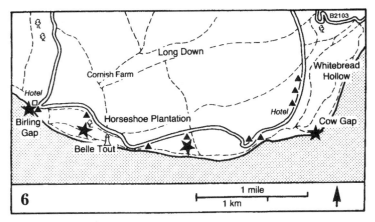

ever, remains, and with the demise of intensive rabbit and sheep grazing, other areas have seen an invasion of scrub and, more recently, ash
and sycamore. The grassland still supports a wide variety of orchids and
other rare *calcicole* plants. Eastbourne Borough Council has been
restoring sheep grazing to the downland, and this is having a greatly
beneficial effect on the chalk plants. Butterflies include chalkhill and
adonis blue, brown argus and marbled white. In years with large numbers of clouded yellows, the grass is dotted with flickering primrose yellow. Much of the grassland is concentrated in a narrow band on the
cliff-top, an area under substantial public pressure as well as cliff erosion.

The scrub varies in density; in some areas such as Whitebread
Hollow, it is very dense indeed. A small plantation, Horseshoe Plantation,
of sycamore, ash, beech and elm at Belle Tout is the only woodland by
the cliff top between Beachy Head lighthouse and Birling Gap, though
the October 1987 storm wreaked havoc with it, many passerines make
for it and scarce or rare migrants are often seen there. Just to the west
of Birling Gap, along the South Downs Way, mature gardens provide
another patch of cover, including wind-clipped trees, and here, too,
migrants seek food and shelter. Other patches of scrub which are well
worth checking are north of the coast road to the west of Beachy Head
Hotel and on Long Down, the latter having the great advantage of being
away from most of the public pressure! The downland to the east of
Belle Tout is managed by the Eastbourne Borough Council, and that to
the west by the National Trust.

Species

Cold winter winds sweep across the open, rolling downland and birds
are at a premium. An occasional Peregrine, Merlin or Hen Harrier slips
over it, putting to flight small groups of Corn Buntings and Yellowhammers, while Fulmars return to their breeding ledges during calm weather in December. If severe weather occurs, substantial movements of
duck, auks or divers may be seen. Spring is slow to arrive, the first signs
include an early March movement eastwards at sea of Red-throated
Divers, followed shortly afterwards by Brent Geese. Mid-month sees the
first summer visitors making their landfall, Wheatears and Chiffchaffs
joining with Black Redstarts and Firecrests by the end of the month.
Each day in April and May brings a new batch of migrants. Light winds

between southwest and east are the best for passerine migrants, with commoner warblers arriving on the more westerly winds, but scarcer species usually need an easterly component. Up to four or five Ring Ouzels, one or two Pied Flycatchers, Redstarts and Wood Warblers and the occasional Hoopoe may help to make a visit memorable. From the low scrub the scolding of breeding Stonechat and Whitethroat can be heard, while from the dense scrub emerges the rattle of Lesser Whitethroats, the full, deep song of the Nightingale, or the hurried notes of the Blackcap.

Rarities are by definition very few indeed, but Beachy Head always attracts its share; every year several Serins fly over or sing for a day before moving on. Other continental overshoots such as Alpine Swifts, Bee-eaters and shrikes have been seen in several years, often not appearing before June. The range of raptors seen most years includes Osprey, Hobby, Marsh Harrier and Buzzard, while Montagu's Harrier and Honey Buzzard sometimes occur. Most raptors pass straight through, undoubtedly the gleaming cliffs are visible from a great dis-

Pied Flycatcher

tance over the Channel and therefore attract such migrants. If a south or east wind blows strongly, eyes turn to the sea; a Force 6 or above southeasterly is ideal. Then the up-Channel passage is pushed towards the south coast of England, and it becomes more concentrated the further east one goes. The species involved change as the season progresses. Throughout April and early May a steady drift of white Sandwich Terns passes by; the most common flock size is three. The significance of this is not known, but has led to speculation about their breeding pattern. At this time both Great and Arctic Skuas pass through, usually in small numbers, but up to 20 and 50 a day respectively can occur: beware of jumping to conclusions about the latter, as Whimbrel beating low into the wind can look remarkably skua-like.

In mid April the first main spring sea passage starts with lines of dark, fast-flying Common Scoters skimming the water, peak days bring up to 12,000 although 1,000 is more normal. Late in the month small numbers of Velvet Scoter may join in with these flocks, or come through by themselves; beware of a flash of pale on the underwing of Common Scoter which might lead to confusion, but the sharp white secondaries of

Velvet Scoter are very distinct when seen. Also late in the month a huge, and very short-lived, movement of Bar-tailed Godwits takes place, between 3,000 and 5,000 pass in five or six days in the period between 20 and 28 April. Many of the flocks are well out to sea, but in those closer inshore, the difference between the smaller, brick-red males and the pale, long-billed females can be seen clearly. From then, and through the first two weeks of May, the passage is at its greatest intensity and diversity. Thousands of 'Commic' Terns move by, as do small flocks of Black Terns and Little Gulls. Increasingly, Mediterranean Gulls are seen passing and loafing around Birling Gap. However, most eyes are seeking the less usual birds, in particular the odd Roseate Tern or Pomarine Skuas. Up to 100 of the latter are seen annually, usually in small groups of two to four, but sometimes 20 or more. Such a flock has a very distinct appearance — heavy birds, many with solid tails, strongly beating their way east, the flock slowly changing shape from a line back to an irregular lump as they pass by. Virtually any scarce seabird might pass by, but winds need to go more south or southwest and be of gale force for shearwaters to appear.

Sea passage slowly trickles to an end by the second week of June. Then we are left with Fulmars drifting along the cliffs to their breeding ledges, the barking of breeding Herring Gulls and the excited yapping of Jackdaws. Sometimes a few Kittiwakes breed, but they can often be seen offshore. Only one or two pairs of Rock Pipits breed, but most of the passerines are in the scrub, the warblers and Stonechats being most obvious. Beachy Head supports high densities of Whitethroats and Lesser Whitethroats as well as Yellowhammers, Corn Buntings and Linnets. The Nightingales soon stop singing and the croak of alarm is about all that reveals their presence. In the rougher grassland Meadow Pipits and a few Skylarks hang on, while here the Green Woodpeckers hunt for ants.

Autumn comes rapidly as August appears. Beachy Head has been shown to be the most important departure point for the *Sylvia* warblers (Blackcap, Garden Warbler, Whitethroat and Lesser Whitethroat) in Britain. Thousands of them gather to feed on the energy-rich and prolific elderberries and blackberries. However, the first birds to show are Willow Warblers in early to mid August — up to 1,500 dot the area moving through the scrub in waves. After that Whitethroats, Garden Warblers and Lesser Whitethroats predominate, followed by Chiffchaffs and Blackcaps in September and October. It is an exciting time when soon after first light the scrub resounds to a range of 'tacs' and 'hooets' from warblers. They do sometimes include scarce species such as Barred or Melodious Warblers, but the sheer number of birds and amount of cover can make finding them hard work. September is a particularly good time, for then Redstarts, Pied and Spotted Flycatchers, Whinchats, Wheatears and Yellow Wagtails are usually prominent, and scarce birds such as Wryneck, Red-backed Shrike, Tawny Pipit and Ortolan Bunting are regularly seen, although the last two may take some finding among the paths, stubble and grass fields inland. Raptors move out from Beachy Head in autumn, so Marsh Harrier, Osprey and Hobby are seen each year. Sea passage is poor although a few skuas, terns, even a Sooty Shearwater and other species pass by.

October is a month of anticipation, as it is at many coastal headlands. Many of the common species have passed through by then and an impressive list of rarities has been noted. Horseshoe Plantation attracts many of them. Yellow-browed Warblers are regular, while that diminutive gem Pallas's Warbler might be seen. In the hawthorn scrub, Ring Ouzels feed, while the sharp, positive call of Firecrests penetrate through the weaker notes of the many Goldcrests. Black Redstarts and Stonechats perch out in the open, sometimes five or ten flicking around together. Overhead the Tree Pipits and Yellow and Grey Wagtails have given way to finches; substantial numbers of Brambling, Siskin and Redpoll are mixed with commoner finches and Meadow Pipits. Late autumn has huge movements of Swallows and House Martins, 10,000 a day are not unusual. If a northerly wind blows many find food below the cliff-tops. Up to 10,000 Woodpigeons may gather and fly out to sea, while winter thrushes and Robins come in. By mid November the leaves have been blown away and migrants have wisely left, leaving the few winter birds to eke out a living.

Timing

This area amply repays a visit in spring, summer and autumn. At all times the early morning is best, due both to the birds' activity and because few sightseers are around. Most species move by offshore in the morning, so by 10.00 am to 11.00 am it can be very quiet. However, skuas can, and do, fly past at any time of day. When large tern movements take place there can be an upsurge of activity in the evening. To see the greatest range of species, seawatching is best between mid April and mid May, particularly the first two weeks of May. It can be a difficult choice as to whether seawatching or searching the bushes is best.

The autumn passage of passerines is much larger than it is in spring. Apart from the chats, wagtails and pipits, which can be seen for much of the day, most other migrants seem to disappear into the undergrowth by about 10.00 am The strong movement of overflying pipits, wagtails and finches ceases even earlier, so it is only seen for the two or three hours after sunrise. Raptors move through at any stage of the day, but many are seen from late morning to mid-afternoon. It is the weather conditions which dictate the number and species of birds present, so a southeasterly is good but a wind between west to north rarely brings in unusual or scarce species.

Access

Beachy Head is designed to receive people, so access is very good indeed. A loop road runs around Beachy Head from the A259 Sussex coast road, leaving it at Eastdean and returning via the B2103 to the west of Eastbourne. Buses run from Eastbourne seafront to the start of the South Downs Way and the Beachy Head Hotel. Extensive car parks with toilets exist both at the hotel and at the Birling Gap Hotel, while other smaller car parks are dotted along the road from Eastbourne to Birling Gap. The South Downs Way runs the whole length of the cliffs and can be joined at any place; there is a criss-cross of other paths through the cliff-top grass and scrub, so it is easy to explore all parts of it. In such a good area for birds it is wise to visit as many parts as possible, with any part of the scrub being likely to produce something of interest. Access to the farmland is more limited although good footpaths exist and are signposted, the best running north from the disused lighthouse at Belle Tout and then turning right to Long Down at Cornish Farm. For seawatching in spring it is best to sit on the less high cliffs either side of Birling Gap as the birds come in from the southwest, while in autumn Cow Gap is better sited for observations of birds coming from the east.

It must be emphasised that the cliff-edge is extremely dangerous. Do not approach too closely. Also it is easy to get cut off by the tide if walking under the cliff-face. The only access points to the beach between Eastbourne and the River Cuckmere are at Birling Gap and Cow Gap, although the access steps are periodically destroyed as the cliff erodes.

Calendar

Resident: Sparrowhawk, Stock Dove, Green Woodpecker, Rock Pipit, Stonechat, Jackdaw, Yellowhammer, Corn Bunting.

December–February: Fulmar, Hen Harrier, Merlin, Peregrine, finch flocks.

March–May: At sea: Red-throated and Black-throated Diver, Fulmar, Brent Goose, Common and Velvet Scoters, Red-breasted Merganser, Grey Plover, Bar-tailed Godwit, Whimbrel, Pomarine, Arctic and Great Skuas, Mediterranean and Little Gulls, terns and auks. On shore: Osprey, Hobby, Common Sandpiper, Turtle Dove, Hoopoe, Yellow and White Wagtail, Nightingale, Black Redstart, Redstart, Whinchat, Wheatear, warblers, Firecrest, Pied Flycatcher, Serin, rarities.

June–July: Quail, Lesser Whitethroat, Whitethroat, Linnet.

August–November: Sooty Shearwater, Marsh Harrier, Osprey, Hobby, Arctic Skua, Short-eared Owl, Wryneck, Tree Pipit, Yellow and Grey Wagtail, Black Redstart, Ring Ouzel, Fieldfare, Redwing, Sedge and Reed Warblers, commoner warblers, Dartford, Melodious and Yellow browed Warblers, Firecrest, Pied Flycatcher, Red-backed Shrike Brambling, Siskin, Redpoll, rarities.

7 CUCKMERE AND SEAFORD HEAD

OS 199
TV 49/59 & 69

Habitat

The lower reaches of all rivers in Sussex have been canalised and the Cuckmere is no exception. Unusually, a new channel was constructed so cutting off the old meanders, which, fortunately, have been retained. Grazing meadows surround the brackish meanders and the river, while on the eastern side of the valley, adjacent to the shoreline, a scrape which contains shallow brackish water has been excavated. The beach at the mouth of the Cuckmere supports a good range of shingle plants such as sea kale and yellow-horned poppy. To the east lie the chalk cliffs of the Seven Sisters which stretch to Beachy Head, while to the west there is the chalk block of Seaford Head, rising to 282 ft (86 m).

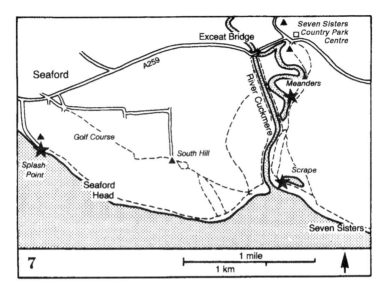

The chalk grassland has a rich flora including a wide range of orchids and a rare umbellifer, the moon carrot. Patches of scrub have developed over this area, particularly on the eastern slope, but sheep grazing has been introduced recently to help keep the grassland in good condition and prevent scrub encroaching further. Inland from the cliff path is a golf course, and further to the east blocks of arable fields. The west of Cuckmere Haven and Seaford Head is a Local Nature Reserve under the management of Lewes District Council, and the land to the east of the meanders is in the Seven Sisters Country Park, managed by the East Sussex County Council.

Species

Most of the interest in winter is concentrated on the Cuckmere Valley, with its wetland and grazing habitats being the attraction. Under normal conditions it attracts reasonable numbers of commoner wildfowl. Several hundred Wigeon graze the meadows, but they take to the meanders for safety when disturbed. Smaller numbers of Teal, Shelduck, Mallard and Tufted Duck are also present, with up to 10 Shoveler or the occasional Goldeneye. Most of the wildfowl are found on the meanders where up to 25 Little Grebes dive for small fish and a dozen Cormorants and Grey Herons look for larger prey. In colder periods much larger numbers of wildfowl are present, and then geese tend to appear on the meadows. Brent, White-fronted and Canada Geese are regular, the last two flying north to roost on Arlington Reservoir 5.5 miles (9 km) away. Sometimes the odd Scaup, Smew, Slavonian Grebe or other scarce waterbirds drop in for a few days. On the beach and the muddy sides of the river, small numbers of Ringed Plovers, Dunlin and other commoner waders forage, and there is usually a wintering Common Sandpiper somewhere along the river.

The meanders attract passerines too; up to 30 Rock Pipits and small numbers of Twite, Meadow Pipits, Yellowhammers and one or two Lapland Bunting, Kingfisher or Stonechat may be located. The patient observer may see, or perhaps more likely hear, the occasional Water

Rail in the bush-fringed dykes along the western side of the river. Kestrels find that the steep sides of the valley provide ideal updraughts to enable them to hang on the wind, while Sparrowhawks flash low across fields. Now Peregrines too are a regular sight, and may be seen in any month of the year.

First signs of spring movements are noted at sea, with Brent Geese and divers moving east. Wheatears, standing boldly upright, and Black Redstarts, tend to be the earliest land migrants, and Firecrests are regular in the bushes on the western side of the valley. By early or mid April small numbers of many migrants can be seen flicking among the patches of scrub on Seaford Head while, in the valley, Yellow and White Wagtails appear and the odd Water/Scandinavian Rock Pipit, coming into their pink summer flush, can be found along the meanders, giving rise to speculation that wintering Rock Pipits may not always be what they seem. The Cuckmere forms a narrow but distinct valley through the Downs and so is a good migration route. In most springs Avocets, Common and Wood Sandpipers and other waders drop into the scrape, while Spoonbills have stopped there on a few occasions. The small pool at Exceat Bridge has proved to be remarkably reliable for Temminck's Stint in mid May; up to seven birds were there in 1993 for example. Little Egrets have now become a regular feature of the valley, with small numbers present in May and up to six in August and September.

Seawatching here is best carried out at Splash Point, at the eastern end of the promenade at Seaford. Because this site is only slightly above beach level and passage birds come close inshore, it can be particularly good for observing terns and skuas. During the last half of April and the first half of May an impressive stream of Bar-tailed Godwit, Whimbrel, 'Commic', Sandwich, Little and Black Terns, Mediterranean and Little Gulls, scoter and Great Arctic and Pomarine Skuas pass by. If your luck is in, there is always the possibility of a Long-tailed Skua in early to mid May! The breakwater at Splash Point seems to attract some of the terns to halt briefly during migration and so give a better chance to separate Arctic from Common Terns than is possible at most seawatching locations. Even so, it is not easy to pick out for certain the Arctic Terns with the partly translucent underside of the wing and the sharply defined narrow black tips to the trailing edge of the primaries. The odd Black Redstart winters around the breakwater and cliffs at Seaford Head too, and visitors in spring and summer will now find some 600 pairs of Kittiwakes on the cliffs.

Small numbers of migrants still trickle through during the first ten days of June. By then the breeding season is well under way with, on Seaford Head, its typical downland scrub species: Whitethroat, Linnet, Yellowhammer and Corn Bunting, singing from prominent songposts on bramble and gorse bushes. From the cliff below can be heard the low chuckle of Fulmars, some 15 pairs of which find a crevice on the crumbling cliff face in which to nest. On the shingle beach one or two pairs of Ringed Plovers attempt to breed with their young seeking security under sea kale from the intense disturbance on an early summer's weekend. Singing Meadow Pipits parachute down onto the grassland, and Skylarks hang for ages high in the sky, but only the odd Yellow Wagtail now remains to breed. Even in the summer Kestrels hunt along the sides of the valley, and Sparrowhawks slip low across the fields from the woodland further north.

Autumn migration time can be very interesting here with many warblers seeking out the scrub on the valley sides and on Seaford Head. An early morning visit, before many people are about, should reveal Willow Warblers flycatching around the bushes where Whitethroats, Lesser Whitethroats, Garden Warblers and Blackcaps feed. Redstarts, and possibly a Pied Flycatcher, may sit on the side of bushes from where they drop down to the turf to take insects. Wheatears seem to like the short turf near the cliff-top but move further inland as the day wears on. Down in the valley groups of up to 30 Yellow Wagtails gather around the grazing animals, feeding on the insects disturbed or attracted by them. Along the mud margins of the meanders a few Grey Wagtails and Meadow Pipits feed, and here scattered Dunlin, Greenshank, Oystercatchers and Green Sandpipers also feed. Other waders, especially Common Sandpipers should be looked for along the river edge. On the scrape up to ten Little Stints and smaller numbers of Curlew Sandpipers and Knot join with about 30 Ringed Plovers and Dunlin. Virtually any species of wader may occur here. As in spring, raptors move through the valley, so Hobbies, Marsh Harriers and Ospreys are seen in most years.

Later on, in September and October, autumn gales bring small numbers of Arctic Skuas and terns inshore, while adult and juvenile Kittiwakes from the nearby colony at Newhaven slide past. Then it is worth checking the exposed mud on the meanders for scarce waders such as Pectoral Sandpiper, while on this relatively sheltered water Grey Phalaropes have stayed for several days picking tiny insects off the water surface. On some days House and Sand Martins and Swallows concentrate in huge numbers also feeding on this bountiful food source, while on the ground the pipits and wagtails rush around snapping up the flies. The wintering wildfowl numbers slowly build up from late October, and the westward passage of Brent Geese and Wigeon can be seen offshore, with the occasional flock stopping off.

Timing

The Cuckmere Haven can be good at any time of the year, although in the few calm and hot days of midsummer and early autumn, it can feel airless and, unless the visit is made in the cool of the early morning, small birds can be difficult to find. An early morning walk is even more important on Seaford Head, where few birds remain in the open after mid-morning. There is little point in searching Seaford Head in winds between north and west, but it can come alive in light winds with a southerly or easterly component. Seawatching usually requires strong winds. Between late March and early May a southeasterly brings the best results, while in autumn a whipping south or southwesterly can force seabirds inshore. Severe winter weather usually brings an influx of wildfowl at least for the first week or two, before ice eventually pushes the birds further west. At this time the beach should be checked and the sea should be scanned, for flocks often sit offshore with a scattering of seabirds.

Access

There are four good car parks in this area. For the Cuckmere it is best to park at Exceat on the east side of the valley. This large car park is locked overnight but it is opened fairly early in the morning. From it one can walk either southwest along the meanders (if very wet, the drainage ditches can be difficult to cross easily in shoes), or southeasterly along a good path. Both lead to the scrape and the beach. It is not advisable to try to wade across the River Cuckmere on the beach so, to look at the west side of the valley, walk along the road to cross the river at Exceat Bridge, and then continue either along the riverbank or the path to the west of the grazing meadows. This path takes one closest to scrub patches on the hillside and can produce better overall birdwatching. From here, too, it is possible to climb up onto Seaford Head. On the opposite side of the road from the car park is the Country Park Centre which is usually open and includes an informative display and leaflets on the natural history of the area. When open, toilets are available.

The easier route on to Seaford Head is to drive to the car park at South Hill Barn. This has to be approached from the housing in Seaford and is most simply reached via Chyngton Road and Chyngton Way, these roads running immediately to the north of the golf course.

Finally, car parking along the eastern end of Seaford seafront is also convenient, particularly if seawatching is to be carried out. A climb up past the ruined fort, with the golf course on your left, leads to a cliff-top path onto Seaford Head. The scattered scrub and grassland can be explored at will. It is extremely important to remember that the chalk cliff is very crumbly and under no circumstances should one approach the cliff edge.

Calendar

Resident: Mute Swan, Kestrel, Sparrowhawk, Grey Partridge, Ringed Plover, Green Woodpecker, Meadow Pipit, Stonechat, Yellowhammer, Reed Bunting, Corn Bunting.

December–February: Red-throated Diver, Little Grebe, Cormorant, Grey Heron, Brent Goose, Shelduck, Wigeon, Teal, Pochard, Hen Harrier, Merlin, Peregrine, Grey Plover, Dunlin, Curlew, Short-eared Owl, Kingfisher, Rock Pipit.

March–May: Black-throated Diver, Slavonian Grebe, Fulmar, Gannet, Shelduck, Eider, Common and Velvet Scoter, Red-breasted Merganser, Hobby, Avocet, Knot, Sanderling, Dunlin, Bar-tailed Godwit, Whimbrel, Common Sandpiper, Turnstone, Pomarine, Arctic and Great Skuas, Mediterranean and Little Gulls, terns including Black Tern, Cuckoo, Water Pipit, Yellow Wagtail, Black and Common Redstarts, Whinchat, Wheatear, *Sylvia* and *Phylloscopus* warblers, Firecrest, Goldfinch, Linnet.

June–July: Fulmar, Yellow Wagtail, Whitethroat, Linnet.

August–November: Osprey, Hobby, Knot, Little Stint, Curlew Sandpiper, Ruff, Greenshank, Common and Wood Sandpipers, Arctic Skua, Kittiwake, Turtle Dove, Short-eared Owl, Swift, Sand and House Martins, Tree Pipit, Yellow and Grey Wagtails, both redstarts, Whinchat, Wheatear, Ring Ouzel, wide range of warblers, Firecrest, Spotted and Pied Flycatchers, Linnet, Goldfinch, Redpoll.

Habitat

There is no wider range of habitats on the great chalk block of the South Downs than can be seen here, where it rises to 706 ft (214 m). To the north around the Tenantry Ground and Windover Hill, which has on its north scarp slope the famous figure of the Long Man of Wilmington cut out of the turf, the downland is relatively closely grazed and supports a good range of chalk-loving plants and butterflies such as chalkhill blue and marbled white. Some of the slopes have suffered from encroaching

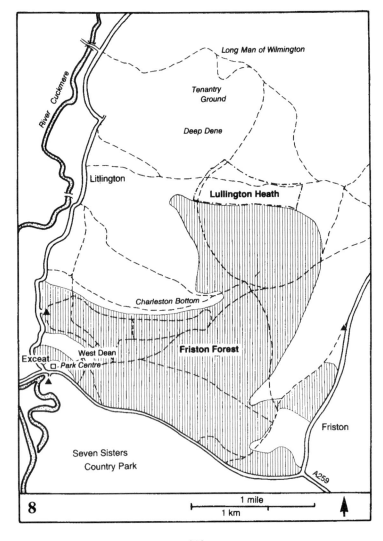

scrub, but this includes valuable berry-bearing shrubs such as wayfaring tree, privet and hawthorn. Further south is the Lullington Heath National Nature Reserve, managed by English Nature. Here a thin, silty soil capping the chalk has provided special conditions for the rare chalk heath plant community to develop. Heather jostles with chalk plants such as dropwort. Over the years dense gorse patches have developed on parts of the heath. Further south again is the large block of commercial forestry of Friston Forest, managed by the Forestry Commission. The planting was of a coniferous nurse crop and beech, much of the former has been removed, but the beech is still rather young and has not yet reached its full potential for wildlife.

Species

Winter on the Downs is harsh; cold winds seem to penetrate every corner with the result that the few birds which remain tend to be very secretive. Small parties of tits with Goldcrests and Treecreepers move out of the woodland to the dense gorse patches. Early in the winter Redwings, Fieldfares and other thrushes from Scandinavia plunder the berries, but these do not last for long and the birds soon seek more sheltered areas. A few Woodcock shelter in the scrub, and Chaffinches with a few Bramblings and other finches feed on the woodland edge.

The only regular predator of birds is the Sparrowhawk, which concentrates on the woodland. Other birds of prey take small mammals, and their appearance depends partly on the prey's cyclical patterns. Kestrels and Short-eared Owls will stay if vole numbers are high, while, in invasion years, a Rough-legged Buzzard is likely to hang around seeking out the many rabbits. Sometimes a Hen Harrier floats across or a Merlin dashes by, but they usually hunt the lower ground nearby during the day.

Common resident species start to become obvious in March, but after very severe winters birds such as Robins, Song Thrushes, Wrens and Dunnocks can be virtually absent on the heath or in the scrub, though they appear to survive slightly better in the woodland. The lucky evening visitor might glimpse or hear the occasional Long-eared Owl, which has bred on the NNR and in Friston Forest. Migration is not particularly obvious here, with just small numbers of Wheatears, Whinchats and one or two Redstarts and Ring Ouzels passing through. In many years a Hoopoe appears, but usually has departed by the next day. Spring migration is more a matter of the breeding birds arriving. In the woodland a Chiffchaff may appear before the end of March, but on the heath it is the first week of April when the first summer visitor, the Willow Warbler, arrives. Steadily other species drop into territory, so by early May the heathland is alive with summery song. Perhaps the speciality is the Nightingale, ten or more of which pour their rich notes from the depths of scrub. Blackcaps, Whitethroats, Lesser Whitethroats and Garden Warblers contribute to the volume of song, while Linnets, which here too are summer visitors, flutter from bush to bush looking for suitable nest-sites. Cuckoos, flying on distinctively downward-angled wings, pass over, perhaps concentrating on the Meadow Pipits nesting on the downland to the north. Late in May, Turtle Doves appear, to emphasise that summer has arrived.

In the heat of summer, ants along forest rides and on the heath attract Green Woodpeckers down, so a flash of a long yellow rump bounding into the woodland is of frequent occurrence. By then song has mostly ceased, but parties of young warblers can be heard calling from all directions, even though the Yellowhammers and Linnets are still feeding young of the second or late broods. Late July and early August see a steady through movement of Willow Warblers as well as early Wheatears from the north. In most years a few Crossbills seek out the more mature pines or larches, and it is at this time of the year that they usually turn up. From mid August to mid September groups of *Sylvia* warblers can be seen on the blackberries and elderberries, but after that few warblers remain; just an occasional Chiffchaff or Blackcap passes through. With the warblers there are a few Whinchats, Redstarts, Spotted Flycatchers and, rarely, a Pied Flycatcher. Raptors passing along the Downs seem to like the mosaic of habitats in this area, so over the years Buzzard, Honey Buzzard, Osprey, Red Kite, all three harriers, Goshawk, Peregrine and Hobby have been seen. The cool days of late October and early November bring substantial finch movements early in the day or, overnight, Redwing and Fieldfares. By then winter is setting in.

Redwings

Timing

There can be little doubt that the best time to visit this area is between mid April and mid September. For birds the first half of the period will give the best results, but the second half can be very good for butterflies and plants. As it is an exposed area, a warm and calm day, especially early in the morning, will be the most enjoyable, but walking on the Downs can be very thirsty work under a strong sun.

Access

There is a plethora of access tracks from the roads which surround this downland block. There is one parking area on the Jevington–Friston road. Others on the A259 between Friston and Exceat involve a long walk through relatively poor woodland if the open northern areas are to be visited. Perhaps the best option is to visit the Seven Sisters Country Park centre at Exceat to pick up the nature trail leaflet and then drive 500 yds (0.5 km) north along the road towards Litlington where there is a good car park on the right. From here take the northern path of the Forest Walk; after 400 yds (0.4 km) the South Downs Way crosses it and takes one north into Charleston Bottom; here join the path going east outside the edge of the woodland and follow this through to the nature reserve 1.5 miles (2.4 km) further on. Two ponds have been recreated on the reserve and Winchester's Pond, in particular, can attract many birds down to drink at it. This route provides the options of following the Woodland Walk or going north from the nature reserve if desired.

Calendar

Resident: Sparrowhawk, Green and Great Spotted Woodpecker, Mistle Thrush, Goldcrest, Long-tailed Tit, Chaffinch and Bullfinch.

December–February: Hen Harrier, Woodcock, Stock Dove.

March–May: Long-eared owl, Nightjar, Hoopoe, Meadow Pipit, Nightingale, Whinchat, Wheatear, Grasshopper Warbler, Lesser Whitethroat, Whitethroat, Garden and Willow Warblers, Chiffchaff, Linnet, Yellowhammer, Corn Bunting.

June–July: Turtle Dove, Jay.

August–November: Unusual raptors, Hobby, Short-eared Owl, Redstart, Whinchat, Stonechat, Wheatear, Fieldfare and Redwing (November), *Sylvia* warblers, Willow Warbler, Chiffchaff, Spotted and Pied Flycatchers, Goldfinch, Linnet, Crossbill, Bullfinch.

9 CISSBURY AND THE ADUR VALLEY

OS 198 TQ 00/10, 01/11, 20/30 & 21/31

Habitat

The River Adur is one of four Wealden rivers which cut through the South Downs to reach the English Channel. It is tidal for the 10 miles (16 km) up to Henfield and from Lancing College to the harbour mouth there are mudflats and saltmarshes dominated by sea purslane. The valley floor from Henfield to Upper Beeding comprises mainly grazing or hay meadows with biologically rich ditches, but further south to the A27 most have been destroyed and winter cereal predominates. Near the mouth lies Shoreham Airport and the estuary through Shoreham is fringed by housing and wharves, but here 25 acres (10 ha) of intertidal habitat is an RSPB reserve. There is a narrow brackish lagoon, Widewater, behind the shingle beach at South Lancing. This provides an interesting area where one can look at coastal and seabird movements.

The South Downs rise steeply from the valley between Upper Beeding and Shoreham and the 8400 acre (3400 ha) downland block to the west, extending nearly to the A24, still contains some floristically good chalk grassland and extensive downland scrub, particularly along Lychpole Hill and at Cissbury. The latter is managed by the National Trust.

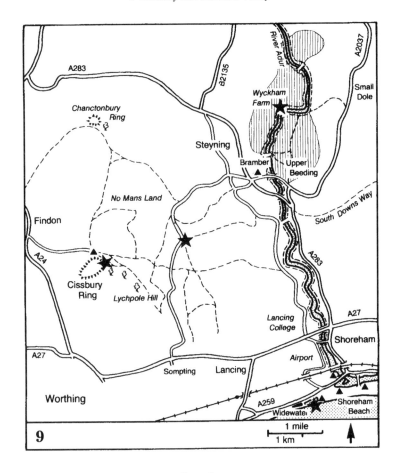

Species

The tidal section of the river around Shoreham is probably of greatest interest to the visiting birdwatcher. Autumn and winter are perhaps the most rewarding times of year, when a good range of waders can be found. The mudflats below the A27 support several hundred Redshank and Ringed Plovers, and up to 1,000 Dunlin throughout the winter. Grey Plover and Oystercatchers are regular in small numbers. Regular wildfowl include Shelduck, Teal and Mute Swans, but ducks are generally thin on the ground unless the weather becomes very cold. Under these circumstances, small numbers of Wigeon can be found on the fields at New Salts Farm, and Goldeneye and Red-breasted Merganser appear on the river itself. Exceptionally small numbers of brent geese may use the airfield, but given the high levels of disturbance rarely stay for very long. Small numbers of Little Grebes are regular on the wider ditches, the occasional Red-throated Diver might occur on the river, or more frequently at the harbour mouth.

Raptors regularly hunt in the valley with Sparrowhawk and Kestrel the most common. Peregrines are now regular and can be seen at close range as they patrol up and down the river. Spring and autumn bring regular Hobby and Ospreys. A few Merlins may winter in the valley, but are more regular on autumn passage. The occasional Hen Harrier can be seen on the Downs, and Rough-legged Buzzards have been recorded in the past.

Typical autumn and winter passerines include small flocks of Corn Buntings, Stonechats on the patches of rough grass and scrub around the airfield and at Widewater. A few overwintering summer visitors are often present such as Chiffchaff, and increasingly Blackcap. The beach, Widewater and the Harbour can hold up to half-a-dozen Black Redstarts, perching on garden fences, the groynes on the beach and the structures around the harbour entrance.

On the sea, Red-throated Divers are regular, and the lucky observer might find the odd Black-throated Diver. Small numbers of Common Scoter occur and these may be accompanied by the occasional Velvet Scoter. Eider and Red-breasted Merganser are regularly seen off Widewater and Shoreham Beach. It is quite possible for any of the five grebes, Razorbill or Guillemot also to be present. The Harbour usually hosts a small flock of up to five purple sandpipers in most winters, and is a regular haunt of wintering Mediterranean Gulls. In windy or cold weather it is always worth a look as sea duck, auks and perhaps a Grey Phalarope can be found and observed at close range.

By mid March, sizeable arrivals of Wheatears are regular along the beach, bringing an early and most welcome start to the spring. Like other coastal sites, a steady trickle of a wide variety of migrants pass through the area. New Salts Farm and the rough ground around Shoreham Airport are probably the best areas to search for Redstarts, Whinchats, Yellow Wagtails and virtually all the warblers. Watching the passage over the sea can be rewarding here, but it hardly compares with the major seawatching stations elsewhere along the South Coast. However, the full range of seabirds are seen most years, including the three common skuas, Little Gulls, Black and Roseate Terns, Manx Shearwater and a wide variety of ducks, terns and waders. As Shoreham Beach is in a bay, it really does require a good southeasterly wind to bring the birds within moderate range. Watching under these conditions brings the inevitable bonuses such as Osprey, Peregrine, Hobby and Marsh Harrier.

Once the migrants are in, the downland scrub is full of Blackcaps, Lesser and Common Whitethroats and Willow Warblers. In line with the national trends, Turtle Doves have probably ceased to be regular breed-

Oystercatchers

ers, although are still recorded as passage migrants. The occasional Nightingale can also be found. Most of the Corn Buntings move up from the valley bottom, and their jangling song can be heard from fenceposts and the tops of the bushes. The South Downs generally are one of the few remaining strongholds for this species in the southeast, although even here local decreases have been recorded. Quail used to be regular but are now much rarer. Down in the river valley the reed-fringed dykes support quite large numbers of Reed Warblers, while those with more scrub are favoured by Sedge Warblers and Reed Buntings. Intensive agriculture has reduced the value of many of the ditches, and these species are best seen around the airport or north of Upper Beeding. Very small numbers of Yellow Wagtail breed in these areas too. The Grey Herons which breed near Henfield are often seen on their feeding flights to or from the lower Adur levels. Coastal breeders are few, but Ringed Plovers hang on despite intense human disturbance.

Flocks of non- or post-breeding Lapwings are already in evidence by mid June, heralding the autumn migration. This is always a time of expectation and Cissbury and Lychpole Hill are particularly good for migrants. Throughout the autumn, passerines feed in the scrubland. Many hundreds of Willow Warblers, Chiffchaffs, Blackcaps, Garden Warblers and both whitethroats pass through, with a scattering of Redstarts, Whinchats, Grasshopper Warblers, Pied and Spotted Flycatchers and Wheatears. A few Firecrests occur with larger numbers of Goldcrests late in the autumn. Overhead, the harsh call of the Tree Pipit is heard frequently, and late in the autumn the hard trill of Redpolls and the wheeze of Siskins are also frequent. During August and September raptors move along the Downs, so Marsh Harrier, Buzzard, Hobby, Osprey and the occasional Montagu's Harrier might be seen. Later the harsh chatter of Ring Ouzels may mix with the 'tac' calls of *Sylvia* warblers as they feed on the abundant elderberries and blackberries. Down in the valley the reedbeds attract roosts of Yellow and Pied Wagtails, Swallows and Corn Buntings, while the mudflats are worth checking for scarcer waders. A visit in August or September should produce Greenshank, and the occasional Curlew Sandpiper, Ruff, Whimbrel or small parties of Little Stints.

On the beach, a trickle of terns and Arctic Skuas are supplemented by a wide range of others if a gale force southwesterly rushes in from the Atlantic. As winter nears in late October and November, finch flocks bounce along the shoreline, mostly comprising Goldfinches and Linnets, but also involving Greenfinches, Siskins, Chaffinches and Bramblings. The persistent observer is likely to find the odd Snow Bunting. At sea, lines of Brent Geese swing westwards as they make for their wintering grounds.

Timing

The area is of interest at all times of the year, although the downland is best from April to October. Inevitably, it is essential to be out early in the day to appreciate fully the scale of passerine migration, by mid-morning most birds have slipped into cover and it can be hard work to locate them. With large numbers of people in this part of Sussex, it is also sensible to get out early to avoid the inevitable disturbance.

The estuarine waders can be watched at all stages of the tide, although they are usually easiest to see during the two hours from mid tide to an hour before high water; the flooding tide pushes them off the lowest levels and from hidden creeks onto upper level mudflats. Seawatching is usually most productive during the morning and evening. It can be difficult at midday when the sun is shining into one's eyes. The southeast winds in spring can bring virtually anything inshore or produce an unexpected migrant, while severe weather in winter certainly produces unusual waterbirds.

Access

The valley is well served by roads. The A283 from Shoreham to Steyning and the A2037 from Upper Beeding to Henfield run along it, while the A27 and A259 cross it near the coast. Additional unclassified roads complete the network.

The riverbank can be walked on either side from the A27 northwards, or on the west bank southwards. Good car parks exist between the east side of Shoreham Airport and the riverbank, just to the north of the Norfolk Bridge, which carries the A259 over the estuary, and in the centre of Bramber. To look at the beach, turn south at the roundabout by New Salts Farm; from there, follow the road eastwards to the car park at the coastguard station on the west of the harbour mouth. Widewater is reached by turning right 80 yds (70 m) from the roundabout and following the signs to the beach car park.

To explore the downland, it is best to find the unclassified road running from the A27 at Sompting to Steyning. Although much of this road is narrow, there are several parking areas on the higher parts. From these, several public footpaths, including the South Downs Way, run west towards Cissbury and Lychpole Hill. Alternatively, one can drive to the A24 and turn east at Findon and up to a small car park on the north side of the Ring.

Calendar

Resident: Cormorant, Grey Heron, Sparrowhawk, Ringed Plover, Little Owl, Corn Bunting.

December–February: Red-throated Diver, Little and Great Crested Grebes, Shelduck, Wigeon, Pochard, Scaup, Goldeneye, Common Scoter, Eider, Red-breasted Merganser, Peregrine, possibly Hen Harrier and Merlin, Grey Plover, Guillemot, Rock Pipit, Kingfisher, Black Redstart, Stonechat, Redwing, Fieldfare, possibly wintering warblers.

March–May: At sea: Black-throated Diver, Fulmar, Gannet, Brent Geese, Common and Velvet Scoter, Red-breasted Merganser, Bar-tailed Godwit, Whimbrel, Sanderling, Arctic, Great and Pomarine Skuas, Mediterranean and Little Gulls, Sandwich, Common, Little and Black Terns, Razorbill. On land: Osprey, Short-eared Owl, Yellow Wagtail, Redstart, Whinchat, Wheatear, warblers, Firecrest.

June–July: Breeding warblers, occasional Nightingale and Quail.

August–November: Brent Geese, Osprey, Hobby, Knot, Little Stint, Curlew Sandpiper, Whimbrel, Bar-tailed Godwit, Kittiwake, Arctic Skua, Grey Wagtail, Tree Pipit, Whinchat, Stonechat, Wheatear, Goldfinch, Siskin.

Habitat

The Arun Valley, which runs north from the A27 at Arundel to the A283 at Pulborough, still provides interest despite increased drainage and agricultural intensification over much of its area. Much of the lowland remains in grazing meadows with fringing woodland and chalk escarpments. The RSPB Reserve at Pulborough Brooks has become a major feature since its establishment in 1989, and now plays a critical role is supporting many of the birds that breed and winter in the valley. In an average winter, the Arun Valley now holds some 25,000 to 35,000 birds, about three quarters of which roost or feed at Pulborough. Breeding waders are still a cause for concern however, and recent surveys reveal continuing declines away from the acknowledged 'hotspots'. The following text divides the valley into six main birdwatching zones, each of which is treated in detail.

ARUNDEL WILDFOWL AND WETLANDS TRUST

Habitat

Although there is a substantial wildfowl collection housed in a series of lagoons, a large natural area has been left and maintained. Here, one of the largest reedbeds in West Sussex fringes other shallow, mud-fringed lagoons with willow and sallow bushes. A good supply of spring water emerges from the chalk downland and feeds the ditches and lagoons, an important feature in severe weather.

Species

In winter, the ducks in the waterfowl collection are in very good plumage and wild birds are drawn into the pools. Wigeon, Teal, Gadwall, Tufted Duck, Pochard and Canada Geese use the grounds in the day, and the dabbling duck mostly flight out at dusk and feed on nearby grassland. During recent hard winters some of the large flock of Bewick's Swans have come to roost in the grounds. With the muddy margins and shallow open water, it is not surprising that one or two Green Sandpipers winter, while in severe weather Water Rails, which normally remain hidden in vegetation, emerge to feed in the open and are frequently seen very well indeed. Snipe and Jack Snipe feed, sometimes the latter can seen gently bouncing on flexed legs on the mud. Passerines are attracted here, too, with one or two Cetti's Warblers, a few Bearded Tits and the odd Chiffchaff or Firecrest eking out an existence in the reeds on the southern edge of the reserve. The reedbeds may attract the occasional Bittern, but these are usually only seen briefly in flight. This part of the reserve attracts roosting Redwings, Reed and Corn Buntings and sometimes finches, while the alders usually support a small flock of Siskins.

On passage many waders stop for a few days. Dunlin, Ringed and Little Ringed Plovers, Greenshank, Common, Green and Wood Sandpipers are annual, with others such as Whimbrel and Curlew seen or heard passing overhead. Hirundines, raptors and many warblers pass

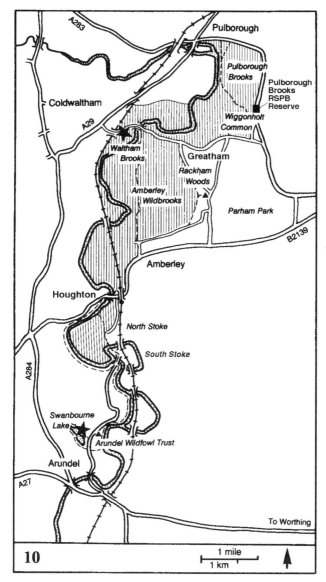

through the area. Summer, too, is an interesting time as large numbers of Reed and Sedge Warblers and Reed Buntings sing from the reedbeds, while Redshank and Lapwing breed.

SWANBOURNE LAKE

Habitat

This clear, shallow, spring-fed lake is part of the wooded Arundel Park and is adjacent to the Wildfowl and Wetlands Trust's reserve. A wide range of mature and over-mature trees and scrubland surrounds the lake, which is bordered in places by a little emergent vegetation. Three small islands provide resting places for wildfowl.

Species

If you have ever wanted to watch Tufted Duck and Pochard swimming under water, this is the place to do it. With between 100 and 200 diving duck on this shallow, crystal clear lake which has a pale bottom, they stand out remarkably clearly. In winter, 50 to 80 Gadwall, feeding on the weed brought to the surface by Coot, can be seen here and even a few remain for the summer. Many gulls drop in to bathe and sometimes a Mediterranean Gull can be picked out. If Bitterns are present at the Wildfowl and Wetland Trust Reserve, they may be seen feeding along the margins of the lake.

As there are large old trees in Arundel Park, it is not surprising that Mandarins, originally escapees from the Wildfowl and Wetland Trust, breed here. They are best seen on, or near to, the middle island, sometimes perched high up on tree branches. A complication is that Wood Duck are also resident and breed here, so the head pattern of the females has to be critically examined if not in the company of a male! With woodland around, resident birds include all three woodpeckers, Marsh Tits, Little and Tawny Owls, Treecreeper and Nuthatch. A walk around the lake adds many passerines to the list of waterfowl. The lake drops into the Mill stream, which runs into the Arun. By the Mill, Kingfisher and Grey Wagtail can often be seen in winter, and the latter usually breeds.

Summer brings in additional woodland warblers. Chiffchaffs, Willow and Garden Warblers and Blackcaps are common, while overhead there is an incessant yapping of Jackdaws. The mournful 'ooo-woo' of Stock Doves and the 'purr' of Turtle Doves can give the summer a very relaxed feeling here.

ARUN VALLEY from ARUNDEL to HOUGHTON

Habitat

For much of its length the banks of the River Arun are lined by dense stands of reed and the dykes, too, are reed-fringed. South of the village of South Stoke there are dense patches of hawthorn along field edges, but to the north it is more open. The fields are mostly grazed by cattle.

Species

From the riverbank footpaths, quite good views can be obtained of this section, but it is not until one reaches the Wildfowl Trust that bird-watching is good. The river attracts diving duck in severe weather, Tufted Duck, Goosander and Goldeneye are regular and Smew occasional; Little and Great Crested Grebes can usually be found, along with a few Cormorants. Up to 180 of this last species form a large roost near South Stoke. They generally fly up the valley from the coast just before sunset. At dusk in winter a ghostly Barn Owl may drift over rough grassland beside the river. During the day large flocks of Redwings and Fieldfares often feed in the fields while, more spectacularly, up to 100 Bewick's join with Mute Swans to graze the meadows to the west of North Stoke.

The breeding season brings many warblers to this section. Blackcaps and Garden Warblers sing from the scrub on the slopes by the river, while Lesser Whitethroats are more frequent in the dense hawthorn hedges in the valley itself and Whitethroats find the open scrub to their liking. Reed and Sedge Warblers concentrate along the reed-fringed ditches and, in some years, a Grasshopper Warbler reels in the reedbeds alongside the Arun.

AMBERLEY WILDBROOKS and WALTHAM BROOKS

Habitat

Most of this section of the Valley remains grassland with cattle grazing predominating. Amberley Wildbrooks is of outstanding importance for its dyke flora, supporting many nationally rare plants but the fields themselves have only limited botanical value. Under the right conditions they can, however, support important numbers of wintering wildfowl but this is entirely dependent on the extent and timing of winter flooding. Not surprisingly, the drainage of the Wildbrooks has been a subject of much debate for many years, and a wide range of interests are still engaged in trying to find a solution to the conflicts that inevitably exist on such sites.

In addition to the open meadows, some wet wooded patches are found, and here willows and sallows predominate, with large mounds of tussock sedge forming an understorey. Waltham Brooks, on the other hand, has a large area of standing water, the level of which usually drops in summer and autumn to reveal a rich, muddy margin. This is a Sussex Wildlife Trust Reserve.

Species

Winter wildfowl are entirely dependent on the location and extent of winter flooding, and their distribution can vary from one year to the next. Nevertheless, Waltham Brooks generally holds most of the key species which include Pintail, Shoveler, Wigeon, Teal, Gadwall, Shelduck, Canada and Greylag Geese. Small numbers of these visit the Wildbrooks from time to time, and here one can find many Lapwings in winter. Water Rails skulk in ditches, especially those with little water, but are best seen in cold weather when they come into the open. The Valley's Bewick's Swans do use the Wildbrooks for feeding when they are flooded. Barn, Little and Short-eared Owls can all be seen here. The river is worth checking in severe winter weather as Smew, Goosander and Red-throated Diver have been seen, and the occasional Great Grey Shrike may frequent the tops of the hawthorns.

Perhaps because of the permanent water Waltham Brooks is an excellent site to look for passage birds. Early in the season brings Sand Martins and the odd Garganey, followed a little later by Little Ringed and Ringed Plovers, Black-tailed Godwits, Ruff, Common, Green and Wood Sandpipers, Greenshank, Black Terns and scarcer species. Among the passerines, Whinchat is regular. Fewer migrants occur on the Wildbrooks, although a small flock of Whimbrel is present in early May on quiet, isolated fields.

In the breeding season, Redshank, Lapwing and a few Snipe can be seen, but numbers of all have decreased markedly over the last decade.

On the grassland, Meadow Pipits and a few Yellow Wagtails are found, while the ditches, especially where some scrub is found, attract Sedge Warblers and Reed Buntings. Breeding wildfowl are not numerous, but include Shelduck, Gadwall, Teal, Shoveler and Greylag Geese. The wet woods on Amberley support a few pairs of Nightingales, several Whitethroats and Willow Warblers and Great Spotted Woodpeckers, as well as Sedge Warblers and the widespread Blackcap and Garden Warblers.

Autumn migration is most obvious on Waltham Brooks, where a range of waders can be seen. The scarcer species have included Marsh and Pectoral Sandpipers. Hobby, too, are often seen hunting for dragonflies in late August and September.

Male Garganey

RACKHAM WOODS

Habitat

This sandstone outcrop right on the edge of Amberley Wildbrooks has been planted with conifers, although old deciduous woodland forms a fringe on its western flank, with willow and sallow woodland extending out into the Wildbrooks themselves.

Species

These provide a sharp contrast to the adjacent grassland. Typical woodland species can be found all year, although they are often most visible in winter and early spring. All three woodpeckers are regular, along with Nuthatch, Long-tailed, Marsh and Willow Tits, Goldcrest and Treecreeper. In winter they are joined by flocks of Siskins, Redpolls and, in some years when numbers are high, by those conifer specialists, Crossbills. Although these and adjacent woods support Woodcock all year, it is not until April, when they start their dusk and dawn roding display flights, that they become obvious. By then the summer visitors are in, with Blackcap, Garden and Willow Warblers and Chiffchaffs being the most obvious. Sometimes a Wood Warbler sings from the birch patches, but they rarely stay long.

PULBOROUGH BROOKS RSPB RESERVE

Habitat

This RSPB reserve was established in 1989, and has rapidly become one of the most popular in the country attracting many thousands of visitors each year. The key to its success has been the dramatic restoration of the grazing meadows adjacent to the River Arun. Through careful water level management and grazing regimes, a remarkable lowland wet grassland has been created which now supports nationally and internationally important numbers of wintering wildfowl. In 1989 the reserve supported only locally important numbers of birds. After seven years of targeted management, the reserve now supports an average wintering population of some 18,500 wildfowl (with a peak count of 24,500 birds), and an important assemblage of breeding waders and ducks. It also supports nationally significant assemblages of other wetland flora and fauna. Away from the water-meadows, the reserve also includes pasture, hedgerows, scrub and mixed woodland.

Species

The reserve is most important for its wintering Lapwing and wildfowl, the key species being Bewick's Swan, Wigeon, Teal and Pintail. Regular raptors include Peregrine, Merlin, Sparrowhawk and passing Hen Harriers. A small flock of Ruff also winter. Breeding birds include Garganey, Shoveler, Teal, Lapwing, Snipe, Redshank and Yellow Wagtail. The surrounding scrub and hedges hold Nightingales and warblers, whilst the nearby woods and heathland support Woodcock and Nightjar. Hobby regularly hunt over the reserve in summer. A wide range of waders pass through on passage, and numbers of Whimbrel in particular can be impressive. Marsh Harrier and Osprey fly through in most years. Notable rarities do occur, and have included Red-footed Falcon, Montagu's Harrier and Hoopoe for example.

Timing

It can be good here at any time of the year, although late September and October can be disappointing over much of the grazing land. To see a wide variety of species it is necessary to explore the many habitats. A calm, sunny day in winter can provide very good birdwatching with a wide range of passerines, wildfowl and raptors. Most areas can be visited at any time of the day, although early morning is best at Swanbourne Lake and the Wildfowl Trust, and evening can be fascinating at both Waltham Brooks and the Wildfowl Trust. With many areas, where a fairly long walk brings the best results, days with strong winds, heavy rain or poor visibility are best avoided. Waltham Brooks is overlooked from the adjacent road, and the late afternoon or evening light gives the best conditions; at other times the sun can restrict good views. For those with little time to explore the Valley, the Pulborough Brooks Reserve is undoubtedly the best stop at any time of year. In addition to the well laid out paths and hides, it has toilets, a tearoom and a shop.

Access

Roads surround the valley and most areas are accessible by using footpaths from car parks.

Arundel Wildfowl Trust, Swanbourne Lake and the Arun Valley to North Stoke are all best served from one centre. A minor road runs from

Arundel town centre just to the east of the castle, to Offham. This leads to the Wildfowl Trust; if visiting this area there is a large car park, but if not, car parking is readily available by the side of the road nearby. The Wildfowl Trust grounds are well laid out and the natural area of pools, reed and sallows to the south is overlooked by three large hides; these give excellent views. Swanbourne Lake is open all day and a hard path runs around the lake and back to the road. This area is very popular on a weekend and it is usually best to visit it early in the day.

Access to the riverbank is by walking 200 yds (183 m) towards Arundel from the Wildfowl Trust and taking the path on the left bank of the mill stream for a further 200 yds (183 m). This takes one to the west bank of the river Arun and the path here turns north. This can be followed for 1.5 miles (2.4 km) to South Stoke where it crosses the river, follows the right bank of the isolated meander before crossing this again in 300 yds (275 m) and going on to North Stoke. However, the path has to be retraced as other routes back are very much longer. Amberley Wildbrooks has only one good public footpath, this runs north from Amberley village. It is a made-up path, mostly of chalk spoil for the first 0.5 mile (0.8 km) but can get very sticky in wet weather. Further north it deteriorates and for much of the winter, especially after wet weather, it can be almost impassable — then wellington boots are essential. The eastern fields can be overlooked from Rackham Woods.

Waltham Brooks lie alongside the unclassified road running from Coldwaltham on the A29 to Greatham. Limited parking is available just to the east of the railway line and by Greatham Bridge. The best views are obtained from the sharp bend 150 yds (138 m) to the east of the railway line.

Rackham Woods are part of the woodland complex including Northpark Wood and Parham Park. Two car parks, particularly the one at the southeastern tip of the woodland, serve it. From this a 0.75 mile (1.2 km) footpath skirts the west of the woodland and returns either along the road or on rides within the wood. Another footpath into Parham Park can be found just 150 yds (138 m) from this car park and a walk along the roads surrounded by woodland can be productive.

The entrance to the Pulborough Brooks Reserve is located on the left hand side of the A283, about two miles north of Storrington village

Calendar

Resident: Grey Heron, Mute Swan, Canada and Greylag Geese, Teal, Gadwall, Tufted Duck, Sparrowhawk, Lapwing, Snipe, Redshank, Woodcock, Stock Dove, Barn, Little and Tawny Owls, Kingfisher, woodpeckers, Grey Wagtail, Marsh and Willow Tits, Yellowhammer, Reed and Corn Buntings.

December–February: Cormorant, Bittern, Bewick's Swan, White-fronted Goose, Wigeon, Pintail, Shoveler, Pochard, in cold weather Goldeneye and Goosander, Hen Harrier, Peregrine, Merlin, Water Rail, Ruff, Green Sandpiper, Short-eared Owl, Redwing, Fieldfare, Cetti's Warbler, Chiffchaff, Firecrest, Bearded Tit, Siskin, Redpoll.

March–May: Shelduck, Garganey, Osprey, Marsh Harrier, Little Ringed and Ringed Plovers, Dunlin, Ruff, Black-tailed Godwit, Whimbrel, Curlew, Greenshank, Wood and Common Sandpipers, Common Tern, Water Pipit, Cuckoo, Nightingale, Whinchat, Wheatear, Wood Warbler, Crossbill.

June–July: Garganey, Redshank, Snipe, Tree Pipit, Yellow Wagtail, Grasshopper Warbler, Sedge and Reed Warblers, Whitethroat, Lesser Whitethroat, Garden Warbler, Blackcap, Spotted Flycatcher.

August–November: In mid autumn: Garganey, Hobby, Little Ringed Plover, Little Stint, Curlew and Pectoral Sandpipers, Ruff, Curlew Greenshank, Green, Wood and Common Sandpipers, Little Gull, Black Tern, Yellow Wagtail, Redstart, Whinchat, Stonechat, Wheatear, many warblers. In late October/November wintering wildfowl appear, especially Wigeon, Shoveler and Bewick's Swans, Short-eared Owl, winter thrushes, Cetti's Warbler, Blackcap, Chiffchaff, Firecrest, Bearded Tit, Goldfinch, Siskin, Redpoll.

11 CLIMPING

OS 197
SU 80/90 & TQ 00/10

Habitat

Gaps in the coastal urban development in West Sussex form important areas for wildlife, as well as providing landscapes and amenity areas for people. One of the few such areas is centred on Climping, and lies between the mouth of the River Arun at Littlehampton and Middleton-on-Sea, some 2.5 miles (4 km) to the west. Much of the hinterland is under cereals, but the southeast corner is a golf course. This is separated from the sea by a line of small sand dunes and a sand and vegetat-

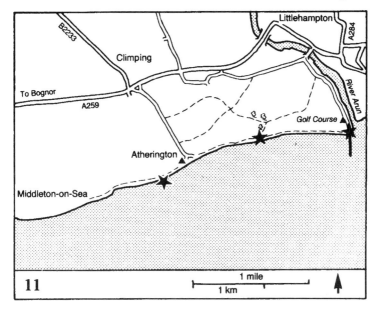

ed shingle beach, but the rest of the beach is shingle with a narrow, artificial bank protecting the farmland. The beach is quite wide at low water and has a patchy mixture of sand, shingle and stony ground. At the eastern end of the beach is a pier some 200 yds (183 m) long. Behind the seawall there are patches of rough ground, blackthorn and hawthorn scrub and small linear private woodlands.

Species

Waders form a prominent feature of the winter bird community. The diverse nature of the foreshore provides many habitats, so there is an unusual combination of 150 Oystercatchers, a very important flock of 150 to 200 Sanderling and 100 plus Grey Plover, plus small numbers of Dunlin, Ringed Plovers, Turnstone and Redshank. The Sanderling feed in small groups at the tide edge but can be very mobile, sometimes moving to the many miles of contiguous beaches, but usually they concentrate on the flooding tide. Small numbers of Purple Sandpipers used to frequent the wooden pier by the mouth of the Arun, but now only occasional singles occur in the winter months. Inland, up to 600 Lapwing feed in the fields along with the occasional Ruff, and marshy spots hide both Snipe and its diminutive relation the Jack Snipe. Here, too, the ditches provide for a few Water Rails.

The sea here sometimes attracts waterbirds. In normal winters a few Great Crested Grebes, Cormorants, Common Scoter, Eider and Red-breasted Merganser feed offshore although, because of the low vantage point, they can be difficult to pick out. Severe weather will result in an increase of duck on the sea, with Wigeon and Teal resting on it during the day and the odd auk or Red-throated Diver being pushed inshore. A flock of up to 30 Mute Swans feeds in the River Arun at Littlehampton. It is well worth checking gulls on the beach or on the pier, for Mediterranean, Glaucous and Iceland have been seen among the many common species.

Agricultural and rough land attracts small flocks of Goldfinches and Linnets, with a few Yellowhammers and Corn Buntings. It is not surprising that Kestrels and Sparrowhawks are seen regularly and Short-eared Owls do occur from time to time. Seeds from the plants growing on the shingle beach provide food for small groups of Greenfinches, which are sometimes joined by a Snow Bunting. On this habitat, too, are small numbers of Rock Pipits and Stonechats, although they feed mainly on the emerging seaweed flies which seem to appear throughout the winter months.

In March, lines of Brent Geese pass by, having just left their important wintering grounds in the harbours a few miles to the west. A Firecrest or Chiffchaff might be seen in the bushes around the golf course, but they could well be wintering birds becoming more obvious. Wheatears can be found here in the first week of March, and these birds are frequently the first recorded in Sussex each year. By mid-month, migrant Chiffchaffs are common and raucous Sandwich Terns can be seen offshore. Spring migration here has not been studied in detail, but a wide variety of warblers, both Common and Black Redstarts, Whinchats and Yellow Wagtails are regular, many being seen around the periphery of the golf course. Seawatching in April and May reveals small numbers of most species, such as Common Scoter, Eider, Whimbrel, Arctic Skua and Little and 'Commic' Terns and can be worthwhile, but it is much more concentrated off Selsey Bill or West Worthing. During the Bar-tailed Godwit movement in late April it is not unusual to see small groups also feeding on the foreshore.

A few warblers, principally Blackcap and Whitethroat, remain to breed in the patches of woodland and scrub, while Meadow Pipits and Skylarks can be found mainly around the golf course. Small numbers of Goldfinches, Yellowhammers and Corn Buntings breed on the farmland, with Great Spotted Woodpeckers in the woods. Reed Buntings, Reed and Sedge Warblers can be found in the dykes.

Passage in autumn can be very good with the whole range of commoner migrants being seen each year. August brings mostly warblers, but in September there is a much greater variety including Pied Flycatchers in most years. Rarer species have been seen, including Icterine, Barred and Aquatic Warblers and Red-backed Shrike. The golf course is particularly attractive to Wheatears, Whinchats and that south coast speciality the Tawny Pipit. A few raptors move through, principally Hobby, although there are several records of Ospreys flying out to sea. Later on in the autumn the morning coastal movement of Goldfinches, Linnets and other finches is prominent, and sometimes includes scarcer species such as Lapland Bunting. Dartford, Yellowbrowed and Pallas's Warblers have all been seen in recent years.

Timing

During spring and autumn migration it is important to be out early in the morning. Not only are the birds feeding more actively and the visible passage prominent, but there are relatively few people around. At weekends and, to a certain extent, on weekdays large numbers of walkers, many with dogs, are about so there is much disturbance. The beach faces south, so for much of the middle of the day birds sitting on the sea are silhouetted against the bright reflected light. It is pointless visiting here in high summer.

In winter a good time to see the waders is about mid-tide, just before the water reaches the steep shingle beach. Wildfowl on the sea are best seen at any stage during the two hours either side of high tide, otherwise they will be far out. So a large tide which is full mid-morning provides a good combination. Strong winds with a distinct southerly component are needed to push passing seabirds inshore, but then other bird watching here is not usually productive.

Access

The A259 coast road delimits the north of this site and access to the two car parking areas is off this road. The main car park is reached via the unclassified road to Atherington. It is possible to drive down to just behind the shoreline here. Alternatively, it is usually possible to take the first turning immediately west of the river and drive down a small road towards the pier or the beach. Toilets are located here. In either case a walk along the foreshore is required before turning inland on the footpath beside the golf course.

Calendar

Resident: Sparrowhawk, Kestrel, Oystercatcher, Stock Dove, Little Owl, Great Spotted Woodpecker, Yellowhammer, Reed and Corn Bunting.

December–February: Great Crested Grebe, Cormorant, Mute Swan, Eider, Common Scoter, Red-breasted Merganser, Water Rail, Lapwing,

Ringed and Grey Plovers, Sanderling, Dunlin, Jack Snipe, Snipe, Turnstone, Short-eared Owl, Rock Pipit, Stonechat, Greenfinch, Goldfinch, possibly Snow Bunting.

March–May: Divers on passage, Gannet, Brent Goose, occasional large raptors (for example, Buzzard, Osprey), Hobby, Bar-tailed Godwit, Whimbrel, Arctic Skua, Sandwich, Common and Little Terns, Turtle Dove, Yellow Wagtail, Black Redstart, Redstart, Whinchat, Wheatear, most warblers, Firecrest.

June–July. Mute Swan, Meadow Pipit, Whitethroat, Blackcap.

August–November: Up to late September good for all the commoner summer migrants including Redstart, Whinchat and Spotted Flycatcher; scarcer species may include Osprey, Hobby, Peregrine, Little Ringed Plover or Tawny Pipit. During October and November the winter birds appear including Red-breasted Merganser, Sanderling, Rock Pipit and Stonechat, while passage migrants include Black Redstart, Firecrest and possibly warblers such as Dartford, Yellow-browed and Pallas's.

12   CHICHESTER GRAVEL PITS   OS 197
SU 80/90

Habitat

Fringing the Chichester by-pass lies the complex of 20 former gravel pits. Others, once good for birds, have been filled with rubbish. The southern group of pits is used intensively at times for water recreation, the northernmost for windsurfing and most for fishing. Despite this pressure, they remain interesting. As with most gravel pits designed many years ago, there is little marginal reed-growth, although the banks of many are clothed in dense willows, sallows and blackberries. Only on Portfield North is any mud, actually sand washings, found regularly, although recently the water level in Portfield South has also been lowered. At their closest the pits are just 2 miles (3 km) from Chichester Harbour and this appears to have some influence on their birds. It is suspected that a proportion of waders and terns, migrating east along the south coast in spring, cut inland via the Chichester gravel pits, so by-passing the Selsey peninsula.

Species

The influx of wildfowl in winter brings 400 of both Tufted Duck and Pochard to the pits; a few Goldeneye and Goosander join them, particularly when the winter is severe elsewhere. Perhaps because Chichester Harbour is close by, Long-tailed Ducks are regularly seen in winter, sliding surreptitiously under the water on characteristically half opened wings and remaining down for what seems to be an age. Dabbling duck

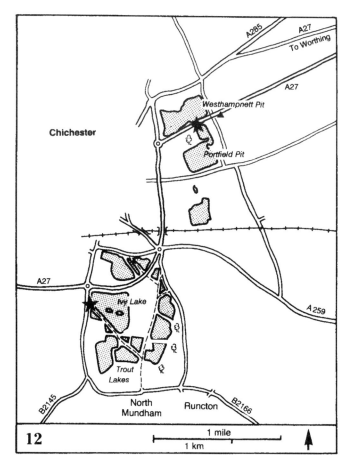

do not find the relatively deep water to their liking, but up to 250 Shoveler with their huge spatulate, sieving bills, are able to glean food from the surface layers, and a similar number of Teal may be found in the shallow Portfield North. The majority of the 1,500 to 2,000 Coot find the trout lakes to their liking where they dive for water weeds. Also present, is a scattering of attendant Gadwall, a duck which has found that it can exploit this otherwise unavailable food source. On an island in Ivy Lake, a roost of Cormorants has developed, the white-bellied juveniles are particularly striking. Storms in late winter often bring in a Red-throated Diver, though, sadly, such birds may show signs that there is chronic oil pollution in the English Channel.

Careful scrutiny of the margins of pits during frosty weather should bring the reward of a hunched and skulking Water Rail, or if very lucky, a Bittern. A scattering of Green Sandpipers remain until high water levels push them to secluded corners.

As spring approaches, the Chiffchaffs wintering in the waterside willows utter a few hesitant phrases and an occasional Blackcap slips through the dense ivy. Soon the flowering pussy willows are full of singing migrants like Chiffchaff, Willow and Sedge Warblers and, later, Reed Warblers sing vigorously from patches of reed. It is one of the best

229

places in Sussex to see early Sand Martins and Swallows, usually over Ivy Lake, where there is always a side sheltered from strong winds for insects to congregate.

By late April, the elegant Common Terns, which breed on rafts put out by the Sussex Ornithological Society, have returned to dip down or to dive into the water. Winds with an easterly component concentrate the strong up-Channel passage of waders, terns and gulls onto the English coast. At such times, summer-plumaged Black Terns or the rosy-flushed Little Gulls are seen frequently, while overhead a trickle of Whimbrel or Bar-tailed Godwits pass. If mud is present, other migrating waders, such as Grey Plover, Temminck's Stint or Sanderling, may drop in for a few hours.

Great Crested Grebe

Ruddy Duck, Pochard, Tufted Duck and Shelduck all breed, although the secretive nature of the first two means that they are often over-looked. Several pairs of Great Crested Grebes try to breed but many are unsuccessful due mainly to fluctuating water levels over their long breeding season and probably predation by pike. At any time of the year, a flash of electric blue reveals a Kingfisher moving between feeding stations on overhanging branches.

Waders reveal a hint of autumn as early as late June, with Green Sandpipers and Lapwings already building up in numbers. Soon, any exposed mud attracts a wide range of waders, including Black-tailed Godwits, Ruff, Little Stint, Greenshank and Redshank. Large concentrations of Swifts may be seen up to early August, with hirundines building up late in the season. On the open water during August, an occasional Black-necked Grebe moulting out of breeding plumage may be picked out from the Little Grebes. Over the water, juvenile Black Terns twist and turn, sometimes they are quite difficult to pick out from masses of feeding hirundines; it is well worth checking all terns for young White-winged Black and Arctic Terns have been seen.

Timing

During migration times and in summer, it is advisable to be out as early as possible. Small birds are active then and even the most secretive waterbirds are more visible. The fishing is mostly carried out from banks, so causes little disturbance in larger pits, but on Ivy Lake there is a water-skiing course. This is used intensively on summer weekends, driving away waterfowl, although terns may remain. Similar disturbance results from sailboarding on Westhampnett Pit.

Access

The A27 Chichester by-pass and several main and minor roads run close to the gravel pit complex and several footpaths provide good viewing points. There are many small areas where it is possible to park and walk, but unless visiting the leisure centre, there are no large car parks. Banks of pits away from roads or footpaths are private, but nevertheless the majority of pits can be seen well.

Calendar

Resident: Great Crested and Little Grebes, Canada Goose, Shelduck, Pochard, Tufted and Ruddy Ducks, Sparrowhawk, Kingfisher, Reed Bunting.

December–February: Cormorant, Shoveler, Wigeon, Teal, Water Rail, Redwing, Lesser and Greater Black-backed Gulls, Grey Wagtail, Chiffchaff, finch flocks, Meadow Pipits and Pied Wagtails on adjacent fields.

March–May: Shelduck, Common and Black Terns, hirundines, Swift, Reed and Sedge Warblers, Willow Warblers, Chiffchaff, Lesser Whitethroat, Whitethroat.

June–July: Redshank, Common Terns, Turtle Dove; from late June, returning Green and Common Sandpipers.

August–November: Wide range of commoner migrant waders, Black Tern, Grey Wagtail, roosting Sand Martins and Swallows, commoner passage warblers.

13 PAGHAM HARBOUR

OS 197
SZ 89

Habitat

There can be few better birdwatching areas in Britain than Pagham Harbour, combining as it does an excellent range of habitats and birds, nearly all easily seen from a plethora of footpaths radiating from car parks.

The harbour itself is very muddy, with extensive, but broken, beds of the rice grass, *Spartina*, adjacent to the seawalls. Two deep creeks drain it and between them lies a high *Spartina*-covered bank. The harbour mouth is guarded by two shingle spits which have been battered by storms and changed shape many times in the past. Coastal defence work has slowed down such changes. A fast flow of water passes through the narrow entrance and over extensive rough gravel deposits on the beach.

Starting on the eastern (Pagham village) side, from the northerly spit at the harbour mouth and moving in an anti-clockwise direction, the first of the main habitats of significance for birds is Pagham Lagoon, a former entrance to the harbour. Between Pagham and Sidlesham, the

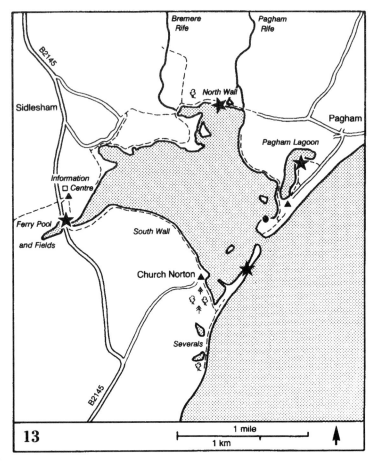

North Wall gives a good view northwards over wet grass fields, with an extensive growth of reed along dykes and some large, mature hedges. The section around the Information Centre was once a rubbish tip, now restored to rough grassland with some trees planted on it. To the west of the B2145, at this point, lies grassland surrounding the Sidlesham Ferry Pool, this area is a nature reserve owned by the Sussex Wildlife Trust and managed by the Warden. The footpath along the south shore initially runs past some linear pools at the harbour edge, with areas of sparse rush and reed. It overlooks cereal fields inland and passes through patches of gorse and blackthorn, before reaching a line of stunted oaks in the hedge. At Church Norton, the churchyard and vegetation around it provides another excellent area, but visitors are requested to respect the graveyard. The shoreline is lined here by willows, sallows and blackthorn, and a little farther south by gorse. Two small pools, the Severals, lie south along the beach. These have open water in the centre and dense reedbeds. Floristically, the Pagham Harbour complex is good. The whole of the harbour and several adjacent areas are managed by the West Sussex County Council, who have declared it a Local Nature Reserve.

Species

It does not matter in which season one visits Pagham. Winter perhaps brings the best birdwatching, with up to 1,000 Grey Plover and a few Spotted Redshank, Greenshank and Avocet joining the 10,000 or more waders out in the harbour. On the flooded fields during the day and roosting around the harbour at night are up to 800 Black-tailed Godwits and 300 Ruffs.

Out on the mudflats or among the saltmarshes at high water is an excellent variety of wildfowl. Regularly up to 3,000 Brent Geese, with an occasional individual of the Pale-bellied race, feed here. Often they move onto the grassland and, sometimes, cereal crops during the late winter. Some damage results and to deter them, blue bags on posts and frequent bangs will probably be encountered. About 400 Pintail, the most elegant estuarine duck, 1,000 Wigeon, 800 Teal and 400 Shelduck are seen. A visit at high tide is best to look for the diving wildfowl in the main channels. This brings small numbers of Scaup, Red-breasted Mergansers, Eiders, Red-necked and Slavonian Grebes in to join the two common grebes. Under severe conditions, Tufted Duck, Pochard and Smew may be seen in the harbour. In most years a Smew or two finds Pagham Lagoon a good home for a few weeks. Divers rarely enter the harbour, but do occur offshore as do most of the grebes, Eiders and mergansers at low tide — beware of assuming that the bobbing rafts of Mallard are Eiders! Severe weather to the east often brings grey geese to the fields, most frequently White-fronted, but Pink-footed, Bean and Greylag have been seen. They spread over a large area inland, but tend to fly high into the harbour at dusk, seeking a safe roost.

Among the scarcer small birds present in winter are Kingfishers, usually seen flashing along the stream by the side of the Ferry Pool. Wintering Firecrests and Chiffchaffs at Church Norton are regular. In most years a few Bearded Tits arrive here from, presumably, eastern England. They may be found in any of the reedbeds, from where the squeals of Water Rails emerge. Often a Snow Bunting takes up residence on the shingle spits. Severe weather pushes a small number of Woodlarks to the coast, so it is well worth checking through all apparent Skylarks feeding along the high tide line. With such a high density of birds, it is not surprising that Hen Harriers, Merlins and Short-eared Owls hunt regularly over the whole area. Gulls provide the service of scavenging with the odd angry-looking Glaucous Gull inhabiting the shingle spits but also drifting between Selsey and Bognor Regis.

In mid March Wheatears can be found sitting on the beach, flicking away low and flashing a white rump. The first of the harsh cries of the Sandwich Terns and a repetitive song of the Chiffchaff are heard at Church Norton. Soon a steady trickle becomes a flood with Willow Warblers and Swallows, followed by a host of summer visitors. Church Norton often attracts a Hoopoe, normally finding one of the fields to its liking for a day. Sometimes the raptors are obliging, with an Osprey sitting on the posts marking the entrance to the harbour, but usually they move straight through. Waders, more obligingly, stop at the Ferry Pool: Temminck's Stints are regular and once seven were here together. Around the feet of nearby cattle, brilliant Yellow Wagtails rush to catch disturbed insects. The pool and streams are worth checking for the most spectacular of duck, the Garganey. Virtually anything can turn up, and does, though it often seems to have been there the day before.

Midsummer is a relatively quiet time. At the mouth of the harbour Little, Common and Sandwich Terns fish in the shallows. Little Terns, in particular, with their rapid clockwork action and sharp plunges, may be seen right up any channel that holds water, even in the saltmarsh. While on the spit, it is worth looking out to sea in case some immature, over-summering Eider are present. Beware of the confusing blackish young males with irregular white blotches on the breast. Even in summer, the odd Arctic Skua or Gannet may be passing offshore. The mudflats are fairly quiet with small groups of Shelduck sitting around, while others are incubating eggs under bushes or in the many rabbit burrows inland. The reedbeds resound to the repetitive song of the Reed Warbler or the more varied and hurried notes of Sedge Warblers. From the dense hedges, the rattling song of the elusive Lesser Whitethroat may be heard. From the private woodland at Church Norton come signs of all three woodpeckers. The loud ringing laugh of the Green Woodpecker

Ringed Plover

can sometimes be contrasted directly with the weaker, flatter, but otherwise similar call of the much scarcer Lesser Spotted. Perhaps the most fascinating area is Sidlesham Ferry where dense breeding populations of Lapwing and Redshank remain and often the delightful downy Lapwing chicks can be seen within a few feet of the road. Inevitably, such a concentration attracts predators, principally Kestrels, which draw massive communal mobbing when they attack. In midsummer, creches of up to 100 young Shelduck, with just a handful of adults, seek food and safety on the pool.

By early July the wader passage is well underway and from now to the end of October a stop each time you pass the Ferry Pool is vital. Flocks of up to 30 Ruff and 80 Black-tailed Godwits, many still in partial breeding plumage, are among early returning birds. By the end of July a wide range may be present, including Little Stints, Curlew Sandpipers and Little Ringed Plovers. This is the best, although not the only area where a rarity may be discovered and over the years most of the North American vagrant waders have passed through here, including Semipalmated, Least, White-rumped and Baird's Sandpipers and Wilson's Phalarope. Eastern rarities are less frequent.

On the grassland, flies and other insects attract parties of Yellow Wagtails, mostly pale juveniles with gorgets of dark smudges on the throat. Most small passerine migrants can be found in the trees and hedges, with those at the Severals, Church Norton and along the South Wall footpath usually being the most productive. Rarely a staid Melodious Warbler stops in the oaks or sallows, its broad and long bill and general shape often resulting in confusion with Reed Warblers which also feed in these trees — they are far from being restricted to reedbeds! Look for the square tail shape, shorter undertail coverts and creamy or yellow washes on the underparts before jumping to conclusions. Check for Whinchats and Wheatears on fenceposts and hedgetops. Early in the morning, migrating wagtails and pipits fly overhead calling loudly, but they never seem to drop down. On the other hand, a Wryneck may be seen down on a footpath, feeding quietly but flicking quickly into nearby cover when disturbed — at times it can sit hidden for long periods. Late autumn passerine migrants such as Firecrests and Black Redstarts tend to be seen around Church Norton and it is here that the tall willows and oaks should be checked for rarer eastern warblers such as Yellow-browed and Booted. In years when Dartford Warblers have bred well inland, one often skulks in the gorse on the southern side of the harbour.

Those birdwatchers with an interest in raptors are often lucky. Osprey, Marsh Harrier, Buzzard and Hobby are seen each year. In addition, the resident Sparrowhawks and Kestrels add to the variety. It is vital to look around the moment panic sets in amongst gulls and waders. Often a Marsh Harrier hunts over the cereal fields between Sidlesham Ferry and Selsey. A strong east or southeast wind brings seabirds in close offshore with Great, Arctic and, occasionally, Pomarine Skuas, many terns and Gannets. Little Gulls and Black Terns often get blown into the harbour, with the former deciding to sit out the storm on the Ferry Pool, along with a Grey Phalarope, if the wind has a westerly component late in the season. This pool is one of the best places to look at juvenile Little Stints and Curlew Sandpipers and compare them with Dunlin. Often in the first two weeks of September all three may be together within 10 yds (9 m) of the road.

Timing

Pagham Harbour is well worth visiting at all times of the year. During migration periods the early morning is by far the best time of day, with birds passing overhead as well as feeding avidly in the vegetation. The area around Church Norton picks up most migrants as they arrive. It always pays to check the Ferry Pool during the early morning when the light is behind you. After midday the sun will be in your eyes and therefore picking out plumage details at the far side will be very difficult. In spring and autumn, many waders from the harbour roost on the Ferry Pool at high tide, so choose a day with high water in the morning. In winter, activity extends throughout the day and it is the tide which is more important. Try to choose a high tide around midday so you watch for the two or three hours either side of it. This brings the waders closer, flushes dabbling duck from the marshes and brings diving duck and grebes into the harbour. If time permits, it can be worth staying out until dusk when any geese and Ruff come in to roost; the latter choose the Ferry Pool in autumn, but the harbour in winter. The best evening places are the North Wall and the Ferry Pool. Pagham Lagoon is normally only good during the winter, as it is heavily disturbed from spring to autumn.

Access

Pagham Harbour is reached via the B2145, which is signposted to Selsey and runs south from a roundabout on the A27 Chichester bypass. Within 1 mile (1.6 km) the B2166 to Pagham turns off left: from which a minor road leads to Pagham Lagoon, but is best left until later.

The best place to start is at Pagham Harbour LNR Information Centre. This is sited on the left-hand side of the B2145, about 0.5 mile (0.8 km) beyond Sidlesham village. Here there is a large car park, a welcome public convenience and, at the Centre, the latest information on which birds are around. From here you should walk south for 150 yds (137 m) to a hide which overlooks the Ferry Pool. This, provided by the Sussex Ornithological Society, is of great value in poor weather. It also has provision for wheelchair birdwatchers and can be reached from the car park on a hard path and level ground. Slightly further on, a gateway through the fence leads to the footpath around the harbour so one can turn either way. To reach Church Norton from here, you can choose to walk east either alongside the rife, checking for birds skulking in the two pools on your right-hand side, or on the seawall footpath the other side of the pools. The seawall gives good views over surrounding fields, so is better in winter. The two paths join at the end of the long pool and then it is 1 mile (1.6 km) to Church Norton. The footpath leaves the seawall and drops onto the foreshore just over halfway along, so it is impassable at high water on large spring tides and is rather muddy at low water: strong boots or wellingtons are recommended.

Alternatively, there is a small car park at Church Norton. This is a popular area which can become quite crowded, so careful parking is required. Note that this car park serves the church and may be closed at times. To reach it, follow the Selsey road from the Information Centre; about 1.5 miles (2.4 km) take a sharp left turn on a right-hand bend, signposted to Church Norton, and follow this narrow lane straight on to the end; the car park is tucked around to the left at the end of it. After checking for migrants around the church, a path leads onto the shingly foreshore. Turn right here to the shingle beach. A walk south will provide views over the Severals and a small grazed field and inland marsh, while in winter it can be worth walking left to the tip of the south shingle spit to look for birds in the entrance channel. (This beach gives the best views here of passing seabirds, although Selsey Bill is much better for them.)

The route north from the Information Centre runs into the village of Sidlesham where, immediately after joining a road, turn right along another road by an arm of the harbour. Where the road kinks away from the harbour, keep straight on by a harbourside stone wall. For a short distance, about 150 yds (137 m), the path on the seawall is very bad and, except at high spring tides, it is best to walk along the foreshore. The path then becomes better and follows the field boundaries giving a good view over the mudflats of the inner harbour before turning sharp right and reaching the North Wall. This gives an excellent view inland over fields, rifes and reedbeds; initially saltmarsh dominates the harbour, but at the eastern end the harbour's outer mudflats and creeks can be seen. Normally there is little point in continuing past the thatched 'Salthouse' cottage which, during summer months, serves as the second Information Centre. But if masses of grebes and diving ducks are present, turn right here along the edge of the foreshore and this gives an excellent vantage point over the water. Slightly further on you will come to Pagham Lagoon, but after scanning it for diving birds, you will have to retrace your steps for the 2 miles (3.2 km) back to the Information Centre.

The easiest way to watch Pagham Lagoon is from the car park at its southern end. To reach this, take the B2166, which leaves the Selsey road near the A27, for 5 miles (8 km) following signs to Pagham. Here the road swings to the right, signposted to 'The Church', but turn sharp left to 'The Sea'. After 0.25 mile (0.4 km), there is a complex junction where you should turn diagonally right across the 'bus turning area' into Beach Road. Follow this road, observing the signs (the unmade road is potholed and has many ramps) and in 0.6 mile (1 km) the car park is reached. Look back at the lagoon, but also go onto the tip of the spit where a superb view of the harbour can be had from the new hide.

Calendar

Resident: Heron, Sparrowhawk, Mute Swan, Shelduck, Oystercatcher, Ringed Plover, Redshank, Little Owl, Barn Owl, Green Woodpecker, Reed and Corn Bunting.

December–February: Slavonian, Great Crested and Little Grebes, Cormorant, Little Egret, Brent Geese, Wigeon, Pintail, Teal, Eider, Red-breasted Merganser, Hen Harrier, Merlin, Water Rail, Avocet, Grey Plover, Dunlin, Ruff, Turnstone, Bar- and Black-tailed Godwits, Curlew, Glaucous and Mediterranean Gull, Short-eared Owl, Stock Dove, Stonechat, Fieldfare, Chiffchaff, Firecrest, Rock Pipit, lark and finch flocks.

March–May: Osprey, Common, Sandwich and Little Terns, Shoveler, Whimbrel, Bar-tailed Godwit, scarce waders and passerines, Willow Warbler, Sedge Warbler, Blackcap, Lesser Whitethroat, Linnet, Goldfinch, Yellow Wagtail, hirundines.

June–July: Late migrants such as Spotted Flycatcher and Garden Warbler, terns, Reed Warbler, Yellow Wagtail.

August–November: Offshore Gannet, Arctic Skua and terns, rapid increase in common ducks and waders through the period, including Little Stint, Curlew Sandpiper, Little Ringed Plover, Greenshank, Spotted Redshank, Ruff, Black-tailed Godwit, Whimbrel, Common and Wood Sandpipers; yellow-legged Herring Gull, Wryneck, Tree Pipit, Yellow and Grey Wagtails overhead, Reed, Sedge and Willow Warblers, Goldcrest, Whinchat, Wheatear, Redstart, Pied and Spotted Flycatchers, passage raptors. During October to November, Red-necked Grebe, Black Redstart, Firecrest, passage finches, especially Goldfinch, Linnet and Siskin.

14 SELSEY BILL AND BRACKLESHAM BAY

Habitat

Protruding about 3.5 miles (5.5 km) from the coast of West Sussex, the shingle point of Selsey Bill is an excellent site from which to observe migration. Although the town of Selsey has developed considerably, at the point where the B2145 reaches the coast and at the end of Grafton Road, there are some large vegetated gardens and a small playing field where passerine migrants gather.

Since early 1989, when the old Pontins holiday camp was demolished, the site has remained undeveloped allowing trees, scrub and grassland to develop. This area, bounded by the playing field, the lifeboat station and the built-up area is in private ownership, but is bisected by a footpath which gives good views in all directions. It has proved to be a magnet for migrants, adding several species to the Selsey list. It seems however that the site may soon be redeveloped.

To the west of Selsey is a shingle beach, backed by grassland, which further inland gives way to cereals. This area is Bracklesham Bay, sometimes known as Selsey West Fields. The intertidal area is of particular interest for its petrified forest, exposed at low water on spring tides.

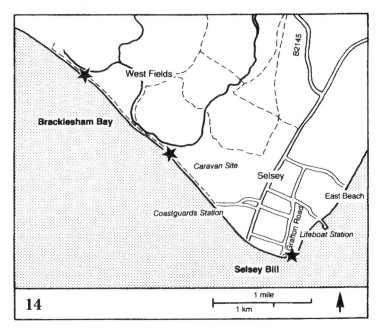

Species

Regular observations have been made at Selsey Bill since the late 1950s and the list of species seen extends to over 260 species. Winter is the time when relatively little passerine migration takes place. However, should severe weather set in many thousands of winter thrushes, Skylarks, Lapwing and Golden Plover may gather in the fields or be seen streaming south or west. In a typical winter it is worth checking along the shoreline from the Bill tip to East Beach. There is usually a Black Redstart to be found feeding on kelp flies emerging in a sheltered spot behind a breakwater, along with a few Rock and Meadow Pipits. Gulls gather around the fishing boats on East Beach, and a Glaucous Gull has been a regular winter feature for a number of years, whilst the occasional Mediterranean Gull may join the more common species. On the sea, especially off the Bill, any of the three divers may be present, with Great Northern being the least regular. Slavonian and Great Crested Grebes, Razorbills, Guillemots, Red-breasted Merganser and Eider can usually be picked out. The strong tides mean that birds drift well offshore at times. Large numbers of divers and other seabirds may occur in severe weather. When the tide is out, gulls scavenge, many flying up with mussels which they drop onto the shingle to crack them open, and small numbers of Oystercatchers and Turnstone feed. The West Fields are best at this time of year. Flocks of Brent Geese graze the grassland and, if the fields are slightly flooded with winter rain, Wigeon, Pintail and Teal may be there. Several thousand Lapwing and Golden Plover feed on the fields plus about 100 Curlew. If fortunate, up to 100 each of Ruff, Black-tailed Godwit and Dunlin can be present as well. Severe weather often brings Grey Geese to these fields. Raptors are often impressive: up to three Hen Harriers, five Short-eared Owls, several Sparrowhawks and a Merlin or Barn Owl might be seen on a single good day. Passerines are not very abundant, but a few Goldfinches, Greenfinches, Skylarks and Linnets feed among the rank vegetation. Along the field boundaries, small numbers of Corn Buntings and Yellowhammers might be seen, together with a Stonechat or two.

Spring migrants are often seen on early dates at Selsey Bill. In most years Wheatears and Black Redstarts are seen in the first week of March. These are soon followed by others and on late March days up to 40 or 50 Wheatears in their sparkling plumage can be seen flicking along the beach and perching on the breakwaters. After that, a steady movement of Swallows, Yellow Wagtails, Willow Warblers and many other typical spring migrants pass through. The playing field often holds Yellow Wagtails (do check for the Blue-headed race) while on the beach it is worth examining the Pied Wagtails for the much greyer continental or northern race, the White Wagtail. Many Meadow Pipits come in off the sea. While seawatching, a remarkable range of scarce species have been seen arriving; from Alpine Swift, Nightjar and Stone Curlew to Honey Buzzard, Hobby and Hoopoe. One or two Serins are seen each spring and sometimes a male will stop to sing in trees and nearby gardens.

The main spring feature is the eastward passage of birds at sea. It follows the pattern described earlier for Beachy Head and involves Brent Geese, Common Scoter and Sandwich Terns up to mid April. In the following month a very wide range of divers, duck, waders, skuas and terns passes by especially on east or southeast winds. The fact that Selsey Bill is well to the west in the county means that there are differences in the range and numbers of each species involved. There tends to be a more 'oceanic' component, with proportionately more Manx Shearwaters, Gannets, Fulmars and auks and fewer skuas, terns and waders than the more easterly sites. It is thought that a proportion of the

Manx Shearwater

waders, such as Whimbrel and Bar-tailed Godwits and 'Commic' and Black Terns, cut off the Selsey Peninsula by flying overland from Chichester to Pagham Harbour. Among the notable species seen recently are the annual flocks of Pomarine Skuas, Long-tailed Skua, a few Roseate Terns and Caspian Tern.

Breeding birds are few. Most of the interest lies on the fields near Bracklesham Bay. Here Lapwing still twist and creak in their display flight, a Redshank or two hangs melodically in the air and a Ringed Plover might be seen. Apart from this group of birds, which are becoming very scarce in Sussex, a scattering of Meadow Pipits and Skylarks breed, with a few Reed and Sedge Warblers and Reed Buntings in the wetter ditches and Whitethroats in the bramble or gorse patches in the low field boundaries.

Autumn migration starts in late July with a few Wheatears and Willow Warblers but picks up quickly. August and September bring a very wide range of migrants, and numbers are rather larger than in spring. Many of the warblers, Redstarts and Pied Flycatchers are seen in the bushes near the Bill tip, but the Whinchats and Wheatears are more frequent on the West Fields. Overhead Yellow and Grey Wagtails, Tree Pipits and many Swifts and hirundines move west or south, out to sea. The West Fields attract passage raptors, so that it is not a surprise to see a Marsh or Montagu's Harrier, a Buzzard or an Osprey drifting through, or a Hobby scything its way out to sea. Easterly winds can bring unusual birds at this time, a Wryneck, Red-backed or Woodchat Shrike, Ortolan Bunting or Tawny Pipit may drop down for a day. A southwesterly gale can be good, bringing Manx and an occasional Sooty Shearwater and Pomarine, Great and Arctic Skuas may be seen fairly frequently. Most of these, especially the shearwaters, pass by about 0.75 mile (1.2 km) out to sea.

From late September to early November passage of most summer migrants starts to wind down; hirundines, Goldfinches, Linnets, Meadow Pipits and, in some years, Siskins and Redpolls pour out south or southwest. A search of bushes may reveal a Firecrest among the Goldcrests, Black Redstarts or a Ring Ouzel or two before, in late October, the winter thrushes appear. Then Brent Geese, Wigeon and other wildfowl start their steady build-up, with flocks flying purposefully westwards to their wintering grounds. Sometimes, too, a Grey

Phalarope will drop in, feeding in the wash around a breakwater and giving superb views, or a Little Auk might splash down.

This is also the time when rarities may appear. In recent years these have included Radde's Warbler, Desert Wheatear, Yellow-browed Warbler and 'Siberian' Stonechat.

Timing

Selsey Bill is undoubtedly at its best from early March until early June, and again throughout August to mid November, when the migration is at its most intense. To find passerine migrants, either in the bushes, on the ground or flying over, it is best to be there early in the morning. Many strollers, dog-walkers and holidaymakers will be around later and will invariably scare some birds away. Seawatching is best when the tide is reasonably well in, for the seabirds tend to fly past further out at low water; if this coincides with early morning, so much the better. A light to moderate wind between northeast and south is required in the spring, while in the autumn the best winds are gales between south and southwest. The West Fields can be excellent when wet in winter, but may turn up virtually any migrant at any time. Like all sites, a light southeast wind is most likely to bring scarcer continental migrants to this area, especially in May and from late August to mid October. In winter good birdwatching can be had, especially at the onset of severe weather, when large movements of birds take place.

Access

Selsey Bill lies at the end of the B2145 where a shingle car park overlooks the sea. A network of private roads (access is permitted) lies to the east of the B2145. Parking is allowed by the road next to the playing field, which lies to the west of the end of Grafton Road (adjacent to the former coastguard tower known as 'Bill's House'. From here it is possible to walk either 1.25 miles (2 km) to the East Beach, or 3 miles (5 km) to the West Fields. The walk along the top of the beach in the latter area gives a good view over the farmland so it is not necessary to seek out the public footpaths across it — neither add materially to the range of birds that can be seen. On high spring tides or when an onshore gale is blowing, it is not advisable to attempt to walk along the foreshore; seek a more accessible route through the many small roads which lead down to the sea.

Calendar

Resident: Sparrowhawk, Ringed Plover, Lapwing, Barn and Little Owls, Yellowhammer, Corn and Reed Buntings.

December–February: Red-throated (and possibly other) Divers, Great Crested, Red-necked and Slavonian Grebes, Brent Goose, Shelduck, Eider, Red-breasted Merganser, Hen Harrier, Merlin, Oystercatcher, Golden Plover, Ruff, Black-tailed Godwit, Turnstone, Mediterranean and Glaucous Gulls, auks, Short-eared Owl, Rock Pipit, Black Redstart, Stonechat.

March–May: Black-throated Diver, Manx Shearwater, Eider, Common and Velvet Scoters, Goldeneye, Osprey, Hobby, Knot, Sanderling, Bar-tailed Godwit, Whimbrel, Common Sandpiper, Pomarine, Arctic and Great Skuas, Mediterranean and Little Gulls, Kittiwake, terns including

Roseate and Black, Cuckoo, Hoopoe, Yellow Wagtail, Redstart, Whinchat, Wheatear, small numbers of warblers, Serin, Goldfinch, Linnet. Look for spring overshoots such as Bee-eater, Alpine Swift or Woodchat Shrike.

August–November: Sooty and Manx Shearwaters, Brent Goose (mid September onwards), Teal, Marsh Harrier, Buzzard, Hobby, Purple Sandpiper, Greenshank, Common Sandpiper, Grey Phalarope, skuas, Little Gull, terns, Little Auk (November), Turtle Dove, Short-eared Owl, Wryneck, Tawny and Tree Pipits, Yellow and Grey Wagtails, Black Redstart, chats, Wheatear (including rare species), Ring Ouzel, common and scarce warblers, Firecrest, Spotted and Pied Flycatchers, Goldfinch, Linnet.

15 CHICHESTER HARBOUR
OS 197
SU 60/70 & 80/90

Habitat

Chichester Harbour comprises four finger-like channels — Emsworth, Thorney, Bosham and Fishbourne — radiating from a southern core area. Part of this 7042 acres (2850 ha) site lies in Hampshire. Most of the intertidal flats are muddy with some eel-grass (*Zostera*) and algae (*Enteromorpha* and *Ulva*) growing on it during the warmer months. South of Thorney Island and, to a limited amount, around the harbour mouth there are areas of sand and shingle. Many of the once extensive marshes of cord grass (*Spartina*) have suffered die-back followed by erosion back to a mud base, but this plant remains the dominant species and is especially prominent in the Chichester Harbour Conservancy's Nutbourne Marshes LNR. Small areas of botanically rich marshes occur scattered around the harbour; in these, the upright yellow-flowered stems of golden samphire, mauve sea aster and three species of sea lavender push through the dominant sea purslane. At the head of the Fishbourne Channel there is a large tidal reedbed.

Most of the land around the harbour is either built-up or intensively farmed. However, a few areas are of special interest, especially as winter roost sites. These are the large sand dune and shingle system at East Head (owned by the National Trust), a small shingle spit at Ellanore, and inland pools and wet grassland behind Chichester Yacht Basin and along the Chichester Canal. The upper reaches of the channel are rewarding. However, the most important complex is Thorney Deeps and Thorney Island, virtually all of which is owned by the Ministry of Defence, but Pilsey Island at the southern tip is an RSPB reserve. The wet grass, scrub and reeds of Thorney Deeps comprise the largest undeveloped area left around Chichester Harbour. Two other shingle and saltmarsh islands, North and South Stakes, lie at the southern limit of the Nutbourne Marshes LNR.

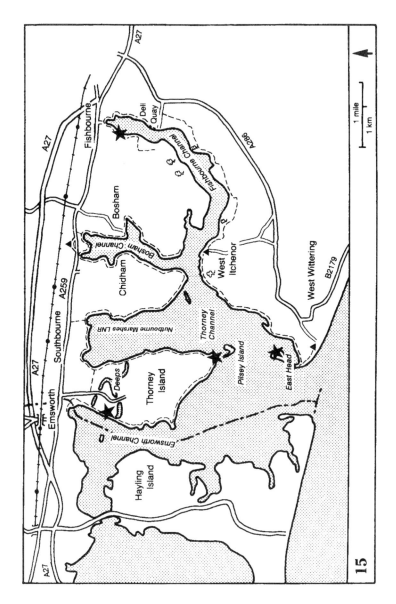

Species

Winter is by far the most important time for birds in the harbour. Then, internationally important numbers of Brent Geese, Ringed and Grey Plover, Dunlin, Bar-tailed and Black-tailed Godwits pour in to feed on its many sheltered mudflats, along with nationally important numbers of Shelduck, Sanderling, Curlew and together with large numbers of many other waterbirds. Most feed on the intertidal flats although many Brent Geese forage inland, principally on grass, but they also graze winter cereals. At high tide spectacular numbers of waders and wildfowl can be seen at close range at the established roost sites, but because of the high levels of disturbance — particularly at weekends — birds do tend to move around. Grey Herons breed nearby and they are seen regularly throughout the year, and Little Egrets have become a regular feature in recent years, with nearly 200 recorded at the main roost site in the early autumn. In the spring and summer, Common, Sandwich and Little Terns and Black-headed Gulls usually breed and can be seen feeding anywhere in the harbour. The margins of the shoreline and the edge of the farmland attract many passerines, both in the winter and the breeding season. The Harbour does not appear to attract major falls of migrants, but small numbers of chats and warblers are recorded regularly, and many other species are noted. Migrant raptors are frequently seen both in spring and autumn, those occurring fairly regularly being Marsh Harrier, Buzzard, Osprey and Hobby. In winter Hen Harrier, Merlin and Peregrine are annual.

Main Birdwatching Zones

Many parts of the harbour are accessible by foot, but just two sections are described here to give the flavour of this excellent birdwatching area.

EAST HEAD to WEST ITCHENOR

The sandy areas around East Head attract a roost of many waders for the winter. There is a tendency for the 100 to 300 Sanderling to be found on the western and northern beaches facing into the harbour mouth. Ringed and Grey Plovers, Dunlin and Redshank, with a scattering of other species, usually concentrate on the sheltered, low saltmarsh area on the inside of East Head. They remain here if only slightly disturbed or if high tide is fairly low, but on spring tides they move to another area, sometimes as far as Pilsey Island. Winter brings a large flock of over 2,000 Brent Geese. Initially they feed in the bay inside the spit, but as the season progresses, the grass by the West Wittering car park is used. To be able to sit in the car and watch this vast flock only a short distance away is a fascinating experience. Up to 100 Shelduck can be found with the Brent Geese on the water. A wide range of other wildfowl are here too — Teal and Wigeon among the dabbling duck — while the channel can hold any of the three diver species, the five grebes or diving duck. In midwinter Great Crested Grebes, Goldeneye and Red-breasted Merganser are always present and a careful search of the bobbing shapes may well reveal a Slavonian or Red-necked Grebe, a Common or Velvet Scoter or a Guillemot.

The adjacent farmland holds both Grey and Red-legged Partridge. These are very prominent in snowy weather when round, black, huddled shapes, often in sevens, are visible in the centre of fields. Both Little and Barn Owls might be seen even in daylight, the former sitting patiently awaiting a move by its prey, while the latter floats over the few patches of rougher ground. Among the many passerines which occur here, it is worth looking for a Stonechat perched on the scrub by the road to the car park, Rock or Meadow Pipits and Greenfinches on the tideline, Goldfinches and Linnets in rough ground (and do keep an eye open for Lesser Spotted Woodpeckers in the hedgerows, often picked up by hearing a firm hammering on a nearby branch). The upper saltmarsh around, and the wet patch in the centre of, East Head sometimes attracts a long-staying Snow Bunting or Shore Lark. The Merlins and Peregrines which frequent Thorney Island often make dashing raids over to East Head, and Sparrowhawks are regular.

Migration through this area has been little studied, but the gorse, blackthorn, tamarisks and brambles can hide virtually any of the commoner warblers, while Wheatears and Whinchats perch along the fences around the car park. Although the beach is not ideally sited to concentrate seabird migrants moving east in spring, quite substantial numbers of 'Commic', Little and Sandwich Terns and a scattering of skuas and waders pass close enough to see reasonably well.

In summer there are a few Reed and Sedge Warblers breeding in the reedbeds and Turtle Doves purring from the bushes along the road to Snowhill. Small numbers of Ringed Plovers, Shelduck and Redshank breed, but generally there are too many people about to make a visit pleasant.

Autumn migration is not particularly noticeable, although quite substantial numbers of Dunlin and Ringed Plovers can be found roosting inside East Head when high water coincides with few dog-walkers. It is well worthwhile checking the plovers carefully, as the odd Kentish Plover may join them. Many passerine migrants move through this area. Although the range is good including Pied Flycatcher, Redstart and Yellow Wagtail, numbers are rarely high. As October and November draw on, there is a return of the flocks of wintering waders and wildfowl.

THORNEY ISLAND

In many ways Thorney provides the best birdwatching areas in Chichester Harbour. It was an island until the saltmarshes between it and the mainland were reclaimed in 1870. These marshes, Thorney Deeps, are now brackish grazing marshes with large areas of open saline water, substantial reedbeds and scrub areas. The island is owned by the Ministry of Defence and there is no public access, but a footpath around the shoreline provides excellent views of the Harbour. A large, mainly disused, airfield here is fringed with small patches of scrub. Mud predominates on the flats to the east and west, but to the south lies the RSPB's Pilsey Island Reserve. It should be noted that there is no access to this important roost site by foot.

Thorney Island is justifiably famous for its winter birds. The Pilsey Island high tide roost hosts up to 15,000 Dunlin, 1,500 Grey Plover, 1,300 Oystercatchers, 800 Bar-tailed Godwits, 200 Sanderling and 600 Ringed Plover gather at high tide, providing some excellent close views of packs of waders. An Avocet or two has become regular in recent winters. On this southern tip wildfowl are much in evidence — up to 1,000 Brent Geese now feed on the mown grass of the airfield or on the harbour. It is worth checking through them for Pale-bellied Brent or White-fronted Geese. Small groups of Shelduck, Pintail and Teal forage among the saltmarshes. Just offshore, at the mouth of the Thorney Channel, diving waterbirds can be much in evidence — Goldeneye, Red-breasted Merganser and Great Crested Grebes are present in moderate numbers with most, up to 30 or more, late on in February/March. Scarcer species often seen include Slavonian, Black-necked and Red-necked Grebes, Eider, Long-tailed Duck and auks. Wildfowl, too, are a feature of

Thorney Deeps. Here up to 10 Mute Swans, 100 Coot, 800 Wigeon, 50 Gadwall and 30 Shoveler join with 500 Teal, up to 500 Redshank and 800 Brent Geese to rest or feed around high water. It is well worth checking carefully through these for Scaup and Smew, while among the waders up to 10 Greenshank, four Spotted Redshank and sometimes a Green or Common Sandpiper may winter.

Brent Geese

In winter, small flocks of Corn Buntings, Yellowhammers, Linnets, many other small passerines and a flock of about 100 Stock Doves, along with the numerous waterbirds, means Thorney attracts many raptors. These include regular Merlins and Peregrines and up to ten Short-eared Owls which hunt over both the Deeps and the southern airfield. Barn and Little Owls and Kestrels are also regulars. In addition Hen Harriers and a few Sparrowhawks are also seen. Severe weather brings flocks of hundreds of Redwings and Fieldfares onto grassland and some of the many Water Rails, which winter in the Deeps, into ditches where they can be seen. Thorney is, however, generally mild so it is not unusual to find a Chiffchaff or two wintering, and some surprising species have overwintered, for example, Temminck's Stint and Yellow-browed Warbler. The southern tip of Thorney is a good place to look for early migrants, for example, Wheatears and Sandwich, Common or Little Terns, and the reedbeds on the Deeps attract early Sedge and Reed Warblers. Many other passerine migrants filter through during the spring. At this time, waders start to assume their breeding plumage, so enhancing the roost at Pilsey. A May passage of up to 250 to 300 Ringed Plovers is notable, and the careful observer may find the odd Kentish Plover. Common Sandpipers, sometimes a Temminck's Stint and a flock of Black-tailed Godwits are among migrant waders to be seen on the Deeps.

There is a diverse breeding bird community here. Perhaps the Deeps prove to be the most productive with breeding Redshank, Lapwing, Shelduck, Mute Swans, Tufted Duck and Little Grebes and a host of passerines. The reedbeds support over 80 pairs of Reed and 45 pairs of Sedge Warblers, while the adjacent scrub includes many Whitethroats, Linnets and Yellowhammers, and a few Turtle Doves. Nightingales unfortunately seem to have declined in recent years from about five pairs to one. On the farmland and scrub edges Lesser Whitethroats, Corn Buntings and many more Whitethroats can be seen or heard. On the southern tip Ringed Plovers and often Oystercatchers nest, but the terns seen there are mostly from colonies on Nutbourne Marshes LNR. After mild winters the rough ground may hold a pair of Stonechats. Most of the waders which spend the summer in Chichester Harbour roost on and around Pilsey, including several hundred Oystercatchers and smaller numbers of Bar-tailed Godwits, Grey Plover and Turnstone.

The rapid return of waders in late July and August is a major feature. On the Deeps up to 150 Greenshank, 1,250 Redshank and small numbers of Spotted Redshank, Green and Common Sandpipers are a regular feature. By September Wigeon, Shoveler and Pintail start to appear. The high tide roost on Pilsey also builds up rapidly with up to 1,200 Ringed Plovers, 600 Bar-tailed Godwit and 2,000 Grey Plover and Dunlin in late August. On a neap tide they roost on the sands, but if there is disturbance or a high spring tide, they take refuge on the airfield. This also attracts early-returning Golden Plover. Up to 500 Black-tailed Godwits also roost on Thorney Deeps in September. Later, in mid October, Brent Geese can be seen feeding on the intertidal flats. The rest of the wintering wildfowl appear soon afterwards. Passerine migration in autumn is good, the reedbeds on the Deeps provide a roost site for several thousand Swallows and Sand Martins and smaller numbers of wagtails. The roosts attract dusk raids by Sparrowhawks and Hobby. The open areas can often be, literally, hopping with Wheatears, Whin-chats and, later on, with Stonechats. Little Egrets have become regular in recent years and peak in the early autumn. They roost on the western side of Thorney Island, and nearly 200 have been counted. It is worth checking through the roosts for any passing Spoonbills or other egrets.

Timing

Chichester Harbour can be good throughout the year, although for waders and wildfowl high tides from August through to May are best. To watch birds fly on and off their roosts it is necessary to be present about two hours either side of high-water. Inevitably, in such an attractive and accessible area, it is best to make a visit as early as possible in the day to minimise disturbance, as well as to coincide with peak activity of smaller species. On very bright sunny days it is difficult to pick up species on the water or mud off the southern tips of Thorney or Chidham, so a slightly overcast day is best, as are very light winds. The relatively exposed nature of the harbour and many fairly long walks means that if there are strong winds and rain, birdwatching can become very uncomfortable. Hard weather can bring in many geese and duck, but it seems to have the opposite effect on Black-tailed Godwit and the plovers, for they decrease in numbers sharply.

Access

Chichester Harbour is bounded to the north by the A259 (Chichester to Havant), to the east by the A286 (Chichester to West Wittering) and to the west by the A3023 on Hayling Island. There are many points of access down to the shore and the Chichester Harbour Conservancy is making a good footpath around most of the 40 miles (65 km) of the harbour's shoreline. Car parking is presently limited. For East Head and West Itchenor car parks and toilets are found both at West Wittering (access to which is found where the A286 meets the B2179) and at West Itchenor. West Wittering is accessible by bus, although Itchenor is not. From both of these, which are 7 miles (12 km) from Chichester, the coastal footpath is clearly marked and runs for 2.5 miles (4 km).

It is usually possible to find a car parking space on the first 500 yds (458 m) along the access road to Thorney Island from the A259, which is just 0.25 mile (0.4 km) east of Emsworth. Failing that, Emsworth provides the best possibility. From the former, take the public footpath by the Emsworth Marina to the west, and it is possible to follow the coastal footpath right around the 5 miles (8 km) of the island before cutting back the 1 mile (1.6 km) on the track alongside the north edge of Thorney Deeps, to the car. Inevitably the walk from Emsworth is slightly longer, but it also includes passing Emsworth Slipper Pond, which may have some interesting birds on it. Emsworth can be reached by bus or train.

Calendar

Resident: Little Grebe, Cormorant, Little Egret, Grey Heron, Mute Swan, Shelduck, Tufted Duck, Sparrowhawk, Water Rail, Oystercatcher, Ringed Plover, Grey Plover, Black and Bar-tailed Godwits, Curlew, Redshank, Turnstone, Stock Dove, Little and Barn Owls, Linnet, Reed and Corn Buntings.

December–February: Great Crested and scarce grebes, Brent Goose, Wigeon, Gadwall, Teal, Pintail, Scaup, Eider, Long-tailed Duck, Scoters, Goldeneye, Red-breasted Merganser, Hen Harrier, Merlin, Peregrine, Avocet, Golden Plover, Knot, Sanderling, Dunlin, Common and Jack Snipe, Guillemot, Short-eared Owl, Rock Pipit, Grey Wagtail, Fieldfare, Redwing, Snow Bunting.

March–May: Marsh Harrier, Grey Partridge, Kentish Plover, Whimbrel, Mediterranean Gull, Sandwich, Common and Little Terns, Cuckoo, White Wagtail, Nightingale, Redstart, Whinchat, Whitethroat, Willow Warbler, Yellowhammer.

June–July: Turtle Dove, Sedge and Reed Warblers and Lesser Whitethroat. Wader numbers start to build up from July onwards.

August–November: Wintering wildfowl appear from late September, Osprey, Hobby, Little Stint, Curlew Sandpiper, Spotted Redshank, Redshank, Greenshank, Green and Common Sandpipers, Little Gull, Black Tern, Kingfisher, Yellow Wagtail, migrant hirundines, warblers and chats, Spotted Flycatcher, Goldfinch.

16 KINGLEY VALE

OS 197
SU 80/90 & 81/91

Habitat

This chalk downland site is of outstanding importance for its impressive dense yew woodland. With massive, twisted trunks some of these huge trees are over 500 years old and form the finest yew forest in Europe.

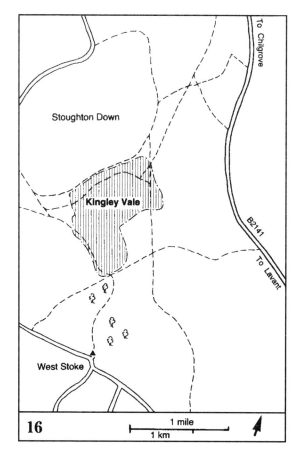

Kingley Vale is, accordingly, a National Nature Reserve — managed by English Nature — and is worth a visit just to experience this unique habitat.

Elsewhere at Kingley Vale there are extensive tracts of scrub, which is excellent for birds until it becomes too dense and tall. Aside from reserve management, the scrub is also grazed by resident fallow deer. Management includes maintaining and enlarging the area of grassland which is of great botanical importance. The wide range of species includes aromatic thyme and marjoram, colourful harebells and vetches and eleven species of orchids including good numbers of early purple, frog and pyramidal. The grassland attracts many butterflies including chalkhill blue, brown argus, dark green fritillary and grizzled skipper, whilst the scrub and deciduous woodland hold purple and green hairstreak, and white admirals can be found in season. Perhaps the most welcome butterfly of all, the yellow brimstone, heralds the start of spring from February onwards.

Species

Much of the birdlife present in the winter months is associated with the wealth of berry-bearing trees and shrubs. In some years an exceptionally heavy crop, particularly of yew and hawthorn, can bring in large numbers of thrushes, finches and tits. In poor crop years much smaller numbers are present.

By late October the first Scandinavian winter visitors, the Redwing and Fieldfare, will be seen. Perhaps their calls will give them away: the Redwing with its thin 'sseeip' and the chuckle of Fieldfare penetrating through the woodland. The former can be very difficult to see, their striking head pattern of a frowning white supercilium and lines of black and white merges into the background of leaves and berries. Fieldfares tend to sit further out on branches, the pale grey rumps contrasting with the black tail. Both continental and British Song Thrushes and Blackbirds also join the feast, while the large, noisy and aggressive Mistle Thrushes can be picked out by their rattling calls and huge white-tipped tails. These rapacious birds work their way through the berry crop and then move out to feed in the nearby fields.

Although the numbers of finches have decreased over the years, flocks of Greenfinches and Chaffinches do occur, with an occasional white-rumped Brambling or the heavy, short-tailed Hawfinch. Tits concentrate in mobile flocks in winter, so it is a matter of patience and searching to locate them. Once found, a careful examination of the flock should reveal Marsh, Long-tailed and Coal as well as the commoner species; associated with them are likely to be a few Goldcrests and Treecreepers.

The common raptors and owls also occur, including Sparrowhawk and Tawny Owl, and an occasional Buzzard. The dense scrub affords protection from the winter weather to small numbers of wintering woodcock, but they are far from easy to locate unless seen flying at dusk.

Migration on the Downs is not obvious and the months of March and April are notable for the steady disappearance of winter visitors, with perhaps a Redwing uttering its weak, but melodic, song from the depths of the woodland late in this period. By early April the thin song of the Chiffchaff heralds the arrival of the spring migrants. It is followed almost immediately by the summery cascade of notes from the Willow Warbler. Throughout April a trickle of Wheatears passes through, feeding on the short turf, while later small numbers of Redstarts and Whinchats perch on the fences, flying down to take insects off the ground. Swallows flick through the valley on their way north. The occasional Hoopoe has been recorded, attracted to the warm south-facing clearings.

Spring merges into summer as the Blackcaps, Whitethroats and Lesser Whitethroats, and the occasional Garden Warbler, appear and sing from the scrub. By far the most difficult to separate are the first and last, not least because a Blackcap in its quieter sub-song can appear to mimic a Garden Warbler. The open patches of scrub attract Whitethroats while the others species prefer the more dense areas. Summer brings the much too brief song period of the Nightingale, a few pairs of which breed on the reserve. Usually it is at its best from late April to mid May; by the end of the month, the marvellous liquid notes, which are given both by day and night, are uttered only sporadically. Other summer visitors that should put in an appearance include the Turtle Dove and Cuckoo. In the dense downland scrub, in addition to the many warblers, such attractive birds as Long-tailed Tits and Bullfinches may be found, while Yellowhammers sing from the more open areas. The pure yew forest sections are remarkably poor for birds, but where it merges with the ash, oak or hawthorn, it is transformed. Several pairs of Tawny Owls are present although they are usually only seen when their downy youngsters emerge in early July to sit in the open, enduring with equanimity the scolding of a host of passerines, or at dusk. At this time of day the lucky observer may catch a glimpse of a roding Woodcock, flying overhead with its peculiar jerky wing beats and distinctive croaking and 'pssit' call-notes. Little Owls may sit on a boundary fencepost watching for large insects and small mammals.

The most colourful species resident here are two with brilliant yellow rumps. The most obvious is the Green Woodpecker, usually seen bounding away when disturbed from hunting for ants on open grassland. The other is the over-gaudy Golden Pheasant, the male so distinctive in its reds and yellows, but the female resembles a small, rather yellowish female Pheasant with a strongly barred tail. These are slowly increasing in numbers and are usually found where ash and yew woodland have a dense shrub understorey in which the pheasants can hide. Patience is needed to see one.

For a short period after the songs cease birds can be difficult to see, but then the hordes of youngsters emerge and join in with the autumn migrants. Many Willow Warblers move through in August followed by passage *Sylvia* warblers taking advantage of the feast of blackberries and elderberries. A few Redstarts, Whinchats, Pied and Spotted Flycatchers and an occasional Black Redstart move through. A Hobby may be spotted overhead, perhaps in fast pursuit of a passing juvenile Swallow or House Martin. By mid October the haws are ripening ready to welcome and provide for the thrushes in winter. Then finches are moving so, in some years, Siskins, Redpolls and others may fly past.

Timing

Summer, with its diversity of birds, insects and plants, is the most pleasant time to visit this area. Early morning reveals most birds, but the butterflies do not appear in numbers until at least mid-morning and sunny days are of course best. In winter it has an unusual attraction even if, at first sight, it appears empty.

Access

The reserve can only be approached on foot from the car park which lies just over 0.75 mile (1.3 km) from its entrance. The car park is at the western edge of the hamlet of West Stoke, itself 2 miles (3.2 km) on a minor road from Mid Lavant (on the A286 Chichester to Midhurst road) to Funtington. On entering the hamlet, the car park is located on the north side of the road, just on a sharp left-hand bend (coming from Mid Lavant). On entering the reserve a 2 mile (3.2 km) nature trail, covering most of the habitats, is signposted. Other footpaths can be taken to explore the area further. Details are available in a nature trail leaflet produced by English Nature.

Calendar

Resident: Sparrowhawk, Kestrel, Golden Pheasant, Tawny Owl, Green and Great Spotted Woodpeckers, Mistle Thrush, Goldcrest, Long-tailed and Marsh Tits, Chaffinch.

December–February: Buzzard, Woodcock, Fieldfare, Redwing, Greenfinch, Hawfinch.

March–May: Stock Dove, Cuckoo, Barn Owl, possibly Hoopoe, Tree Pipit, Nightingale, Redstart, Whinchat, Wheatear, *Sylvia* warblers, Chiffchaff, Willow Warbler.

June–July: Woodcock, Turtle Dove, *Sylvia* warblers, Yellowhammer, Corn Bunting.

August–November: Hobby, Black Redstart, Redstart, Whinchat, Stonechat, Wheatear, warblers, Spotted and Pied Flycatchers, Siskin, Redpoll.

17 IPING AND STEDHAM COMMONS

OS 197
SU 82/92

Habitat

Iping and Stedham Commons represent some of the best remaining open heathland in West Sussex. They are situated on a band of greensand that sweeps south and east from the Hampshire/West Sussex border at Liss, to Pulborough in West Sussex. It's geological and biological interest make it an integral part of the Wealden Heaths, which whilst now highly fragmented, still comprise a highly distinctive landscape and habitat in these two counties and southwest Surrey.

Much of the former heathland in this area has been reclaimed for agriculture, planted with conifers or mined for sand and gravel. Succession on the remaining areas is an ever present threat, but is currently held at bay by the co-operative efforts of the Sussex Downs

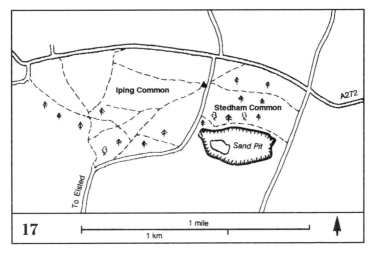

Conservation Board, English Nature, West Sussex County Council, the Sussex Wildlife Trust, the National Trust and local landowners. Iping and Stedham Commons are perhaps the most accessible and provide the visitor with a flavour of what these once-extensive heathlands must have been like.

Species

Taken as a whole, the Wealden Heaths are one the most important sites in Britain for the three heathland specialists — Nightjar, Woodlark and Dartford Warbler — and all three can be found at Iping and Stedham.

The Woodlark's evocative song can be heard as early as February, when the males re-establish their breeding territories. Early mornings are best, and on some occasions it is possible to find up to five males in the air at one time. The lucky birdwatcher may catch a glimpse of a passing Hen Harrier too, quartering the heath with its wings held in the classic shallow 'V', and moving south to the Downs. Sparrowhawks can be seen around the Commons at any time of year, but are perhaps most obvious in the winter months when they hunt in the open more often, perhaps hunting the flocks of Meadow Pipits which occur on the heath in the winter.

As the days lengthen the heaths' Stonechats become more obvious, calling and singing from the tops of the gorse bushes. Green Woodpeckers regularly frequent the open heath, and the nearby birch and conifer woodland also supports Great Spotted Woodpeckers, and very occasionally Lesser Spotted Woodpeckers too. A typical woodland bird community can be found here, including most of the tits, Nuthatch, Treecreeper and Goldcrest. The birches around the heath provide winter feeding for flocks of Redpoll and Siskin, some of which probably stay to breed in the surrounding woodlands.

March and April brings Chiffchaffs and Willow Warblers, followed soon after by Tree Pipits whose parachuting songflight becomes a characteristic feature of the heath in spring and summer. The odd Wheatear and Whinchat also pass through. The warmer days encourage the male Dartford Warblers to sing from the tops of the gorse bushes and heather, and on calm days to indulge in their fluttering songflights. Other breeders include Yellowhammer, Linnet and Reed Bunting in the wetter areas.

By early to mid May the first of the Nightjars will have arrived, and at dusk their eerie churring song can be heard across the heath. It is best to arrive about half an hour before sunset, and wait for the birds to start calling. Wait for the churring to stop — which usually means the bird has taken flight — and listen for the loud slap of the males wing-clapping display. The patient observer can then pick out the the the white wing patches and tail spots as they fly between songposts. The roding woodcock's 'piss-p' call adds to the special atmosphere of heathlands in summer.

The patient observer is likely to be rewarded by views of Hobby which hunt insects and hirundines over the heath, and Buzzards are now seen with increasing regularity.

Early autumn is marked by the steady movement of Swallows and House Martins as they follow the Downs east to Beachy Head. Wheatears and Whinchats may be seen on the heath, and the surrounding scrub and woodland may hold Spotted Flycatchers, Lesser Whitethroats and other common passerine migrants. The nearby gravel pit sometimes holds the odd Greenshank or Green Sandpiper, for example, but few remain there for long. By late October and November the movement of finches, Chaffinches, Siskins and Redpolls in particular, or Redwing and Fieldfare becomes a feature of the area, but the heath itself gradually becomes progressively quieter.

Timing

Spring and early summer is the best time to visit this heathland. To hear Nightjars, it is more practical to arrange a dusk visit on a warm and calm evening; arrive about sunset so you can be in position well before they start calling. For virtually all other species, an early morning visit will give by far the best results. Then birds are at their most vocal and active, and few visitors will have arrived on the reserve to walk, jog or exercise their dogs.

Access

Iping and Stedham Local Nature Reserve is 1.5 miles (3 km) west of Midhurst on the A272. There is a car park provided by the County Council, situated 0.1 mile (0.2 km) down the road to Elsted on the right-hand side. Iping Common lies to the west, Stedham to the east. It has a height barrier to prevent entry of tall vehicles. From here a network of paths, some on firebreaks, radiate out with the main one leading west northwest towards the highest part of the Common; this goes through a good range of habitat types. To look at woodland it is best to walk 200 yds (183 m) further down the road to where a track leads off to the east. This track skirts both coniferous and deciduous woodland and the sand pit.

Calendar

Resident: Sparrowhawk, Green and Great Spotted Woodpeckers, Skylark, Meadow Pipit, Dartford Warbler and Stonechat (both in mild winters), Nuthatch, Goldcrest, Long-tailed, Marsh and Coal Tit, Treecreeper.

November–March: Hen Harrier, Meadow Pipit.

March–May: Cuckoo, Woodlark, Tree Pipit, Stonechat, Whitethroat, Willow Warbler, Linnet, Yellowhammer, Reed Bunting.

June–July: Hobby, Nightjar, Turtle Dove, Woodcock.

August–November: Buzzard, hirundines, Whinchat, Wheatear, Redwing and Fieldfare (November), Lesser Whitethroat, Chiffchaff, Redpoll, Siskin.

ADDITIONAL SITES

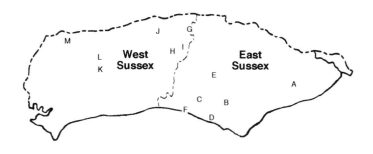

Key & Site	Habitat	Birds of Interest	Peak Season	Nearest Town
A Fore Wood	Deciduous woodland, coppice	Sparrowhawk, woodpeckers warblers, Hawfinch	Spring/ summer	Crowhurst
OS 199 TQ 752130	*An RSPB reserve. Car parking possible at village hall opposite Crowhurst Church (TQ 765126). Can be very muddy after heavy rain.*			
B Arlington Reservoir	Reservoir, scrub, reeds, farmland	Great Crested Grebe, wigeon, passage waders, terns, gulls, passerines, Osprey	All year	Polegate
OS 199 TQ 533075	*South East Water LNR. Good car park and toilets off B2108. Circular path (1.75 miles) with hide in northeast corner and disabled access to dam. Car park has toilets but note closes at dusk. Handy railway station at Berwick. Groups wishing to visit should contact South East Water's Conservation and Recreation Department on 01323 870810.*			
C Lewes Levels	Wet grassland, ditches	Yellow Wagtail, migrants, wildfowl	Spring/ winter	Lewes
OS 198 TQ 420080	*Main area is to west of River Ouse. Footpaths along banks of river and running out from A26 Lewes/Newhaven road. Birds dependent on amount of shallow surface flooding.*			
D Newhaven Tidemills	Shingle beach, grassland, harbour	Seabird passage, sea-duck, Purple Sandpiper, Kittiwake	All year	Newhaven
OS 198 TQ 458002	*Access from car parks on A259 Newhaven to Seaford road or at west end of Seaford promenade. Wintering Purple Sandpipers best viewed from east arm of harbour at high tide. Autumn flocks of terns can be viewed off Newhaven beach.*			
E Chailey Common	Heathland	Cuckoo, Tree Pipit, Stonechat, warblers	Spring/ summer	Haywards Heath
OS 198 TQ 390215	*An East Sussex County Council LNR. Car parks situated off roads crossing the common.*			

Key & Site	Habitat	Birds of Interest	Peak Season	Nearest Town
F Brighton Marina	Marina, with views out to sea	Winter grebes, divers, Shag, Purple Sandpiper, passage sea-duck, waders and seabirds, Kittiwake, Rock Pipit, Black Redstart	Spring/ autumn/ winter	Brighton
OS 198 TQ 330034	*Car park inside marina. Spring seawatching is best from western arm with a good south-easterly. Eastern arm worth checking for wintering divers, Shags, auks.*			
G Weir Wood Reservoir	Reservoir with shallow water, woodland and scrub	Grebes, wildfowl, Osprey, passage waders, warblers	All year	East Grinstead
OS 187 TQ385343	*The western end is crossed by an unclassified road, and another runs to the south, with a car park at the southwestern corner and path to hide. The western section is a LNR.*			
H Ardingly Reservoir	Reservoir, wood-land	Grebes, wildfowl, Sparrowhawk, war-blers		Haywards Heath
OS 198 TQ 330295	*Owned by South East Water. Car parking is provided near the dam, and two hides are available for public use. Can be viewed from causeway on minor road between Ardingly and Balcombe, but note parking is restricted.*			
I Wakehurst Place	Woodland, park-land, lakes	Woodland birds, finches (winter)	All year	Balcombe
OS 187 TQ 340315	*The grounds of this old house are owned by the National Trust and managed by Kew Gardens. Access is via a large car park off the B2028. Free entry for NT members, charge for non-members. Access to the Loder Valley Nature Reserve is by permit only from the Wakehurst Place administration.*			
J Buchan Park	Woodland, meadows, ponds, heathland	Sparrowhawk, Woodcock, Lesser Spotted Woodpecker, passerines, Siskins, Redpolls	All year	Crawley
OS 187 TQ 245315	*A Country Park managed by West Sussex County Council. The car park is situated just off the A2220 Crawley/Horsham road. The centre has toilets, and refreshments are available at weekends and Bank Holidays.*			
K Burton Mill Pond	Lake, woodland, reedbed	Wildfowl inc. Goldeneye, Goosander, Hobby, Kingfisher, all three woodpeck-ers, Grey Wagtail, woodland passerines	All year	Petworth
OS 197 SU 997180	*A LNR managed by the Sussex Wildlife Trust and West Sussex County Council. Parking is available by the mill — please do not park on the road. View from the road and pub-lic footpaths.*			
L Ebernoe Common	Pasture, wood-land, grassland, ponds, hedge-rows	Little Grebe, Mandarin, Woodcock, all three woodpeckers and Nuthatch, Nightingale, warblers	Spring	Northchapel
OS 197 SU 975278	*The reserve car park is located off the minor road to the east of the A283 at the grid ref-erence indicated. An information board shows public footpaths through the woodland.*			

Key & Site	Habitat	Birds of Interest	Peak Season	Nearest Town
M Blackdown	Woodland, scrub, ponds, heathland	Sparrowhawk, Woodcock, woodpeckers, Tree Pipit, warblers, Nightjar (?)	Spring/ summer	Haslemere
OS 197 SU 920293	*This afforested hill is managed by the National Trust, who are restoring parts of the site to heathland. It provides an excellent vantage point over the surrounding countryside.*			

SYSTEMATIC LIST OF SPECIES

This species list, which follows the sequence and scientific nomenclature of *The Birds of the Western Palearctic* (Cramp *et al.* 1977–94), includes all species recorded in Kent, Surrey and Sussex during the period 1900–1996 inclusive. A brief description of the status of each species follows, based on the records published in *Birds of Kent* (1981), *Birds in Surrey* (1972), *Birds of Sussex* (1996) and the annual county reports. For species that provide a spectacle for birdwatchers, and those with local or restricted distributions, a few sites are identified where these birds may be anticipated.

Red-throated Diver   *Gavia stellata*
Annual winter visitor and passage migrant off the coast. Occasional on inland waters.
Sites: Kent — 3, 9. Sussex — 1, 6, 7, F.

Black-throated Diver   *Gavia arctica*
Scarce but annual winter visitor to coastal waters. Occasional inland. Regular passage migrant off the coast.
Sites: Kent — 9. Sussex — 6, 7.

Great Northern Diver   *Gavia immer*
Scarce but annual winter visitor to coastal waters. Rare inland. Small but regular spring passage off the coast.

White-billed Diver   *Gavia adamsii*
Very rare vagrant.

Little Grebe   *Tachybaptus ruficollis*
Widespread breeding species. Forms large wintering flocks in late autumn.
Sites: Kent — 1.

Great Crested Grebe   *Podiceps cristatus*
Widespread breeding species, mainly at inland freshwater sites, passage migrant and winter visitor. Flocks gather around the coast.
Sites: Kent — 3, 9, 11, 12. Surrey — 3, 4, 5, 8. Sussex — 3, 12, B, H.

Red-necked Grebe   *Podiceps grisegena*
Annual winter visitor to coastal waters and inland. Scarce passage migrant around the coast.
Sites: Kent — 9, 12. Sussex — 3, 13, 14, 15.

Slavonian Grebe   *Podiceps auritus*
Annual winter visitor to coastal waters, rarer inland. Scarce passage migrant around the coast.
Sites: Kent — 2, 9. Sussex — 13, 14, 15.

Black-necked Grebe *Podiceps nigricollis*
Annual visitor, less common in winter than the previous two species, but seen more frequently at other times of the year, apart from mid-summer. Has bred.
Sites: Kent — 9. Sussex — 12, 15.

Fulmar *Fulmarus glacialis*
Passage migrant and breeding species on coastal cliffs. Scarce in late autumn. Very rare inland.
Sites: Kent — 6, 8. Sussex — 2, 6, 7.

Cory's Shearwater *Calonectris diomedea*
Rare vagrant.

Great Shearwater *Puffinus gravis*
Very rare vagrant.

Sooty Shearwater *Puffinus griseus*
Scarce but regular in autumn on coast.

Manx Shearwater *Puffinus puffinus*
Annual passage migrant, mainly during May–October, on coast. Occasional inland following gales.
Sites: Kent — 3, 6, 9. Sussex — 14.

Mediterranean Shearwater *Puffinus yelkouan*
Scarce but regular passage migrant in summer and autumn on coast. Has occurred inland.
Sites: Kent — 9.

Little Shearwater *Puffinus assimilis*
Very rare vagrant.

Storm Petrel *Hydrobates pelagicus*
Rare autumn and winter vagrant, mainly after severe gales.

Leach's Petrel *Oceanodroma leucorhoa*
Scarce but regular in late autumn. Rare inland, usually after gales.
Sites: Kent — 1, 3, 6, 9, D.

Gannet *Sula bassana*
Passage migrant, most numerous in autumn on coast. Rare inland.
Sites: Kent — 3, 6, 7, 9. Sussex — 6, 7.

Cormorant *Phalacrocorax carbo*
Increasingly widespread, commonly seen on inland waters. Recently established breeding colonies.
Sites: Kent — 9. Surrey — 4. Sussex — 2, 9, 10.

Shag *Phalacrocorax aristotelis*
Passage migrant and mainly winter visitor on coast, occasional on inland waters.
Sites: Sussex — 3, F.

Bittern   *Botaurus stellaris*
Scarce winter visitor, occasionally remaining to late spring. Has bred.
Sites: Kent — 5, 9, 12.   Surrey — 9.

American Bittern   *Botaurus lentiginosus*
Very rare vagrant.

Little Bittern   *Ixobrychus minutus*
Very rare vagrant.

Night Heron   *Nycticorax nycticorax*
Rare vagrant.

Squacco Heron   *Ardeola ralloides*
Very rare vagrant.

Cattle Egret   *Bubulcus ibis*
Very rare vagrant.

Little Egret   *Egretta garzetta*
Increasingly regular visitor in late summer and early autumn. Wintering
in small numbers.
Sites: Kent — 1.   Sussex — 7, 9, 13, 15.

Great White Egret   *Egretta alba*
Very rare vagrant.

Grey Heron   *Ardea cinerea*
Widespread resident.
Sites: Kent — 1.   Surrey — 1, 3, 4, 13.   Sussex — 5, 9, 15.

Purple Heron   *Ardea purpurea*
Rare, mainly spring vagrant.

Black Stork   *Ciconia nigra*
Very rare vagrant.

White Stork   *Ciconia ciconia*
Rare vagrant.

Glossy Ibis   *Plegadis falcinellus*
Very rare vagrant.

Spoonbill   *Platalea leucorodia*
Almost annual visitor in small numbers, most frequent in spring and
autumn. Rarer inland.

Mute Swan   *Cygnus olor*
Widespread resident. Large non-breeding flocks form during summer.
Sites: Kent — 3, 5, H.   Surrey — 4.   Sussex — 5, 10.

Bewick's Swan   *Cygnus columbianus*
Regular passage migrant and winter visitor to traditional sites. Occasional
elsewhere.

Sites: Kent — 1, 3, 5, 9, H.   Sussex — 10.

Whooper Swan   *Cygnus cygnus*
Scarce passage migrant and winter visitor.

Bean Goose   *Anser fabalis*
Scarce passage migrant and winter visitor.

Pink-footed Goose   *Anser brachyrhynchus*
Scarce passage migrant and winter visitor.

White-fronted Goose   *Anser albifrons*
Regular passage migrant and winter visitor.
Sites: Kent — 1, 3.

Lesser White-fronted Goose   *Anser erythropus*
Very rare vagrant.

Greylag Goose   *Anser anser*
Increasingly widespread resident feral populations. Scarce passage migrant and winter visitor.

Snow Goose   *Anser caerulescens*
Very rare vagrant, but status unclear as a result of escapes.

Canada Goose   *Branta canadensis*
Increasingly widespread resident feral populations.

Barnacle Goose   *Branta leucopsis*
Scarce winter visitor. Occasional cold weather influxes. An increasing feral resident.

Brent Goose   *Branta bernicla*
Regular passage migrant and winter visitor.
Sites: Kent — 2, 3, 9.   Sussex — 13, 15.

Red-breasted Goose   *Branta ruficollis*
Very rare vagrant.

Egyptian Goose   *Alopochen aegyptiacus*
Rare feral visitor.

Ruddy Shelduck   *Tadorna ferruginea*
Rare vagrant, but status unclear as a result of escapes. Feral birds occasionally breed.

Shelduck   *Tadorna tadorna*
Common resident, passage migrant and winter visitor to coast. Breeds inland annually.
Sites: Kent — 2.   Sussex — 10, 13, 15.

Mandarin   *Aix galericulata*
Increasing introduced resident.
Sites: Kent — 11, M.   Surrey — 4, 9, 11.   Sussex — 4, 10, L.

Wigeon *Anas penelope*
Common passage migrant and winter visitor. Has bred.
Sites: Kent — 3, 9. Surrey — 4. Sussex — 3, 10, 13, 15.

American Wigeon *Anas americana*
Very rare vagrant.

Gadwall *Anas strepera*
Scarce but increasing breeding species. Passage migrant and common winter visitor.
Sites: Kent — 1, 5, 12. Surrey — 3. Sussex — 1, 3, 10.

Teal *Anas crecca*
Scarce breeding species. Passage migrant and common winter visitor.

Mallard *Anas platyrhynchos*
Widespread breeding species, passage migrant and winter visitor.

Black Duck *Anas rubripes*
Very rare vagrant.

Pintail *Anus acuta*
Regular passage migrant and winter visitor mainly to coastal areas. Occasionally summers and has bred.
Sites: Kent — 1, 2, 3. Surrey — 1, 4. Sussex — 10, 13, 15.

Garganey *Anas querquedula*
Passage migrant and scarce summer visitor. A few pairs breed almost annually.
Sites: Kent — 1, 3, 5. Surrey — 4, 9. Sussex — 3, 5, 10.

Blue-winged Teal *Anas discors*
Very rare vagrant.

Shoveler *Anas clypeata*
Widespread but thinly distributed breeding species. Common passage migrant and winter visitor.
Sites: Kent — 1, 2, 3, 9. Surrey — 1, 4. Sussex — 1, 10, 12, 15.

Red-crested Pochard *Netta rufina*
Scarce passage migrant and winter visitor. Status undoubtedly confused by escapes and feral breeding population.

Pochard *Aythya ferina*
Passage migrant and winter visitor. Uncommon breeding species.
Sites: Kent — 1, 9, 12. Surrey — 4. Sussex — 12.

Ring-necked Duck *Aythya collaris*
Very rare vagrant.

Ferruginous Duck *Aythya nyroca*
Rare vagrant. True status confused by escapes.

Tufted Duck *Aythya fuligula*
Widespread breeding species and winter visitor. Passage migrant.

Scaup *Aythya marila*
Passage migrant and winter visitor mainly to coastal waters. Scarce inland.
Sites: Kent — 2, G. Sussex — 1.

Eider *Somateria mollissima*
Winter visitor, passage migrant and non-breeding summer visitor to coast. Very rare inland.
Sites: Kent — 3, 6, 7, 9. Sussex — 2, 5, 13, 15.

King Eider *Somateria spectabilis*
Very rare vagrant.

Long-tailed Duck *Clangula hyemalis*
Uncommon but regular passage migrant and winter, mainly to coastal areas. Occasional on inland waters.

Common Scoter *Melanitta nigra*
Common spring passage migrant and winter visitor, less common non-breeding summer visitor to coast. Scarce inland.
Sites: Kent — 3, 6, 9. Sussex — 1, 6, 7, 14.

Surf Scoter *Melanitta perspicillata*
Very rare vagrant.

Velvet Scoter *Melanitta fusca*
Regular passage migrant and winter visitor in small numbers on coast. Has summered. Very rare inland.
Sites: Kent — 9. Sussex — 1, 6, 7, 14.

Goldeneye *Bucephala clangula*
Regular passage migrant and winter visitor in small numbers.
Sites: Kent — 1, 2, 9, 11. Surrey — 3, 4. Sussex — 3, 10, 12, 15.

Smew *Mergus albellus*
Scarce but regular winter visitor. Occasional cold weather influxes.
Sites: Kent — 9. Surrey — 4. Sussex — 1, 3.

Red-breasted Merganser *Mergus serrator*
Regular passage migrant and winter visitor to coast. A few summer annually. Scarce inland.
Sites: Kent — 2, 3, 9. Sussex — 13, 15.

Goosander *Mergus merganser*
Uncommon but regular winter visitor and passage migrant. Occasional cold weather influxes.
Sites: Kent — 9, 11. Surrey — 3, 4, 6. Sussex — 3, 10, 12.

Ruddy Duck *Oxyura jamaicensis*
Uncommon introduced breeding species and winter visitor.
Sites: Kent — 1, 9, 11. Surrey — 4. Sussex — 12.

Honey Buzzard *Pernis apivorus*
Scarce but increasing spring and autumn passage migrant. Has bred.

Black Kite *Milvus migrans*
Rare mainly spring passage migrant.

Red Kite *Milvus milvus*
Scarce but annual visitor, mainly in spring and autumn.

White-tailed Eagle *Haliaeetus albicilla*
Very rare winter visitor.

Marsh Harrier *Circus aeruginosus*
Passage migrant showing a marked increase in recent years. Now breeding and wintering regularly.
Sites: Kent — 3. Sussex — 1, 13, 15.

Hen Harrier *Circus cyaneus*
Regular winter visitor and passage migrant. Forms roosts in winter months. Has bred.
Sites: Kent — 1, 3, 5, H. Surrey — 7, 9. Sussex — 1, 4, 5, 14, 17.

Montagu's Harrier *Circus pygargus*
Scarce but regular passage migrant. Occasionally breeds.

Goshawk *Accipiter gentilis*
Scarce but increasing. A few pairs now breed.

Sparrowhawk *Accipiter nisus*
Widespread. Increasing breeding species, common passage migrant and winter visitor.

Buzzard *Buteo buteo*
A rare breeding resident. Increasing passage migrant and winter visitor.

Rough-legged Buzzard *Buteo lagopus*
Rare winter visitor and passage migrant.
Sites: Kent — 3.

Osprey *Pandion haliaetus*
Annual spring and autumn passage migrant. Occasional summer records.

Lesser Kestrel *Falco naumanni*
Very rare vagrant.

Kestrel *Falco tinnunculus*
Widespread breeding species. Passage migrant in small numbers.

Red-footed Falcon *Falco vespertinus*
Rare vagrant.

Merlin *Falco columbarius*
Passage migrant and annual winter visitor.
Sites: Kent — 1, 3. Surrey — 7, 9. Sussex — 5, 15.

Hobby *Falco subbuteo*
Increasing breeding summer visitor and passage migrant.
Sites: Kent — 5. Surrey — 7, 9. Sussex — 1, 10, 17.

Gyr Falcon *Falco rusticolus*
Very rare vagrant.

Peregrine *Falco peregrinus*
Increasing as a passage migrant and winter visitor. A few pairs now breed.
Sites: Kent — 3. Sussex — 7, 13, 15.

Black Grouse *Tetrao tetrix*
Formerly bred. Introductions survived until the 1930s.

Red-legged Partridge *Alectoris rufa*
Widespread resident, locally common.

Grey Partridge *Perdix perdix*
Widespread but decreasing resident.

Quail *Coturnix coturnix*
Scarce summer visitor, recorded in variable numbers from year to year.
Sites: Kent — 7.

Pheasant *Phasianus colchicus*
Common and widespread resident. Numbers boosted each year by release of birds for shooting.

Golden Pheasant *Chrysolophus pictus*
Scarce introduced resident.

Water Rail *Rallus aquaticus*
Regular passage migrant and winter visitor. Uncommon breeding species.
Sites: Kent — 5, 12. Surrey — 9. Sussex — 10, 15.

Spotted Crake *Porzana porzana*
Scarce mainly autumn passage migrant.

Sora Rail *Porzana carolina*
Very rare vagrant.

Little Crake *Porzana parva*
Very rare vagrant.

Baillon's Crake *Porzana pusilla*
Very rare vagrant.

Corncrake *Crex crex*
Rare passage migrant, occasionally heard in summer. Formerly bred.

Moorhen *Gallinula chloropus*
Common and widespread resident.

Coot *Fulica atra*
Common, widespread resident and winter visitor.

American Coot *Fulica americana*
Very rare vagrant.

Crane *Grus grus*
Rare passage migrant and winter visitor.

Little Bustard *Tetrax tetrax*
Very rare vagrant.

Great Bustard *Otis tarda*
Very rare vagrant.

Oystercatcher *Haematopus ostralegus*
Regular breeding species, passage migrant and winter visitor to coast.
Scarce inland.
Sites: Kent — 3, 7, 9. Sussex — 1, 13, 15.

Black-winged Stilt *Himantopus himantopus*
Rare mainly spring vagrant.

Avocet *Recurvirostra avosetta*
Increasing passage migrant, winter and breeding summer visitor.
Rare inland.
Sites: Kent — 1, 2, 3, 9. Sussex — 1, 13, 15.

Stone Curlew *Burhinus oedicnemus*
Rare passage migrant. Formerly bred.

Cream-coloured Courser *Cursorius cursor*
Very rare vagrant.

Collared Pratincole *Glareola pratincola*
Rare vagrant.

Oriental Pratincole *Glareola maldivarum*
Very rare vagrant.

Black-winged Pratincole *Glareola nordmanni*
Very rare vagrant.

Little Ringed Plover *Charadrius dubius*
Regular passage migrant, but scarce breeding summer visitor.
Sites: Kent — 1, 9, 11. Surrey — 4, 13. Sussex — 10, 13.

Ringed Plover *Charadrius hiaticula*
Common coastal breeder, passage migrant and winter visitor. Scarce
inland, breeding irregularly.
Sites: Kent — 1, 2, 7. Surrey — 4. Sussex — 1, 13, 15.

Killdeer *Charadrius vociferus*
Very rare vagrant.

Kentish Plover *Charadrius alexandrinus*
Scarce but regular passage migrant in spring and autumn.
Sites: Kent — 7, 9. Sussex — 15.

Greater Sand Plover *Charadrius leschenaultii*
Very rare vagrant.

Dotterel *Charadrius morinellus*
Scarce but regular passage migrant in spring and autumn.

American Golden Plover *Pluvialis dominica*
Very rare vagrant.

Pacific Golden Plover *Pluvialis fulva*
Very rare vagrant.

Golden Plover *Pluvialis apricaria*
Widespread passage migrant and winter visitor. Commonest around coastal areas.
Sites: Kent — 1, 3, 7, H. Surrey — 4. Sussex — 5, 14.

Grey Plover *Pluvialis squatarola*
Common passage migrant and winter visitor to coast. Scarce inland.
Sites: Kent — 3. Sussex — 13, 15.

Sociable Plover *Chettusia gregaria*
Very rare vagrant.

Lapwing *Vanellus vanellus*
Widespread but declining breeding species. Common passage migrant and winter visitor.

Knot *Calidris canutus*
Common passage migrant and winter visitor to coast. Rare inland.
Sites: Kent — 1, 3, 7, 9. Sussex — 15.

Sanderling *Calidris alba*
Common passage migrant and winter visitor to coast. Scarce inland.
Sites: Kent — 6, 7, 9. Sussex — 1, 11, 15.

Semipalmated Sandpiper *Calidris pusilla*
Very rare vagrant.

Little Stint *Calidris minuta*
Regular passage migrant, more common in autumn.
Sites: Kent — 1, 3, 7, 9. Surrey — A. Sussex — 1, 9, 12.

Temminck's Stint *Calidris temminckii*
Scarce but regular passage migrant.
Sites: Kent — 1, 3, 7, 9. Sussex — 7.

Least Sandpiper *Calidris minutilla*
Very rare vagrant.

White-rumped Sandpiper   *Calidris fuscicollis*
Rare vagrant.

Baird's Sandpiper   *Calidris bairdii*
Very rare vagrant.

Pectoral Sandpiper   *Calidris melanotos*
Scarce but regular autumn vagrant.

Sharp-tailed Sandpiper   *Calidris acuminata*
Very rare vagrant.

Curlew Sandpiper   *Calidris ferruginea*
Scarce spring passage migrant, regular in autumn.
Sites: Kent — 1, 3, 7, 9.   Sussex — 1, 13.

Purple Sandpiper   *Calidris maritima*
Regular local winter visitor to a few coastal sites. Rare inland.
Sites: Kent — 6, F.   Sussex — 2, 9, D, F.

Dunlin   *Calidris alpina*
Abundant winter visitor and common passage migrant. Scarce in summer and inland.
Sites: Kent — 1, 2, 3.   Sussex — 13, 15.

Broad-billed Sandpiper   *Limicola falcinellus*
Rare mainly spring vagrant.

Stilt Sandpiper   *Micropalama himantopus*
Very rare vagrant.

Buff-breasted Sandpiper   *Tryngites subruficollis*
Very rare vagrant.

Ruff   *Philomachus pugnax*
Regular passage migrant and winter visitor.
Sites: Kent — 3, 9.   Surrey — 4, A.   Sussex — 10, 13, 14.

Jack Snipe   *Lymnocryptes minimus*
Scarce but regular winter visitor and passage migrant.
Sites: Sussex — 5, 10, 11.

Snipe   *Gallinago gallinago*
Declining local breeding species. Widespread passage migrant and winter visitor.
Sites: Kent — 5.   Surrey — 9.   Sussex — 5, 10.

Great Snipe   *Gallinago media*
Very rare autumn vagrant.

Long-billed Dowitcher   *Limnodromus scolopaceus*
Very rare vagrant.

Woodcock *Scolopax rusticola*
Widespread breeding species. Common winter visitor and passage migrant.
Sites: Kent — 4, 10, J, K, N. Surrey — 7, 9, M. Sussex — 4, 10, 17, L, M.

Black-tailed Godwit *Limosa limosa*
Locally common winter visitor and passage migrant. A few pairs now breed.
Sites: Kent — 1, 2, 3. Sussex — 13, 15.

Bar-tailed Godwit *Limosa lapponica*
Common passage migrant and winter visitor to coast. Scarce inland.
Sites: Kent — 3, 7, 9. Sussex — 6, 7, 15, F.

Whimbrel *Numenius phaeopus*
Regular passage migrant.
Sites: Kent — 1, 3, 7, 9. Sussex — 1, 5, 6, 7, 10, F.

Curlew *Numenius arquata*
Common winter visitor and passage migrant. Scarce inland, but breeds annually.
Sites: Kent — 1, 2, 3, 7. Surrey — 9. Sussex — 1, 4.

Upland Sandpiper *Bartramia longicauda*
Very rare vagrant.

Spotted Redshank *Tringa erythropus*
Passage migrant, more numerous in autumn than spring. Small numbers overwinter.
Sites: Kent — 3. Sussex — 13, 15.

Redshank *Tringa totanus*
Widespread but declining breeding species away from the coast. Common passage migrant and winter visitor.
Sites: Kent — 1, 2, 3. Sussex — 10, 13, 15.

Marsh Sandpiper *Tringa stagnatilis*
Rare vagrant.

Greenshank *Tringa nebularia*
Regular passage migrant. Small numbers overwinter.
Sites: Kent — 1, 2, 3, 7. Surrey — 4, A. Sussex — 15.

Greater Yellowlegs *Tringa melanoleuca*
Very rare vagrant.

Lesser Yellowlegs *Tringa flavipes*
Very rare vagrant.

Solitary Sandpiper *Tringa solitaria*
Very rare vagrant.

Green Sandpiper *Tringa ochropus*
Regular widespread passage migrant. Small numbers overwinter.

Wood Sandpiper   *Tringa glareola*
Regular passage migrant, more common in autumn. Scarcer inland.
Sites: Kent — 1, 3, 5, 9.   Surrey — 6, A.   Sussex — 1, 5, 7, 10.

Terek Sandpiper   *Xenus cinereus*
Very rare vagrant.

Common Sandpiper   *Actitis hypoleusos*
Widespread passage migrant. Small numbers overwinter. Has bred.
Sites: Kent — 1, 7, 11.   Surrey — 1, 4, A.   Sussex — 15.

Spotted Sandpiper   *Actitis macularia*
Very rare vagrant.

Turnstone   *Arenaria interpres*
Common winter visitor and passage migrant. Scarce inland.
Sites: Kent — 3, 6.   Sussex — 1, 13, 15.

Wilson's Phalarope   *Phalaropus tricolor*
Very rare vagrant.

Red-necked Phalarope   *Phalaropus lobatus*
Scarce passage migrant, more common in autumn.

Grey Phalarope   *Phalaropus fulicarius*
Scarce autumn and rare winter visitor.

Pomarine Skua   *Stercorarius pomarinus*
Passage migrant, regular in spring along south coast and in autumn more often on the north coast. Rare in winter and inland.
Sites: Kent — 1, 3, 6, 9, D.   Sussex — 6, 7, 14, D, F.

Arctic Skua   *Stercorarius parasiticus*
Common coastal passage migrant in spring and autumn. Scarce in winter and inland.
Sites: Kent — 1, 3, 6, 9, D.   Sussex — 6, 7, 14, D, F.

Long-tailed Skua   *Stercorarius longicaudus*
Scarce passage migrant, more regular in autumn. Very rare inland.

Great Skua   *Stercorarius skua*
Regular passage migrant, more common in autumn. Scarce in winter and inland.
Sites: Kent — 1, 3, 6, 9, D.   Sussex — 6, 7, 14, D, F.

Mediterranean Gull   *Larus melanocephalus*
Increasingly regular around the coast and at a few inland sites. Breeding numbers also increasing.
Sites: Kent — 6, 9, F.   Sussex — 1, 6, 7, 9, 14, F.

Laughing Gull   *Larus atricilla*
Very rare vagrant.

Franklin's Gull *Larus pipixcan*
Very rare vagrant.

Little Gull *Larus minutus*
Regular spring and autumn passage migrant. Small numbers occur in winter and summer.
Sites: Kent — 3, 9. Surrey — 4. Sussex — 12.

Sabine's Gull *Larus sabini*
Scarce but regular autumn passage migrant on the coast. Rare inland.

Bonaparte's Gull *Larus philadelphia*
Very rare vagrant.

Black-headed Gull *Larus ridibundus*
Common breeding species around the coast. Widespread passage migrant and winter visitor.

Slender-billed Gull *Larus genei*
Very rare vagrant.

Ring-billed Gull *Larus delawarensis*
Rare vagrant.

Common Gull *Larus canus*
Common passage migrant and winter visitor. Small local breeding population.
Sites: Kent — 9.

Lesser Black-backed Gull *Larus fuscus*
Widespread passage migrant and winter visitor. A few pairs breed regularly.

Herring Gull *Larus argentatus*
Common breeding resident, passage migrant and winter visitor.

Iceland Gull *Larus glaucoides*
Scarce winter visitor and passage migrant.

Glaucous Gull *Larus hyperboreus*
Scarce but regular winter visitor and passage migrant.
Sites: Kent — 6, 7, 9. Sussex — 1, 14.

Great Black-backed Gull *Larus marinus*
Common winter visitor and passage migrant. Small numbers summer.

Kittiwake *Rissa tridactyla*
Common passage migrant and winter visitor. Large local breeding populations. Scarce inland.
Sites: Kent — 8. Sussex — 7.

Ivory Gull *Pagophila eburnea*
Very rare vagrant.

Gull-billed Tern *Gelochelidon nilotica*
Now a very rare vagrant.

Caspian Tern *Sterna caspia*
Rare vagrant.

Royal Tern *Sterna maxima*
Very rare vagrant.

Lesser Crested Tern *Sterna bengalensis*
Very rare vagrant.

Sandwich Tern *Sterna sandvicensis*
Common passage migrant and summer visitor, scarcer inland. Breeding
colonies recently re-established. Occasionally overwinters.
Sites: Kent — 7, 9. Sussex — 1.

Roseate Tern *Sterna dougalii*
Rare summer visitor and passage migrant.
Sites: Kent — 9. Sussex — 1, 14.

Common Tern *Sterna hirundo*
Common passage migrant and summer visitor. A few pairs breed
inland; larger colonies present around the coast.
Sites: Kent — 1, 5, 9. Surrey — 4. Sussex — 1, 12, 15.

Arctic Tern *Sterna paradisaea*
Regular passage migrant in spring and autumn.
Sites: Kent — 9. Surrey — 4.

Forster's Tern *Sterna forsteri*
Very rare vagrant.

Bridled Tern *Sterna anaethetus*
Very rare vagrant.

Sooty Tern *Sterna fuscata*
Very rare vagrant.

Little Tern *Sterna albifrons*
Passage migrant and summer visitor. Small numbers breed locally
around the coast. Scarce inland.
Sites: Kent — 1, 3, 5, 7, 9. Sussex — 1, 13.

Whiskered Tern *Chlidonias hybridus*
Very rare vagrant.

Black Tern *Chlidonias niger*
Passage migrant, regularly seen on inland waters.
Sites: Kent — 3, 9. Surrey — 4, 9. Sussex — 1, 12.

White-winged Black Tern *Chlidonias leucopterus*
Rare vagrant, more often in autumn around the coast.

Guillemot   *Uria aalge*
Common passage migrant and winter visitor to coast. Formerly bred.
Rare inland.
Sites: Kent — 1, 3, 6, 9.   Sussex — 9, 14.

Razorbill   *Alca torda*
Passage migrant and winter visitor to coast, less common than
Guillemot. Rare inland.
Sites: Kent — 3, 6, 9.

Black Guillemot   *Cepphus grylle*
Rare vagrant.

Little Auk   *Alle alle*
Scarce but regular late autumn passage migrant.

Puffin   *Fratercula arctica*
Scarce passage migrant.

Pallas's Sandgrouse   *Syrrhaptes paradoxus*
Very rare vagrant.

Feral Rock Dove   *Columba livia*
Widespread resident, particularly in association with human habitation.

Stock Dove   *Columba oenas*
Widespread resident.

Woodpigeon   *Columba palumbus*
Abundant resident and winter visitor.

Collared Dove   *Streptopelia decaocto*
Widespread resident.

Turtle Dove   *Streptopelia turtur*
Passage migrant and widespread summer visitor.

Ring-necked Parakeet   *Psittacula kramari*
Locally common introduced resident.
Sites: Kent — 6.   Surrey — 3, 4.

Great Spotted Cuckoo   *Clamator glandarius*
Very rare vagrant.

Cuckoo   *Cuculus canorus*
Widespread summer visitor and passage migrant.

Yellow-billed Cuckoo   *Coccyzus americanus*
Very rare vagrant.

Barn Owl   *Tyto alba*
Thinly but widely distributed resident.
Sites: Kent — 1, 3.   Sussex — 5, 10, 15, 16.

Scops Owl   *Otus scops*
Very rare vagrant.

Snowy Owl   *Nyctea scandiaca*
Very rare vagrant. Status confused by escapes.

Little Owl   *Athene noctua*
Widespread resident.

Tawny Owl   *Strix aluco*
Widespread resident.

Long-eared Owl   *Asio otus*
Thinly distributed but widespread breeding species, passage migrant and winter visitor.
Sites: Kent — 1.   Sussex — 8.

Short-eared Owl   *Asio flammeus*
Scarce breeding species. Passage migrant and winter visitor mainly to coastal areas.
Sites: Kent — 1, 3.   Surrey — 4, A.   Sussex — 1, 5, 15.

Nightjar   *Caprimulgus europaeus*
Locally common summer visitor, rarely seen on passage.
Sites: Kent — 4, 10, K, N.   Surrey — 7, 9, H, M.   Sussex — 4, 8, 10, 17.

Common Nighthawk   *Chordeiles minor*
Very rare vagrant.

White-throated Needletail   *Hirundapus caudacutus*
Very rare vagrant.

Swift   *Apus apus*
Widespread summer visitor and passage migrant.

Pallid Swift   *Apus pallidus*
Very rare vagrant.

Alpine Swift   *Apus melba*
Scarce but almost annual vagrant.

Kingfisher   *Alcedo atthis*
Widespread resident.

Blue-cheeked Bee-eater   *Merops superciliosus*
Very rare vagrant.

Bee-eater   *Merops apiaster*
Rare vagrant. Has bred.

Roller   *Coracias garrulus*
Very rare vagrant.

Hoopoe   *Upupa epops*
Scarce but regular passage migrant. Occasional winter records. Has bred.

Wryneck   *Jynx torquilla*
Scarce but regular passage migrant, more often in autumn. Formerly bred.

Green Woodpecker   *Picus viridis*
Widespread resident.

Great Spotted Woodpecker   *Dendrocopos major*
Widespread resident. Autumn passage migrant on coast.

Lesser Spotted Woodpecker   *Dendrocopos minor*
Thinly distributed but widespread resident.

Short-toed Lark   *Calandrella brachydactyla*
Very rare vagrant

Crested Lark   *Galerida cristata*
Very rare vagrant.

Woodlark   *Lullula arborea*
Locally common and increasing breeding species. Passage migrant mainly on coast in autumn.
Sites: Kent — 8, 9.   Surrey — 7, 9, G.   Sussex — 17.

Skylark   *Alauda arvensis*
Widespread but declining resident. Common passage migrant and winter visitor.

Shore Lark   *Eremophila alpestris*
Scarce winter visitor and passage migrant.

Sand Martin   *Riparia riparia*
Common passage migrant and local breeding summer visitor.

Crag Martin   *Ptyonoprogne rupestris*
Very rare vagrant.

Swallow   *Hirundo rustica*
Widespread summer visitor and passage migrant.

Red-rumped Swallow   *Hirundo daurica*
Scarce spring and autumn vagrant.

House Martin   *Delichon urbica*
Widespread summer visitor and passage migrant.

Richard's Pipit   *Anthus novaeseelandiae*
Rare but regular autumn vagrant, very rare in spring.

Blyth's Pipit   *Anthus godlewskii*
Very rare vagrant.

Tawny Pipit *Anthus campestris*
Scarce but regular passage migrant in both spring and autumn.

Olive-backed Pipit *Anthus hodgsoni*
Very rare vagrant.

Tree Pipit *Anthus trivialis*
Local breeding summer visitor and passage migrant.
Sites: Kent — 4, 10, E, P. Surrey — 7, 9, 10, 12. Sussex — 4, 17, E, M.

Meadow Pipit *Anthus pratensis*
Widespread breeding species, particularly around the coast. Common
passage migrant and winter visitor.

Red-throated Pipit *Anthus cervinus*
Very rare vagrant.

Rock Pipit *Anthus petrosus*
Scarce local breeding species, passage migrant and winter visitor. Rare
away from coast.
Sites: Kent — 1, 2, 3, 6, 7, 8, F. Sussex — 6, 7, 9, F.

Water Pipit *Anthus spinoletta*
Scarce winter visitor and passage migrant.
Sites: Kent — 5, 7. Surrey — 5. Sussex — 5.

Yellow Wagtail *Motacilla flava*
Widespread but local summer visitor and passage migrant.
Sites: Kent — 5. Surrey — A. Sussex — 5, 10.

Citrine Wagtail *Motacilla citreola*
Very rare vagrant.

Grey Wagtail *Motacilla cinerea*
Widespread resident and passage migrant, particularly in autumn.
Sites: Kent — L, M. Surrey — 5. Sussex — 4.

Pied Wagtail *Motacilla alba*
Widespread resident and passage migrant.

Waxwing *Bombycilla garrulus*
Scarce winter visitor.

Dipper *Cinclus cinclus*
Rare winter vagrant.

Wren *Troglodytes troglodytes*
Abundant resident.

Dunnock *Prunella modularis*
Widespread resident.

Alpine Accentor *Prunella collaris*
Very rare vagrant.

Rufous Bush Robin   *Cercotrichas galactotes*
Very rare vagrant.

Robin   *Erithacus rubecula*
Abundant resident and winter visitor.

Thrush Nightingale   *Luscinia luscinia*
Very rare vagrant.

Nightingale   *Luscinia megarhynchos*
Locally common summer visitor. Infrequently seen passage migrant.
Sites: Kent — 1, 4, 12, I, J.   Surrey — 9, 11, 14, K.   Sussex — 10, 16, L.

Bluethroat   *Luscinia svecica*
Scarce passage migrant.

Red-flanked Bluetail   *Tarsiger cyanurus*
Very rare vagrant.

Black Redstart   *Phoenicurus ochruros*
Scarce breeding species. Regular passage migrant and occasional winter visitor.
Sites: Kent — 6, 7, 8, 9.   Surrey — 1, 4, 6.   Sussex — 2, 6, 9, 14, F.

Redstart   *Phoenicurus phoenicurus*
Local breeding summer visitor and passage migrant.
Sites: Kent — 4, P.   Surrey — 7, 9, 12.   Sussex — 4.

Whinchat   *Saxicola rubetra*
Widespread passage migrant, particularly in autumn. Has bred.

Stonechat   *Saxicola torquata*
Local breeding species, passage migrant and winter visitor.
Sites: Kent — 1, 3, 7, 9, 10, N, P.   Surrey — 7, 9, G.   Sussex — 4, 6, 7, 9, 17, E.

Isabelline Wheatear   *Oenanthe isabellina*
Very rare vagrant.

Wheatear   *Oenanthe oenanthe*
Very local breeding summer visitor and common passage migrant.
Sites: Kent — 9.

Pied Wheatear   *Oenanthe pleschanka*
Very rare vagrant.

Black-eared Wheatear   *Oenanthe hispanica*
Very rare vagrant.

Desert Wheatear   *Oenanthe deserti*
Very rare vagrant.

Rock Thrush   *Monticola saxatilis*
Very rare vagrant.

Swainson's Thrush   *Catharus ustulatus*
Very rare vagrant.

Ring Ouzel   *Turdus torquata*
Regular passage migrant, more common in autumn.

Blackbird   *Turdus merula*
Abundant resident, passage migrant and winter visitor.

Black-throated Thrush   *Turdus ruficollis*
Very rare vagrant.

Fieldfare   *Turdus pilaris*
Common passage migrant and winter visitor.

Song Thrush   *Turdus philomelos*
Widespread resident, passage migrant and winter visitor.

Redwing   *Turdus iliacus*
Common passage migrant and winter visitor. Has bred.

Mistle Thrush   *Turdus viscivorus*
Widespread resident and partial migrant.

American Robin   *Turdus migratorius*
Very rare vagrant.

Cetti's Warbler   *Cettia cetti*
Scarce breeding resident and occasional passage migrant.
Sites: Sussex — 10.

Grasshopper Warbler   *Locustella naevia*
Scarce and declining summer visitor and passage migrant.

Savi's Warbler   *Locustella luscinioides*
Very rare local breeding species and passage migrant.

Aquatic Warbler   *Acrocephalus paludicola*
Scarce autumn passage migrant.

Sedge Warbler   *Acrocephalus schoenobaenus*
Locally common summer visitor and passage migrant.
Sites: Kent — 5.   Surrey — 5.   Sussex — 5, 10, 15.

Paddyfield Warbler   *Acrocephalus agricola*
Very rare vagrant.

Marsh Warbler   *Acrocephalus palustris*
Scarce but regular breeding summer visitor and passage migrant.

Reed Warbler   *Acrocephalus scirpaceus*
Locally common summer visitor and passage migrant.
Sites: Kent — 5.   Surrey — 9.   Sussex — 5, 10, 15.

Great Reed Warbler   *Acrocephalus arundinaceus*
Rare vagrant.

Booted Warbler   *Hippolais caligata*
Very rare vagrant.

Icterine Warbler   *Hippolais icterina*
Scarce passage migrant.

Melodious Warbler   *Hippolais polyglotta*
Scarce passage migrant.

Dartford Warbler   *Silvia undata*
Locally common resident, partial autumn migrant and winter visitor.
Sites: Kent — 9.   Surrey — 7, 9.   Sussex — 4, 6, 17.

Subalpine Warbler   *Silvia cantillans*
Rare vagrant.

Sardinian Warbler   *Silvia melanocephala*
Very rare vagrant.

Desert Warbler   *Silvia nana*
Very rare vagrant.

Barred Warbler   *Silvia nisoria*
Scarce autumn passage migrant.

Lesser Whitethroat   *Silvia curruca*
Common summer visitor and passage migrant.

Whitethroat   *Silvia communis*
Widespread summer visitor and passage migrant.

Garden Warbler   *Silvia borin*
Widespread summer visitor and passage migrant.

Blackcap   *Silvia atricapilla*
Widespread summer visitor and passage migrant. A few overwinter.

Greenish Warbler   *Phylloscopus trochiloides*
Rare vagrant.

Arctic Warbler   *Phylloscopus borealis*
Very rare vagrant.

Pallas's Warbler   *Phylloscopus proregulus*
Rare but regular late autumn vagrant.

Yellow-browed Warbler   *Phylloscopus inornatus*
Scarce but regular vagrant, mainly in autumn.
Sites: Kent — 3, 6, 7, 8, 9.   Sussex — 6, 11, 13.

Radde's Warbler *Phylloscopus schwarzi*
Very rare autumn vagrant.

Dusky Warbler *Phylloscopus fuscatus*
Very rare autumn vagrant.

Bonelli's Warbler *Phylloscopus bonelli*
Very rare vagrant.

Wood Warbler *Phylloscopus sibilatrix*
Local breeding summer visitor and passage migrant.

Chiffchaff *Phylloscopus collybita*
Widespread summer visitor and passage migrant. Small numbers over-winter.

Willow Warbler *Phylloscopus trochilus*
Widespread summer visitor and passage migrant.

Goldcrest *Regulus regulus*
Widespread breeding species and passage migrant.

Firecrest *Regulus ignicapillus*
Rare breeding species and scarce but regular passage migrant. A few overwinter.
Sites: Kent — 6, 7, 8, 9, E. Sussex — 2, 6, 9, 13.

Spotted Flycatcher *Muscicapa striata*
Widespread summer visitor and passage migrant.

Red-breasted Flycatcher *Ficedula parva*
Rare spring vagrant, scarce but regular in autumn.

Collared Flycatcher *Ficedula albicollis*
Very rare vagrant.

Pied Flycatcher *Ficedula hypoleuca*
Scarce spring and regular autumn passage migrant. Has bred.

Bearded Tit *Panurus biarmicus*
Local breeding species, passage migrant and winter visitor.
Sites: Kent — 5.

Long-tailed Tit *Aegithalos caudatus*
Widespread resident.

Marsh Tit *Parus palustris*
Widespread resident.
Sites: Kent — 4, I. Surrey — 9, 10, 11. Sussex — 4, 10, 16.

Willow Tit *Parus montanus*
Thinly distributed resident.
Sites: Kent — I, J. Surrey — 8, 9, 14. Sussex — 10.

Crested Tit *Parus cristatus*
Very rare vagrant.

Coal Tit *Parus ater*
Widespread resident.

Blue Tit *Parus caeruleus*
Abundant resident.

Great Tit *Parus major*
Common resident.

Nuthatch *Sitta europaea*
Widespread resident.

Wallcreeper *Tichodroma muraria*
Very rare vagrant.

Treecreeper *Certhia familiaris*
Widespread resident.

Short-toed Treecreeper *Certhia brachydactyla*
Very rare vagrant.

Penduline Tit *Remiz pendulinus*
Rare vagrant.

Golden Oriole *Oriolus oriolus*
Scarce but regular spring migrant. Has bred. Rare in autumn.
Sites: Kent — 5, 7, 9.

Isabelline Shrike *Lanius isabellinus*
Very rare vagrant.

Red-backed Shrike *Lanius collurio*
Scarce passage migrant. Formerly bred.

Lesser Grey Shrike *Lanius minor*
Very rare vagrant.

Great Grey Shrike *Lanius excubitor*
Scarce winter visitor and passage migrant.
Sites: Kent — 5.   Surrey — 9, G.   Sussex — 4.

Woodchat Shrike *Lanius senator*
Rare vagrant.

Jay *Garrulus glandarius*
Widespread resident. Passage migrant in varying numbers. Occasionally
irruptive.

Magpie *Pica pica*
Widespread resident.

Nutcracker *Nucifraga caryocatactes*
Very rare vagrant.

Jackdaw *Corvus monedula*
Widespread resident.

Rook *Corvus frugilegus*
Locally common resident.

Carrion Crow *Corvus corone*
Widespread resident.

Raven *Corvus corax*
Status unknown due to incidence of escapes or released birds.

Starling *Sturnus vulgaris*
Common resident, passage migrant and winter visitor.

Rose-coloured Starling *Sturnus roseus*
Rare vagrant.

House Sparrow *Passer domesticus*
Common resident.

Tree Sparrow *Passer montanus*
Declining breeding species. Passage migrant and winter visitor.
Sites: Surrey — A.

Red-eyed Vireo *Vireo olivaceous*
Very rare vagrant.

Chaffinch *Fringilla coelebs*
Common resident, passage migrant and winter visitor.

Brambling *Fringilla montifringilla*
Passage migrant and winter visitor. Occasionally in large numbers.
Sites: Kent — 4, 10. Surrey — 4, 6, 9.

Serin *Serinus serinus*
Scarce but regular passage migrant.
Sites: Kent — 6, 9. Sussex — 6, 14.

Greenfinch *Carduelis chloris*
Widespread resident, passage migrant and winter visitor.

Goldfinch *Carduelis carduelis*
Widespread breeding species and partial migrant. Smaller numbers winter.

Siskin *Carduelis spinus*
Widespread winter visitor and passage migrant. Small numbers breed annually.
Sites: Kent — 5, 10, L, M. Surrey — 4, 5, 9, 10. Sussex — 10, 17.

Linnet *Carduelis cannabina*
Widespread resident and partial migrant. Wintering flocks favour coast.

Twite *Carduelis flavirostris*
Scarce winter visitor and passage migrant.
Sites: Kent — 3, 7. Sussex — 7, 13.

Redpoll *Carduelis flammea*
Widespread but declining breeding species, passage migrant and winter visitor.

Arctic Redpoll *Carduelis hornemanni*
Very rare vagrant.

Two-barred Crossbill *Loxia leucoptera*
Very rare vagrant.

Crossbill *Loxia curvirostra*
Scarce passage migrant and winter visitor, occurring in large numbers in irruptive years. Breeds irregularly.
Sites: Kent — 4, 10, E, K. Surrey — 7, 9, 10, G. Sussex — 4, 8.

Parrot Crossbill *Loxia pytyopsittacus*
Very rare vagrant.

Trumpeter Finch *Bucanetes githagineus*
Very rare vagrant.

Scarlet Rosefinch *Carpodacus erythrinus*
Rare but increasing vagrant.

Pine Grosbeak *Pinicola enucleator*
Very rare vagrant.

Bullfinch *Pyrrhula pyrrhula*
Widespread resident.

Hawfinch *Coccothraustes coccothraustes*
Thinly distributed resident.
Sites: Kent — 4, 10. Surrey — 11. Sussex — 4, A.

Golden-winged Warbler *Vermivora chrysoptera*
Very rare vagrant.

Blackpoll Warbler *Dendroica striata*
Very rare vagrant.

Common Yellowthroat *Geothlypis trichas*
Very rare vagrant.

Dark-eyed Junco *Junco hyemalis*
Very rare vagrant.

White-throated Sparrow *Zonotrichia albicollis*
Very rare vagrant.

Lapland Bunting *Calcarius lapponicus*
Regular passage migrant and winter visitor. Rare inland.
Sites: Kent — 1, 3, 7.

Snow Bunting *Plectrophenax nivalis*
Scarce passage migrant but regular winter visitor.
Sites: Kent — 3, 7, B, D. Surrey — 4. Sussex — 1, 9, 11.

Pine Bunting *Emberiza leucocephalos*
Very rare vagrant.

Yellowhammer *Emberiza citrinella*
Widespread resident.

Cirl Bunting *Emberiza cirlus*
Formerly a scarce breeding species; now a very rare vagrant.

Rock Bunting *Emberiza cia*
Very rare vagrant.

Ortolan Bunting *Emberiza hortulana*
Scarce passage migrant.

Rustic Bunting *Emberiza rustica*
Very rare vagrant.

Little Bunting *Emberiza pusilla*
Very rare vagrant.

Reed Bunting *Emberiza schoeniclus*
Locally common resident, passage migrant and winter visitor.

Pallas's Reed Bunting *Emberiza pallasi*
Very rare vagrant.

Black-headed Bunting *Emberiza melanocephala*
Very rare vagrant.

Corn Bunting *Miliaria calandra*
Locally common resident, particularly in coastal areas.
Sites: Kent — 1, 3, 7, H. Sussex — 1, 6, 9, 10.

Northern Oriole *Icterus galbula*
Very rare vagrant.

GLOSSARY OF TERMS

A number of words and expressions used in the text may not be familiar to the reader. Most are commonly used by birdwatchers and have a precise ornithological meaning.

Auk
A seabird of the Razorbill/Guillemot family.

Aythya hybrids
Hybrids between ducks of the genus *Aythya*, normally involving a Tufted Duck or Pochard, which can have a confusing resemblance to scarcer members of the genus, such as Scaup and Ferruginous Duck.

Backing
An anticlockwise change of wind direction.

BOU
British Ornithologists' Union.

Bunding
Creating an artificial embankment to retain water.

Coasting
Flying along the line of the coast, usually involving birds on migration, often against a headwind.

Common woodland passerines
Those small birds resident in most English woods and parks, eg. Wren, Dunnock, Robin, thrushes, tits, Nuthatch, Treecreeper and Chaffinch.

Creche
An assembly of still dependent young of several families. Creches of young Canada Geese and Shelduck form in June and July.

Dabbling duck
A surface feeder such as Mallard and Shoveler.

Diving duck
A species which feeds by swimming underwater like Tufted Duck and Pochard.

Drumming
This word describes two different activities: *a*) a rapid bill-tapping sound made by both sexes of Great and Lesser Spotted Woodpeckers, essentially to attract mates; and *b*) the flight display of the Snipe, a sound produced by the vibration of the outer tail feathers.

Eclipse plumage
The dull, camouflaged plumage obtained by male ducks during their post-breeding moult.

Fall
Mass arrival of passerine night-migrants, usually along the coast.

Feral
Introduced by man and now living in a wild state, eg. Canada Goose, Ruddy Duck.

Gravel or sand pit	A pit worked for gravel or sand. Exhausted pits normally fill with water if left unpumped and are then sometimes turned into Nature Reserves, or used for sailing or fishing.
Heligoland trap	A large, funnel-like trap of wire mesh, in which birds are caught for ringing — an important part of the study of bird migration.
Hirundine	A bird of the swallow or martin family.
Irruption	An arrival of certain specialised feeders from the continent, eg. Waxwing or Crossbill, when their population is high and food runs short in their native areas. Irruptions vary greatly in size and are more marked in eastern Britain.
LNR	Local Nature Reserve.
Migrant	A bird that summers in one part of the globe and winters in another.
Mist-netting	Another means of catching birds for the purpose of ringing — a fine, black net is strung between poles.
NNR	National Nature Reserve.
Passerine	A small perching bird; used to describe all small land birds.
Race	A word used synonymously with 'subspecies'. Britain's Pied Wagtail *Motacilla alba yarrelii* and the Continental White Wagtail *Motacilla alba alba* are races of the species *Motacilla alba*.
Raptor	A diurnal bird of prey such as the Kestrel or Buzzard; excludes owls.
Reservoir	In the Thames Valley these are large, embanked (bunded) structures built for the storage of pumped water. Elsewhere they may be created by damming river valleys.
Roding	The display flight of the Woodcock, usually seen at dawn or dusk.
Sawbill	A duck with a serrated bill edge to grasp fish — Red-breasted Merganser, Goosander and Smew.
SBBO Census Area	The Sandwich Bay Bird Observatory recording area for which daily counts of species present are made.
Seabird	One of the mainly pelagic or coastal species, not normally seen inland, such as Manx Shearwater, Gannet, Common Scoter or Arctic Skua.

Seawatching — Scanning the sea to observe passing seabirds.

Shorebird — A wading bird, more usually associated with the coast, such as Dunlin or Sanderling, but usually used synonymously with 'wader' to describe all such species.

SSSI — A site notified by English Nature as being a Site of Special Scientific Interest. Not necessarily notified for its birds.

Thermalling — The use of rising, warm air currents to gain height. Most often associated with raptors, but not exclusively so — gulls often thermal.

Trip — A collective term for a group of Dotterel.

Veering — A clockwise change of wind direction.

Wader — A bird which feeds on mud, water or marsh, eg. Dunlin, Curlew, including some plovers and Woodcock which have adapted to drier ground but excluding herons, etc.

Acrocephalus Warbler — Those warbler species normally associated with reeds, like Sedge and Reed Warbler of the genus *Acrocephalus*.

Phylloscopus Warbler — A 'leaf warbler', eg. Willow, Wood, Chiffchaff and scarce related species of the genus *Phylloscopus*.

Sylvia Warbler — One of the scrub-haunting warblers, eg. Blackcap, Whitethroat of the genus *Sylvia*.

Waterbird — A collective term for birds normally found on or near inland water.

Waterfowl — A collective term more particularly for ornamental collections of swans, geese and duck.

Wildfowl — A collective term usually applied to duck and geese.

Winter thrushes — Those which come across from northern Europe to Britain for the winter, chiefly Fieldfare and Redwing flocks, but Blackbirds and Song Thrushes also arrive to join local birds.

FURTHER READING

Clark, JM. *Birds of the Hants/Surrey Border* (1984). Hobby Books, Aldershot.

Drewett, J. *The Nature of Surrey* (1987). Barracuda Books, Buckingham.

Dymond, JN, Fraser, PA & Gantlett, SJM. *Rare Birds in Britain and Ireland* (1989). Poyser, Waterhouses.

Gibbons, DW, Reid, JB & Chapman, RA. *The New Atlas of Breeding Birds in Britain and Ireland* (1993). Poyser, London.

Gillham, EH & Homes, RC. *The Birds of the North Kent Marshes* (1950). Collins, London.

Harrison, JG & Grant, PJ. *The Thames Transformed* (1976). Andre Deutsch, London.

James, P. *Birds of Sussex* (1996). Sussex Ornithological Society.

Lack, P. *The Atlas of Wintering Birds in Britain and Ireland* (1986). Poyser, Waterhouses.

Oliver, PJ. *Birdwatching on the North Kent Marshes* (1991). Peter Oliver, Oxted.

Parr, D, Editor. *Birds in Surrey* (1972). Batsford, London.

Pemberton, JE, Editor. *The Birdwatcher's Yearbook and Diary 1997* (1996). Buckingham Press, Buckingham.
   This is an annual fact-filled publication which no birdwatcher can afford to be without. Names & addresses of organisations, tide tables, book reviews, schedule I species, articles, etc.

Sharrock, JTR. *The Atlas of Breeding Birds in Britain and Ireland* (1976). British Trust for Ornithology, Tring.

Taylor, DW, Davenport, DL & Flegg, JJM. *The Birds of Kent* (1981). Kent Ornithological Society, Meopham.

Taylor, DW. *Birding in Kent* (1996). Pica Press, Mountfield, near Robertsbridge.

USEFUL ADDRESSES

Bird Observatories

Dungeness Bird Observatory (DBO)
The Warden, Dungeness Bird Observatory, Romney Marsh, Kent TN29 9NA (tel: 01797 321309)

Sandwich Bay Bird Observatory (SBBO)
The Warden, Sandwich Bay Bird Observatory, Guilford Road, Sandwich, Kent CT13 9PF (tel: 01304 617341)

Reserves

Church Wood, Blean
The Warden, 11 Garden Close, Rough Common, Canterbury, Kent CT2 9BP (tel: 01227 462491)

Dungeness
The Warden, Boulderwall Farm, Dungeness Road, Lydd, Romney Marsh, Kent TN29 9PN (tel: 01797 320588)

Elmley
The Warden, Kingshill Farm, Elmley, Sheerness, Isle of Sheppey, Kent ME12 3RW (tel: 01795 665969)

Fore Wood
The Warden, Crown House, Petteridge Lane, Matfield, Tonbridge, Kent TN12 7LT

Northward Hill
The Warden, RSPB Office, Northward Hill Reserve, Bromhey Farm, East-borough, Cooling, Kent ME3 8DS (tel: 01634 222480)

Pagham Harbour LNR
The Warden, 10 Horsefield Road, Selsey, Chichester, West Sussex

Pulborough Brooks
The Warden, Uppertons Barn Visitor Centre, Wiggonholt, Pulborough, West Sussex RH20 2EL (tel: 01798 875851)

Rye Harbour LNR
The Warden, 2 Watch Cottages, Nook Beach, Winchelsea, East Sussex TN36 4LU

Sevenoaks Wildfowl Reserve
John Tyler, Tadorna, Bradbourne Vale Road, Sevenoaks, Kent TN13 3DH (tel: 01732 456407)

Thursley NNR
The Warden, Uplands Stud, Brook, Godalming, Surrey GU8 5LA

Bird and Wildlife Organisations

Hants and Surrey Border Bird Report
John Clark, 4 Cygnet Court, Old Cove Road, Fleet, Hants GU13 8RL

Haslemere Natural History Society
Haslemere Educational Museum, High Street, Haslemere, Surrey GU27 2LA

Kent Ornithological Society (KOS)
Secretary: Keith Derrett, 14 Chestnut Avenue, Staplehurst, Kent TN12 ONH (tel: 01580 892220)
County Recorder: Ian Hodgson, Whitgift House, Hardy Close, Canterbury CT2 8JJ (tel: 01227 784303)
Annual *Kent Bird Report* from Membership Secretary: Steve Davies, 13 Crown Lane, Bromley BR2 2PG (tel: 0181 289 0378)

Kent Wildlife Trust (KWT)
Tyland Barn, Sandling, Maidstone, Kent ME14 3BD (tel: 01622 662012)

London Natural History Society
Ornithological Section Secretary: Vicki Harley, 30 Margett St, Cottenham, Cambridge CB4 4QY

English Nature (Kent)
South East Regional Countryside Management Centre: Coldharbour Farm, Wye, Ashford, Kent TN25 5DB (tel: 01233 812525)

English Nature (Surrey and Sussex)
Howard House, 31 High Street, Lewes, East Sussex BN7 2LU (tel: 01273 476595)

Royal Society for the Protection of Birds (RSPB)
South East Regional Office: Scan House, 8 Church Street, Shoreham-by-Sea, West Sussex BN4 5DQ (tel: 01273 463642)

Surrey Bird Club
Secretary: Mrs G. M. Cook, 'Moorings', Vale Wood Drive, Lower Bourne, Farnham, Surrey GU10 3HW
Annual *Surrey Bird Report* available from: J. V. P. Hutchins, 6 Gorse Court, Guildford, Surrey GU4 7XZ

Surrey Wildlife Trust
School Lane, Pirbright, Woking, Surrey GU24 0JN (tel: 01483 488055)

Sussex Ornithological Society
Secretary: David Golds , 63 Sullington Gardens, Worthing, West Sussex BN15 0HS
Annual *Sussex Bird Report* available from: J. E. Trowell, Lorrimer, Main Road, Icklesham, Winchelsea, East Sussex TN36 4BS

Sussex Wildlife Trust
Woods Mill, Henfield, West Sussex BN5 9SD (tel: 01273 492630)

Other useful addresses

Birdwatching on the Medway Estuary
Derek Tutt, Barn Owl Travel, 21 Heron Close, Lower Halstow, Kent ME9 7EF (tel: 01795 844464)

Ministry of Defence Ranges
Ash Range Office (tel: 01252 25233)

National Trust (Kent and East Sussex)
The Estate Office, Scotney Castle, Lamberhurst, Tunbridge Wells, Kent TN3 8JN

National Trust (Surrey and West Sussex)
Southern Region, Polesden Lacey, Dorking, Surrey RH5 6BD

National Rivers Authority (Southern Region)
Recreation and Conservation Officer, Guildbourne House, Chatsworth Road, Worthing, West Sussex BN11 1LD

National Rivers Authority (Thames Region)
Kings Meadow House, Kings Meadow Road, Reading, Berks RG1 8DQ

Thames Water Utilities Ltd
Nugent House, Vastern Road, Reading, Berks RG1 8DB (tel: 01734 591159)
This is the address to write to for a birdwatching permit which gives admittance to the Barn Elms, Kempton Park West, Queen Mary and Walton Reservoirs.

CODE OF CONDUCT FOR BIRDWATCHERS

Today's birdwatchers are a powerful force for nature conservation. The number of those of us interested in birds rises continually and it is vital that we take seriously our responsibility to avoid any harm to birds.

We must also present a responsible image to non-birdwatchers who may be affected by our activities and particularly those on whose sympathy and support the future of birds may rest.

There are 10 points to bear in mind:
1. The welfare of birds must come first.
2. Habitat must be protected.
3. Keep disturbance to birds and their habitat to a minimum.
4. When you find a rare bird think carefully about whom you should tell.
5. Do not harass rare migrants.
6. Abide by the bird protection laws at all times.
7. Respect the rights of landowners.
8. Respect the rights of other people in the countryside.
9. Make your records available to the local bird recorder.
10. Behave abroad as you would when birdwatching at home.

Welfare of birds must come first

Whether your particular interest is photography, ringing, sound recording, scientific study or just birdwatching, remember that the welfare of the bird must always come first.

Habitat protection

Its habitat is vital to a bird and therefore we must ensure that our activities do not cause damage.

Keep disturbance to a minimum

Birds' tolerance of disturbance varies between species and seasons. Therefore, it is safer to keep all disturbance to a minimum. No birds should be disturbed from the nest in case opportunities for predators to take eggs or young are increased. In very cold weather disturbance to birds may cause them to use vital energy at a time when food is difficult to find. Wildfowlers already impose bans during cold weather: birdwatchers should exercise similar discretion.

Rare breeding birds

If you discover a rare bird breeding and feel that protection is necessary, inform the appropriate RSPB Regional Office, or the Species Protection Department at the Lodge. Otherwise it is best in almost all circumstances to keep the record strictly secret in order to avoid disturbance by other birdwatchers and attacks by egg-collectors. Never visit known sites of rare breeding birds unless they are adequately protected. Even your presence may give away the site to others and cause so many other visitors that the birds may fail to breed successfully.

Disturbance at or near the nest of species listed on the First Schedule of the Wildlife and Countryside Act 1981 is a criminal offence.

Copies of Wild Birds and the Law are obtainable from the RSPB, The Lodge, Sandy, Beds. SG19 2DL (send two 2nd class stamps).

Rare migrants

Rare migrants or vagrants must not be harassed. If you discover one, consider the circumstances carefully before telling anyone. Will an influx of birdwatchers disturb the bird or others in the area? Will the habitat be damaged? Will problems be caused with the landowner?

The Law

The bird protection laws (now embodied in the Wildlife and Country-side Act 1981) are the result of hard campaigning by previous genera-tions of birdwatchers. As birdwatchers we must abide by them at all times and not allow them to fall into disrepute.

Respect the rights of landowners

The wishes of landowners and occupiers of land must be respected. Do not enter land without permission. Comply with permit schemes. If you are leading a group, do give advance notice of the visit, even if a formal permit scheme is not in operation. Always obey the Country Code.

Respect the rights of other people

Have proper consideration for other birdwatchers. Try not to disrupt their activities or scare the birds they are watching. There are many other people who also use the countryside. Do not interfere with their activities and, if it seems that what they are doing is causing unneces-sary disturbance to birds, do try to take a balanced view. Flushing gulls when walking a dog on a beach may do little harm, while the same dog might be a serious disturbance at a tern colony. When pointing this out to a non-birdwatcher be courteous, but firm. The non-birdwatchers' goodwill towards birds must not be destroyed by the attitudes of bird-watchers.

Keeping records

Much of today's knowledge about birds is the result of meticulous record keeping by our predecessors. Make sure you help to add to tomorrow's knowledge by sending records to your county bird recorder.

Birdwatching abroad

Behave abroad as you would at home. This code should be firmly adhered to when abroad (whatever the local laws). Well behaved bird-watchers can be important ambassadors for bird protection.

This code has been drafted after consultation between The British Ornithologists' Union, British Trust for Ornithology, the Royal Society for the Protection of Birds, the Scottish Ornithologists' Club, the Wildfowl Trust and the Editors of *British Birds*.

Further copies may be obtained from The Royal Society for the Protection of Birds, The Lodge, Sandy, Beds. SG19 2DL.

INDEX OF SPECIES

This index of selected species includes those that are usually without a county site reference in the Systematic List, but omits others that are widespread and commonly seen. It refers to pages on which species are mentioned in the text, but excludes reference to the seasonal calendar lists. Pages 15–102 concern Kent, 103–178 Surrey and 179–257 Sussex.

INDEX OF SITES AND PLACE NAMES

Page references are given for all sites and place names included in the text. Site titles and place names on the maps are shown in bold print